Virginia Hamilton

Virginia Hamilton has written many,

many books—both fiction and non-

fiction. An excerpt from one of her

books appears in this book. To read

more about Virginia Hamilton and her

views on writers and writing, just turn

the page.

Someone once said that we all have a story to tell. How many stories do you have? How do your stories come to you?

To Virginia Hamilton, it can happen like this.

"One day there appears out of nowhere a small visual piece, a glimpse say, of a small child struggling to put on rubber galoshes. At once the image disappears around the corner of my mind. So curious, so surprising it was, coming as it did from nowhere, that I have to chase after it to see where it's going. I may not discover another image like it for some time, but what of it? By then, I've been at the typewriter for hours. By that time I've explained why the child is putting on the galoshes; that the hour is the middle of the night and she needs the galoshes to get through heavy snow to find her dad, whom she hears singing while he sleds down a nearby hill; that her hungry need for her father is greater than her large fear of the cold, dark outside—I'm into the book. I need no more glimpses; I may not yet know what the story has to do, but I've caught it, like a fever, or it's caught me. In another instance, there is a whole story in the shape of the dreams and fears of one character, who appears in the mind fully realized."

Virginia Hamilton has stories to tell. And she has been telling them beautifully and regularly since the publication of *Zeely*, her first book, in 1967. *Zeely* grew out of a story that she wrote in college. She felt that the historical connections with Africa that run through the book were important for her to explore at that particular time in her life.

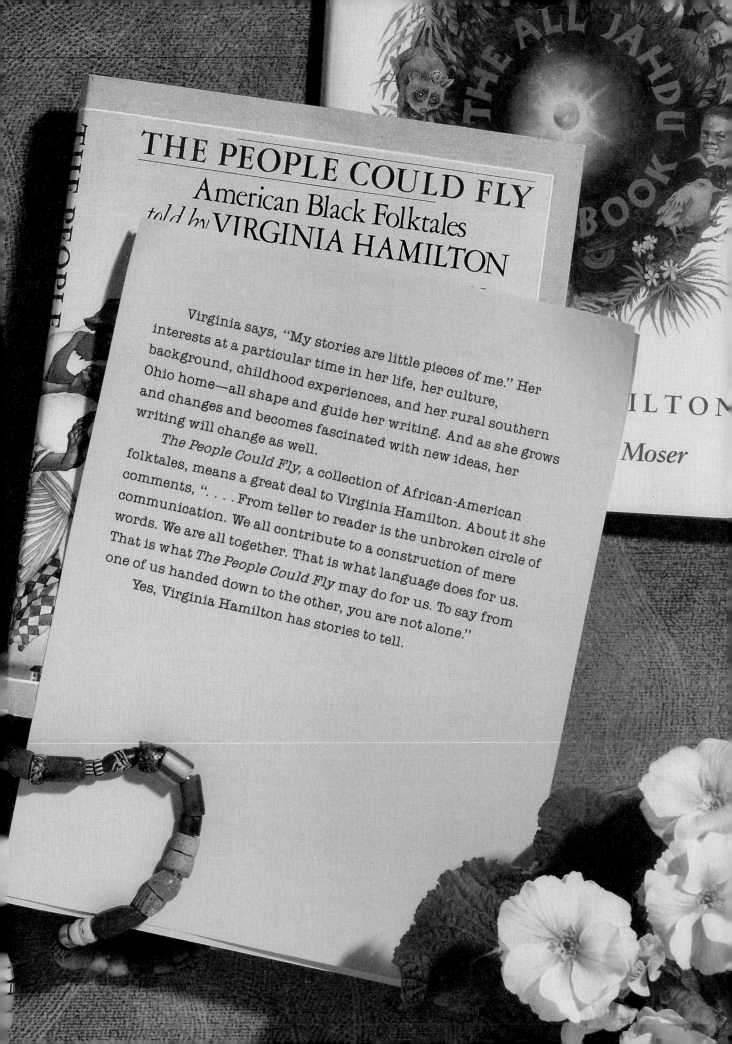

THE PEOPLE COULD FLY
American Black Folktales
told by VIRGINIA HAMILTON

Virginia says, "My stories are little pieces of me." Her interests at a particular time in her life, her culture, background, childhood experiences, and her rural southern Ohio home—all shape and guide her writing. And as she grows and changes and becomes fascinated with new ideas, her writing will change as well.

The People Could Fly, a collection of African-American folktales, means a great deal to Virginia Hamilton. About it she comments, ". . . . From teller to reader is the unbroken circle of communication. We all contribute to a construction of mere words. We are all together. That is what language does for us. That is what *The People Could Fly* may do for us. To say from one of us handed down to the other, you are not alone."

Yes, Virginia Hamilton has stories to tell.

DEDICATIONS FROM THE DEVELOPMENT TEAM

*To my parents Juliet Chew Yat and Yukio, ever inspiring
their daughters to question and wonder, and to
Leon Hewitt. May you, too, see your wonders and
capture your dreams.*
—Lynn Yokoe

*To the greatest teachers we ever had—our mothers—
Nancy B. Randall, Vernon F. Cox, and Mary N. Boltz.
—Cindy Randall, Mary Farley Cox, Bob Boltz.*

ACKNOWLEDGMENTS

Reading/Language Arts Authors Elaine Mei Aoki, Virginia Arnold, James Flood, James V. Hoffman, Diane Lapp, Miriam Martinez, Annemarie Sullivan Palincsar, Michael Priestley, Nancy Roser, Carl B. Smith, William H. Teale, Josefina Villamil Tinajero, Arnold W. Webb, Peggy E. Williams, Karen Wood

Write Idea! is a Writing/Language Arts Program that incorporates a writing workshop approach and helps students to extend reading experiences through writing. The approach to writing in the Macmillan/McGraw-Hill Reading/Language Arts Program is based on the strategies and approaches to composition and conventions of language in *Write Idea!*

Multicultural and Educational Consultants Yvonne Beamer, Joyce Buckner, Alma Flor Ada, Helen Gillotte, Cheryl Hudson, Narcita Medina, Susan Monken, Lorraine Monroe, James R. Murphy, Gail Powell, Sylvia Peña, Ramón Santiago, Cliff Trafzer, Mary Tripp, Hai Tran, Esther Lee Yao

Literature Consultants Joan I. Glazer, Paul Janeczko, Margaret H. Lippert

Teacher Reviewers Gail Farrier, Phoenix, Arizona; José Garcia, New York, New York; Jeri Montiegel, Grand Rapids, Michigan; Carla Phillips, Phoenix, Arizona *(Acknowledgments continue on page 419.)*

Copyright © 1993 Macmillan/McGraw-Hill School Publishing Company

Macmillan/McGraw-Hill School Division
10 Union Square East
New York, New York 10003

Printed in the United States of America.

ISBN 0-02-243808-4

4 5 6 7 8 9   RAI   99 98 97 96 95 94

Write Idea!

AUTHORS

Elaine Mei Aoki ○ James Flood ○ James V. Hoffman

Diane Lapp ○ Ana Huerta Macias ○ Miriam Martinez

Ann McCallum ○ Michael Priestley ○ Nancy Roser ○ Carl B. Smith

William Strong ○ William H. Teale ○ Charles Temple

Josefina Villamil Tinajero ○ Arnold W. Webb ○ Peggy E. Williams

MACMILLAN/McGRAW-HILL SCHOOL PUBLISHING COMPANY

New York   Chicago   Columbus

Take the Flip Trip!

Welcome to *Write Idea!* And what is *Write Idea!* you may be asking. Well, it's a very special writing/language arts book that's sure to help you to become the best writer and user of language that you can possibly be. That's what *Write Idea!* is.

Write Idea! is organized into three parts. A book that is organized into three parts may be a different kind of book for you. For that reason, you can read about the three parts and what's in each part.

PART ONE

Writers and Writing

Part 1 begins with an Introduction that, you guessed it, introduces the book and gives you all sorts of information about reading, writing, and speaking. The Introduction is followed by a special unit about Journals, Logs, and Notebooks—a writer's best friends. Other units, 11 of them, will help you with many different kinds of writing— story, report, and poetry, to name just a few.

Writers and Writing

PART TWO

Writer's Workshop

Part 2 is filled with strategy, writer's craft, and language lessons. These lessons include all sorts of activities designed to help you become strategic writers and users of language. Most of the activities can be used with a partner or in a small group. Remember, cooperation counts!

PART THREE

Information Instantly

In Part 3 you will find all sorts of reference information. Do you want to replace an overworked word with a more colorful one? You could check the Thesaurus. Unsure of a comma rule? You can consult the Grammar, Mechanics, and Usage Handbook. You can find a Glossary and Spelling Tips in Part 3, too. Check it out!

Note the Notes!

Write Idea! has a special feature that you might not have seen in a language arts book before. You might have seen a feature like it in other books or magazines, though.

Are you curious? Good! That feature involves information. In the margins on some pages, you will find tips, pointers, and references to other parts of the book. Learning to find information is an important skill. Using *Write Idea!* will give you good practice.

REVISING STRATEGIES

Guidelines for the strategic writer

F A S T F O C U S

Pointers for the expert editor

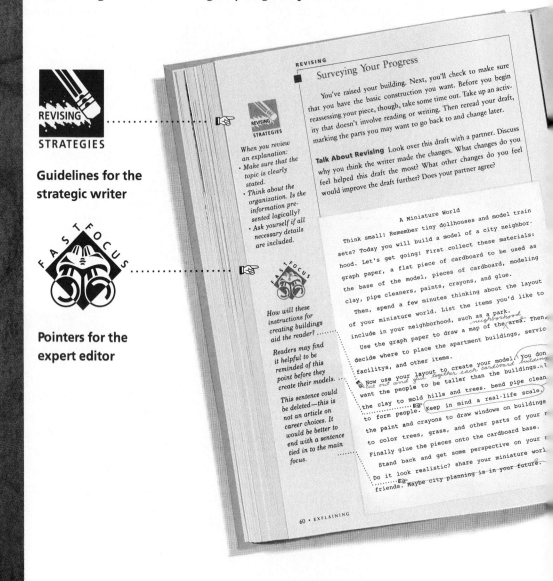

ON YOUR OWN Reread your draft. Look again at the places where you marked your paper. How could you clarify the points for your readers? Think about whether an absolute novice to your topic could follow your explanation. Is the information organized so that it makes sense? Ask your partner to read your draft. A different pair of eyes can always help! In addition, ask yourself the following questions so that your ideas are presented precisely and clearly.

■ Does my topic sentence contain the main idea of my explanation?

■ Do my supporting details—the facts, reasons, or steps in my process—provide the information that develops my topic?

■ If my draft explains how to do something or how something works, have I used chronological (time) order—the easiest order for a reader to follow?

■ Do the time-order words and phrases in my explanation, such as *first, next, at this point, after that,* and *later,* help show readers how the ideas in my explanation are connected?

■ Have I included all that my audience needs to know in order for me to accomplish my purpose? Should I delete any information that does not suitably guide my readers?

■ Have I concluded my explanation effectively? Have I summarized the information, restated the topic sentence in different words, or left my audience with an important point to consider?

CONFERENCING STRATEGIES

When you and your partner discuss explanations, you may want to say things such as:
• I could easily follow each step, but I'd like to know more about _____.
• Does this section really go before (or after) _____?

Look for the positive aspects of the piece as well as the areas that can be improved. Point out at least one thing you learned from reading the piece.

For more advice about conferencing, see page 229.

EXPLAINING • 61

CONFERENCING STRATEGIES

Tips for the perfect partner

Using the notes in the margins is sure to make you a whiz at locating and using the information you need to become an expert writer and language user. Improving your language strategies will help you in all your subjects. And that's a very bright idea!

PART 1

Writers
and Writing

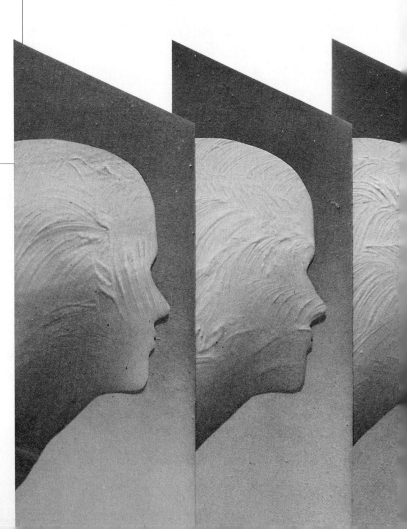

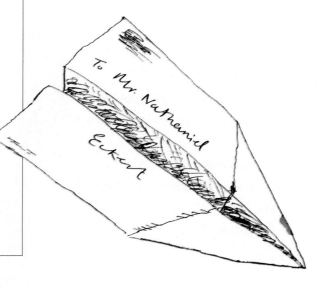

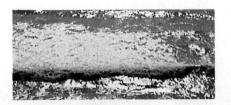

PART 2

Writer's Workshop

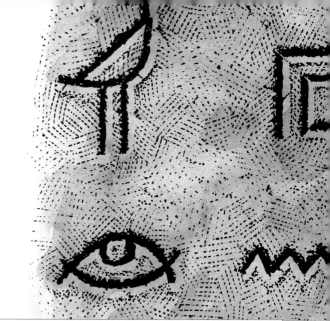

WRITER'S CRAFT 239

USING LANGUAGE 301

PART 3

Information Instantly

P A R T

1

Writers and Writing

I like writing. I'm fairly prolific; it's a daily activity for me. And that keeps the youth and the imagination going. If I were to stop, I would be in serious trouble.
— Gary Soto
author

What's in a Word?

What's in a word? In a word, everything. Think about what life would be like if human beings didn't use words to communicate with each other. Imagine how you would do these things without language:

- sing a song
- tell a story
- explain the rules of a game

For some simple activities you could try drawing pictures or using body language to communicate your messages to other people. You would probably find, however, that these methods were very time-consuming and unsuitable for all but the simplest messages. Life would be like an endlessly frustrating game of charades!

No matter what language they're in, the words of human speech are some of our most powerful and valuable tools. You need these tools every day to express complicated needs, thoughts, and feelings to others. When you put words together to say just what you mean, you express your individual self.

Every language on earth grows and changes. Listen carefully to some of the words your grandparents use or think about the dialog as you watch an old movie on TV. The chances are that you will hear some phrases or words that are quite different from the speech you use today.

There are limitless ways to use words, so try to make them your own. The power of words is yours to harness, so that you can share your knowledge, your feelings, and your dreams.

Talk About Communicating Have you ever thought about what a wonderful tool language really is? Begin a list, jotting down all the ways you can think of that you've used language since you got out of bed this morning. Then compare lists with a partner. Make a list of the ways in which other people have used language to communicate messages to each of you today.

WRITERS ON

WRITING

I always liked to write; I had never had any difficulty writing. Some people play the piano. I can't, but I can write.

– Nicholasa Mohr author and illustrator

From Speaking to Writing

Since prehistoric times the power of human speech has made communication possible among humans. The invention of writing, however, immensely expanded people's ability to communicate. Before writing was invented, people could express themselves only to others who were nearby. With the written word, information and ideas could be shared with people who might be distant either in place or time.

Even in the earliest of societies, humans needed to store information. More than five thousand years ago, peoples such as the Sumerians used a system of writing for counting and record keeping. At first, people drew signs and pictures on clay tablets to represent objects and ideas in their spoken language. There was one sign for each word. Later, the meanings and often the sounds of the main parts of words—syllables—came to be signified by symbols. This was basically the system that the ancient Egyptians expanded into their hieroglyphics. The Chinese also developed a system using about fifty thousand word symbols that continues to be used today.

Some languages changed when the Greeks, among others, developed a new system based on an alphabet. The alphabet helped to make written language more economical to use. Using only 24 letters, one for each separate sound in the Greek language, a writer could record anything he or she could say. Learning the alphabet was simple, compared to mastering hundreds or thousands of word symbols. Almost anyone could now become a writer!

As a writer today, you've inherited the long development of language history. You can record your ideas and feelings for the benefit of other people. Best of all, with inventions like erasers, self-correcting typewriters, and word processors, reworking and polishing your ideas before you share them with others has never been easier!

IN YOUR JOURNAL Look at the covers of a few paperback books at home, in the library, or in a bookstore. Choose a cover that makes you want to read the book. In your Journal, jot down some thoughts about the words in the book's title and the images on the cover. Tell why you think the cover is so powerful.

WRITING

I think it is important for children to know that a good part of the reward of being a writer is the process itself.

– Patricia MacLachlan author

Writing as a Process

We know from modern science that every human being is unique. In the same way, no two writers are exactly alike. The thoughts and feelings of each individual are unique, and every writer has distinctive ideas and a personal style.

Even though each writer is different, most follow the same basic writing process, although the order of the steps can be as unique as the writer. In this process, writers start with an idea and end up with a finished piece of writing they can share.

> What territory do you want to cover with your writing? Where will you dig up the best ideas? To whom will you communicate these ideas, and why?

Prewriting At the beginning, writers are like explorers in a new territory. They make notes about their observations and thoughts to help them plan their next step. Writers also think about who might be interested in and appreciate their ideas.

> As you record each idea, ask yourself how it relates to what you've already put on paper. If you get stuck, look at your prewriting notes. Is there anything else you can include?

Drafting The purpose of drafting is to record your ideas on paper as completely as you can. Don't worry about the form or order of your ideas yet. Instead, get your thoughts down on paper where you can take another look at them and think about them more clearly.

Revising As a writer, you take the time at this stage to see if your work makes sense. Each writer has a different way of revising: some change a little, some revise a lot, while many writers seek the opinions of friends. It's a good idea to check your prewriting notes when you revise. See if you think you've achieved your purpose. You may even decide to explore new ideas that have occurred to you while writing your draft.

Who might give you a useful, reliable opinion about your work? How can a partner play a valuable role in the writing process?

Proofreading This is the stage when you check your work for all the small but important flaws, such as errors in punctuation, spelling, and grammar. Correcting these mistakes will make your writing clear and professional.

As a writer, how will you check that your work is error-free?

Publishing Many writers enjoy publishing — sharing their work. They find it rewarding to see the effect their words have on other people. There are a number of ways to publish, including delivering your work aloud, presenting it in written form, or combining it with art.

How will you display your next writing project?

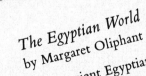

The Egyptian World
by Margaret Oliphant

What did the ancient Egyptians eat? Were they often at war? These answers and much more can be found in *The Egyptian World* by Margaret Oliphant. This book is a very complete source of information about daily life in ancient Egypt. The text is accompanied by many photographs of wall paintings and hieroglyphics which help bring the information to life. If you want to go on an archaeological dig without getting your hands dirty, this is the book for you.

If you want to use the power of writing to share your thoughts and ideas, you don't need to go on an archaeological dig and mount an exhibit in a museum! All you need are your own ideas and feelings, plus a method of recording them. If you decide to develop a routine for saving your writing, here are some helpful suggestions.

Keeping a Journal A journal is a flexible kind of diary. You don't need to keep a daily record of events. Instead, you can use a journal or notebook to jot down your thoughts, observations, feelings, and notes about interesting information. You may or may not record notes about the time and place of your thoughts. You may make several entries on one day and no entries for several days at a time. You can organize your journal in whatever way works best — by time period, by topic, or by a method of your own choice. You can make drawings or record quotations in your journal. In short, your journal can be a permanent, private record of your inner thoughts. Whenever you wish, you can reread your notes. Who knows what writing ideas may come out of your notes — maybe weeks or months after you first made them!

I learned so many things on the field trip today.

Establishing a Working Folder You'd be surprised at the different kinds of papers that writers can pile up in the course of a writing project: file cards with notes or prewriting ideas, slips of paper with lists or diagrams, articles, one or more working drafts, even photographs! Establishing a working folder for each current writing project will help you keep your materials organized. You might use a separate folder for each project, or you might organize different projects in a multipocket folder. You'll probably find that your thoughts are more organized as your work becomes more organized.

Create a Permanent Portfolio Artists and photographers put their better pieces in a permanent portfolio—a collection of the finished paintings and photos that have special meaning for them or that represent their best work. Why should writers be any different? If you make writing a habit, you'll soon accumulate a collection of favorite poems, stories, and other pieces. You can store these in a permanent portfolio.

Each time you finish a writing project, set it aside for a few days. Then decide whether or not you think it's good enough to go into your portfolio. You can change the pieces in your portfolio whenever you like. The more you write, the more interesting and satisfying your portfolio will be.

Talk About Communicating Take a look at the list you created of all the ways you've used language today. Then get together with a partner and review your lists. As you discuss them, see if they give you some ideas about how to use the power of words for your next project.

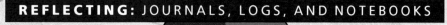

REFLECTING: JOURNALS, LOGS, AND NOTEBOOKS

UNIT 1

At the age of seven I started my first journal, using a pastepot to secure on the page pictures cut from magazines. The visual aids were the troops to back up my small vocabulary on the front line. I wanted to capture all my thoughts and adventures and keep them safe within the diary. As I grew up, I continued to record my life's outward events as well as my inward reflections. In the evolution of the journals, I made small watercolors and drawings as windows in my text.

— Laurel Lee
from *Signs of Spring*

■ Writers at Work

Almost everyone enjoys thinking about exploring. Wherever explorers go, they carefully observe their surroundings to discover interesting things in the world around them. Scientific researchers often record their observations in a special notebook called a log. Entries can be made several times an hour, as the researchers watch and record the results of their work. The log entries often prove useful as researchers continue their explorations. Sometimes researchers and explorers keep diaries—detailed accounts of each day's events.

Writers are explorers, too. Not everyone can hop on a ship, but everyone can explore some personal thoughts and feelings about everyday and familiar surroundings. One way in which writers explore this personal geography is by keeping a writer's notebook or journal—a written record of thoughts, feelings, and ideas. Keeping a journal is a good way to preserve impressions and observations that you otherwise could lose or forget.

Read and compare the following pieces of writing. What do they suggest about the value of keeping a writer's notebook or journal?

Twenty-second day: We set out from last night's harbor. Mountains are visible in the far distance. A boy of eight—looking even less than his years—was amazed to discover that, as our boat moves, the mountains appear to move with us. He composed this poem:

Viewed from a moving boat,
    even mountains move—
But do the mountain pines know
    this?

It is a fitting poem for a child.

Today the sea is rough. Around the rocks the foam is like driving snow, and the waves themselves are flowers in bloom:

A wave is but a single thing,
    we're told; but from its hue
You'd think it was a mixture—
    flowers and snow!

—Ki no Tsurayuki
from The Tosa Diary

The writer who postpones the recording of his thoughts uses an iron which has cooled to burn a hole with.

*– Henry David Thoreau
essayist*

February 5, 1918

There was an apple tree with many apples on it, looking especially red because the sky above was so blue. The tree was on the other side of a brick wall, but there was a ladder leaning against the wall. It was a high wall, but the ladder was high, too, and its top reached right up into the tree. I started to climb up the ladder. It was so real that I could feel the way my hands grasped the rungs and my toes curled around them. I climbed and climbed toward the red apples and the blue sky. Then I woke up.

– Elizabeth Yates
from My Diary—My World

EMOTIONS

This was to be an objective diary. It stops here! I don't care how much I rave if only I could get down to keep _a little_ the feeling of what has happened last week....

The best I can do is to piece together painstakingly the small superficial details, all – everything I can remember, everything no matter how little – and rather blindly hope that a miracle will happen, that this conglomerate, patched collection of fragments may ignite somehow – at least for me – and that some glimmering of the indescribable feeling may be relit in me.

– Anne Morrow Lindbergh
from Bring Me A Unicorn

If you were to scan my own notebooks, here are the kinds of things you would see on one side of the center line or the other:

- lists of memories
- descriptions of places and people in my childhood
- conversations from my childhood
- reflections on my writing process
- letters to myself from my ancestors
- family stories
- notes I have taken from TV programs, newspapers, books, magazines, speeches
- freewriting
- mapping to show how a piece might be organized
- drafts
- quotations from writers, artists, musicians, scientists, any creative people
- art postcards from museums
- blue, yellow, or rainbow-hued pages
- photographs from my childhood
- newspaper clippings
- titles of books I want to read or have read
- imaginary letters to or from my family or childhood friends
- writing schedules that help me with deadlines

I go nowhere without my notebook.

—June Gould from *The Writer in All of Us*

The Writer's Craft All of these writers used a journal or notebook to preserve impressions and ideas. Maybe some things they recorded weren't useful right away, but many observations could have become part of the writers' creative efforts later on. How did you feel about exploring these writers' thoughts?

Your thoughts and reflections are worth recording, too. What do these pieces suggest to you about starting a journal of your own?

A writer's notebook or journal:
- is a place to record personal feelings.
- saves thoughts and observations.
- can be used for writing ideas.

Observing, Imagining, and Reflecting

From the moment you wake up to the moment you fall asleep, you receive countless sensory impressions. No one can remember them all—but everyone *can* learn to be a good observer. Test yourself: What do you notice and feel when you see a beautiful butterfly or hear a new song or smell freshly baked bread? Whatever it is, jot it down in your Journal. Then, whenever you want to relive those moments, all you have to do is look up your observations.

A journal is also a place to let your imagination run free. So use your Journal to think aloud on paper and to try out ideas. Someday you might develop those ideas into something that you'll want to share with the world!

An Entry a Day Deciding to keep a journal will help you only if you get around to using it. After all, you wouldn't want to lose a great idea just because you didn't take a minute to jot it down.

Make writing a habit. Even if you think that you have nothing new to say, open your Journal every day and write *something*. In fact, it's probably a good idea to visit your Journal around the same time every day.

QUICK BITS

phrases, lists, or even short sentences to help you with grammar

DREAMSCAPES

daydreams or night dreams (best recorded first thing in the morning!)

LIST LIST

songs, books, TV shows—your favorite and your least favorite (and why)

IS THIS ME?

thoughts and impressions about yourself as a writer

If you have trouble starting, look over some recent entries and jot down your impressions of them. Try doodling until your ideas start to flow. A journal is one place where spelling, grammar, and neatness aren't all that important. What matters is that you write down the things that are important to *you*.

Getting It Together Sometimes you'll want to sort through your observations and reread them or use them in your writing. The way you organize your Journal can make this easier. Some people like to record their impressions each day in a loose-leaf notebook. Others prefer keeping note cards in a file box or using a folder. Within their journals, some people use different colors of ink for different subjects. Whether you organize your writing as daily diary entries or gather your ideas in a folder, use a system of organization that you find comfortable.

Are you thinking about how you could organize your own Journal? Maybe these headings will help you. Remember—the best way to organize your Journal is the way that works best for you!

It's perfectly okay to record bits and pieces of ideas in your Journal, but as you write, you may hit upon a subject you have a lot to write about. Then you can use your Journal to make more detailed plans. Those plans could include lists, diagrams, charts, and even pictures or sketches.

You can find out more about these planning techniques on pages 213–224.

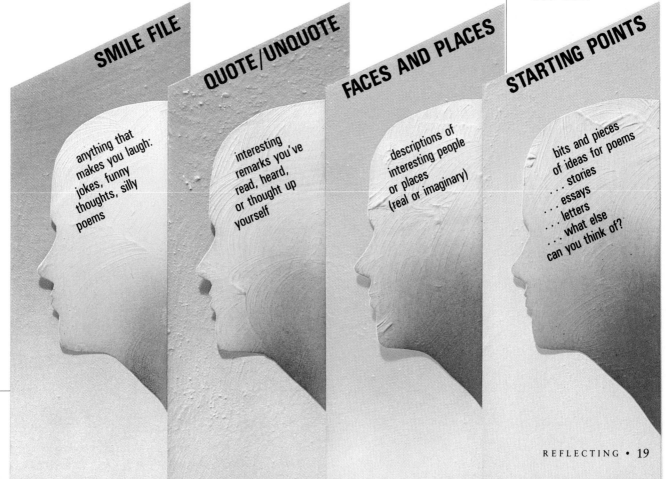

SMILE FILE
anything that makes you laugh: jokes, funny thoughts, silly poems

QUOTE/UNQUOTE
interesting remarks you've read, heard, or thought up yourself

FACES AND PLACES
descriptions of interesting people or places (real or imaginary)

STARTING POINTS
bits and pieces of ideas for poems
... stories
... essays
... letters
... what else can you think of?

Listening to Yourself

The words you choose and the way you put them together reflect your personal perspective. Writing in your Journal every day can help you to discover the things you're really interested in and the special way you can write about them.

*A way to define the writer's voice is personal style. Many things go into developing a personal style, and you can read about them in **Writer's Craft** on pages 239–281.*

All of the entries in your Journal or notebook are discoveries from your personal explorations. When you make your entries, you're using your writer's voice to tell about them. With each entry that voice becomes clearer and stronger and eventually will be heard in the writing you share. Let your Journal be a place to listen to yourself before you speak out loud.

Letting It Out—Sometimes! A journal is private. When you write in it, you don't have to be concerned about pleasing an audience. When friends are stumped for writing ideas, you may want to skim through your Journal for ideas to suggest. Sometimes, however, you may want to share parts of your Journal with friends or family members. People who care about you are naturally curious about what's on your mind, and sharing journal entries can be a way to let them know. Consider reading parts of your Journal out loud or copying out the passages you want to share. Can you think of other ways to share parts of your Journal?

Talk About Journals With one or more friends, share some of your thoughts on keeping a daily journal. How could a journal help you to develop ideas for your own writing projects? For example, what kinds of journal entries could help you to write a story? a poem? an essay? As you talk, share ideas for organizing your Journals, too.

UNIT 2

He rode easily, relaxed in the saddle, leaning his weight lazily into the stirrups. Yet even in this easiness was a suggestion of tension. It was the easiness of a coiled spring, of a trap set.
— Jack Schaefer from *Shane*

Paint a Portrait

- *Have I ever had to depend on a description to identify something? What kind of description was it?*
- *How would I describe myself to someone who has never met me?*

When artists paint portraits of people, they look beyond facial features and color of hair. Truly great portraits capture a look at the inner life of the person. This is what writers strive to do when they write a character sketch. How does the person feel, and how does the person make others feel? What makes that person stand out and occupy a special place in the artist's or writer's heart?

IN YOUR JOURNAL Think of the most amazing person you've ever met. Why is that person amazing? In your Journal, jot down a few descriptive words that come to mind. How would you describe that person to someone else? Is there something unique about his or her personality? Take a few minutes to sketch a quick drawing of the person in your Journal.

On August 6, 1973, Roberto Clemente was inducted into the Baseball Hall of Fame. Clemente led an inspirational life on and off the field. He won twelve Gold Glove Awards, played in twelve All Star games, and was the eleventh player to get 3,000 hits. He helped the Pittsburgh Pirates win two World Series. Clemente also helped numerous humanitarian causes. He died in a plane crash during a relief mission for earthquake victims.

Meet William Brewer

What do these things have in common: History class, spaghetti, *Into a Dream,* basketball, and poetry? All five are favorites of William Brewer. William attends Hally Open Middle School in Detroit, Michigan.

Have you ever had a tough time coming up with topics or ideas for writing? William suggests writing in a journal about things that happen each day. He remembers, ''Some days I have nothing to write about—like if nothing interesting happened that day. I can still think of an idea by reading my school journal. . . . Another thing I do is look at books and get ideas from them. It's kind of interesting learning and writing about topics you don't know much about.''

An excerpt from William's writing appears on page 24. William shares, ''I wrote this piece because there are a lot of things I don't know about space and space travel. I want to know what life was like for Mr. Bluford especially.''

Maria Tallchief was one of the first American ballerinas to gain international fame. She began dancing with the Ballet Russe de Monte Carlo, but her career flourished with the New York City Ballet. She created many roles through her thirteen years with the company.

In 1955 Rosa Parks refused to give up her seat to a white man on a bus in Montgomery, Alabama. Her subsequent arrest sparked a 380-day bus boycott and galvanized the civil rights movement. Her quiet courage made her a symbol of the growing movement for the rights of African Americans in the United States.

■ Writers at Work

Once you're into a story everything seems to apply—what you overhear on a city bus is exactly what your character would say on the page you're writing. Wherever you go, you meet part of your story. I guess you're tuned in for it, and the right things are sort of magnetized—if you can think of your ears as magnets.

*- Eudora Welty
author*

When painting a portrait, artists look carefully at their models to capture the unique qualities of each subject: the arch of an eyebrow, the gesture of a hand, the glance of an eye.

Instead of using charcoal and watercolors, writers describe people and places with vivid language and specific details that help the readers picture the subject in their own minds. Notice how the writers of the following descriptions have captured the specific qualities of each subject.

Guion S. Bluford, Jr., was born in West Philadelphia, Pennsylvania, on November 22, 1942. Guion lived with his parents, Guion Sr. and Lolita, and his brothers, Kenneth and Eugene, in an integrated rowhouse neighborhood on Media Street. Guion's nickname was "Bunny." He was mostly called that by his family. Guion was shy and preferred working out puzzles or brain-teasers to playing outside. He was interested in airplanes and was more interested in the aerodynamics of flight than actually flying an airplane.

By junior high, Guion Bluford decided to be an aerospace engineer. Fortunately for Guy Bluford (short for Guion), he didn't take the advice of a high school teacher who thought he wouldn't do well in college. In 1960 Bluford enrolled in Penn State University. . . In January 1972, Guion Bluford was accepted by NASA as a Group 8 astronaut. Bluford became the first Afro-American to travel in space. At 2:30 A.M on August 30, 1983, Bluford and his crew members took off for outer space. That was the first night launch in shuttle history. . .
— William Brewer   Hally Middle School   Detroit, MI

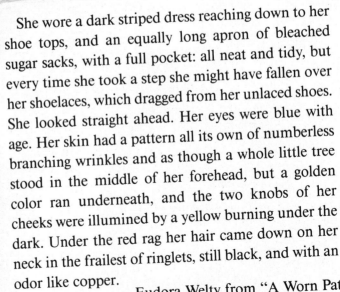

She wore a dark striped dress reaching down to her shoe tops, and an equally long apron of bleached sugar sacks, with a full pocket: all neat and tidy, but every time she took a step she might have fallen over her shoelaces, which dragged from her unlaced shoes. She looked straight ahead. Her eyes were blue with age. Her skin had a pattern all its own of numberless branching wrinkles and as though a whole little tree stood in the middle of her forehead, but a golden color ran underneath, and the two knobs of her cheeks were illumined by a yellow burning under the dark. Under the red rag her hair came down on her neck in the frailest of ringlets, still black, and with an odor like copper.
— Eudora Welty from "A Worn Path"

The Writer's Craft Each of these descriptions conveys a specific impression or feeling about its subject. What impression does each description convey? To create this impression, each writer has used details that appeal to one or more of the senses. What descriptive details help to create the main impression in each piece? Which description do you think gives the best picture of its subject? Why?

He put down his reed pipes when he saw me and with six of his arm-legs slowly pushed himself off the portico. He seemed surprised and walked around me. He walked delicately on two arm-legs like a ballet dancer imitating an old man, with his six other arm-legs stretched out to balance his overpuffed body. He stepped back in front of me and examined me boldly, even though Argans usually kept their eyelids down low because they knew how their eyes bothered humans. Argans have myriads of tiny eyes on their orbs. They shine like clouds of stars in dim light and it takes some getting used to—it's like being watched by a one-man crowd.

— Laurence Yep from *Sweetwater*

The City Is So Big

The city is so big
Its bridges quake with fear
I know, I have seen at night

The lights sliding from house to house
And trains pass with windows shining
Like a smile full of teeth

I have seen machines eating houses
And stairways walk all by themselves
And elevator doors opening and closing
And people disappear.

— Richard García

WRITERS' GALLERY

For more examples of descriptive writing, turn to page 192.

Word Pictures

Writing a description is like painting a picture. You have an image in your mind, and you want others to see it. How do you start?

Think of the colorful impressions, sensory textures, or other characteristics of a person or place you find interesting or special. Vivid words can help you to paint a picture—a word picture—of that person, place, or even a feeling. Writing a description can help you to share with others the pictures and images in your mind.

For example, consider writing a character sketch of someone special to you. What aspects of a person could you describe: physical features, personality, or the way that person talks or walks? What makes that person unique?

Brainstorm: Purpose and Audience As a writer, you need to think about your purpose and audience before starting to write. What is your purpose? What do you want your audience to know about the person or thing you describe? Who is your audience? Are you writing this piece for a friend or for a group of people you've never met before? Discuss the purpose of your description with your partner. Then brainstorm together and create a list of possible audiences for your piece.

Take a look at what the writer on page 27 did to get started. The cluster, which is one way to explore details about a subject, provided a good jumping-off point. What can you tell about Coach Jennigan from the cluster? You may want to use lists, charts, or diagrams to spark your ideas. Think about using any method that will help you start your creative thoughts going. Use your memory and your imagination.

IN YOUR JOURNAL In this unit you will see how description can make a character come to life. You'll have an opportunity to write a character sketch of your own. If you'd prefer, you may choose another kind of descriptive writing. See the Writer's Project File on page 36 for help in making another choice. Once you've made your choice, start planning your description in your Journal. You may want to draw your own cluster, or you can use any number of planning methods. Turn to page 219 for more information about clusters.

Descriptive writing:
- *gives the reader an overall impression or feeling about the subject.*
- *uses figurative language, such as simile and metaphor, which helps the reader form vivid images of the subject through comparison.*
- *includes specific details to help create a colorful, in-depth picture.*

For more help in:
- *choosing a topic, turn to pages 213–215.*
- *selecting a planning strategy, turn to pages 216–224.*
- *self-selecting, turn to the Writer's Project File on page 36.*

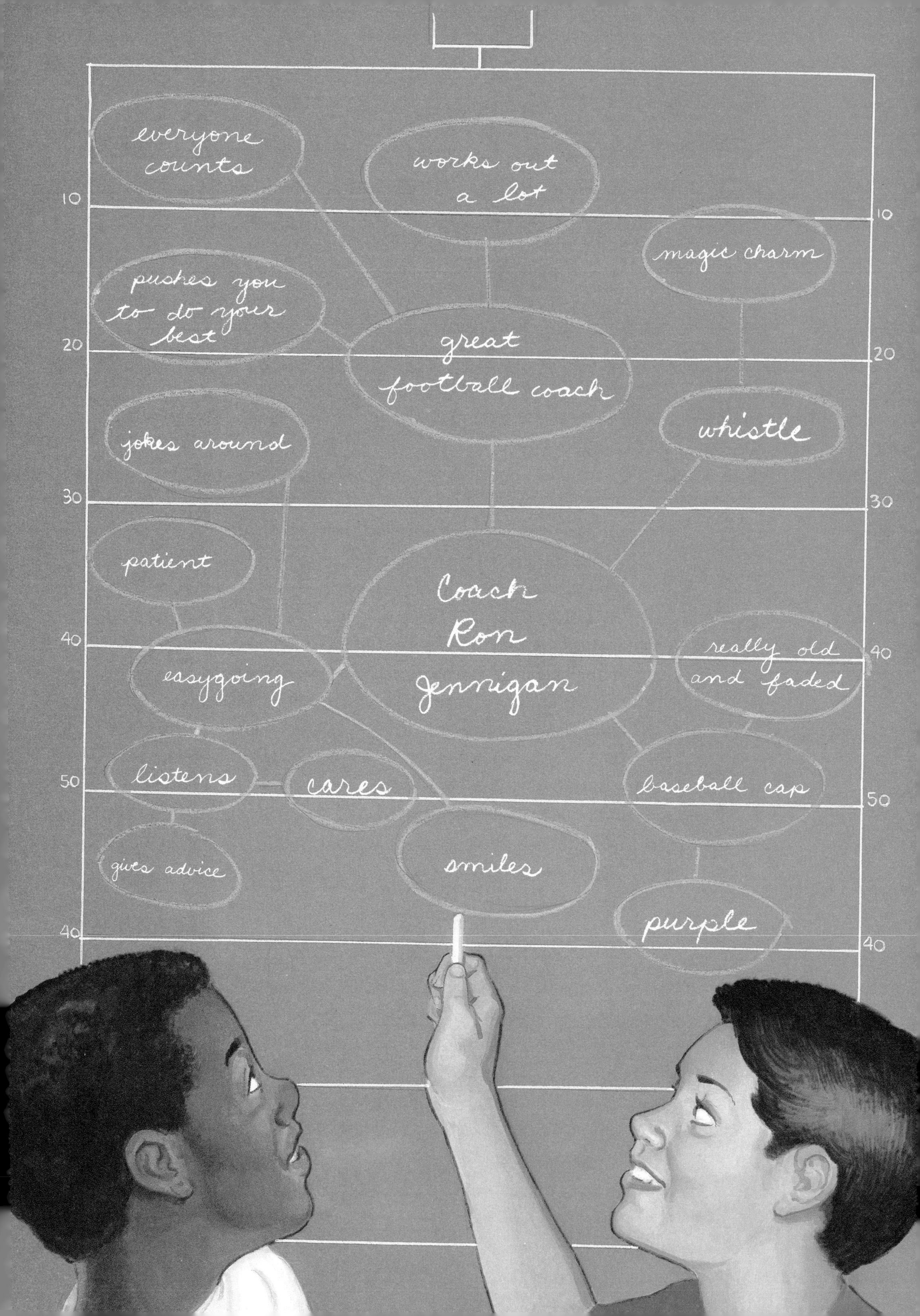
everyone counts
works out a lot
magic charm
pushes you to do your best
great football coach
jokes around
whistle
patient
Coach Ron Jennigan
really old and faded
easygoing
listens
cares
baseball cap
gives advice
smiles
purple
10
10
20
20
30
30
40
40
50
50
40
40

A Rough Sketch

A painter uses brushes and paints to create a picture. What do you have? As a writer, you may have random words and phrases, notes, drawings, plans, and even some organized ideas. How do you turn your materials into a work of art?

Think of lightly sketching an image. Begin writing and keep going until you get all of your ideas on paper. Take a look at the *Prescription for a Description* for tips.

Prescription for a Description

- Think about your purpose and audience. Ask yourself these questions:
  - What do I hope to accomplish with this piece?
  - Who will read it?
- To create an overall impression, visualize the person, place, or thing you are going to describe. Imagine how you want the description to sound. Do you have a vivid picture in your mind's eye?
- Use specific details that stand out and make your subject special or unique. Include sensory details—details that appeal to one of the five senses. Sensory details describe how things look, sound, taste, feel, or smell.
- Give the details a logical order. You may want to describe a scene from near to far or from one side to the other. This organizing technique can help the reader follow your description. Phrases such as *in front, to the right,* and *in the distance* lend spatial order to your description. Learn more about spatial order on page 251.
- Think about using figurative language, such as simile, metaphor, or personification, to create striking images. Here are a few examples:
  - My brother Paul is as quiet as spring rain. (simile)
  - Paul's eyes are an ocean of blue. (metaphor)
  - The birds in the trees laughed at Paul's attempt to fly the kite. (personification)

  For a further discussion of simile, metaphor, and personification, see pages 277–278.

Talk About Drafting Here is a draft for a character sketch. Look it over and discuss it with a partner. What is your overall impression of Coach Jennigan? Which details do you find especially descriptive? Are there any places that you think could use more work?

CRITICAL THINKING

Have you ever heard someone described as being as stubborn as a mule?

Writers use simile and metaphor to describe subjects by comparing them to related subjects. See page 278 for more about simile and metaphor.

In this description, how does comparing the coach's whistle to a magic charm add to the overall impression of the coach?

Turn to the Writers at Work selections on pages 24-25. Which of the authors used simile or metaphor for comparison?

```
    Is it that he works out as hard as anyone else on the
team or that he really cares about his players welfare?
People ask what makes Mr. Ron Jennigan my football coach
so cool. Starters and bench-warmers alike know that
Coach gives each person his all. He pushes you to do your
best and tackle your weak spots--whether you want to or
not! If you need someone to talk to, he gets all serious
and seems to know what to say. Of course, if you ask
Coach, he just smiles that big smile. "People count, he
says.
    He leans quietly against the fence, waiting for
football practice to begin. A faded purple baseball cap
that's as old as Wrigley Field sits on Coach's head. He
laughs as the team members arrive with their jokes. He
always has a new joke or too himself. Coach is a great
guy. When Coach blows his whistle, the sound works like
a magic charm, and the team quickly lines up. Then comes
the toughest workout you can imagine.
    What's Coach's secret? It's not just his easygoing
manner and great jokes. It's that he really believes that
every person counts. He makes all of us believe that
we do.
```

ON YOUR OWN Using whatever plans you've made, try drafting a description of the subject you've chosen. Don't worry about making every word count. You have plenty of time to fix any mistakes or add to your description later.

Taking a Fresh Look

Now you've written your draft. What's next? Take a break! Think about something else, ride a bike, or run an errand.

When you come back to your draft, you'll be able to give it a fresh look, with a refreshed mind. Don't be afraid to make changes. This is a chance to add color, depth, and clarity to your piece.

Talk About Revising With a partner, look over these revisions made on the draft. Discuss why you think the changes were made. What changes would you make? Does your partner agree?

The writer wants to start off the piece by introducing the reader to the subject. Is this a good idea? Why or why not?

How do these specific details make the description clearer?

Why do you think the writer removed this sentence? (Hint: Does it add to the overall impression?)

∧Is it that he works out as hard as anyone else on the team or that he really cares about his players welfare? People ask what makes Mr. Ron Jennigan my football coach so cool. Starters and bench-warmers alike know that Coach gives each person his all. He pushes you to do your best and tackle your weak spots--whether you want to or not! If you need someone to talk to, he gets all serious *when to listen and when to give advice.* and seems to know what to say. Of course, if you ask Coach, he just smiles that *crooked* big smile. "People count, he says.

He leans quietly against the fence, waiting for football practice to begin. A faded purple baseball cap that's as old as Wrigley Field sits on Coach's head. He laughs as the team members arrive with their jokes. He always has a new joke or too himself. ~~Coach is a great guy.~~ When Coach blows his whistle, the sound works like a magic charm, and the team quickly lines up. Then comes the toughest workout you can imagine.

What's Coach's secret? It's not just his easygoing manner and great jokes. It's that he really believes that every person counts. He makes all of us believe that we do.

ON YOUR OWN You may want to make some notes in your Journal about changes you'd like to make in your description. If you are unable to decide exactly how to change the text, just mark the parts that don't seem quite right so that you can come back to them later. Then ask a partner to read your description and to suggest places where the draft might need work. Finally, ask yourself questions such as these:

- Does my lead or opening sentence immediately capture the interest of my readers?

- Do my descriptive details create a strong, vivid, and accurate overall picture of the subject? Can my readers see what I see?

- Where should I provide more specific details that will help my readers understand my subject more clearly?

- What sensory details can I add to enrich my description? How do things look, sound, taste, feel, and smell?

- Are the details in my description arranged clearly? If I chose to describe something in spatial order, such as from left to right or from top to bottom, did I stick to that logical order?

- Where can I add figurative language, including similes, metaphors, and personification, to help bring my subject to life?

- Can I delete any sentences that do not contribute to the overall impression I am trying to create?

CONFERENCING STRATEGIES

When you work with a partner, you may want to say:
- *I especially enjoyed the detail about _____.*
- *I'd like to know more about _____.*

Read the entire piece before you make any comment. Criticism is best received when it is positive and helpful.

For more advice about conferencing, see page 229.

REVISING STRATEGIES

When you review a description:
- *Reread the passage. Has a strong overall impression been created?*
- *Notice if figurative language helps make the subject come to life.*
- *Think about the details. Are they vivid and specific? Do they give insight into the subject?*

The Finishing Touches

You've revised your draft. You're thinking about sharing your piece with an audience. Before you do, you'll want to give your work one last look. Proofreading is like putting the final brush strokes on your painting.

Before writers make a clean, final copy of their work, they must be sure that there are no spelling, grammar, or punctuation mistakes.

Talk About Proofreading Discuss proofreading corrections on page 33 with a partner. What punctuation errors were fixed? Why were the corrections made? Do you need to make any of them in your own work?

ON YOUR OWN Think about whether you would like to publish your writing. If you would, read through your descriptive piece, checking for any errors. Are there particular punctuation errors in your own writing that you need to be on the lookout for? What grammar corrections can you make? You may want to use the following questions as a guide to help you proofread your description:

- Did I indent every paragraph?

- Did I correctly punctuate each sentence?

- Are there any run-on sentences or sentence fragments that I should correct? (For more information about correcting run-ons and fragments, see page 303.)

- Did I use adjectives correctly to describe my subjects?

- Did I use adverbs correctly to bring the action in my description to life?

- If I included dialog, did I use quotation marks correctly? (To learn more about using quotation marks, see page 356.)

- What words do I tend to misspell?

After you've proofread, you may want to exchange pieces with a friend for a look by another pair of eyes. This way you have an even better chance of catching everything.

PROOFREADING

CHECK-UP

ᒧIs it that he works out as hard as anyone else on the

team or that he really cares about his players⌄welfare?

People ask what makes Mr. Ron Jennigan⌃my football coach⌄

so cool. Starters and bench-warmers alike know that

Coach gives each person his all. He pushes you to do your

best and tackle your weak spots--whether you want to or

not! If you need someone to talk to, he gets all serious

when to listen and when to give advice.

and seems to know ~~what to say~~. Of course, if you ask

⌃   *crooked*

Coach, he just smiles that ~~big~~ smile. "People count, ᵛhe

says.

He leans quietly against the fence, waiting for

football practice to begin. A faded purple baseball cap

that's as old as Wrigley Field sits on Coach's head. He

laughs as the team members arrive with their jokes. He

two

always has a new joke or (too) himself. ~~Coach is a great~~

~~guy~~. When Coach blows his whistle, the sound works like

a magic charm, and the team quickly lines up. Then comes

the toughest workout you can imagine.

What's Coach's secret? It's not just his easygoing

manner and great jokes. It's that he really believes that

every person counts. He makes all of us believe that

we do.

- *Check your capitalization and punctuation by using the **Mechanics Handbook** on page 353.*
- *Are you having any grammar problems? Check page 301.*
- *Circle misspelled words. Use the **Word Finder** on pages 368–369 or your dictionary.*

Proofreader's Marks

∧	Add.	⟨	Check the spelling.
ℓ	Take out.	⊙	Add a period
≡	Make a capital letter.	⋏	Add a comma.
/	Make a lower-case letter.	⌄⌄	Add quotation marks.
⌗	Indent the paragraph.	∽	Reverse the order.

DESCRIBING • 33

Sharing Your Work of Art

Publishing is a chance to share your creativity. Publishing gives family, friends, or the general public an opportunity to experience your insights and ideas. How would you like to publish your work?

Talk About Publishing The character sketch of Coach Jennigan was published in a school yearbook. The author titled the piece "A Coach for All Seasons." What kind of effect do you think the character sketch will have on the audience it reaches?

To add variety and interest to their writing, writers often use different types of sentences.

This character sketch contains questions, an exclamatory sentence, and complex sentences. How can you use sentence variety in a writing project of your own?

For more help in:
• *deciding how to publish your work, turn to page 237.*

A Coach for All Seasons

People ask what makes Mr. Ron Jennigan, my football coach, so cool. Is it that he works out as hard as anyone else on the team or that he really cares about his players' welfare? Starters and bench-warmers alike know that Coach gives each person his all. He pushes you to do your best and tackle your weak spots—whether you want to or not! If you need someone to talk to, he gets all serious and seems to know when to listen and when to give advice. Of course, if you ask Coach, he just smiles that crooked smile. "People count," he says.

He leans quietly against the fence, waiting for football practice to begin. A faded purple baseball cap that's as old as Wrigley Field sits on Coach's head. He laughs as the team members arrive with their jokes. He always has a new joke or two himself. When Coach blows his whistle, the sound works like a magic charm, and the team quickly lines up. Then comes the toughest workout you can imagine.

What's Coach's secret? It's not just his easygoing manner and great jokes. It's that he really believes that every person counts. He makes all of us believe that we do.

ON YOUR OWN If you decide to publish, think about the best way to communicate your original purpose to your audience. Should your piece be read aloud so that you can add suspense to certain parts? Be creative. Your work is an original piece of art.

How does your finished work compare with the Model for Self-Evaluation on page 282?

SELF-CHECK

Here are some ideas for descriptive writing. Does one of them catch your interest? Think about how you would write the piece. Let your imagination go, and put your descriptive powers to work.

Flashback

The local theater company is presenting *Blues in the Night,* a play about Paul Robeson, during its yearly festival. Research Robeson's life, and write a description of him.

Seasonal Favorite

Think about your favorite season. What do you like about it? Which colors, smells, and sounds do you associate with it? Jot down some notes and write about your thoughts and opinions. You may want to write a poem.

Extra! Extra! Read All About It!

You've decided on a career as a photojournalist. Choose a magazine or newspaper photograph that you find inspiring. What is the feeling, tone, and mood? What details or insights come to mind? Write a critique of the photograph for your fellow students.

Chef for a Day

As a famous chef, you are putting together a Feast of International Foods. Imagine which foods you will serve. Think about it for a few minutes. Then write a menu with entries describing each food in detail. You might begin with an appetizer such as guacamole: a soft, creamy, cool, olive-green avocado dip studded with chunks of tangy onion and topped with a dab of thick sour cream.

BALLAD OF THE
MORNING STREETS

The magic of the day is the morning
I want to say the day is morning high
and sweet, good
morning.

The ballad of the morning streets, sweet
voices turns
of cool warm weather
high around the early windows grey to blue
and down again amongst the kids and
broken signs, is pure love magic, sweet day
come into me, let me live with you
and dig your blazing

— Amiri Baraka

◼ Express Yourself

SELF-SURVEY

- *Has a friend ever shared a poem with me? What was it about?*
- *What's my favorite song? Does it seem like a poem to me?*
- *If I wanted to hit a reader right between the eyes with a poem, what would I write about?*

Have you ever seen an eagle soaring through open blue skies that never seem to end? Picture the eagle's graceful lines as it glides through the glimmering sun and the red-orange mountains. What could the magnificent creature be thinking of?

What do you think of when you have a moment all to yourself? What have you discovered about your inner self during those quiet times? What is your vision as you reflect on your hopes and your dreams? Take a few minutes now to look at your immediate feelings and thoughts.

IN YOUR JOURNAL Writers often share their inner selves through their poetry. Have you ever read a poem that hit you right between the eyes—one that made you think, "Hey, I know what that poem means! I've felt that way, too"? A poem like that is likely to become one of your favorites. Do you have a favorite poem? If so, jot it down in your Journal and make a quick note about what it means to you. If you haven't yet found a favorite poem, make notes in your Journal about why you like certain poems and not others.

Meet Jesse Russon

Jesse Russon attends Evergreen Junior High School and lives in Salt Lake City, Utah. Some of Jesse's favorite moments are spent outdoors, climbing mountains, exploring rivers, and just hanging out with his friends.

Jesse often draws on his travels to help him with his writing. He pictures scenes from his experiences in his mind and then describes them in his writing. One of Jesse's poems appears on page 40. "The idea for it just came to my mind. I've been in California, and I used to go to the beach a lot. I was just thinking about how it was at dawn before all the people came."

When asked what advice he might give other seventh-graders, Jesse shares, "Sometimes I get stuck and can't figure out what to say next, or what I'm writing doesn't sound right to me. So I put it down anyway, and later I reread it and fix it or check it again."

BEACH

Writers at Work

WRITERS' GALLERY

For more examples of poetry, turn to page 193.

Even the most active people take time for reflection now and then—to think quietly about the world around them, their own experiences, their hopes, and their dreams. Some people put their reflections on paper, where their thoughts may blossom into poems.

Each of the lyric poems on these pages expresses the poet's feelings about something. A lyric poem often has a songlike quality and sometimes rhymes. As you read the poems, think about the different ways the poets found to tell you about their thoughts. What feelings does each poet express? What mood comes through?

Tide overriding the glistening land,
Leaving curdles in the glazing sand,
Light, breezy gushes in the air,
Blowing bits of sand everywhere.
But,
Being alone is not possible here—
Animals crawling about so near,
Not just on the land,
But in the water too.
Swimming around in the deep, deep blue,
Whoosh, shoosh, are the sounds of the waves
As you view the dark gloomy caves.
And up to the sky as the clouds float by,
You think to yourself—
Peace, Peace,
While you lie.

— Jesse Russon
Evergreen Junior High School
Salt Lake City, Utah

space

privacy that no one owns
a silent moment
outdoors, in the city
the shade of a tree at a park
a vacant table at a library
your own office window with your own view
beaches and sea
body-free
your own breath of air
an expansive horizon
viewed by many
but singularly

— Evangelina Vigil-Piñón

The Writer's Craft These poems are quite different from one another. What makes each poem stand apart from the others? What thoughts and reflections do the poets share?

Choose one poem that you enjoyed. What pictures did the poem bring to mind? How did the poet create those pictures? Was it by describing or by making comparisons? Did the poet provide images and details that let you know how something looked, felt, or sounded? Think about how you could use similar methods to create pictures in your own writing.

Writing, I find, goes on in the mind for a long time before you really put anything down on paper. . . . I try to do it every day and get an early start when I think my energies are at their very best.

–N. Scott Momaday poet, author, and painter

kidnap poem

ever been kidnapped
by a poet
if i were a poet
i'd kidnap you
put you in my phrases and meter
you to jones beach
or maybe coney island
or maybe just to my house
lyric you in lilacs
dash you in the rain
blend into the beach
to complement my see
play the lyre for you
ode you with my love song
anything to win you
wrap you in the red Black green
show you off to mama
yeah if i were a poet i'd kid
nap you

— Nikki Giovanni

The Serenity in Stones

I am holding this turquoise
in my hands.
My hands hold the sky
wrought in this little stone.
There is a cloud
at the furthest boundary.
The world is somewhere underneath.
I turn the stone, and there is more sky.
This is the serenity possible in stones,
the place of a feeling to which one belongs.
I am happy as I hold this sky
in my hands, in my eyes, and in myself.

— N. Scott Momaday

Exploring New Territory

Lyric poetry:
- *reflects on feelings and emotions, such as love and grief, often with songlike rhythm and rhyme.*
- *uses imagery to make ideas come alive and figurative language, such as metaphors, to help readers to understand people, things, and feelings in the poems.*
- *includes sensory details to help readers to see, to hear, to feel— maybe even to taste and to smell—as they read.*

When you move to a new neighborhood, what's the first thing you do? Would you explore to find out everything you can about the new area? That's the way to explore the territory of poetry, too. Experience the many forms, feelings, and thoughts of poetry.

Read this poem and see how Langston Hughes paints a vivid word picture of a mother's life and feelings.

Mother to Son

Well, son, I'll tell you:
Life for me ain't been no crystal stair.
It's had tacks in it,
And splinters,
And boards torn up,
And places with no carpet on the floor—
Bare.
But all the time
I'se been a-climbin' on,
And reachin' landin's,
And turnin' corners,
And sometimes goin' in the dark
Where there ain't been no light.
So, boy, don't you turn back.
Don't set down on the steps
'Cause you find it kinder hard.
Don't you fall now—
For I'se still goin', honey,
I'se still climbin',
And life for me ain't been no crystal stair.
— Langston Hughes

What kind of a life has the mother had? You know the answer when she states, "Life for me ain't been no crystal stair." This kind of comparison, which doesn't use *like* or *as,* is a metaphor. What details tell you that the stairway of the mother's life has not been easy?

Langston Hughes helps you to hear and to feel the message of this poem by using rhythm. The rhythm of the lines is determined by the patterns of weak and strong beats. This rhythm pattern is called meter. Does the stop-and-start rhythm give you clues about the uneven rhythm of the mother's life?

The author's use of repetition tells you about the mother's life. For example, you know that she makes progress despite life's problems by the way so many lines begin with *and*. Repetition like this can clarify meaning; it also plays a part in rhythm. Phrases and even whole lines can repeat, too.

Do sounds in the poem repeat? Reread the poem and listen for words with the same vowel sound—for example, the sound of *i* in the words *in* and *splinter*. How many examples of this *i* sound can you find? (Hint: You're listening for the *sound;* you might find it in words that don't have an *i*.) Repetition of a vowel sound is called assonance.

Brainstorm: Purpose and Audience Ask yourself, "Why might I want to write a poem? How would I feel about sharing it? Who might my audience be?" When all your questions about purpose and audience are answered, you're ready to push ahead!

Goals
Hopes
Plans
Possibilities

Possibilities
Plans
Success
(Probable)
Maybe?
Choices

Choices
Chances
Holding on
Taking Chances
Suppose I...?

Somewhere in you, the beginning of a poem is waiting to flourish. All you have to do is open your mind, so you can set it in motion. You could try making a list like this one, which a writer created. One of the broad topics jotted down in the first column sparked ideas pursued in the second column. One of these ideas led to the ideas in the third column. Turn to page 217 to learn more about making lists.

IN YOUR JOURNAL In this unit a lyric poem takes shape. How about writing one yourself? If you'd rather work on a different kind of poem, see the Writer's Project File on page 50. Make your choice —then begin! Jot down your ideas and plans in your Journal.

FOR MORE HELP

For more help in:
- *choosing a topic,* turn to pages 213–215.
- *selecting a planning strategy,* turn to pages 216–224.
- *self-selecting,* turn to the **Writer's Project File** on page 50.

Putting Down Stakes

Why is lyric poetry usually written from the first-person point of view?

Point of view is the perspective from which a poem is told: first-person (I), third-person (he or she), or omniscient (all-knowing). (See page 280.) Since much lyric poetry is intensely personal, using the first-person perspective is natural because it allows readers to share the poet's thoughts and feelings directly.

What is the point of view in each of the Writers at Work poems on pages 40–41? How could a change in the point of view affect your responses to a poem?

You've learned quite a bit about lyric poetry. Now you can put down your stakes and begin writing. *Landmarks for Lyric Poems* gives you some reminders that may help you.

Landmarks for Lyric Poems

- Get off to a good start. Decide *what* (you want to write), *why* (you want to write it—your purpose), and *who* (will read it—your audience).

- The mood and tone you set for the poem can help you to accomplish your purpose and reach your audience. For more about mood and tone, turn to pages 279–281.

- What type of organization will you use? Will you write your lyric poem as a continuous thought like Langston Hughes's "Mother to Son"? Will you use stanzas, which function like paragraphs in a piece of prose?

- Lyric poems often rhyme. Do you want your poem to rhyme? If so, decide on a rhyming pattern. See page 273 to learn about different rhyming patterns.

- Lyric poems often have rhythm that lends a musical sound pattern to the work. Will you use meter—will your poem have a pattern of accented and unaccented syllables? How can you use assonance or other sound effects? Would repetition help the rhythm?

- Use imagery and figurative language. What would help your readers to form mental pictures of your subject and to understand your meaning? Ask yourself these questions:
  - What mental pictures do I have when I think about _____?
  - Should I use a metaphor, or do I want to make the same comparison in the form of a simile (using *like* or *as*)? Turn to page 278 to read more about metaphor and simile.

- Use sensory details that will help your reader react with any of the five senses. Seeing, hearing, feeling, touching, and tasting all help the reader to share in the feelings of a lyric poem.

Talk About Drafting Here is the draft of a lyric poem. Read it first; then discuss it with your partner. What thoughts or reflections does the poet share with the reader? What is the mood and tone of the poem? How does the poem make you feel? Talk about the imagery the poet uses. Do you notice any figurative language?

ON YOUR OWN It's time to take your plans, to check out the *Landmarks for Lyric Poems,* and to dig right in. Write a draft of your poem. Don't worry now about getting lost in words. Keep writing until you have all your thoughts down on paper. You can always retrace your steps and make everything more to your liking later. As you're writing, keep in mind that poetry is different from prose. Poets don't have to structure their writing around complete sentences. This is an opportunity for you to really relax and play with language.

Possibles, Probables, and Supposes

some kids collect butterflies,
Others bugs or roses.
I collect possibles
Probables, perhapses, and supposes.

I keep them in two small jars,
All sorted out so neat —
The possibles sit on the left,
The others on the right.

The probables are what I'll be.
The possibles are what I might.
If I don't keep the lids shut tight,
They'll get away from me

So I guard them very carefully
Because who knows
When I might need a possible
A probable, or a suppose?

Making Adjustments

REVISING STRATEGIES

Take a few minutes to reflect on your poem. Do you like the way it sounds? You can adjust your poem in any way you like—even put it away and write a different one instead. You're in charge!

Talk About Revising What do you and your partner think of the revisions the poet made in this draft? Have the changes improved the poem? What changes would the two of you have made?

When you review a lyric poem:
- *See if the poem helps you to form mental images. See page 276.*
- *Examine the figurative language. Do the metaphors or similes make sense?*
- *Check the sensory details.*

How does this deletion help the rhythm of the poem?

Changing those two little words made a big difference! What do you think is the reason for the change?

The words <u>might</u> and <u>tight</u> rhyme in this stanza. Why do you think the writer moved this sentence?

> Possibles, Probables, and Supposes
>
> Some kids collect butterflies,
> Others bugs or roses.
> I collect possibles
> Probables, ~~perhapses~~ and supposes.
> I keep them in ~~two~~ jelly ~~small~~ jars,
> All sorted out by type ~~so neat~~—
> The possibles sit on the left,
> The others on the right.
>
> The probables are what I'll be.
> The possibles are what I might.
> If I don't keep the lids shut tight,
> They'll get away from me
>
> So I guard them very carefully
> Because, you see, who knows
> When I might need a possible
> A probable, or a suppose?

ON YOUR OWN Now look at your poem. Have you given your audience the gift of mental pictures? Check your rhythm, rhyme, and meter. Did your plans shift as you wrote your draft? Continue revising until your poem sounds right to you.

The Finishing Touches

You're a poet! As you look over your poem, remember that you needn't strictly adhere to grammar and punctuation rules. You can bend punctuation and grammar to suit your expressive needs. You can use punctuation marks to help to create the poem's rhythm. Just make sure that your writing appears as you intend it to appear.

Talk About Proofreading The poet who wrote "Possibles, Probables, and Supposes" found some errors to correct. See if you or your partner can explain the reason for each change.

Poetry is a very personal form of writing. Read the piece as a whole, and point out parts you liked. For more about conferencing, see page 229.

Possibles, Probables, and Supposes

some kids collect butterflies,
Others bugs or roses.
I collect possibles,
Probables, ~perhapses~ and supposes.
I keep them in two *jelly* small jars,
All sorted out *by type* so neat —
The possibles sit on the left,
The others on the right.

The probables are what I'll be.
The possibles are what I might.
If I don't keep the lids shut tight,
They'll get away from me.

So I guard them very carefully
Because, *you see,* who knows
When I might need a possible,
A probable, or a suppose?

Proofreader's Marks

∧	Add.
ℯ	Take out.
≡	Make a capital letter.
/	Make a lower-case letter.
ℂℍ	Indent the paragraph.
○	Check the spelling.
⊙	Add a period.
∧	Add a comma.
⌄⌄	Add quotation marks.
∽	Reverse the order.

CHECK-UP

- *Check your capitalization and punctuation by using the **Mechanics Handbook** on page 353.*
- *Circle misspelled words. Use the **Word Finder** on page 368 or your dictionary.*

ON YOUR OWN If you plan to publish, proofread your work. A small error, such as a misplaced comma, could change the rhythm or meaning of your poem. Does it read and look the way you want it to?

Hang Up Your Hat! You're Home!

Maybe the best part of exploring something new happens when you begin to feel at home. You've been through idea-gathering, drafting, adjusting, and polishing, so you know your way around poetry, and you have a wonderful product for all of your efforts: a unique poem. Now you can think about publishing your poem and sharing it with others. Who do you think would be interested in reading the poem? Whom would you want to share it with?

Talk About Publishing Talk with your partner about the final version of the poem on page 49. Do all the parts now add up to one successful whole? The poet illustrated the piece and displayed it on the Careers bulletin board in the writing center. What audience did the poem reach? How would you have published it?

ON YOUR OWN Have you decided to publish your poem? If you have, how will you do it? One good idea is to rewrite it in beautiful script, mount it on stiff paper, and present it to someone special as a gift. You may want to copy it into your own personal poetry book and save it for your own reflections in a few months. Will your thoughts on your chosen subject have changed? What other publishing ideas do you have?

In the second stanza, the word type doesn't exactly rhyme with right. Such a close call is often referred to as a slant rhyme. Slant rhymes occur when the vowels in the words have the same sound, but the consonants don't. What sound do you hear when you pronounce the y in type and the i in right? Do you have any slant rhymes in your work?

DID YOU NOTICE?

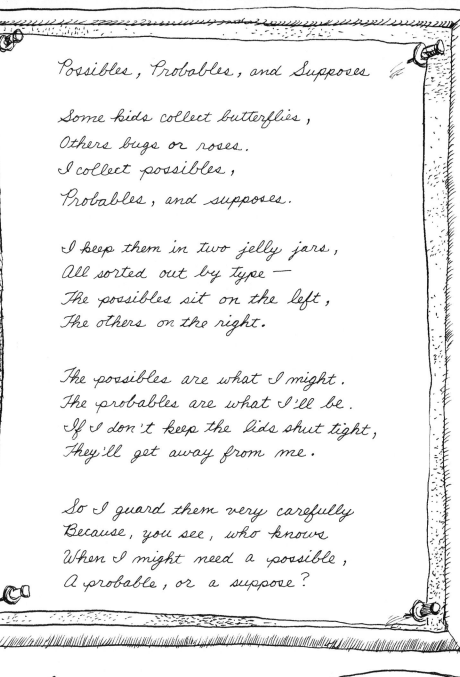

Possibles, Probables, and Supposes

Some kids collect butterflies,
Others bugs or roses.
I collect possibles,
Probables, and supposes.

I keep them in two jelly jars,
All sorted out by type —
The possibles sit on the left,
The others on the right.

The possibles are what I might.
The probables are what I'll be.
If I don't keep the lids shut tight,
They'll get away from me.

So I guard them very carefully
Because, you see, who knows
When I might need a possible,
A probable, or a suppose?

FOR MORE HELP

For more help in:
· **deciding how to publish your work**, turn to page 237.

SELF-CHECK

How does your finished poem compare with the **Model for Self-Evaluation** on page 283?

Here are some ideas for poems you could write. Choose one that interests you. Through your poem, express your feelings, thoughts, and opinions. Remember that your poem can have any form you like.

To the Editor

Science and technology are steadily chipping away at the mysteries of the universe. Choose an object in space —perhaps a quasar or a black hole—and write a poem that explains what the object is and how you feel about it being out there in space. Send your poem to the science editor of your local newspaper.

Ignorance Isn't Bliss

Have you noticed that people are most likely to be suspicious of those whose customs they don't understand? Research the foods, games, and folktales of different groups. Then plan a poster campaign that will educate others about groups outside their own. For each poster, write a short poem. Maybe your poems will become slogans for an age of understanding.

Simply the Best

Who is your favorite musician or actor? Write a tribute to that person in the form of a poem. Tell why you think this star is so special, and try to explain how he or she makes you feel. Imagine yourself reading your poem at an awards ceremony at which your star will be presented with an award.

Poet Laureate

Imagine that you have been dubbed, unofficially, the town's poet laureate (an honorary position given to a poet). For your first duty as poet laureate, write a poem praising what you find remarkable about your town.

EXPLAINING: HOW-TO GUIDE

UNIT

4

I was scared to death. . . . When the stone arrived,
I studied it for hours before I even made a scratch.
I made four full-size drawings, a profile from each
side and a front and a back view. I hung a plumb
so that it pointed directly to the center of the head
and from this point I took all measurements.
                              —Allan Houser
                                 interview in *Southwest Art*

Knowledge Builders

Look at the scene on these pages. How would you describe the feelings that abound: anticipation, the excitement of dreams coming true, the energy of hard work, the hum of creativity? How would you explain what's going on?

Recall other groundbreaking scenes you have witnessed. Think back to what your community was like five, seven, or even nine years ago. What changes and new beginnings have taken place over the years? How would you explain the changes to a new friend?

IN YOUR JOURNAL Sharing your knowledge with others can be rewarding. Often, explaining what you know can give you a special kind of self-confidence. Try to remember a recent explanation you gave. Perhaps it was simple, like giving a friend directions to your house. Maybe you explained something more complicated, like a multistep math problem. In your Journal, freewrite or make some other notes about that memory. If your notes spark ideas about other explanations you've given, jot those down, too.

Meet Vincent Chin

Do you think you could learn how to street skateboard from a book? Vincent Chin thinks you can—just as long as you give yourself time and lots of practice. He wrote a how-to guide for skaters. An excerpt of the piece appears on page 54.

Vincent is a student at Dr. Sun Yat-sen Intermediate School in New York, New York. He enjoys sports of all kinds and through the year participates in football, basketball, and baseball leagues. Vincent also volunteers his time after school helping first and second graders with their homework.

Where does Vincent get his writing ideas? He draws on things that are happening in his life or from topics he's reading about in school. He shares, "The most important thing is to get your ideas down on paper and express what you think about the subject. Later you can always figure out how to piece it all together—kind of like putting together a puzzle." He encourages getting input from friends; he also reads his work to his parents and his sister "just to get a second opinion." He emphasizes, "Getting your point across is just about the best thing a writer can do."

SELF-SURVEY

- *What TV programs have I seen that give instructions or other kinds of explanations?*
- *When I'm learning how to do something, which do I find more helpful—reading instructions by myself or having someone show me?*
- *What activity do I do very well: skateboarding, debating, or making pancakes? How could I explain this activity to someone who is having difficulty?*

Writers at Work

Sometimes . . . it takes me an entire day to write a recipe, to communicate it correctly. It's really like writing a little short story.

–Julia Child chef and author

What do these things have in common?
· instructions for a board game
· a newspaper column with gardening tips
· a recipe card
· a "call in and ask the expert" radio program

What's the answer? They're all resources for building your knowledge. They all offer explanations. What other resources can you think of?

Think of writers of explanations as knowledge builders. As you read the explanations below, think about the building blocks of knowledge that each writer has provided.

One trick to get you started is an ollie. To do an ollie on a skateboard, keep your knees slightly bent. Bring your front foot to the middle of your board, and your back foot higher up the back of your board. Your body weight should be on your front foot and on the <u>front part of your back foot.</u>

The next steps are tricky so follow carefully. First, quickly shift your weight to the front part of your back foot and push the back of the board down, so the front comes up. Then, spring off your back foot allowing the board to come off the ground. Right after lifting your front foot, use the side of your front foot to kick the front of your board down, leveling the board out. Keeping your knees slightly bent, land on your board as it lands on the ground.

All these steps must be done in order and in stride to successfully land the trick. Keep practicing until you can do the trick well. Good luck!

—Vincent Chin
Dr. Sun Yat-sen
Intermediate School
New York, New York

Purée of Parsnips

To go with roast duck, goose, pork, or turkey. For 4 to 6 servings (more than you need for the zucchini boats, but the purée is so good and reheats so well, I am suggesting almost double the necessary amount)

2 pounds (1 kg) parsnips
5 Tb cream   Salt
Pepper   2 Tb butter

Trim and peel the parsnips and cut into slices about 1/3 inch (1 cm) thick. Place in a saucepan with water barely to cover and a teaspoon of salt. Bring to the boil, cover pan, and boil slowly 20 to 30 minutes or until parsnips are tender and water has almost entirely evaporated. Using a vegetable mill or food processor, purée, and return to saucepan. Beat in the cream and butter, and season to taste with salt and pepper. Set pan in another containing simmering water, cover, and let cook 20 to 30 minutes more—note the subtle change in taste that takes place. Correct seasoning before serving. May be cooked in advance and reheated over simmering water.

—Julia Child from
Julia Child & Company

The Writer's Craft Now that you've read these explanations, what new knowledge do you have? Compare the examples once more, noting their different forms. Which pieces are clear and interesting? Which pieces leave little nagging questions in the back of your mind? How would you improve those pieces?

WRITERS'
GALLERY

For more examples of writing that explains, turn to page 194.

Of the 2,573 registrants, 1,421 submitted designs, a record number for such a design competition. When the designs were spread out for jury selection, they filled a large airplane hangar. The jury's task was to select the design which, in their judgment, was the best in meeting these criteria:

- a design that honored the memory of those Americans who served and died in the Vietnam War.
- a design of high artistic merit.
- a design which would be harmonious with its site, including visual harmony with the Lincoln Memorial and the Washington Monument.
- a design that could take its place in the "historic continuity" of America's national art.
- a design that would be buildable, durable, and not too hard to maintain.

. . . The jury spent one week reviewing all the designs in the airplane hangar. On May 1 it made its report to the Vietnam Veterans Memorial Fund: the experts declared Entry Number 1,026 the winner.

　　　—Brent Ashabranner
　　　from *Always to Remember*

Contest Rules

1. Your contest entry must be your very own original work. Ideas and words should not be copied.
2. To enter a competition, you cannot be older than fourteen.
3. You must have your parent's or guardian's permission to send your entry. Each entry must be signed by your parent, guardian, or teacher, saying it is your own original work and that no help was given.
4. Be sure to include your name, age, and full address on each entry.
5. Do not send any poems, drawings, stories, or photographs on subjects other than those described on this contest page.
6. If you want your work returned, enclose a self-addressed, stamped envelope with each entry.
7. Incomplete entries cannot be considered. Your entry will be incomplete if you forget to include your age or the signature of your parent, guardian, or teacher.
8. Your entry must be received by 25 April. We will publish as many of the prizewinning entries as possible in the July 1990 issue of *Cricket*.
9. Send entries to Cricket League, P.O. Box 300, Peru, Illinois, 61354.

　　　—from *Cricket Magazine*
　　　April 1990

Drawing the Blueprints

Writing that explains:
• *sharply focuses on a specific topic.*
• *organizes information so that the reader can follow the explanation easily.*
• *uses facts and clear, precise language to help readers understand the explanation.*

For more help in:
• *choosing a topic, turn to pages 213–215.*
• *selecting a planning strategy, turn to pages 216–224.*
• *self-selecting, turn to the **Writer's Project File** on page 66.*

Are you an explanation expert? Some people are, you know. They share information in such useful ways that you wish they were always around to help. You can be an explanation expert, too.

Writing an explanation is much like constructing a building. First, you need to create blueprints. With any explanation, you need to begin by planning what you are going to write. Suppose you want to explain how to do something, such as teach a younger child how to ride a bicycle. You'll want to think through the steps before you make your explanation so the child won't fall down quite so much.

Brainstorm: Purpose and Audience Before writers actually start writing, they usually think about what they want to accomplish. They have a purpose for writing. They also think about the people for whom they want to write—their audience. Spend a few minutes talking with your partner about the purpose of the explanation you want to write and a possible audience for it.

What helps you churn out ideas: talking to friends, perhaps, or daydreaming? Do you like to make lists or draw pictures? On page 57 the writer used a flowchart to help organize ideas for an explanation. A flowchart helps the writer visualize a step-by-step process: Begin with the directions in the top box; follow the arrow to the information in the next box. What is the writer planning to explain? What title might you give to the completed piece? If you'd like to know more about flowcharts, turn to page 220.

IN YOUR JOURNAL In this unit you will see an explanation unfold that tells how to build a model of a city neighborhood. This explanation is written in the form of a how-to guide. Is there an activity you'd like to explain? You can choose to write a how-to guide, too. If you would rather write a different kind of explanation, browse through the Writer's Project File on page 66. Whatever you choose, begin to plan your piece. Feel free to write notes, draw pictures, or make clusters. You may want to work out a flowchart in your Journal to help you begin. Which method works best for you?

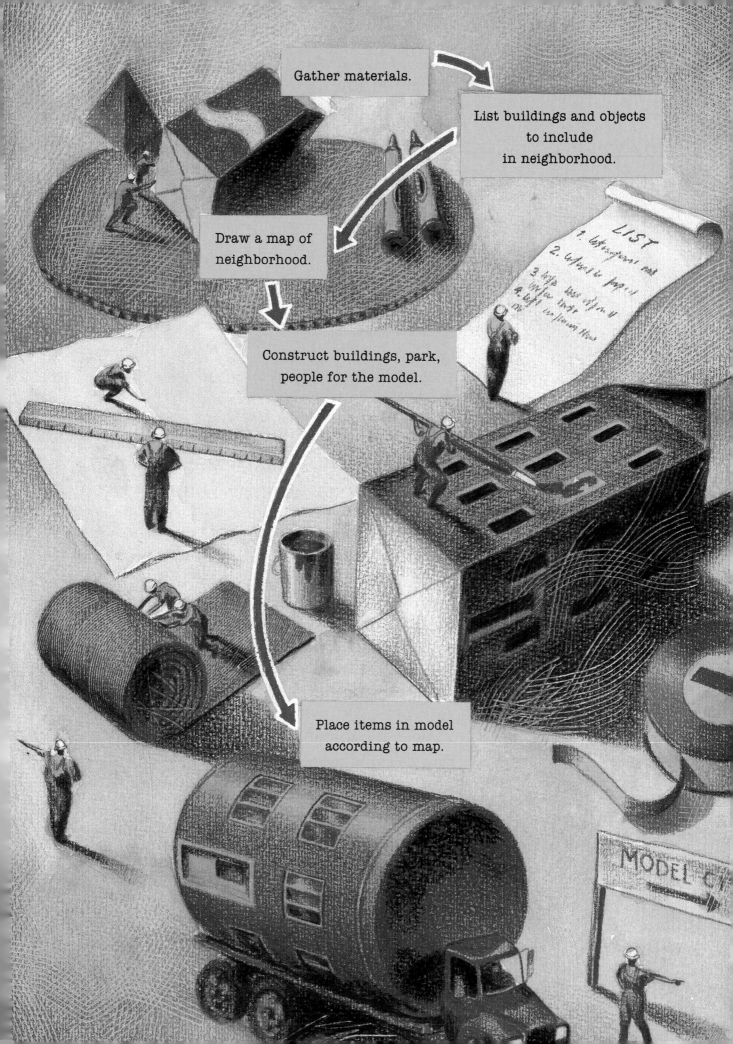

■ # Raising the Frame

For a writer, choosing a topic and developing a plan is like a contractor's completing the blueprints and foundation for a building. The next step is to raise the frame of the building—it's time to write a draft. Read through *Building Blocks* for some helpful tips about how to put your draft on paper.

Building Blocks

■ To focus in on your purpose and audience, ask yourself these questions:

- What will my writing explain?
- For whom am I writing?
- Why is it important for my readers to learn to do this activity?

■ Present your topic clearly to your readers. To keep this in mind, try completing this sentence: When my readers have finished reading my explanation, they will know _____.

■ Think about the best way to present your information. Will you write your step-by-step explanation in article form or as a poem? Use the form that best suits your purpose and audience.

■ Try to keep your explanation flowing. Arrange your information in obvious, logical order. Pay attention to the sequence of the steps in your explanation.

- State the main idea early in an explanation. Tell the readers right away what you are going to explain in your topic sentence.
- Use time-order words such as *first, second, next, now, then,* and *finally* to help your readers follow the steps.
- Try listing all the materials your reader will need before you begin your explanation.

■ Double-check your facts and the order of your steps by asking yourself the following questions:

- If I did not know how to do this activity, would I be able to follow these instructions?
- Have I provided sufficient background information?

■ Let readers know whether or not they're on the right track. Point out potential trouble spots. Offer encouragement or advice, such as "At this point, your diagram should look like this" or "Make sure the paint is dry before you go on."

Talk About Drafting With a partner, read through and discuss this draft. Compare the draft with the flowchart plan on page 57. Were all the steps included in the explanation? Is the how-to guide easy to follow? What do you think of the way the piece is organized?

```
                    A Miniature World

    Think small! Remember tiny dollhouses and model train

sets? Today you will build a model of a city neighbor-

hood. Let's get going! First collect these materials:

graph paper, a flat piece of cardboard to be used as

the base of the model, pieces of cardboard, modeling

clay, pipe cleaners, paints, crayons, and glue.

    Then, spend a few minutes thinking about the layout

of your miniature world. List the items you'd like to

include in your neighborhood, such as a park.

    Use the graph paper to draw a map of the area. Then,

decide where to place the apartment buildings, service

facilitys, and other items.

    Now use your layout to create your model. You don't

want the people to be taller than the buildings. Use

the clay to mold hills and trees. bend pipe cleaners

to form people. Keep in mind a real-life scale. Use

the paint and crayons to draw windows on buildings and

to color trees, grass, and other parts of your model

Finally glue the pieces onto the cardboard base.

    Stand back and get some perspective on your model.

Do it look realistic? share your miniature world with

friends. Maybe city planning is in your future.
```

CRITICAL THINKING

How can you organize your how-to explanation so that it is easy to understand?

Clear, logical sequencing helps your readers to follow your explanation accurately. To learn more about time order, see page 250.

Look at the Writers at Work examples on pages 54–55. Do you see methods of organization that you could use in your own writing?

ON YOUR OWN It's time to write! Like a builder, you have all your tools and materials gathered. Your plans are at your disposal. The fun of building begins—write freely and put all your thoughts on paper. For now, you don't have to worry if you write down some steps in the wrong order. You can change the sequence later.

Surveying Your Progress

REVISING STRATEGIES

When you review an explanation:
- *Make sure that the topic is clearly stated.*
- *Think about the organization. Is the information presented logically?*
- *Ask yourself if all necessary details are included.*

FAST FOCUS

How will these instructions for creating buildings aid the reader? ....

Readers may find it helpful to be reminded of this point before they create their models. ...

This sentence could be deleted—this is not an article on career choices. It would be better to end with a sentence tied in to the main focus. ....

You've raised your building. Next, you'll check to make sure that you have the basic construction you want. Before you begin reassessing your piece, though, take some time out. Take up an activity that doesn't involve reading or writing. Then reread your draft, marking the parts you may want to go back to and change later.

Talk About Revising Look over this draft with a partner. Discuss why you think the writer made the changes. What changes do you feel helped this draft the most? What other changes do you feel would improve the draft further? Does your partner agree?

A Miniature World

Think small! Remember tiny dollhouses and model train sets? Today you will build a model of a city neighborhood. Let's get going! First collect these materials: graph paper, a flat piece of cardboard to be used as the base of the model, pieces of cardboard, modeling clay, pipe cleaners, paints, crayons, and glue.

Then, spend a few minutes thinking about the layout of your miniature world. List the items you'd like to include in your neighborhood, such as a park.

Use the graph paper to draw a map of the *neighborhood* area. Then, decide where to place the apartment buildings, service facilitys, and other items.

Now use your layout to create your model. *Cut out and glue together each cardboard building.* You don't want the people to be taller than the buildings. Use the clay to mold hills and trees. bend pipe cleaners to form people. Keep in mind a real-life scale. Use the paint and crayons to draw windows on buildings and to color trees, grass, and other parts of your model Finally glue the pieces onto the cardboard base.

Stand back and get some perspective on your model. Do it look realistic? share your miniature world with friends. Maybe city planning is in your future.

ON YOUR OWN Reread your draft. Look again at the places where you marked your paper. How could you clarify the points for your readers? Think about whether an absolute novice to your topic could follow your explanation. Is the information organized so that it makes sense? Ask your partner to read your draft. A different pair of eyes can always help! In addition, ask yourself the following questions so that your ideas are presented precisely and clearly.

■ Does my topic sentence contain the main idea of my explanation?

■ Do my supporting details—the facts, reasons, or steps in my process—provide the information that develops my topic?

■ If my draft explains how to do something or how something works, have I used chronological (time) order—the easiest order for a reader to follow?

■ Do the time-order words and phrases in my explanation, such as *first, next, at this point, after that,* and *later,* help show readers how the ideas in my explanation are connected?

■ Have I included all that my audience needs to know in order for me to accomplish my purpose? Should I delete any information that does not suitably guide my readers?

■ Have I concluded my explanation effectively? Have I summarized the information, restated the topic sentence in different words, or left my audience with an important point to consider?

When you and your partner discuss explanations, you may want to say things such as:
· *I could easily follow each step, but I'd like to know more about _____.*
· *Does this section really go before (or after) _____?*

Look for the positive aspects of the piece as well as the areas that can be improved. Point out at least one thing you learned from reading the piece.

For more advice about conferencing, see page 229.

Safety Inspection

A newly completed building must be inspected for safety before it can be opened to the public. Is the wiring connected correctly? Are the doors and windows in place? Think about your explanation. Would you like to share it with the public? If you publish, your writing must be inspected to make sure that the spelling, grammar, and punctuation are correct.

Talk About Proofreading With a partner, review the proofreading corrections in "A Miniature World" on page 63. Talk over the reasons why the changes were made. Have you ever had to make those changes in your own writing?

A Miniature World

Think small! Remember tiny dollhouses and model train sets? Today you will build a model of a city neighborhood. Let's get going! First, collect these materials: graph paper, a flat piece of cardboard to be used as the base of the model, pieces of cardboard, modeling clay, pipe cleaners, paints, crayons, and glue.

Then, spend a few minutes thinking about the layout of your miniature world. List the items you'd like to include in your neighborhood, such as a park.

Use the graph paper to draw a map of the *neighborhood* area. Then, decide where to place the apartment buildings, service *facilities* facilitys, and other items.

Now use your layout to create your model. *Cut out and glue together each cardboard building.* You don't want the people to be taller than the buildings. Use the clay to mold hills and trees. bend pipe cleaners to form people. Keep in mind a real-life scale. Use the paint and crayons to draw windows on buildings and to color trees, grass, and other parts of your model. Finally, glue the pieces onto the cardboard base.

Stand back and get some perspective on your model. Do it look realistic? share your miniature world with friends. Maybe city planning is in your future.

- Check your capitalization and punctuation by using the **Mechanics Handbook** on page 353.

- Are you having any verb problems? Check page 318.

- Circle misspelled words. Use the **Word Finder** on page 368 or your dictionary.

Proofreader's Marks

∧	Add.
ℓ	Take out.
≡	Make a capital letter.
/	Make a lower-case letter.
¶	Indent the paragraph.
○	Check the spelling.
⊙	Add a period.
∧	Add a comma.
⌄⌄	Add quotation marks.
∽	Reverse the order.

ON YOUR OWN Give some thought to publishing your piece. Talk through your publishing ideas with a classmate. How would you like to share your writing with the audience you've chosen? If you decide to publish, proofread your explanation. If you wish, ask a partner to proofread your piece as a final check.

FOR MORE HELP

For more help in:
· *deciding how to
publish your
work, turn to
page 237.*

PUBLISHING

Open House!

Now that your explanation is proofread, it's ready for the public! Here is an opportunity to share your knowledge with others. Think about the many ways there are to publish. Then picture in your mind the audience you'd like to reach. What publishing method do you think will have the greatest impact on your audience?

Talk About Publishing With your classmate, take some time to discuss the published explanation on page 65 of how to build a neighborhood model. This how-to guide was printed in the crafts section of a monthly magazine for teenage writers. Can you think of any other publishing opportunities for this explanation? What would you have done?

ON YOUR OWN Would you like to publish your explanation? If so, where would you like to see it appear? Is there a crafts section in the local newspaper? What about turning your explanation into a video, using real-life props and your favorite music? Any method of publishing you choose is fine, so be creative!

*How does your finished work compare with the **Model for Self-Evaluation** on page 284?*

A Miniature World

Think small! Remember tiny dollhouses and model train sets? Today you will build a model of a city neighborhood. Let's get going! First, collect these materials: graph paper, a flat piece of cardboard to be used as the base of the model, pieces of cardboard, modeling clay, pipe cleaners, paints, crayons, and glue.

Then, spend a few minutes thinking about the layout of your miniature world. List the items you'd like to include in your neighborhood, such as a park.

Use the graph paper to draw a map of the neighborhood. Then, decide where to place the apartment buildings, service facilities, and other items.

Now use your layout to create your model. Keep in mind a real-life scale. You don't want the people to be taller than the buildings. Cut out and glue together each cardboard building. Use the clay to mold hills and trees. Bend pipe cleaners to form people. Use the paint and crayons to draw windows on buildings and to color trees, grass, and other parts of your model. Finally, glue the pieces onto the cardboard base.

Stand back and get some perspective on your model. Does it look realistic? Share your miniature world with friends.

Look over these ideas for explanations to write. Do you see a topic that appeals to you? Forge ahead with it, using your knowledge and your imagination to write your explanation.

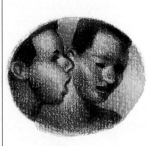

Folksplanations

Before there were written languages, folks passed along information through storytelling. Their legends and stories often explained mysteries of nature, such as why the sun rises. Write an explanation of a natural phenomenon, such as the northern lights. Then tell your folksplanation to a group of friends.

Musical Message

Have you ever encountered someone who doesn't like the music you and your friends think is phenomenal? Write a letter to a pen pal in Egypt who has never heard your favorite albums. Tell your pen pal what the music means to you and what it tries to do. Then tell why it's your favorite type of music.

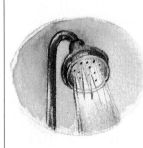

Water Waste Ban

In periods of drought, the public is urged to conserve water. Find out how different conservation methods work. For example, how does putting a brick in the toilet tank save water? Plan a poster series for use in the next water emergency. Each poster should give an explanation of how one measure will save water. The explanation should be scientifically correct.

Have I Got a TV Show for You!

Imagine you are a TV producer with a fantastic idea for a new game show. Sell your idea to the networks. Write a proposal explaining the game show: the rules, the prizes awarded, the target audience, and a catchy title.

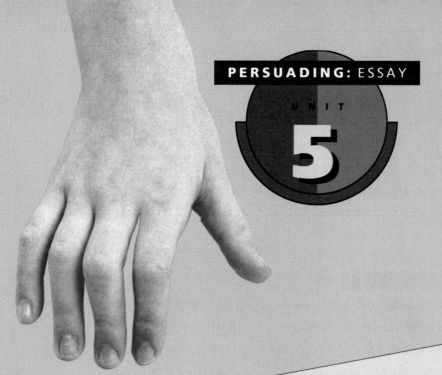

Think of your fellow man; lend him a helping hand—
Put a little love in your heart.
You see, it's getting late; oh, please don't hesitate!
Put a little love in your heart.

And the world will be a better place,
And the world will be a better place
For you and me.
You just wait and see.
Put a little love in your heart.

— Jimmy Holiday, Randy Myers, and Jackie DeShannon
from "Put a Little Love in Your Heart"

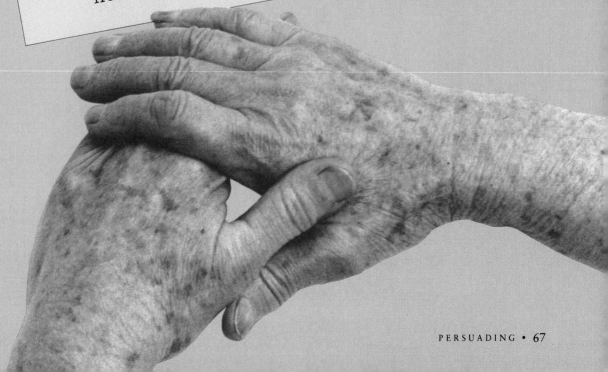

Taking a Stand

"I think it's great that so-and-so is helping so-and-so." "I don't think that what so-and-so is doing is right." How often do you voice your opinions? Speaking your mind and urging others to agree with you is a priceless gift every person can give. By speaking up and utilizing the art of persuasion, you can help to make the world a better place in which to live.

IN YOUR JOURNAL What topic do you have an opinion on that you would like others to consider? Think about issues and ideas that you have heard people debating. Which issues are the most important to you? List them in your Journal and make some notes about your own opinions on these issues.

- *What TV commercial sticks out in my mind? What product does it try to persuade me to buy? What does it say about the product? Do I believe everything the commercial claims?*
- *What arguments helped me to influence a friend's opinion? How successful was I? What could I have done differently?*

Meet Tamara Thomas

"You can turn writing into an adventure." This is how Tamara Thomas approaches writing.

Tamara lives in Glenwood, Illinois, and attends Brookwood Junior High School. She enjoys math and is thinking about becoming an accountant. Tamara also likes reading, skating, and spending time with her toy poodle, Hershey.

When Tamara writes, her favorite form is the mystery story. For students who might have a hard time writing, she suggests, "Writing can be fun if you put your mind to it—I put myself in the story and think of all the fun things that might happen to me. As I'm thinking, I write notes. Then I sit down and start really writing."

Tamara wrote a persuasive essay about why she thinks skating is the best way to spend your spare time. Her essay "In My Spare Time" appears on page 70.

WRITERS' GALLERY

For more examples of persuasive writing, turn to page 195.

Writers at Work

Language is power. Words have persuaded people to negotiate peace rather than to fight wars, to buy products, to help those in need, and to travel into the unknown.

You yourself have contact with the power of persuasion every day. How do you and your friends decide what to do after school? Do you watch TV? Has a commercial jingle ever stuck in your mind? Do your teachers share their opinions with the class? As you reading each piece below, think about how effectively these writers persuade you to agree with their opinions or beliefs. What facts and logical reasons do they present to support their positions? Look for words or phrases that seem especially persuasive.

THE PERSUADER

In My Spare Time

In my spare time I like to go skating. I like to skate because I get to see my friends, I get exercise, and it also relaxes me.

First, I like to skate because I get to see my friends. We have fun watching people fall; we also enjoy getting boys' phone numbers. After we finish skating, we dance for about twenty minutes. After dancing we go to McDonald's to get something to eat. Then we go home.

Second, I like to skate because I get exercise. Skating makes my leg muscles bigger, and it helps me lose weight.

Finally, and most important, I get relaxed from it. It takes my mind off things. I also go skating when I am mad at something or someone because it relieves me from being stressed out.

In my opinion, skating is a very enjoyable and relaxing activity to do.

— Tamara Thomas
Brookwood Junior High School
Glenwood, IL

Habitat destruction is the greatest threat to wildlife today. Adopt An Acre allows you to insure the survival of millions of species of plants and animals, preserving wild places for future generations.

The Rio Bravo Conservation Area in northwest Belize is a lush tropical forest rich in wildlife. Your contribution will save jaguars, tropical butterflies, spider monkeys, and toucans. 100% of all funds goes directly to the purchase and protection of ecosystems and endangered species in the tropics.

The Ecosystem Survival Plan is a special program working in partnership with zoos, aquariums, and conservation organizations and is dedicated to promoting global conservation through the acquisition of threatened habitat around the world. Save an acre. It's habitat forming!

— from an ad in *Zoo Life*

The Writer's Craft All of these writers want you to agree with their points of view. Which piece seems most convincing to you? How did the writer persuade you? Think of additional reasons to support some of the points of view being expressed. How would you try to persuade someone to agree with your point of view on one of the issues presented in the selections?

By the age of seven this Black female was possessed by a magnificent devotion to language, a fascination with its resources, its potential. Blackness and love of language have been the executives of my life, have nourished and verified my life, have coordinated my portion of the field.

– Gwendolyn Brooks author and poet

COMMUNITY NEWSPAPER

A dispute arose between the North Wind and the Sun, each claiming that he was stronger than the other. At last they agreed to try their powers upon a traveller, to see which could soonest strip him of his cloak. The North Wind had the first try; and, gathering up all his force for the attack, he came whirling furiously down upon the man, and caught up his cloak as though he would wrest it from him by one single effort: but the harder he blew, the more closely the man wrapped it round himself. Then came the turn of the Sun. At first he beamed gently upon the traveller, who soon unclasped his cloak and walked on with it hanging loosely about his shoulders: then he shone forth in his full strength, and the man, before he had gone many steps, was glad to throw his cloak right off and complete his journey more lightly clad.
Persuasion is better than force.

— "The North Wind and the Sun"
Aesop's Fables

Poetry is still in the world, and children are colliding with some of it. They reach, touch lovely words and strong words with excitement and timid respect. They work hard to merit ownership. Looking at poetry and saluting it, they realize that in the world there is beauty. That there is horror they know and have always known. New bombs are crafted most carefully. Hatreds are here, and multiply. Modern ice and iron marry, and offer presently a frightening progeny. But children know also that there are flowers. They are not ashamed to speak to daisies and dandelions. Children of course commit platitudes a-plenty. Often our young poets address their readers and, more sorrowfully, them*selves*, in a cliché-ridden manner that they assume is "right for poetry." But they are capable, also, of exaltation and thought and emotion and expression that do them honor. Their nature is not frugal, it is expansive and lifting. It reacts. It reacts to clouds, sunshine. It reacts to dryness, waste, oppression.

— Gwendolyn Brooks
from "45 Years in Culture and Creative Writing"

Pros and Cons

Writing that persuades:
- *presents the writer's point of view and tries to convince the reader to agree with it.*
- *gives facts and logical reasons in support of the writer's position.*
- *uses persuasive language and formal language. To learn more about formal language, see* **Writer's Craft** *on page 279.*

Should I work part-time after school?
Why is studying history important?
How could I help someone disadvantaged?

Answering questions like these involves making some tough decisions about important issues. Chances are, you already have some strong ideas about these questions. If you're a bit of a persuader, writing can introduce others to your way of looking at the world. In the process, you could discover the power of words.

Begin by focusing on an issue, a situation, or an idea that is meaningful in your life.

Brainstorm: Purpose and Audience What issues or ideas are important to you? Why do you feel that way? Whom might you like to win over to your way of thinking? Think about whether your readers are likely to have strong ideas of their own before they hear yours. Talk with a classmate about your ideas for a persuasive piece. Think about the audience you want to reach.

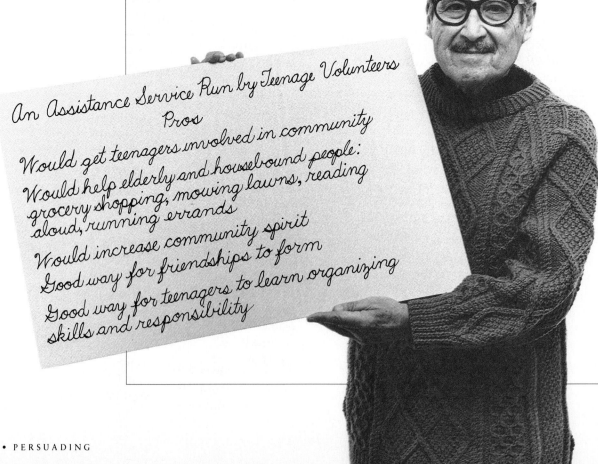

An Assistance Service Run by Teenage Volunteers

Pros
Would get teenagers involved in community
Would help elderly and housebound people: grocery shopping, mowing lawns, reading aloud, running errands
Would increase community spirit
Good way for friendships to form
Good way for teenagers to learn organizing skills and responsibility

Once you choose a topic, write down as many arguments as you can think of to support your opinion. Ask a few friends for their input. Then sit down with a partner and consider the writer's plans on pages 72–73. The writer used this list of pros and cons to help plan a persuasive essay about the value of a volunteer program run by teenagers. Why might a writer want to list arguments opposing as well as supporting his or her point of view? How can anticipating your audience's objections help you to strengthen your own arguments?

IN YOUR JOURNAL   In this unit you'll see how one writer wrote a persuasive essay by developing arguments to support a particular position. You could use some of the ideas you jotted down in your Journal as the topic of your own persuasive essay. If you're interested in exploring other kinds of persuasive writing, look through the Writer's Project File on page 82 for a few ideas.

Making a list of pros and cons is one way to start thinking about your topic. For more information about lists, see page 217. If you think you'll need several paragraphs to cover your ideas, you could take your plans a step further and make a brief working outline. Take a seat and begin writing plans in your Journal. Use whatever planning method feels most comfortable to you.

For more help in:
- *choosing a topic,* *turn to pages 213–215.*
- *selecting a planning strategy, turn to pages 216–224.*
- *self-selecting, turn to the **Writer's Project File** on page 82.*

An Assistance Service Run by Teenage Volunteers
Cons
Teenagers may be too busy to volunteer
Volunteers might be unreliable
Impractical—volunteers would need to drive, and many teenagers can't drive

Stating Your Case

CRITICAL THINKING

Do you believe everything you read? Some writers try to appeal to the reader's emotions rather than using facts and logical reasons to support their opinions.

Watch out if a writer says, "You should do this because everyone is doing it" or "If you don't do this, you'll be in real trouble."

Check things you read and hear— and your own work — for faulty reasoning.

Look over the persuasive writing in **Writers at Work** *on pages 70–71. Do the authors use facts and logical reasoning to support their opinions?*

Like a court lawyer, you've prepared your case by thinking carefully about an issue and by gathering material to support your viewpoint. Now you're ready to state your case by writing a draft of your persuasive piece. Remember that this is just a draft—later, you can always reorganize your ideas, put some back in, throw some out, or bring in some new ones. Right now, just get your opinions down on paper. Check out *The Persuasive Pen*. You'll find helpful tips about the structure and language of persuasive writing.

The Persuasive Pen

- Consider your purpose and audience. Complete this sentence: I want to persuade _____ that _____.

- Keep in mind the overall point of view you want to present.

- Think of your essay as having three parts: an introduction, a body, and a conclusion. You may find it helpful to read more about organizing your essay in Beginning, Middle, and End in Writer's Craft on page 248.

- In the introduction, try to get your readers' interest and be sure to state your personal belief about the topic. See page 240 for more information about leads and endings.

- In the body of your essay, include the reasons you have for your opinion or belief. Be sure that your opinions are supported with facts, resource materials, or logical reasons. Try to think like your readers. Figure out what they might object to and provide answers to their objections.

- Summarize your main points or tie your ideas together in the conclusion of the essay.

- Use persuasive language to influence your audience's opinion. State your reasons as clearly and as convincingly as possible. Use phrases that will help your audience believe what you do.

- Use language that fits your purpose. Avoid slang and use formal language to communicate that you are serious about your topic.

Talk About Drafting Think about the draft shown below and share your thoughts with a partner. How well does the writer support the opinion about a teenage volunteer service? Which arguments do you think are the most persuasive? How do you think the writer could make an even stronger case?

ON YOUR OWN Now is your opportunity to pick up your own persuasive pen and wield some word power. Begin drafting a persuasive piece. Don't worry about mistakes at this stage. Your main goal now is to transfer your best ideas from your head to the page. Write any ideas that will help you to state your case fully.

Team Up with Us

I never thought much about what it means to be part of a community. A visit with my grandfather He could not have managed living at home by himself without Team Up. Team Up are an organization of teenagers who help older or housebound people with tasks such as shopping, yard work, and other errands.

Groups like Team Up could pop up all over the country. Although teenagers have busy schedules, they could make a big deal in someone's life with one hour a week.

I think the best part of an organization like this is that it meets everyone's needs. Also, even young teenagers could be a part of the program. After all, volunteers would not need a car to get around neighborhood stores. Teenagers who want a chance to get out into the real world would find a challenge in setting up a program like this. Most of all, the community as a whole would benefit. It is clear to my grandfather and I that working together would give a community more spirit. He likes Team Up.

Where does the writer give the most important reason to support groups like Team Up? Some writers start off slowly and build up steam. Others jolt their audience into listening right away by giving the most important reason first. For more on order of importance, see page 253. In what order will you give your arguments?

The writer introduces another point of view in the second paragraph. Words and expressions such as <u>although</u>, <u>however</u>, <u>most of all</u>, and <u>on the other hand</u> help your readers know what to expect. See page 245 for more about transition words and phrases.

■ Recess to Rethink

Lawyers frequently take recesses to solve problems and talk over points that arise in a court trial. A short break can often shed new light on a stubborn problem.

To get a fresh perspective on the ideas and language you have used in your draft, take a break and have a partner read over your work. Ask him or her to identify strengths and weaknesses in your draft. How can you make your case more persuasive?

Talk About Revising Here is a revised draft about a teenage volunteer service. Look at the changes that the writer made. How do the changes make the essay more effective? Meet with a classmate and talk about the reasons why you think the author made each change. What other changes would you make?

When you and your partner discuss persuasive writing, you may want to say:

• *When I read your persuasive essay, I thought your main point was to make me believe _____. Was that really your purpose?*

• *I think another reason why people should support your point of view is _____.*

For more advice about conferencing, see page 229.

Team Up with Us

Until last summer,

I never thought much about what it means to be part of a community. A visit with my grandfather ~~He~~ could not have managed living at home by himself without Team Up. Team Up are an organization of teenagers who help older or housebound people with tasks such as shopping, yard work, and other errands.

Groups like Team Up could ~~pop up~~ *be a model for communities* all over the country. Although teenagers have busy schedules, they could make a big ~~deal~~ *difference* in someone's life with one hour a week.

I think the best part of an organization like this is that it meets everyone's needs. *Also, even young teenagers could be a part of the program. After all, volunteers would not need a car to get around neighborhood stores.* Teenagers who want a chance to get out into the real world would find a challenge in setting up a program like this. *Older and younger people can learn from each other.* Most of all, the community as a whole would benefit. It is clear to my grandfather and I that working together would give a community more spirit. ~~He likes Team Up.~~

Why did the writer get rid of the slang? See page 270 to read more about using slang.

This information overcomes an objection that readers may have. Why did the writer decide to move it?

This new argument adds support to the writer's opinion. That's smart!

REVISING STRATEGIES

When you review writing that persuades:
- *Think about the piece as a whole. Is the writer's point of view clearly stated?*
- *Consider the supporting arguments. Are they logical?*
- *Look for ways to use persuasive language. Does the tone reflect the writer's purpose?*

ON YOUR OWN You and a partner can help one another by asking questions about each other's draft. Think about points in the draft that you would like to know more about. Decide which suggestions to include in your piece. Then put your ideas for changes to work. Feel free to make as many changes as you like.

Final Proof

Everything needs to be in your favor if you're trying to win over an audience. You want to prove to your readers that you are a careful and thoughtful person, someone who is serious about the ideas and beliefs you express. Your audience may not take you as seriously as you hope if they catch proofreading errors in your work. The best persuaders give their best effort.

Talk About Proofreading With a partner, review this revised, proofread essay. Discuss the types of errors the writer found and corrected. What punctuation and spelling errors were corrected? What methods do each of you use to make sure that you catch all punctuation, spelling, capitalization, and grammar errors in your work?

Look at the first paragraph of the draft. Why was the sentence fragment "A visit with my grandfather" corrected? What other method can you think of to correct a sentence fragment? (To learn more about sentence fragments, turn to page 303.) What other grammar corrections were made in the draft? Why were they made? Think for a moment about the various proofreading corrections. Have you ever had to make similar corrections in your own work?

Team Up with Us

¶ *Until last summer,* I never thought much about what it means to be part of a community. A visit with my grandfather ∧ *changed all that.* He could not have managed living at home by himself without Team Up. Team Up *is* ~~are~~ an organization of teenagers who help older ⌐ housebound people with tasks such as shopping, yard work, and other errands.

Groups like Team Up could pop up ∧ *be a model for communit—* all over the country. Although teenagers have busy schedules, they cou— make a big ~~deal~~ *difference* ∧ in someone's life with one hour a week.

I think the best part of an organization like this — that it meets everyone's needs. Also, even young teenagers could be a part of the program. After all, volu— teers would not need a car to get around neighborhood stores. Teenagers who want a chance to get out into the real world would find a challenge in setting up a program like this. ∧ *Older and younger people can learn from each other.* Most of all, the community as a whole would benefit. It is clear to my grandfather and ~~I~~ ∧ *me* that working together would give a community more spirit. ~~He~~ ~~likes Team Up.~~

Proofreader's Marks

∧ Add.

ℓ Take out.

≡ Make a capital letter.

/ Make a lower-case letter.

¶ Indent the paragraph.

◯ Check the spelling.

⊙ Add a period.

∧ Add a comma.

❝❞ Add quotation marks.

∽ Reverse the order.

PROOFREADING CHECK-UP

- *Check your capitalization and punctuation by using the* **Mechanics Handbook** *on page 353.*
- *Are you having any verb problems? Check page 317.*
- *Circle misspelled words. Use the* **Word Finder** *on page 368 or your dictionary.*

ON YOUR OWN Think about whether or not you would like to publish your persuasive piece. If you decide to publish, proofread your persuasive writing. Keep an eye out for those spelling, punctuation, and grammar errors that you may have a tendency to make. Then ask a classmate to read through the piece as a last check for errors.

■ Stand and Deliver

For more help in:
• *deciding how to publish your work, turn to page 237.*

If you decide to publish your work, think about how you can encourage readers to respond to what you've written. Aren't you curious to know what people will think of your ideas? Remember that you can't expect everyone in the audience to agree with you, no matter how persuasive you are. However, you can be certain that you'll enjoy wielding the power of a persuasive pen even if it's just by sparking a lively discussion.

Talk About Publishing The essay on page 81 was published in the school paper. Read the essay and talk about it with a partner. How persuasive do you think it is? Do you think the method of publishing was effective? Will the essay reach the intended audience? Would you consider starting or joining a group of volunteers after reading it?

ON YOUR OWN Are you thinking about publishing your piece of persuasive writing? If you would like to publish, begin considering specific ways to reach your audience. What method would be most effective? Should your piece be read aloud? Will you submit it to the local newspaper? Think about all of your options. Then decide the best way to publish your work.

*How does your finished work compare with the **Model for Self-Evaluation** on page 285?*

THE INFORMER

Team Up with Us

Until last summer, I never thought much about what it means to be part of a community. A visit with my grandfather changed all that. He could not have managed living at home by himself without Team Up. Team Up is an organization of teenagers who help older or housebound people with tasks such as shopping, yard work, and other errands.

Groups like Team Up could be a model for communities all over the country. Although teenagers have busy schedules, they could make a big difference in someone's life with one hour a week. Also, even young teenagers could be a part of the program. After all, volunteers would not need a car to get around neighborhood stores.

I think the best part of an organization like this is that it meets everyone's needs. Teenagers who want a chance to get out into the real world would find a challenge in setting up a program like this. Older and younger people can learn from each other. Most of all, the community as a whole would benefit. It is clear to my grandfather and me that working together would give a community more spirit.

Here are some ideas that will give you a chance to test your powers of persuasion. Choose a project that interests you and try to figure out the best way to win an audience over to your side.

A Winning Pep Talk

Your softball team has lost every game of the season. The coach is grumpy; in fact, the players are so discouraged that they want to cancel the rest of their season. Write the inspirational pep talk that could be the turning point of the game. What words of wisdom could urge your teammates back into the game?

A Job in the Media

Wow! There's an advertisement in the newspaper for the part-time job you've always wanted! Write a persuasive letter telling something about yourself and your interest in the job. You'd like to be one of the applicants who will be called for an interview.

You've Got to Try It!

Can you think of a product that you've tried recently and really liked? Consider an item such as a poncho that has its origins in another culture. Write a persuasive piece to sell the product on the radio or on TV. You may want to try composing a catchy jingle.

A New Invention

What would be your first reaction if you were alive when the telephone was invented? Express different points of view about the telephone or another invention. Write one persuasive piece as though you are skeptical of the invention. Write the other as though you were the inventor. Persuade the public to try your invention.

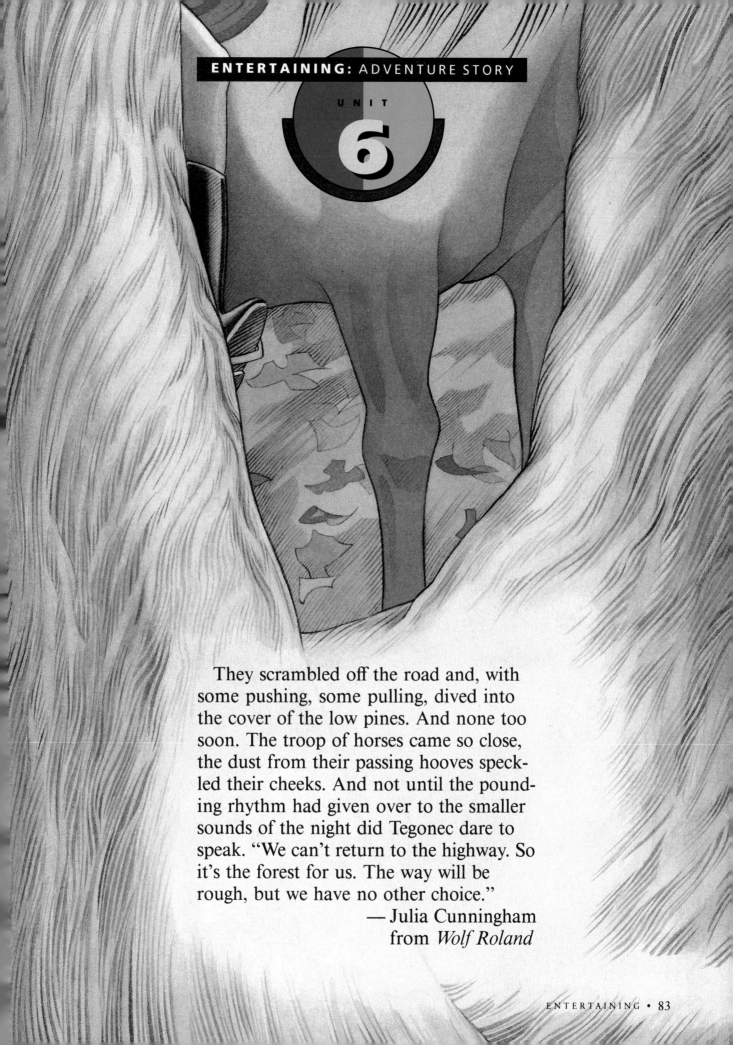

They scrambled off the road and, with some pushing, some pulling, dived into the cover of the low pines. And none too soon. The troop of horses came so close, the dust from their passing hooves speckled their cheeks. And not until the pounding rhythm had given over to the smaller sounds of the night did Tegonec dare to speak. "We can't return to the highway. So it's the forest for us. The way will be rough, but we have no other choice."
— Julia Cunningham
from *Wolf Roland*

Key to Adventure

SELF-SURVEY

- *What do I think of when I hear the word <u>adventure</u>?*
- *If I were a film-maker, what kind of adventure would I want to create? Where would the movie's location be? Who would be the lead adventurer?*

Where do your daydreams take you? Imagine yourself solving the greatest mystery of all time. Picture what it would be like to travel among the stars, encountering unchartered planets with incredible life forms. Compelling adventure stories pull you out of your every-day habits and plop you right in the middle of another world. Enter these unique worlds and create one yourself!

IN YOUR JOURNAL   Think about the kinds of stories you find most exciting. How do you feel about everyday people who accomplish phenomenal things against great odds? Are you drawn to action-packed biographies that portray the real-life adventures of someone just like you? Do you like stories about superheroes facing desperate situations or hilarious predicaments?

Think about why you like these adventure stories. Picture the characters in your mind. Why do the situations appeal to you? Make some notes in your Journal about stories you've found especially en-tertaining. Write the reasons why you found them exciting.

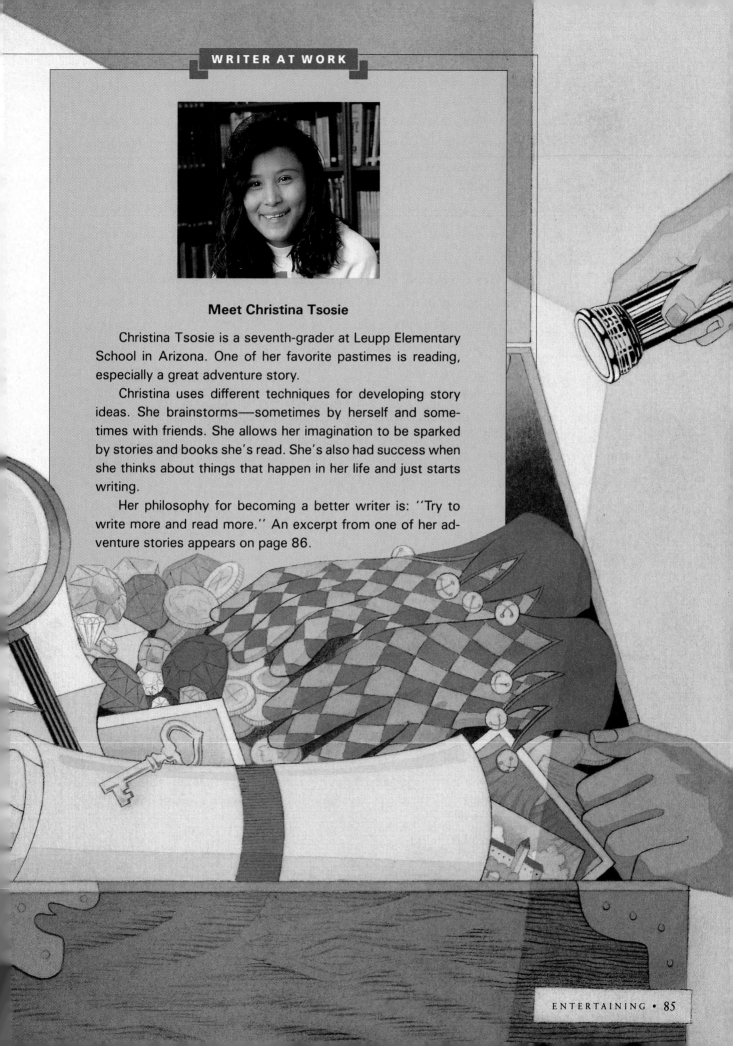

Meet Christina Tsosie

Christina Tsosie is a seventh-grader at Leupp Elementary School in Arizona. One of her favorite pastimes is reading, especially a great adventure story.

Christina uses different techniques for developing story ideas. She brainstorms—sometimes by herself and sometimes with friends. She allows her imagination to be sparked by stories and books she's read. She's also had success when she thinks about things that happen in her life and just starts writing.

Her philosophy for becoming a better writer is: "Try to write more and read more." An excerpt from one of her adventure stories appears on page 86.

Writers at Work

I am a teller of tales, in part, because of the informal way I learned from Mother and her relatives of passing the time, which they also utilize for transmitting information, for entertainment, and for putting their own flesh and blood in the proper perspective.

— Virginia Hamilton author

People have always enjoyed being entertained. Long before books appeared on the scene, people told stories. Tales of faraway lands, of leaders and heroes, of scoundrels and tricksters were passed along from parent to child. People today still love to be entertained. Through stories, books, movies, and plays they can leave their everyday worlds and travel to places they may have imagined but never seen.

See what kind of adventure each excerpt takes you on. Think about the way in which the author pulls you into the story. How does each piece make you feel?

Bear Cub stood up on one hind leg. He hopped in circles, bumping into White-Tailed Fawn and stepping on Baby Otter. Bear Cub sang a wordless song.

Woochuck, Raccoon Girl, and Wolf Child wandered away into the piny woods and were lost. Other little animals sat down on the path. They moaned and trembled all over.

It took Jahdu an hour to gather all the animals on the path again. He tied a rope around them and led them to a good, safe place. There, he let them loose.

I'd better get back to that first path, Jahdu thought. I'd better find out what could cause little animals to stop, hop around, and fall down.

— Virginia Hamilton
from *The All Jahdu Storybook*

Ryan took off his cap and wiped the sweat off his forehead. He turned on the air conditioner.

The man looked at his watch impatiently. With a sour look on his face, he said, "Here, keep the change." At the same time he handed Ryan a $20 bill. Then he opened the door and got out. Carrying his briefcase, he walked across the crosswalk. He mixed in with a crowd of swarming people, and disappeared quickly.

"Keep the change," Ryan mimicked with the same sour look on his face. The cars moved slowly. Ryan managed to squeeze the cab into a quiet alley. He stopped the car, then reached under his seat · · ·

— Christina Tsosie
Leupp Elementary School
Flagstaff, Arizona

The Writer's Craft Writers of entertaining material find many ways to grab the reader's attention. In these selections, each writer has a different way of holding the audience's interest. What makes you curious to find out what happens next in each selection? If you were to write entertaining material, how would you capture your audience's attention?

WRITERS' GALLERY

For more examples of entertaining writing, turn to page 196.

"Hold her!" Mr. High Bear yelled.

Thought she'd step in a prairie-dog hole. Grandpa's voice echoed in Hank's mind, reminding the boy of the danger of a runaway. Hank forced his hands from the horn, leaned back in the saddle, braced and pulled as hard as he could on the reins.

Babe's neck arched as she fought the bit, but her run gradually slowed to a jouncing trot, making Hank grab for the saddle horn again. "Whoa, whoa," he called, steadily tightening the reins until Babe slowed to a walk; then, flanks heaving, she stopped.

Hank, as sweaty as the horse, felt his heart throb in his ears. The horizon shimmered dizzily before him as his breathing became short, quick gasps. Deliberately he took a deep breath and exhaled slowly again and again until the roaring in his ears stopped.

"Old Babe thought she was a filly again," Mr. High Bear laughed as he and the others caught up to Hank. "Ain't seen her run like that for years." His eyes betrayed his concern. "You did okay," he praised, and Hank managed a weak smile, not trusting his voice to speak.

— Virginia Driving Hawk Sneve
from "The Slim Butte Ghost"

Somewhere behind the opaque blind windows a light burned dimly far in the rear of the post office, and I had an impression of subdued activity back there. But the lobby itself was dim and silent, and as I walked across the worn stone of its floor, I knew I was seeing all around me precisely what Brooklynites had seen for no telling how many generations long dead.

— Jack Finney
from "The Love Letter"

ENTERTAINING • 87

Opening Doors

All kinds of ideas live in your imagination. All you have to do is open the doors along the twisting corridors and secret passageways. If you open one door, a hermit might step out, holding an old metal box. Open another door—maybe you'll see someone rowing furiously on the high seas, trying to escape in a leaky boat. Yet another door may give you a glimpse of a man with a talking dog.

Things from the real world and things from your dream world are just waiting behind all those doors in your mind. They're waiting for you to let them out and put them into a story that will be uniquely yours. What can you see through the doors of your imagination?

Brainstorm: Purpose and Audience An adventure story lifts the reader out of the everyday world. What kind of story would you like to tell? Why would you write an adventure story? Whom would you like to reach with an adventure? How would you like your readers to feel? Talk with your partner about your reasons for writing an adventure story. Share your thoughts about an audience.

setting → the treasure room of a medieval castle

characters → Justine, the court jester's sister   Grimspell, a thief who never laughs

conflict → She thinks she is as funny as her brother.   He takes some of the king's jewels and is ready to disappear.

They make a deal—he'll return the jewels if she can find him and make him laugh.

She tries some of her favorite jokes. ← She searches and searches. She finds him.

resolution → On her third and last try, Justine makes Grimspell laugh.

Look at the writer's plans on page 88 for a story about a thief and a court jester's sister. The detailed conflict chart shows the challenge that Justine faces and the way the story is resolved. The plot of a story often centers around a conflict, or a problem, that is resolved in the course of the story.

Why do you think it's so important to set up a conflict when you're planning a story? How could you work out the details of your story by focusing on the conflict? To learn more about organizing your story with a chart, see page 220.

IN YOUR JOURNAL In this unit you will follow the steps a writer takes to write an adventure story. You could take the first step of your own adventure by planning a story, too. When you write an adventure story, it can be particularly important to plan the details of your plot. If you plan your story around a central conflict, a conflict chart could be the perfect planning tool. If you plan your story around events, situations, or characters, an outline or a cluster may be helpful. Choose the method that you think works best and write some plans in your Journal.

Other kinds of writing besides stories can entertain, too. You can check the Writer's Project File on page 98 for ideas.

WHAT'S THE POINT?

Writing that entertains, such as story writing:
- *chooses the right tone and voice to create a special mood—such as excitement, suspense, or humor—for the piece.*
- *uses colorful language to make characters and situations come alive.*
- *develops believable characters.*

CUT-OUT CASTLE

STEPS

CASE

DRAW BRIDGE

BOAT

SPIRAL STAIRCASE

TREASURE ROOM

FOR MORE HELP

For more help in:
- *choosing a topic, turn to pages 213–215.*
- *selecting a planning strategy, turn to pages 216–224.*
- *self-selecting, turn to the Writer's Project File on page 98.*

Imagination at Play

Now that you have ideas for your story, let your imagination run free. Your characters can battle fierce enemies, discover lost worlds, or make your audience laugh. Begin with *Approach to Adventure*.

Approach to Adventure

■ Remember your purpose and audience. Ask yourself why you are writing an adventure story. Think about who will read it and how to keep that audience intrigued and entertained.

■ Keep in mind that your story should have a beginning, a middle, and an end. The beginning captures the reader's interest. The middle develops the characters and their adventure. The end reveals what the characters accomplished or how they changed.

■ Plot, characters, and setting add richness and believability to your writing. The plot is *what happens,* the characters are the *people in the story,* and the setting is the *time or location*.

■ Think about what you want the most exciting moment in your story to be. Will that moment be suspenseful? unexpected? humorous? Some writers plan the most exciting moment, the climax, first. The story conflict is resolved at the climax of a story. See page 249 for more about organizing your story structure.

■ Consider the mood, tone, and voice of your story. (See page 279 for more about mood, tone, and voice.) What tone will your story have? Will you use formal or informal language? What point of view will you use: first person, third-person limited, or third-person omniscient? What mood would you like to convey?

■ Use dialog to give your characters presence and originality. Dialog can help your readers feel as though they are actually meeting the characters and participating in the story action.

Talk About Drafting Discuss this draft with a partner. What makes the story entertaining? How does the setting help to emphasize the conflict? Discuss what you think is the story's most exciting moment and how it leads to the story's resolution.

CRITICAL THINKING

How can a writer help readers to feel the mood of a story? How can writers help their readers to picture settings and feel as if they have met the characters?

*Writers convey this information by making decisions about which words and images to use. Turn to the excerpt from "The Love Letter" in **Writers at Work** on page 87. How does Jack Finney's word choice affect the mood of the scene? For more about mood, see page 281.*

Justine woke with a start. She had felt safe sleeping in the king's treasure room, yet something was wrong. Then she gasped. From behind the drapes strode Grimspell. Watch out! In all of the kingdom there was no better thief, nor one more grumpier.

Jester's sister," he said, "I'll give you three chances to make me laugh. If you do, I'll return the jewels. If you don't, they're mine. I plan to disappear right before your eyes. As you know, I have never smiled in my life. You'll have to find me first."

So she threw on a cloak. The kingdom was vast, but she knew all the hiding places. She climbed mountains and swam streams. At last, she found Grimspell crouched behind a trunk in the treasure room.

Panting, Justine began her first joke. "My brother is one of the best jesters in the country. He's just not so good in the city!" Grimspell gave no response, so Justine asked, "Why did the fool cross the road?" She paused and continued, "He thought he was a chicken!"

Grimspell's face stayed hard as granite. "Two."

This was Justine's last chance. "My brother refuses to work for the king anymore. And after what the king said, you can't blame him."

Grimspell seemed interested. "What did he say?"

Justine said "You're fired!"

The thief smiled and soon was rolling on the floor. Justine grinned, knowing the treasure was safe.

The writer of the story about the jester's sister used dialog to develop the characters. The thief reveals his personality by the blunt and humorless way he speaks. How will your characters reveal their personalities?

ON YOUR OWN Is a story taking shape in your mind? Now it's time to write your own draft. If you let your imagination soar, your characters may take you on a journey that isn't quite on your map. Stay with it—you can decide later which parts you want to keep.

Reshaping Your World

When you and your partner discuss writing that entertains, you might make such comments as:

* *I'm surprised this character did this. I thought he (or she) would be more _____. What's the main thing about this character you want the reader to see?*
* *I think the most exciting part of the story was when _____. Could you add some details to help build the suspense?*

For more advice about conferencing, see page 229.

The world that you just brought to life may take you by surprise. It can seem so real! Maybe your audience will be able to step right into your story and completely forget that there's another world outside. However, if you have the feeling that some parts just aren't colorful or exciting enough to keep your audience there every second, remember that you still have the key. You can sneak back in there and change things.

Talk About Revising With a partner, examine the revised draft of "The Jester's Clever Sister." Do the revisions improve the piece? What new information do they give us about the characters? How do the revisions help the reader picture more clearly what is going on? Does the title help to enhance the story? Discuss the mood of the story. How does the writer maintain the chosen atmosphere?

Remember that in a good story the plot, the setting, and the characters all work together to entertain the reader and to help the reader picture precisely what is going on. Discuss with your partner ways in which "The Jester's Clever Sister" succeeds in entertaining you. What revisions do you think could make it even more entertaining?

ON YOUR OWN Pretend that you've never seen your draft before and that you don't even know who wrote it. Are there any parts that don't seem to work the way you think they should? Can you let the characters' words and actions tell more of the story? As you revise your story, imagine that you're watching the action take place right in front of you. Then ask a couple of friends to read your piece. What are their reactions?

The Jester's Clever Sister

Justine woke with a start. She had felt safe sleeping in the king's treasure room, yet something was wrong. Then she gasped. From behind the drapes strode Grimspell. ~~Watch out!~~ In all of the kingdom there was no better thief, nor one more grumpier.

Jester's sister," he ~~said,~~ *snarled* "I'll give you three chances to make me laugh. If you do, I'll return the jewels. If you don't, they're mine. I plan to disappear right before your eyes. As you know, I have never smiled in my life. You'll have to find me first."

Justine knew she was a funny woman. So she threw on a cloak. The kingdom was vast, but she knew all the hiding places. She climbed mountains and swam streams. At last, she found Grimspell crouched behind a trunk in the treasure room.

Panting, Justine began her first joke. "My brother is one of the best jesters in the country. He's just not so good in the city!" Grimspell gave no response, so Justine asked, "Why did the fool cross the road?" She paused and continued, "He thought he was a chicken!"

Grimspell's face stayed hard as granite. "Two."

This was Justine's last chance. "My brother refuses to work for the king anymore. And after what the king said, you can't blame him."

Grimspell seemed interested. "What did he say?"

Justine said "You're fired!"

The thief smiled and soon was rolling on the floor. Justine grinned, knowing the treasure was safe.

... *How does this more colorful word tell you something about Grimspell's character?*

... *How does moving this sentence emphasize the problems and conflicts between the two main characters?*

... *How does this added information give you a better idea of what Justine is like?*

REVISING STRATEGIES

When you review writing that entertains:
- *Consider whether the audience will feel the mood you tried to create.*
- *Look for colorful language that vividly describes the setting, plot, and characters.*
- *See if you can picture the characters. Can you use dialog to develop their personalities?*

One More Look

When you invent an imaginary world, everything in it is usually just the way you want it to be. No one knows about your world but you. However, when you put that world on paper for all to see, you must make sure your description of it is exactly right. Be sure to proofread your writing carefully. In its final form there should be no grammar, spelling, or punctuation errors.

Talk About Proofreading Talk with a partner about the proofreading corrections in the story shown on page 95. How has each change improved the quality of the writing?

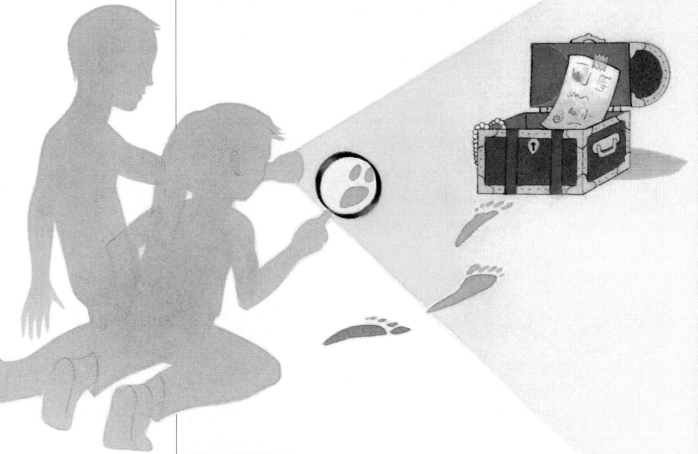

ON YOUR OWN If you think you'd like to publish your piece, proofread it for spelling, grammar, and punctuation errors. If your work includes dialog, you may want to check the rules for punctuating dialog on page 356. Seeing your work in final form may give you some ideas for publishing your piece. Write them down in your Journal.

The Jester's Clever Sister

Justine woke with a start. She had felt safe sleeping in the king's treasure room, yet something was wrong. Then she gasped. From behind the drapes strode Grimspell. ~~Watch out!~~ In all of the kingdom there was no better thief, nor one ~~more~~ grumpier.

¶ Jester's sister," he ^snarled ~~said,~~ "I'll give you three chances to make me laugh. If you do, I'll return the jewels. If you don't, they're mine. I plan to disappear right before your eyes. As you know, I have never smiled in my life. You'll have to find me first."

Justine knew she was a funny woman.
So she threw on a cloak. The kingdom was vast, but she knew all the hiding places. She climbed mountains and swam streams. At last, she found Grimspell crouched behind a trunk in the treasure room.

Panting, Justine began her first joke. "My broth[er] is one of the best jesters in the country. He's just so good in the city!" Grimspell gave no response, so Justine asked, "Why did the fool cross the road?" S[he] paused and continued, "He thought he was a chicken!"

Grimspell's face stayed hard as granite. "Two."

This was Justine's last chance. "My brother refu[sed] to work for the king anymore. And after what the ki[ng] said, you can't blame him."

Grimspell seemed interested. "What did he say?"

Justine said, "You're fired!"

The thief smiled and soon was rolling on the floor. Justine grinned, knowing the treasure was safe.

• *Check your capitalization and punctuation by using the* **Mechanics Handbook** *on page 353.*
• *Are you having any adverb or adjective problems? Check pages 339–342.*
• *Circle misspelled words. Use the* **Word Finder** *on page 368 or your dictionary.*

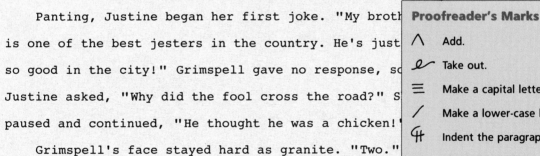

Proofreader's Marks

∧	Add.
ℓ	Take out.
≡	Make a capital letter.
/	Make a lower-case letter.
¶	Indent the paragraph.
○	Check the spelling.
⊙	Add a period.
∧	Add a comma.
⌄⌄	Add quotation marks.
∽	Reverse the order.

Giving Others the Key to Your World

For more help in:
· *deciding how to publish your work,* turn to page 237.

How does your fin-ished work compare with the Model for Self-Evaluation on page 286?

Now you can let others into the world you just created. If you publish your work, you'll give your audience a chance to take a unique adventure—one that only you could make possible.

Talk About Publishing Read the final version of "The Jester's Clever Sister," on page 97. Do you like the way the story turned out? This story was entered in a short-story contest, where it won second prize. It was published in the magazine that sponsored the contest.

Discuss with your partner whether you think this was a good way to publish the story. Did that form of publication accomplish the author's purpose? Did it help the story reach its intended audience? If other stories about Justine and Grimspell were published, would you read them, too? Think about your own piece. What is the best way to present your work to the audience you want to reach?

ON YOUR OWN How can you best present your finished work? Who do you think might enjoy it the most? What could be an effective way to reach that audience? Perhaps you could read your story aloud or send photocopies to friends. You might even work with a group of friends to act it out at a nearby children's hospital. You could take a role for yourself, or you might want to be the director.

The Jester's Clever Sister

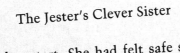

Justine woke with a start. She had felt safe sleeping in the king's treasure room, yet something was wrong. Then she gasped. From behind the drapes strode Grimspell. In all of the kingdom there was no better thief, nor one grumpier.

"Jester's sister," he snarled, "I'll give you three chances to make me laugh. As you know, I have never smiled in my life. If you do, I'll return the jewels. If you don't, they're mine. I plan to disappear right before your eyes. You'll have to find me first."

Justine knew she was a funny woman. So she threw on a cloak. The kingdom was vast, but she knew all the hiding places. She climbed mountains and swam streams. At last, she found Grimspell crouched behind a trunk in the treasure room.

Panting, Justine began her first joke. "My brother is one of the best jesters in the country. He's just not so good in the city!" Grimspell gave no response, so Justine asked, "Why did the fool cross the road?" She paused and continued, "He thought he was a chicken!"

Grimspell's face stayed hard as granite. "Two."

This was Justine's last chance. "My brother refuses to work for the king anymore. And after what the king said, you can't blame him."

Grimspell seemed interested. "What did he say?"

Justine said, "You're fired!"

The thief smiled and soon was rolling on the floor. Justine grinned, knowing the treasure was safe.

If an idea entertains you, chances are you can make it entertaining for others, too. Choose one of these ideas for writing that entertains, and follow your imagination wherever it takes you.

Singing for Your Supper

Picture yourself as a traveling singer in medieval times. You arrive at a small cottage where you are offered dinner in exchange for a song. Write a poem in the form of a song that will entertain your hosts. Tell a story about your amazing exploits fighting dragons, shamelessly flatter your hosts, or describe what you hope to eat! Read or sing your song to your classmates.

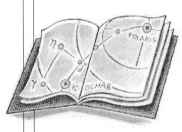

Star-Struck

Imagine you are a scientist of the future who travels to other planets, exploring each new world to see if it would be suitable for human existence. Write a couple of journal entries describing your most exciting missions.

"Lite" Ideas

A widespread interest in health has led to many theories about what is healthful and what is not. Some theories are supported by scientific evidence; others are questionable. Present a theory of your own that makes absolutely no sense, such as "People should avoid eating things that they don't know how to spell." Support your theory with your own brand of evidence.

It's Your Newspaper Column

Some newspapers publish humor columns which present political or social issues with a chuckle! Write an entertaining essay for a humor column. Present a holiday or custom you celebrate. Keep in mind that your audience grew up in another culture.

Our dear Sisi

...it's always pure pleasure to be fully accepted throughout a village, district or even several districts occupied by your clan as a beloved household member, where you can call at any time, completely relax, sleep at ease and freely take part in the discussion of all problems, where you can even be given livestock and land to build free of charge.

As you know I was barely ten when our father died, having lost all his wealth. Mother could neither read nor write and had no means to send me to school. Yet a member of our clan educated me from elementary school right up to Fort Hare and never expected any refund. According to our custom I was his child and his responsibility. I have a lot of praise for this institution, not only because it's part of me, but also due to its usefulness. It caters for all those who are descended from one ancestor and holds them together as one family.

— Nelson Mandela
from a letter to his cousin

Informing Others

- *What are some situations that would cause me to write a business letter?*
- *What kind of language would I use in a business letter? How would it differ from the language I use when I talk to a friend?*
- *What are some of the things I could learn from reading business letters?*

Every day you make choices on how you want to communicate information. What do you want to say? How important is it? Should you say it face-to-face, on the phone, or in a note? If what you have to say is important enough, you want to make sure the information is communicated as clearly and completely as possible.

Writing a letter helps you to take the time to organize your thoughts so that you communicate exactly what you want to say. You can also decide how you want to get your points across—how to order them and whether to express them in formal or informal language. A letter can also serve as a record of information that can be referred to later.

IN YOUR JOURNAL There are many types of letters—letters to friends, thank-you notes to relatives, letters to the editor, requests for information. Think about different types of letters you've written in the past year. In your Journal, write some notes about why you wrote each one. In what ways were the letters different? How were they similar?

Meet Nathan Dwyer

Nathan Dwyer attends Bernardo Heights Middle School in San Diego, California. He lives in San Diego, too. Nathan plays a lot of baseball and enjoys collecting baseball cards.

When it comes to writing, Nathan especially enjoys writing stories that make people laugh and fantasy stories. He shares, ''I hope my audience can see what I see when I write these stories. I hope they can actually relate with the character I write about.''

Nathan tells other student writers, ''Stick with your writing, with what's comfortable to you. It's the biggest part of writing.

''For ideas, I take a subject, and I branch it out. If one thing sounds good, I'll keep writing and see if I feel comfortable with it. If I don't, I just start again. I get to something I really think I can write with, and I just keep going.''

Nathan wrote a letter to Walter Dean Myers, the author of a book he enjoyed reading. The letter is on page 102.

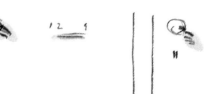

WRITERS'
GALLERY

*For more examples
of informative
writing, turn to
page 197.*

Writers at Work

Letters can highlight important information or just serve as a way for one person to reconnect with another. As you read these letters, notice how each writer organized the information. Can you identify the purpose of each letter?

1234 Main Street
San Diego, CA 92128
March 20, 1991

Walter Dean Myers
c/o Scholastic, Inc.
730 Broadway
New York, NY 10003

Dear Mr. Myers:

I just finished your book, <u>The Legend of Tarik</u>. This book is very exciting! I enjoyed the action scenes a lot, especially the final battle between Tarik and El Muerte. Yet during the course of the book, I really hated Jad the Unclean. How did you come up with this book? It would take me years to come up with something like that. I really didn't dislike any part of this book.

I've looked in bookstores, and I haven't seen this book. I hope to be seeing it soon!

Yours truly,
Nate Dwyer

— Nathan Dwyer
Bernardo Heights Middle School
San Diego, CA

Dear Editor:

Your July "Pro & Con" question on bicycle helmets caught my eye. Three years ago, I almost died when my bike collided with a moving pickup truck. I wasn't wearing a helmet. I was knocked unconscious and was in a coma for three days. I suffered temporary memory loss and weakening of my right side. It took me almost two years to fully recover. We're not sure if a helmet would have saved me completely, but it likely would have saved me some injury.

My only hope is that through reading this letter someone might think twice about not wearing a helmet. The head is a very delicate thing. Yes, helmets are heavy and cumbersome, but I would much rather wear one than die. So please be careful and always wear a helmet.

— Amanda Jayne Harkrader, 15
Radford, Virginia
from *Sports Illustrated for Kids*

The Writer's Craft These letters have different purposes, but each makes its point quickly and clearly. Which letter accomplishes its purpose best? Is the language suitable for its audience?

Nilda remembered her own note, that first day back at school. Her mother had still been upset after the funeral, so Nilda had written the note herself, and her mother had signed it absentmindedly.

Dear Mrs. Fortinash,

   Please excuse my daughter Nilda Ramírez for being absent from school. Her father died and she got lots of things to take care of at home. That is our custom. Thank you.

                         Very truly yours,
                         Lydia Ramírez

           —Nicholasa Mohr from *Nilda*

                          25 W. 43
                          New York, N.Y.
                          26 December 1952

Dear Pupils of 5-B:

   I was delighted to get your letters telling me what you thought about "Charlotte's Web." It must be fine to have a teacher who is a bookworm like Mrs. Bard.

   It is true that I have a farm. It is on the sea. My barn is big and old, and I have ten sheep, eighteen hens, a goose, a gander, a bull calf, a rat, a chipmunk, and many spiders. In the woods near the barn are red squirrels, crows, thrushes, owls, porcupines, woodchucks, foxes, rabbits, and deer. In the pasture pond are frogs, polliwogs, and salamanders. Sometimes a Great Blue Heron comes to the pond and catches frogs. At the shore of the sea are sandpipers, gulls, plovers, and kingfishers. In the mud at low tide are clams. Seven seals live on nearby rocks and in the sea, and they swim close to my boat when I row. Barn swallows nest in the barn, and I have a skunk that lives under the garage.

   I didn't like spiders at first, but then I began watching one of them, and soon saw what a wonderful creature she was and what a skillful weaver. I named her Charlotte, and now I like spiders along with everything else in nature.

   I'm glad you enjoyed the book, and I thank you for the interesting letters.

                          Sincerely,
                          E. B. White

WRITERS ON WRITING

I fell in love with the sound of an early typewriter and have been stuck with it ever since. I believed then, as I do now, in the goodness of the published word: it seemed to contain an essential goodness, like the smell of leaf mold.

—E. B. White author

Getting Down to Business

Writing that informs:
• *clearly pinpoints its audience.*
• *conveys information in a well-organized format.*
• *communicates information in a straightforward, clear, and polite manner.*

FOR MORE HELP

For more help in:
• *choosing a topic, turn to pages 213–215.*
• *selecting a planning strategy, turn to pages 216–224.*
• *self-selecting, turn to the Writer's Project File on page 112.*

Information is all around us. It is conveyed in a great many ways, to be read by a great many people. People have been writing letters for centuries; today letters remain an important and efficient way to communicate information.

The business letter is one kind of informative letter. A business letter communicates its message in a direct and clear manner. It states what is wanted or expected from the recipient.

The business letter format has certain features that help to make it an efficient instrument of communication. The heading contains your street address; your city, state, and zip code; and the date. The inside address includes the name and address of the person or company you are writing to. The salutation is the greeting of your letter. You may need to use the phrase *To Whom It May Concern*. The body of the letter contains your message. Choose a formal closing, such as *Sincerely* or *Yours truly*. Sign the letter and print or type your name under your signature. You may wish to print any appropriate association name or title below your name, too.

778 Fulton Street
Edmonds, WA 98020
September 3, 1993

Ms. Joyce Kasner
Brady-Drake, Inc.
1422 North Skiker
Seattle, WA 98004

Dear Ms. Kasner:

I am writing to confirm the order I placed with you over the telephone this morning.

We expect shipment of 35 drafting tables, Model #34-16, within the next two weeks. As we discussed, 15 of these tables will be black, and 20 will be off-white in color.

Thank you for your prompt and courteous attention to this matter.

Sincerely,

Haruo Ikeda

Haruo Ikeda
Ikeda Architects

Mr. Ikeda wrote this letter to record his telephone order. In very few lines he covered everything important: who wrote it, whom it was written to, the date, the type of drafting tables ordered, and when shipment was to be made. Ms. Kasner was able to read this letter quickly, yet know exactly what Mr. Ikeda requested.

Brainstorm: Purpose and Audience Talk over with your partner the type of business letter you're going to write and the person to whom you will write. You might want to ask for information, order something, join an organization, or register your opinion.

```
Purpose:
To get a summer job at the Maryville Daily Gazette

Audience:
Person in charge of summer hiring

Organization:
Paragraph 1: Why I'm writing
Paragraph 2: My background
          A. My newspaper experience
          B. I can get a recommendation from Ms.
             Jimenez.
Paragraph 3: Summation-I'd enjoy working there.
Paragraph 4: Thank you

Tone:
Clear, straightforward, polite, and enthusiastic

Form:
Must have these parts: 1. my address; 2. date;
3. recipient's name and address; 4. salutation followed
by a colon (:); 5. body (the above four paragraphs);
6. closing; 7. signature; 8. my name.
```

This writer made a chart to organize the main points of her business letter. For more about charts, turn to page 220.

IN YOUR JOURNAL In this unit you'll watch a seed of an idea grow into a full-blown business letter. If you'd like to write another type of letter, look at the Writer's Project File on page 112. Use your Journal to begin planning your letter.

Adding Weight to Your Idea

You've got the bare bones of an idea. In your draft you'll be expanding on that—making all the parts add up to an impressive whole by writing out your thoughts in a logical order. Look at *Letter-Perfect Points* to help your letter inform in the best possible way.

Letter-Perfect Points

- Ask yourself why and to whom you are writing the letter. For example, is the purpose to make a request, to supply or correct information, to make a complaint, to express thanks, or to compliment someone? Who will read the letter?

- Make sure the tone of your letter is appropriate. Is the language straightforward, to the point, and polite even when you make a complaint? See page 279 to learn more about formal language.

- Be certain that you have included all the essential information and that this information is accurate. Have you included the correct dates, order number, and receipt number? Have you included the names of all people, places, and times that may be necessary to communicate your point?

- Eliminate unnecessary words. Does each sentence include or support a main point of information?

- Include all parts of a business letter.
  - Start by writing your address and the date in the heading.
  - Write the name and address of the recipient; include a zip code.
  - Include a more formal greeting, such as *Dear Ms.* (or *Mr.*), followed by the last name; *To Whom It May Concern*; or *Dear Madam* (or *Sir*). Follow the greeting with a colon.
  - Indent each paragraph of the body.
  - Capitalize the first letter of the first word of the closing, and use a comma after the closing. Write your signature in full, followed by your name typed or printed clearly. You may want to add an appropriate title or identifying organization below your name.

Talk About Drafting Look over the draft of a letter. With your partner, discuss how the writer lets the employer know she is qualified for the job. Has the writer included all the necessary parts of a business letter? What do you think about the tone of the letter?

CRITICAL THINKING

Letters to the Editor sections of newspapers and magazines publish persuasive letters. The writers use fact and opinion to support their views. A fact is a statement you can prove to be true. An opinion is a belief or a judgment that cannot be proven to be correct or incorrect.

Look at the letter from Amanda Jayne Harkrader in Writers at Work *on page 102. How does she use both fact and opinion to persuade her audience to agree with her view?*

1431 Harbor Drive
Clayton, MO 63105
March 6, 1993

Mr. Nathaniel Eckert
Maryville Daily Gazette
1 Newport Place
Maryville, MO 62119

Dear Mr. Eckert,

I am writing to apply for the Maryville Daily Gazette summer apprentice program. I am 12 years old, and I have been writing for our school newspaper all year as a roving reporter. I saw the notice on our school bulletin board, and I think I would be a very good candidate for the position.

My news articles covers lots of meetings. Also the teachers' meetings. I helped get our school recycling program off the ground, too. I help fix the stories that come in each month, too. I will be working on the newspaper again next year. The faculty adviser, Ms. Jimenez, said that she would write a reccomendation for me.

I would enjoy working for your newspaper this summer. I know I would learn a lot there. I would like to be a newspaper reporter when I'm older.

Thank you for your consideration.

Sincerely,

Violeta Gomez

When you review writing that informs, keep in mind these points:
- *Organize with a logical order.*
- *Use specific words to express ideas.*
- *Keep your audience in mind.*

This information belongs in the second paragraph with the writer's qualifications. ....

Why did Violeta specify the type of meetings she covered? ....

Violeta's work in support of the recycling program has little to do with the job she is applying for. ....

Shaping Up

Now it's time to nurture your draft. Begin by stepping back a bit and regrouping your thoughts. Then come back to your draft. Revising is your opportunity to reshape what you've written so that your final letter really suits your purpose and your audience.

Talk About Revising Talk over the changes in the section of a letter below with your partner. Do you think the changes in the letter strengthen the writer's chances of getting the job? Try explaining to each other why each of the changes was made. What additional changes would you make?

ON YOUR OWN Read your own letter carefully. Are there places where you could be more specific? Is the tone of the letter appropriate for your audience? Try to eliminate unnecessary information.

Dear Mr. Eckert,

I am writing to apply for the <u>Maryville Daily Gazette</u> summer apprentice program. I am 12 years old, and I have been writing for our school newspaper all year as a roving reporter. I saw the notice on our school bulletin board, and I think I would be a very good candidate for the position.

My news articles covers *the student council* ~~lots of~~ meetings. Also the teachers' meetings. ~~I helped get our school recycling program off the ground, too.~~ I help *edit* ~~fix~~ the stories that come in each month, too. I will be working on the newspaper again next year. The faculty adviser, Ms. Jimenez, said that she would write a reccomendation for me.

I would enjoy working for your newspaper this summer. I know I would learn a lot there. I would like to be a newspaper reporter when I'm older.

In the Best Shape

You've filled out the body of your letter and included all of the necessary parts. You've also revised your letter. Now you are thinking about whether or not to mail it. Wouldn't it be a shame to put the letter in the mailbox and then remember that you forgot to proofread it? A letter is your representative; it should show you at your best.

Talk About Proofreading With your partner, read over the corrections made in this part of the letter. Make sure you each understand the reasons for every change. Are there any kinds of errors you should be especially watchful for in your writing? What are they?

ON YOUR OWN Using the proofreader's marks, correct any punctuation, spelling, grammar, and capitalization errors in your letter. You may want to show your letter to a friend for a second proofreading.

When you and your partner discuss writing that informs, you may want to say things such as:

- *Your piece is very well organized, but do you think this sentence really belongs in the third paragraph?*
- *This sentence seems vague. Could you word it more clearly?*

For more advice about conferencing, see page 229.

CHECK-UP

- *Check your capitalization and punctuation by using the **Mechanics Handbook** on page 353.*
- *Are you having any verb problems? Check page 318.*
- *Circle misspelled words. Use the **Word Finder** on page 368 or your dictionary.*

Dear Mr. Eckert͜:

    I am writing to apply for the <u>Maryville Daily Gazette</u> summer apprentice program. I am 12 years old, and I have been writing for our school newspaper all year as a roving reporter. I saw the notice on our school bulletin board, and I think I would be a very good candidate for the position.

    My news articles ~~covers~~ *cover the student council and* lots of meetings. Also the teachers' meetings. ~~I helped get our school recycling program off the ground, too.~~ I help *edit* ~~fix~~ the stories that come in each month, too. I will be working on the newspaper again next year. The faculty adviser, Ms. Jimenez, said that she would write a *recommendation* (reccomendation) for me.

    I ... ummer. I kn... be a newsp...

Proofreader's Marks

∧	Add.	ⵔ	Check the spelling.
ꬲ	Take out.	⊙	Add a period.
≡	Make a capital letter.	⋏	Add a comma.
/	Make a lower-case letter.	ᵛᵛ	Add quotation marks.
¶	Indent the paragraph.	∽	Reverse the order.

Here's a hint to help you make your writing more specific. Imagine you're a newspaper reporter. Keep in mind the following questions: Who? What? Where? When? Why? How? As you write, make sure you answer each question specifically. For example, you should say, "I worked as a baby-sitter for two years" rather than "I have experience as a baby-sitter."

FOR MORE HELP

For more help in:
• *deciding how to publish your work, turn to page 237.*

■ Off and Running!

You can now consider sending your letter. Publishing and mailing a letter can produce rewarding results. Violeta Gomez may be chosen as a summer apprentice at her local newspaper. If you mail a letter of complaint about a defective product, you may receive a replacement or a refund. Most businesses answer correspondence promptly. Maybe the person to whom you wrote will respond to your letter by sending you a business letter.

Talk About Publishing The writer of this letter had a definite reason for composing her letter: She was applying for a job. Sending the letter to the contact person whose name was on the bulletin board was the obvious way for Violeta Gomez to publish her writing. Discuss with your partner her finished letter on page 111. Did Ms. Gomez represent herself well in her letter?

ON YOUR OWN If you have decided to publish, what methods could you use besides sending the letter through the mail? Are there other, possibly better, methods? Is it a suitable letter for publication in a magazine or newspaper? Would a radio or TV station be interested in reading it over the airwaves? What other possibilites can you think of?

If you've decided to send your letter, you may want to see page 294 and review how to address envelopes. Before you seal the envelope, decide if you want to make a copy of your letter. It's possible you will need to refer to it later.

*How does your finished letter compare with the **Model for Self-Evaluation** on page 287?*

1431 Harbor Drive
Clayton, MO 63105
March 6, 1993

Mr. Nathaniel Eckert
Maryville Daily Gazette
1 Newport Place
Maryville, MO 62119

Dear Mr. Eckert:

I am writing to apply for the Maryville Daily Gazette summer apprentice program. I saw the notice on our school bulletin board, and I think I would be a very good candidate for the position.

I am 12 years old, and I have been writing for our school newspaper all year as a roving reporter. My news articles cover the student council meetings and also the teachers' meetings. I help edit the stories that come in each month, too. I will be working on the newspaper again next year. The faculty adviser, Ms. Jimenez, said that she would write a recommendation for me.

I would enjoy working for your newspaper this summer. I know I would learn a lot there. I would like to be a newspaper reporter when I'm older.

Thank you for your consideration.

Sincerely,

Violeta Gomez
Violeta Gomez

SELF-CHECK

INFORMING • 111

Here are some ideas for writing an informative letter that you may find enjoyable to use. Read through the suggestions to find one that sparks your interest. Then jot down your ideas and start planning!

Reporter-at-Large: News About Zoos

Your school newspaper editor has asked you to write an open letter to the community about the opening of the new town zoo. The zoo has a monkey house, an exotic bird sanctuary, and a Great Cats reserve. Choose two species from these categories. Do some research about the animals or birds. Write a letter informing your readers of the zoo's special features and displays. Include your research about the animals and let your readers know what they can learn by visiting the zoo.

Station K-N-E-W

Do you have a favorite radio deejay? Write a letter to the deejay expressing your appreciation. Include a jingle, a little poem that can be set to music, that would make a catchy theme for the deejay's show.

Colonial Days

You've just visited a colonial home. You enjoyed the demonstrations of weaving and butter churning. Research life in another time period or culture. Write your information into a letter that highlights any customs that might be useful in your life today.

Dishpan Hands

The town's fanciest restaurant needs a chef's assistant to work during lunches in the summer months. Think how much you'd learn, working alongside top-flight chefs! Write a clear, organized letter in which you try to convince the owner that he or she should hire you.

UNIT

8

Like other whales, dolphins have their own special "language." They communicate with each other by using a wide range of underwater sounds, or pulses. Dolphin noises include clicks and whistles. Researchers aided by computers have tried to learn the dolphin language and to teach dolphins human speech, either by word or translated into whistles.

— Deborah G. Felder
from *The Kids' World Almanac of Animals and Pets*

■ Facts in Focus

- *What scientific phenomenon have I witnessed—a falling star, a lunar eclipse, or a solar eclipse? How would I explain the event to a friend?*
- *What scientific phenomenon puzzles me? How would I find an explanation for it?*

All around us, amazing wonders in nature are taking place. The smallest blade of grass processes sunlight into food; entire islands grow larger as erupting lava flow hardens. New species develop; others near extinction.

As we take in new information each day, our minds search for order and explanation. We search for the similarities these unknown quantities or qualities may have with things we already know about. We puzzle over the differences. Through these processes, explanations develop. Then the *How? Why? Who? Where?* answers may open the door for even more questions. And so the search for explanations continues.

IN YOUR JOURNAL To explore a topic in science, you can go on a nature hike in your own private park—your Journal!

Think of a science topic that's of interest to you. It could be the ocean, space, or perhaps prehistoric animals. Whatever captures your interest, write it down in your Journal. Then, write five questions about your subject. For example, if your topic is the ocean, one question you might have is "What's the oldest kind of creature living in the sea?" Be adventurous as you explore the unknown.

Meet Cristina Septien

Who is smarter, a human being or a computer? Is it even fair to compare the two? Cristina M. Septien tries! On page 116 she points out some of the similarities and differences between humans and computers.

Cristina, a student at Elisabeth Morrow School in Englewood, New Jersey, knows a thing or two about computers. She uses one when writing. In addition, Cristina stores ideas for future writing pieces in the computer. She says that it's easier to review her ideas this way, and she doesn't lose any of them!

When Cristina is working on a writing draft, she often shares her work-in-progress with her mom and dad. Her parents then make suggestions for revisions. Cristina also rereads her own work and sometimes adds whole paragraphs "that I think will fit in."

Cristina likes to write and tells other writers, "Have fun with writing; don't make it all serious!"

Writers at Work

WRITERS' GALLERY

For more examples of writing that explains, turn to page 198.

WRITING

I suppose my proclivity to see things with this other imaginative eye is the source of all the books I have made and will be making both for children and for grown-ups.

– Mitsumasa Anno author and illustrator

When writers explore new areas, they find that there's much more to explaining a topic than just listing facts. Writers need to focus on a thesis statement, or main idea, and present information in a well-organized and clearly stated way. Writers use organizing techniques such as comparison, which explains similarities, and contrast, which explains differences.

As you read these selections, notice how each writer uses specific details to help explain the topic.

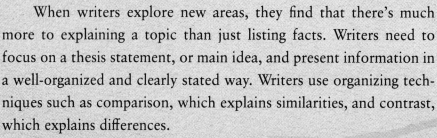

It is noon when the Sun is on the meridian. If two places are located along the same longitude, no matter how far apart (north to south), both have the same meridian, and it is noon at the same moment in both places.

Places west of you have noon a bit later. New York City, at about longitude 75°, is in the Eastern time belt or zone; Chicago, in the Central time belt at about longitude 90°, has noon one hour later; in Denver (about longitude 105°), which is in the Mountain time belt, noon is two hours later; in Los Angeles (about longitude 120°), in the Pacific time belt, noon is three hours later. Alaska and Hawaii (about longitude 150°), are *five* hours later. Other countries or areas have their own "standard time."

— Mitsumasa Anno
from *Anno's Sundial*

Computers are very much like people. They have a "brain" that retains a lot of information. They give off information by putting it on the screen like we talk to people to give them news. Computers have to be shut off properly, and they can't work for a very, very long time like we can't work for a very long time. We have to rest. Computers also have to be kept clean like people or else they can go blank or "forget" a lot of important information.

— Cristina Septien
Elisabeth Morrow School
Englewood, NJ

The Writer's Craft What all these writers have in common is a curiosity about the world around them. They search for explanations to unfold the mysteries of life. What specific focus does each writer have? Which piece of writing do you like best? Why? If these explanations were yours to write, what types of comparisons and contrasts would you make?

Science reports often utilize vivid details that appeal to our five senses. Notice how the writer Jacci Cole appealed to our sense of hearing. Which details do you find most effective?

Jacci Cole from *Animal Communication*

Cats also have several clear ways of communicating with other cats. Moyes says, "The lick is the most basic experience of a cat's life because the rasp of his mother's rough tongue is the first sensation a newborn kitten experiences." Though licking is used for grooming and cleaning, it is also a means for communicating comfort to other cats.

Moyes says that cats don't usually vocalize much when communicating with other cats; they do their talking with their bodies. However, during courtship and mating the male cat will croon softly and gently to the female. And we have all heard the ear-piercing screeches of the fighting rival males!

Our pets, no doubt, save most of their meowing to communicate with us. Moyes believes that different kinds of meows have different meanings. Some of the different meows she has identified are: the welcome—a series of short, chirruping mews, each running from high to low tones; the demand —a high pitched, sustained, incessantly repeated noise; and the informational meow—a series of fairly short but unhurried meows, often interspersed with purring.

On a rain-forest walk, I once came upon a vibrant aqua-blue-and-yellow arrow-poison frog, covered with a poisonous substance. Tiny but pungent with death, it sat right out on a felled tree and let me get close enough to breathe on it.

In temperate northern forests, one finds fewer species of plants in a given area, but many of each species; it's not unusual to see large glades of hemlock or maple. But in the rain forest there are kaleidoscopic numbers of different species, and very few samples of each one. When you look at such a forest, it has depth, texture, variety. But the members of each species are spaced far apart.

— Diane Ackerman
from "Golden Monkeys"

Diving into Your Topic

Writing that explains:
- *expresses clearly and accurately, often in a thesis statement, what the subject of the explanation is.*
- *can develop its main idea through comparison and contrast or another clear plan of organization.*
- *provides specific and accurate details to support the main idea.*

A diver can't begin to explore the ocean depths without taking that first plunge into the water. Writers begin to work in a very similar way. Once you make that first dive, you'll be swimming right along—exploring, gathering, and sorting out information for your explanation.

Brainstorm: Purpose and Audience You have a lot to explore and to explain. Can you narrow your subject? What will be your purpose in explaining? Who will your audience be—friends, family members, people in the community? Will the audience be made up of young children or people of all age groups? Be as specific as possible about your purpose and audience.

Writers have many ways to plan their work. One writer made the Venn diagram shown below for a report on deep-sea creatures. This organizing method is often used for explanations that compare and contrast related subjects. The section of the diagram where the two circles overlap shows the items that fall into both categories. What information does the Venn diagram show? For more information about diagrams, see page 221. You may want to use another planning method. Some writers prefer to make lists. Others scribble outlines or draw charts. What method works best for you?

Fish That Produce Light

To Attract Prey

bearded angler

devil angler

deep-sea angler

Lantern Fish

To Defend Themselves

viperfish

deep-sea shrimp

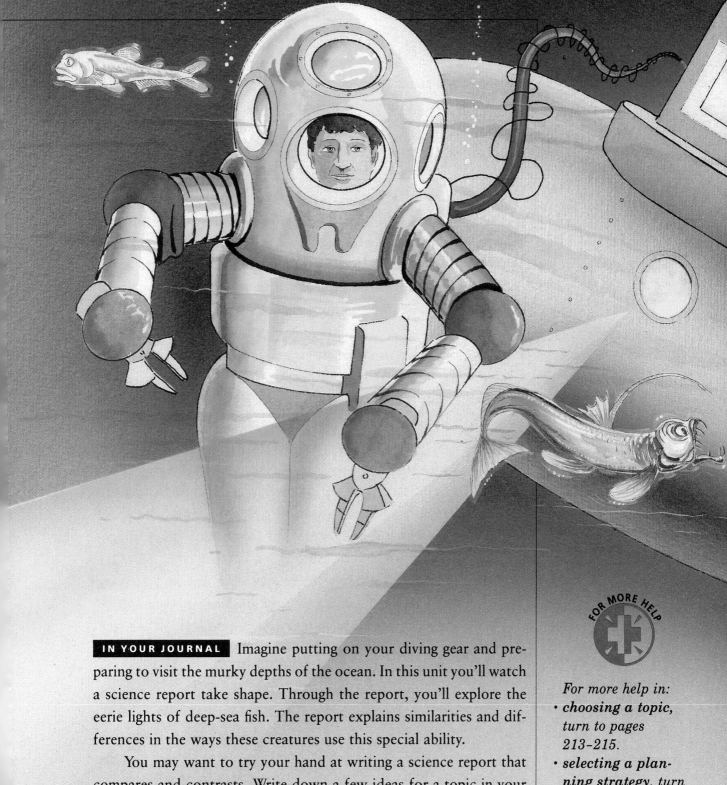

IN YOUR JOURNAL Imagine putting on your diving gear and preparing to visit the murky depths of the ocean. In this unit you'll watch a science report take shape. Through the report, you'll explore the eerie lights of deep-sea fish. The report explains similarities and differences in the ways these creatures use this special ability.

You may want to try your hand at writing a science report that compares and contrasts. Write down a few ideas for a topic in your Journal. If you'd like to try another kind of explanatory writing, take a look at the Writer's Project File on page 128. Whatever you decide, begin planning your writing. You could make a Venn diagram, a chart, or a cluster to explore your ideas.

FOR MORE HELP

For more help in:
- *choosing a topic,* turn to pages *213–215.*
- *selecting a planning strategy,* turn to pages *216–224.*
- *self- selecting,* turn to the *Writer's Project File* on page *128.*

Exploring Your Ideas In Depth

Now you're ready to start a draft. Venture through *Exploring Explanations* and think about the points raised along the way. Writing a draft gives you a chance to plunge right into your topic. As you write, explore your ideas—feel your way around your subject.

Exploring Explanations

- Decide on your purpose for writing the explanation and who your audience will be.

- Narrow your topic so that you have a clear thesis statement, a clear main idea. Complete this sentence to focus your ideas: When my readers finish my explanation, they will have learned the reasons why _____.

- Develop the thesis statement by presenting specific, accurate details to support it. Consult reference books, science articles, and textbooks for facts, quotes from experts in the field, and other information that will help you to write a clear explanation.

- Try using comparison and contrast to organize the explanation. Decide how to use this organizing plan. Will you first give all the similarities between two or more aspects of the topic and then give all the differences? Will you alternate similarities and differences throughout the explanation? To learn more about comparison and contrast, turn to page 252.

- Help the reader to follow your explanation by using transition words and phrases that express relationships between ideas. A few examples are *in addition, on the other hand, in the same way, however, similarly,* and *in contrast.*

- Make sure that your explanation has a clear beginning (the introduction), middle (the body of the explanation, with examples and details), and end (the conclusion, with a summary of the main idea). See page 248 to read more about an effective beginning, middle, and end.

Talk About Drafting With a small group or a partner, discuss the draft on page 121. What is the thesis statement of this science report? How did the writer use comparison and contrast to explain ideas? Is the draft effective? Which details do you find most interesting?

Deep-Sea Lights

How do deep-sea creatures manage to survive in the darkness two thousand feet under the ocean, many fish that live at great depths produce red, green, or blue lights. Some biologists, such as Richard Goldsby from the University of Maryland, believe this mysterious process may be controlled by a creature's hormonal system. Deep-sea fish use bioluminescence for a variety of purposes.

Some fish produce light to attract prey for food. The bearded angler has a light glowing in a "beard" dangling from its chin and curious prey are lured by it. Similarly, the devil angler uses light to attract food; however, the source of its glow are just above its mouth. The deep-sea angler fish uses a light on a flexible stalk that protrudes from its snout.

Fish can also use their light as a defense against predators. Like the bearded angler and the devil angler, the lantern fish uses its light to attract prey. In addition, its light helps hide it from predators. Through a special disguise, the lantern fish can't be seen from underneath. In contrast, the viperfish confuses its enemies by flashing on and off, while the deep-sea shrimp surrounds itself with a glowing cloud so predators can't see it. No one knows exactly how the viperfish uses all its lights.

Sea creatures glow for other reasons, too. Some fish also light up to attract mates. For a variety of purposes, deep-sea creatures glow and glimmer with erie lights far below the ocean's surface.

ON YOUR OWN You've completed your planning. Now it's time to develop your ideas by writing your draft. Divers have a term for letting oxygen flood through the mouthpiece without regulating it. It's called free flow. You'll be doing something similar when you write your draft. Just let your ideas flow. You can clean up the draft later.

○○○ **CRITICAL THINKING**

Why is comparison and contrast useful as an organizing technique for an explanation?

When you compare related subjects, you bring out their similarities. When you contrast two subjects, you show their differences. (See page 252.)

Comparison and contrast help the reader form a clearer picture of the subject. This technique also connects the subject with topics the reader is already familiar with.

*How does Diane Ackerman contrast a temperate northern forest and a rain forest in the **Writers at Work** excerpt on page 117?*

Coming Up for a New Tank of Air

When divers come up for a new tank of air, they take the opportunity to rest a bit, relax, and reflect on their explorations so far.

Try revising the same way. Let a little time go by, and get a breath of fresh air. When you go back to your draft, you may discover something new you'd like to include. You'll probably see things you'd like to change a bit. Take a few minutes to read your draft. Flag any parts that you think need help.

Talk About Revising With your partner, read over the changes in the draft on page 123. Do you think the added information improves the report? Why? Talk over the other revisions. Is there anything else you would change if this were your draft?

REVISING STRATEGIES

When you review writing that explains:
* *Check to see that the purpose is clearly expressed in a thesis statement that summarizes the topic.*
* *Make sure specific language and accurate details are used. Does the piece need facts or other sources to support the main idea? (See page 244 for more about main idea and details.)*
* *Notice if comparison and contrast help define the subject. How are the similarities and differences organized?*

ON YOUR OWN Review your own draft with a friend. Fish around for comments. Replace vague words with facts or precise expressions. Look for places to add sentences that more fully explain a point, and make sure you have focused on a thesis statement. How did you utilize comparison and contrast? Did you fully explain the examples? Use the suggestions that you find most helpful.

As you revise, you may even decide to switch directions and change the focus of your writing. If you get stuck for ideas or supporting details, head for the library. You may find some unusual facts and figures that will intrigue your readers.

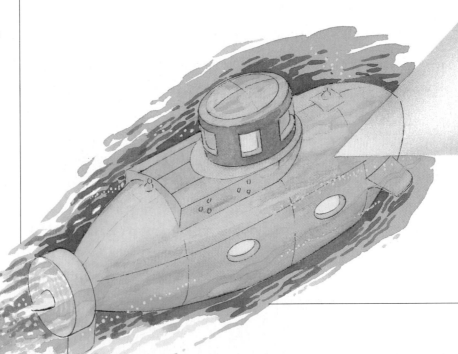

Deep-Sea Lights

How do deep-sea creatures manage to survive in the darkness two

thousand feet under the ocean, many fish that live at great depths

through a chemical process called bioluminescence.

produce red, green, or blue lights. Some biologists, such as Richard

Goldsby from the University of Maryland, believe this mysterious

process may be controlled by a creature's hormonal system. Deep-sea

fish use bioluminescence for a variety of purposes.

Some fish produce light to attract prey for food. The bearded angler

has a light glowing in a "beard" dangling from its chin and curious prey

are lured by it. Similarly, the devil angler uses light to attract food;

however, the source of its glow are just above its mouth. The deep-sea

angler fish uses a light on a flexible stalk that protrudes from its snout.

Fish can also use their light as a defense against predators. Like the

bearded angler and the devil angler, the lantern fish uses its light to

lure   *Since its light matches the strength of sunlight*

attract prey. In addition, its light helps hide it from predators. Through a

through water,

special disguise, the lantern fish can't be seen from underneath. In

contrast, the viperfish confuses its enemies by flashing on and off, while

the deep-sea shrimp surrounds itself with a glowing cloud so predators

can't see it. No one knows exactly how the viperfish uses all its lights.

Sea creatures glow for other reasons, too. Some fish also light up

to attract mates. For a variety of purposes, deep-sea creatures glow and

glimmer with erie lights far below the ocean's surface.

An important point was left out. How does this addition help clarify the thesis statement?

Why do you think the writer moved this sentence closer to the beginning of the paragraph?

Vague language was replaced with a specific detail. How does this change improve the writing?

When you and your partner discuss explanations, you may want to say things such as:

· *I'm not sure I understood this comparison. How are the two things similar?*

For more advice about conferencing, see page 229.

▪ Double-Check Your Findings

WRITERS ON "" WRITING

An all-round knowledge of the subject is bound to shine through in your writing. It does more: it gives you confidence, and that comes through like a searchlight.

– David Woodbury from <u>Writing About Science</u>

It's checkup time! If you think you may want to publish your work, you'll need to proofread your writing to make sure you've caught any errors. Your audience will then focus on what you're saying rather than on any mistakes that may have slipped into your writing.

Talk About Proofreading With a partner, discuss each correction in this draft. What kinds of corrections were made? What marks were used to show each change? What types of errors do you need to watch out for most in your writing?

ON YOUR OWN If you'd like to publish your work, think about different publishing possibilities. What method could help you reach your audience? Then take some time to proofread your writing. You may also want to have a friend read your explanation to catch any errors you may have missed.

Deep-Sea Lights

How do deep-sea creatures manage to survive in the darkness two thousand feet under the ocean? many fish that live at great depths *through a chemical process called bioluminescence.* produce red, green, or blue lights. Some biologists, such as Richard Goldsby from the University of Maryland, believe this mysterious process may be controlled by a creature's hormonal system. Deep-sea fish use bioluminescence for a variety of purposes.

Some fish produce light to attract prey for food. The bearded angler has a light glowing in a "beard" dangling from its chin, and curious prey are lured by it. Similarly, the devil angler uses light to attract food; however, the source of its glow *is* just above its mouth. The deep-sea angler fish uses a light on a flexible stalk that protrudes from its snout.

Fish can also use their light as a defense against predators. Like the bearded angler and the devil angler, the lantern fish uses its light to *lure Since its light matches the strength of sunlight* attract prey. In addition, its light helps hide it from predators. Through a *through water,* special disguise, the lantern fish can't be seen from underneath. In contrast, the viperfish confuses its enemies by flashing on and off, while the deep-sea shrimp surrounds itself with a glowing cloud so predators can't see it. No one knows exactly how the viperfish uses all its lights.

Sea creatures glow for other reasons, too. Some fish also light up to attract mates. For a variety of purposes, deep-sea creatures glow and *eerie* glimmer with erie lights far below the ocean's surface.

- *Check your capitalization and punctuation by using the* **Mechanics Handbook** *on page 353.*
- *Are you having any verb problems? Check page 324.*
- *Circle misspelled words. Use the* **Word Finder** *on page 368 or your dictionary.*

Proofreader's Marks	
∧	Add.
ℓ	Take out.
≡	Make a capital letter.
/	Make a lower-case letter.
¶	Indent the paragraph.
◯	Check the spelling.
⊙	Add a period.
∧	Add a comma.
♥♥	Add quotation marks.
∽	Reverse the order.

Back on Land to Share Knowledge

For more help in:
• **deciding how to publish your work,** turn to page 237.

How does your finished work compare with the Model for Self-Evaluation on page 288?

Transition words and phrases help to link related ideas. Notice how the word <u>similarly</u> helps the writer compare two types of angler fish. What other transition words and phrases in this report help the writer compare and contrast aspects of the topic?

Out of your wet suit, back in your jeans—you've come a long way since you took that first plunge! With your explorations and writing finished, you can now share with others the explanation you've developed. Publishing your explanation means that a wide audience can benefit from the efforts you've put into developing your work.

Talk About Publishing With a partner or in a small group, discuss the published report "Deep-Sea Lights" on page 127. This science report was posted on the local aquarium's "Student Bulletin Board." Is the report clearly organized? What main idea comes through? What audience would enjoy reading the report? Do you think the publishing method will be effective in reaching that audience? What other publishing ideas can you suggest for this work?

ON YOUR OWN If you want to share your work, choose a form of publication that you think is suitable. Keep your purpose and audience in mind. What form would your audience find most useful? You may decide to get together with other members of your class and begin a Student's Encyclopedia. How about making a student bulletin board for a local pet store? What other ideas for publishing can you consider? It's your work, so decide the best way to share it.

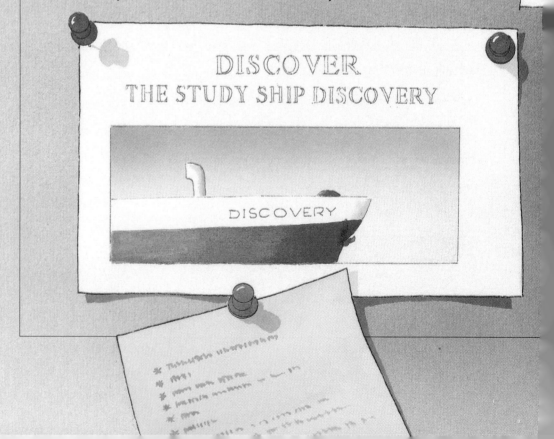

Deep-Sea Lights

How do deep-sea creatures manage to survive in the darkness two thousand feet under the ocean? Many fish that live at great depths produce red, green, or blue lights through a chemical process called <u>bioluminescence</u>. Deep-sea fish use bioluminescence for a variety of purposes. Some biologists, such as Richard Goldsby from the University of Maryland, believe this mysterious process may be controlled by a creature's hormonal system.

Some fish produce light to attract prey for food. The bearded angler has a light glowing in a "beard" dangling from its chin, and curious prey are lured by it. Similarly, the devil angler uses light to attract food; however, the source of its glow is just above its mouth. The deep-sea angler fish uses a light on a flexible stalk that protrudes from its snout.

Fish can also use their light as a defense against predators. Like the bearded angler and the devil angler, the lantern fish uses its light to lure prey. In addition, its light helps hide it from predators. Since its light matches the strength of sunlight through water, the lantern fish can't be seen from underneath. In contrast, the viperfish confuses its enemies by flashing on and off, while the deep-sea shrimp surrounds itself with a glowing cloud so predators can't see it.

Sea creatures glow for other reasons, too. Some fish also light up to attract mates. For a variety of purposes, deep-sea creatures glow and glimmer with eerie lights far below the ocean's surface.

GO ON A MINI-SUB ADVENTURE

Here are some ideas for writing projects that explain. Find one that interests you. Then let your imagination soar!

From Town to Town

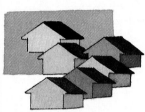

How would you explain the advantages and disadvantages of living in your area? Compare and contrast your town with a neighboring community. Include information about schools, historic sites, parks, and shopping areas.

First Prize

A teacher in your school will receive an award for excellence in teaching. Choose the lucky teacher! Write an essay that explains why your teacher was chosen.

The Evening News

You are a television reporter sent to cover the devastating effects of a natural disaster on a nearby area. You have inspected the damage, interviewed survivors, and spoken to rescue workers and other experts. Explain the situation in a report, and deliver your news broadcast to your classmates.

Cultural Awareness Day

Your community is holding a Cultural Awareness Day, where people share and learn about diverse cultures. Select a culture different from your own. Research the history and culture of the people. What are some contributions the people have made to the building of our country? What examples of courage and perseverance can you recount? What customs are unique to that culture? Write a report for the student panel at the Cultural Awareness Day.

UNIT

9

Based on the author's childhood in Mississippi, the book tells of the struggle to retain black land rights when lumbermen try to force the family to sell beautiful old trees.

—summary of
Song of the Trees
by Mildred Taylor

SONG

Hit the Highlights

SELF-SURVEY

- *What kinds of information do I look for in a summary of a story? Do I just want facts, or do I also look for a taste of the action or the suspense?*
- *How can I communicate my excitement about a book I like so that others will want to read it, too? What elements of the book—characters, plot, setting, dialog—would I highlight in a summary?*

A story summary describes a puzzling mystery and hints that there is a surprising twist in the plot; you decide to read the story. A preview on TV promises live footage of a journey to the North Pole; you decide to watch the show. Summaries and previews hit the highlights. They pique your curiosity and pull you to pick up a certain book or to watch a specific show. Once your interest has been sparked, you'll take it from there.

IN YOUR JOURNAL Have you read a book recently that you would recommend to a friend? What stands out that you like about the book? Why did it interest you? In your Journal, jot down some things you remember most about the book. Get to the heart of it! Do you recall, for example, an unusual character, some heightened moments of tension or tenderness, something special about the story's plot or its setting? Why would you want your friend to read the book?

Meet Thomas Mills

Read any good books lately? Thomas Mills has. He describes the book *Ransom* on page 132.

Thomas attends Hally Open Middle School and lives in Detroit, Michigan. Like a lot of other seventh-graders, Thomas likes to spend his spare time playing basketball and video games.

Thomas keeps a journal at home and writes in it often. "I just like to get my thoughts down on paper." Once in a while he looks back at his journal for writing ideas. Thomas looks for ideas in other ways, too. "What I write about depends on how I feel that day. I just walk around in my neighborhood and think about all the stuff that's going on and use that for ideas."

He enjoyed writing his description of *Ransom* by Lois Duncan because he liked reading the book. Finding a good book that you really like makes all the difference in the world.

WRITERS ON "" WRITING

■ Writers at Work

A story is an investment. Instead of investing dollars, however, you invest the time it takes to read the story—the minutes, hours, or even days. Like any smart investor, you probably need some questions answered before you take the plunge. This is where a story summary can help. Which of the following stories seem worthy of your time and attention? How can a summary spark your interest? Decide which stories will make the best investments.

Educationally I am the product of a wide and complex interplay of university and traditional Indian training. I am disinclined to talk about my education and many other personal details of my life because I feel they have no relationship to my writing. I often quote W. B. Yeats: "Art is the public act of a private person."

- Jamake Highwater author

REVIEWER

Ransom by Lois Duncan starts out with a school bus full of students on their way home from school. They are part of the way home before they realize that the bus driver is a new driver. The bus driver lets all of the students off the bus except the last five, who live in the rich section of the town. The driver never lets them off the bus. After he has taken them to a cabin in the mountains, they overhear the kidnappers talking about killing the other bus driver. . . .

The five students were rescued by Rod, Marianne's stepfather, who was the one to take the ransom to the kidnappers. He took his pistol with him which turned out to be a good idea because it helped save everyone's life. A fight at the cabin happened, and the kidnappers were taken over by Rod and the five students. The police were called, and the kidnappers were no longer a problem.

This was a good adventure story. I enjoyed reading it. It was a mystery full of suspense. There was never a clue about how it was going to end until the final chapter and the final page. I believe that all five of the students will always be friends because of what they went through together.
—Thomas Mills
Hally Open Middle School
Detroit, Michigan

Traditional Native American tales make up a heritage that all North Americans should take pride in and pass on to future generations. In his collection of traditional Native American tales, *Anpao: An American Indian Odyssey*, Jamake Highwater compares the teller of Native American folktales to a weaver whose designs are the threads of his or her personal saga, as well as the history of his or her people. These stories of the Native American oral tradition have been passed from one generation to the next and often mingled with tales from other tribes.

—summary of *Anpao: An American Indian Odyssey*
by Jamake Highwater

The Writer's Craft At the beginning of a TV news program, a reporter gives a snappy preview to keep viewers glued to their sets. A story summary functions in much the same way. It grabs the attention of the audience and excites its curiosity. How? A summary provides a thumbnail description of the plot and introduces the main characters. It may tell briefly about some of the events that take place. It tells you just enough and not too much. If the summary interests you, you'll want to experience the whole work. Did these story summaries capture your interest? What parts of the story summaries were particularly intriguing to you?

WRITERS' GALLERY

REVIEWER

After old Ned got such a terrible beatin' for prayin' for freedom, he slipped off and went to de North to join de Union Army.
— Mingo White, ex-slave
from *Voices from Slavery*

Author Joyce Hansen was inspired by this and other quotes from original sources to write a story about black participation in the Civil War. Though the characters are fictional, *Which Way Freedom?* is based on actual events and circumstances, including the massacre at Fort Pillow, Tennessee, in 1864.

Some 200,000 blacks fought in the Civil War. Historically, their contributions have been neglected. This book approaches the subject realistically, revealing little-known details about the survival skills and tactics of the runaways. It is a sensitive account of a young man's search for freedom and the complicated adjustments he is forced to make as he adapts to his new life.
—summary of
Which Way Freedom?
by Joyce Hansen

Although Ryan White was born with hemophilia, the boy and his family were determined that he live as normal a life as possible. But, given contaminated blood in a transfusion, Ryan contracted AIDS. Most Americans are familiar with the ensuing headline-making facts: his school barred his attendance, neighbors and former friends shunned him and his family. Moving from Kokomo, Ind., to friendlier Cicero, Ryan struggled for the right to be educated and treated like any other kid even as he fought a daily battle against AIDS and hemophilia. Until his death in April 1990, Ryan was an eloquent spokesperson for all AIDS patients. This understated, affecting first-person account is no mere saccharine tearjerker about a "victim." Early on, Ryan resolved to be the "first kid with AIDS to speak out, fight back—and win." Hearing Ryan's often strong, sometimes hurting, always faith-filled voice in these pages, readers will know that his hopeful, heroic spirit did ultimately triumph.
—summary of *Ryan White: My Own Story*
by Ryan White and
Ann Marie Cunningham

What's It About?

Your best friend is on the telephone. She wants to describe a story she's just read. It's fantastic—maybe the best thing she's ever read. It made her laugh and cry, sometimes at the same time!

It sounds great. However, there's one thing you have to know before you decide to read the story yourself. What's it about? A story summary answers that question. It also gives you a quick peek at the characters—a Who's Who in the book.

Brainstorm: Purpose and Audience With a partner, discuss a summary you would like to write. It might be a story summary, like the one in this unit, or it might be something different: a summary of a recent trip or maybe a summary of the rules of a new game.

Before you begin writing, think about the purpose of your piece. Why do you want to write it? Who is the audience you are writing for? What effect do you want to have on your audience?

Story summaries:
- *use vivid details to draw the reader into the story.*
- *provide critical information about the events in a story.*
- *organize information about the story in an orderly manner.*

Question 1:
How could I describe the main character in the story?
Meribah Simon, a 14-year-old girl, Goodnough's friend, a survivor

Question 2:
When and where does the story take place? What does the setting look like?
the Gold Rush of 1849; across deserts, prairies, and mountain ranges from Pennsylvania to California

The writer of the questions below intends to write a story summary of the book *Beyond the Divide* by Kathryn Lasky. You can ask a series of focusing questions like these to help you plan your own writing. Use your questions to organize your thoughts on the topic you choose. Jot down as many answers as you can for each question. You can decide later which of the answers you will use in your summary. Turn to page 218 for more information about focusing questions.

For more help in:
• **choosing a topic,** turn to pages 213–215.
• **selecting a planning strategy,** turn to pages 216–224.
• **self-selecting,** turn to the **Writer's Project File** on page 142.

IN YOUR JOURNAL In this unit you will see how the story summary of *Beyond the Divide* develops. You, too, will write a story summary, unless you choose to write another type of summary. Several suggestions are provided in the Writer's Project File on page 142. If you decide to write a story summary, you can start by making notes in your Journal. For example, you could list some of your favorite books and then choose one as the subject of your story summary. What is it about the book that interests you? Jot down some ideas and impressions. Then start planning your summary. You could write focusing questions, or you might prefer to organize your ideas in the format of a chart or an outline.

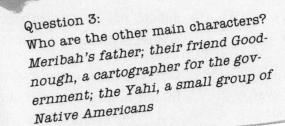

Question 3:
Who are the other main characters?
Meribah's father; their friend Goodnough, a cartographer for the government; the Yahi, a small group of Native Americans

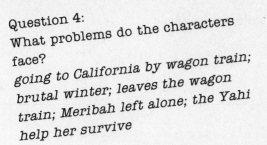

Question 4:
What problems do the characters face?
going to California by wagon train; brutal winter; leaves the wagon train; Meribah left alone; the Yahi help her survive

The Story in Brief

You're on your way to writing a description, such as a story summary. Check your plans and Journal notes, and take a careful look at *Making a Long Story Short*. You'll find good advice to help you describe a story summary. Then you'll be ready to write your draft. The key point to remember is that a summary must contain enough information to pique the audience's interest. At the same time, you want to withhold some information so that the audience feels the need to experience the work itself.

Making a Long Story Short

- Review your purpose before you start. Remember, you do not have to write a long, all-inclusive summary. Include only enough information to arouse the reader's interest. Then choose an audience. Think specifically about what your audience would like to know as you write the summary.

- Start out with something catchy—a startling fact, a bold statement, a penetrating observation—to grab your audience's attention.

- Organize your summary so that, like a story, it has a beginning, a middle, and an end. See page 248 to read more about beginning, middle, and end.

- Carefully summarize the plot, describing key events, but be careful not to give away too much; you certainly want to avoid revealing the ending. What will be the reader's overall impression?

- Think about the way you want to organize your summary. Who are the main characters? Where does the story take place? What is the central event of the story?

- Make the characters come alive. Let the reader see them in action. Is there a quote that reveals a character's personality?

- Use vivid details and colorful language.

CRITICAL THINKING

How do writers of story summaries decide whether they have described a story well enough to inform readers without giving away too many details?

Writers try to answer these questions:
- *Who is the central character, and what is his or her goal?*
- *Who or what gets in the way of that character's goal, creating conflict?*
- *How does the conflict develop? See page 249 about story conflict.*

Reread the Writers at Work summaries on pages 132–133. Do you think each summary provides enough but not too much information?

Talk About Drafting With a partner, discuss the draft that follows. Can you tell from this summary what the book is about? What facts stand out in the summary? What is your overall impression of the story? Do you think you'd like to read the book?

<u>Beyond the Divide</u>

by Kathryn Lasky

When fourteen-year-old Meribah Simon leaves Pennsylvania with her father to travel to California, she has no way of knowing the challenges she will face. It's 1849, and many people are heading to California by wagon train because gold has been discovered there. The cross-country route is arduous, and many find it too difficult to complete.

When circumstances force Meribah and her father to leave the wagon train, they face a brutal winter stranded high in the Sierra Nevada. Meribahs wagon train traverses desolate prairies, burning deserts and perilous mountain ranges. It was a hard trip. Meribah and her father set up a camp in the cold wilderness with their friend. Suddenly, Meribah finds herself alone. They must survive the winter through her own efforts and with the help of the Yahi, a small group of Native Americans.

ON YOUR OWN Ready, get set, draft! Keep your purpose and your audience clearly in mind, and make good use of your plans. At the same time, remember that a draft is a work in progress; it isn't meant to be perfect. You'll be able to polish your writing later.

Taking the Long View

Now that you've finished your draft, a good investment of your time may be to put it away for a while. Stepping away from your writing now will help you to see it in a fresh way later.

Before starting your revision, you may wish to share your draft with a friend and ask for comments. Reading the draft aloud to yourself is another way to find out whether or not you like what you've written. By carefully listening to your words, you can identify places where you'd like to make some changes.

Talk About Revising With a partner, discuss this section of a draft. What revisions did the writer make that will help to catch and to hold the reader's attention? Do you think these changes work? What other changes do you think still need to be made?

When you review a story summary:
- *Look at the piece as a whole. Is it well organized?*
- *Think about the information you included, such as the characters, the plot, and the setting.*
- *Consider the main ideas. Did you include all of the important details?*

The organization of the paragraph could be better. Why did the writer change the order of these sentences?

This sentence is repetitive. What is the effect of leaving it out?

The writer chose to elaborate here. How does this information add to the overall effectiveness of the summary?

> When circumstances force Meribah and her father to leave the wagon train, they face a brutal winter stranded high in the Sierra Nevada. Meribahs wagon train traverses desolate prairies, burning deserts and perilous mountain ranges. ~~It was a hard trip.~~ Meribah and her father set up a camp in the cold *snowbound* wilderness with their friend ^*Goodnough, a cartographer for the government.* Suddenly, Meribah finds herself alone. They must survive the winter through her own efforts and with the help of the Yahi, a small group of Native Americans.

ON YOUR OWN Reread your own draft. First, look at the big picture. Does the draft achieve the right balance between telling the audience enough and not too much? Are you satisfied with its organization and flow? Then, look at the details. Were any important details left out? Put them in, and take out the ones that aren't really necessary.

A Close Inspection

By now you've invested time and energy in your writing. You've revised your draft to make it clear, interesting, and accurate. You're almost ready to share your writing with your audience. This is the time to avoid letting proofreading errors come between you and your audience. You'll want to check your piece carefully and then write a clean copy that is free of spelling, punctuation, and grammar errors.

Talk About Proofreading With a partner, look at this part of the proofread story summary. Why was each correction made? Why is it necessary to keep your writing as error-free as possible?

ON YOUR OWN Look again at the piece you've written. Would you like to share your enthusiasm with others and introduce them to the subject of your piece? If you decide to publish, proofread your description. Check to make sure everything is letter-perfect.

CHECK-UP

- *Check your capitalization and punctuation by using the **Mechanics Handbook** on page 353.*
- *Are you having problems with pronouns? Check page 334.*
- *Circle misspelled words. Use the **Word Finder** on page 368 or your dictionary.*

When circumstances force Meribah and her father to leave the wagon train, they face a brutal winter stranded high in the Sierra Nevada. Meribahs wagon train traverses desolate prairies, burning deserts and perilous mountain ranges. It was a hard trip. Meribah and her father set up a camp in the cold *snowbound* wilderness with their friend. *Goodnough, a cartographer for the government.* Suddenly, Meribah finds herself alone. *She* They must survive the winter through her own efforts and with the help of the Yahi, a small group of

Proofreader's Marks

∧	Add.	⊃	Check the spelling.
ℰ	Take out.	⊙	Add a period.
≡	Make a capital letter.	⋏	Add a comma.
/	Make a lower-case letter.	ᐯᐯ	Add quotation marks.
⌘	Indent the paragraph.	∪	Reverse the order.

When you and your partner discuss a story summary, you might want to make such comments as:

- *I would like to get a clearer picture of _____. Do you think you could elaborate on that part of your summary?*

For more advice about conferencing, see page 229.

■ ## Mission Accomplished

For more help in:
• *deciding how to publish your work, turn to page 237.*

When you invest time in your writing, there are lots of rewards. A sense of pride and accomplishment comes from writing something you feel good about. Your piece is something that only you could have written, something you have tried to present in the best possible way. Think about how writers must feel when they see their names in print for the first time. Who knows where that publication might lead? Someday your writing might even change someone's life!

Talk About Publishing Go over the published summary on page 141. Do you think it turned out well? Does it make you want to go out and read the book *Beyond the Divide?* This summary was presented as a video preview of the book. The writer drew storyboards, which she captured on film, and read her summary aloud. With a partner, begin to think about different ways you could publish your own summary. What unusual ways of publishing could you explore?

ON YOUR OWN Decide how you could submit your story summary for publication. Perhaps a library in your community would be interested in displaying your writing on a bulletin board, complete with illustrations of scenes from the book. You could get together with friends in the neighborhood and have a story-storming session, at which each of you reads a summary aloud. Then the group could discuss the books. How many participants would be intrigued enough to read the other books summarized? Before heading off for vacation, you and your friends may wish to swap story summaries of good books to read while away from school. What other ideas for ways of publishing can you come up with?

SELF-CHECK

How does your finished work compare with the **Model for Self-Evaluation** *on page 289?*

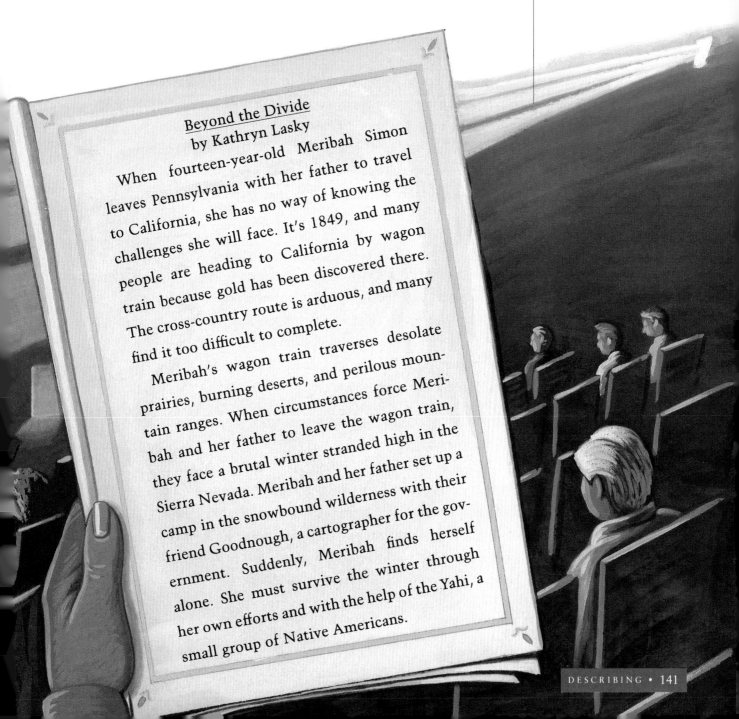

Beyond the Divide
by Kathryn Lasky

When fourteen-year-old Meribah Simon leaves Pennsylvania with her father to travel to California, she has no way of knowing the challenges she will face. It's 1849, and many people are heading to California by wagon train because gold has been discovered there. The cross-country route is arduous, and many find it too difficult to complete.

Meribah's wagon train traverses desolate prairies, burning deserts, and perilous mountain ranges. When circumstances force Meribah and her father to leave the wagon train, they face a brutal winter stranded high in the Sierra Nevada. Meribah and her father set up a camp in the snowbound wilderness with their friend Goodnough, a cartographer for the government. Suddenly, Meribah finds herself alone. She must survive the winter through her own efforts and with the help of the Yahi, a small group of Native Americans.

Would you like to try some other type of descriptive writing? Here are some suggestions for topics to write about. You may wish to write your description in the form of a letter, an ad, or a poem.

Play Ball!

Can words describe the feeling you got when you saw a professional baseball game for the first time—the greenness of the grass, the crack of the bat, and how impossibly high the ball went, even on a foul pop-up? Describe the experience in a summary.

Our Shrinking World

If you could visit any place in the world, where would it be? You can visit any country—in the comfort of your home or your library! Choose one country, and do some research on it. Can you interview acquaintances who once lived or visited there? Write a descriptive summary of one aspect of the country that interests you—fashion, food, theater, or sports.

The Year of Living Typically

Congress has declared a Year of the Teenager. You have been chosen to address the House and the Senate about your experiences as a typical teenager. These legislative bodies are planning programs designed for teenagers. Write a summary that describes your life.

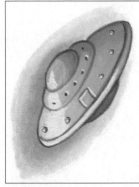

A *Strange* Magazine

Imagine you are a writer for a new magazine, *Strange, Stranger, Strangest!* Write a description of a fantastic person, place, or thing. Let it come alive with a description that only you can supply. Will it be a visitor from outer space or a food item that is full of surprises? Have fun describing your creative concoction.

For whatever happens to the beasts, soon happens to man. All things are connected.

You must teach your children that the ground beneath their feet is the ashes of your grandfathers. So that they will respect the land, tell your children that the earth is rich with the lives of our kin.

Teach your children what we have taught our children, that the earth is our mother.

Whatever befalls the earth befalls the sons of the earth. If men spit upon the ground, they spit upon themselves.

— Chief Seattle
from "Letter to the U.S. Government"

Influencing Others

- *Who has changed my mind about an issue recently? What helped me to "see the light"?*
- *How can I encourage my family to do something I think should be done? Why do I think so?*

Every day we learn new things about the world around us. Some events and issues concern us; some don't. Maybe you feel strongly about the fast-approaching extinction of grizzly bears and zebras. Maybe you advocate more parks in your city or town.

How do your friends and family feel about the things that are important to you? How have your opinions influenced their views? As a writer, you have the power of persuasion at your fingertips. What issues will you address? What opinions will you voice?

IN YOUR JOURNAL Is there something in your community you'd like to change? Community members like yourself often voice their concerns in the pages of a newspaper. The editorial section offers different viewpoints on current affairs or local controversies. If you were making plans to publish your own newspaper, what issues would you write editorials about? List a few of them in your Journal.

Meet Heather Peterson

"Don't just be satisfied with the first draft!" This advice comes from Heather Peterson, a student who lives in Beaverton, Oregon, and attends Mountain View Intermediate School. Heather revises her writing until it reflects her personal style. She likes writing poetry best, because she can express her thoughts in any way she wants.

Heather suggests going to the library to find help with ideas for stories and reports. "Just walk around looking at books until you find a book that looks good. Think about the story or the pictures and brainstorm your own story."

She adds, "The hardest thing about writing to me is trying to figure out how to end whatever it is I'm writing. It helps when I think about all the different ways I can end it, including what happens to all of the characters, and then choose one."

A selection from Heather's persuasive piece titled "Undercover" appears on page 146.

**WRITERS'
GALLERY**

*For more examples
of writing that per-
suades, turn to
page 200.*

Writers at Work

You read examples of persuasive writing every day—in ads, in letters, and even in this book. Persuasive writing presents the writer's opinion or point of view about something and encourages the reader to agree. Facts and logical reasons count, too—they give backbone to any persuasive piece. How do the writers on these pages express their opinions? How do they use facts and logical reasons? Why are some phrases especially persuasive?

We have to recreate a world in which we are known.
We fight against anonymity at the grocer's, the
dry-cleaner's, newsstand, the coffee shop—and are
often thwarted by the supermarket, the
discount pharmacy, the fast-food counter. . . .
I don't suppose any visitor cares if he is known
in a strange city. But many of us live our whole
lives as if we were just passing through.
And if we are all tourists, where are the
natives to teach us how to wave?

— Ellen Goodman
from ''Waving Good-bye to the Country''

I first learned to read when I was four years old, during a daily ''quiet hour'' we used to have when my sisters and I were younger. I had no idea then how important books and reading would become to me. For one thing, books are a never-ending supply of free knowledge on any subject you could ever want to investigate. Books can teach you about history, geography, science, the arts, or maybe just pull you out of the real world for a while into their own harmonious sphere.

Many of my views and values have been started and encouraged by books. Sometimes they even gave me a new point of view or just enhanced my own perspective.

A book can take you anywhere in the world that you want to go. It can take you back through time to places and events that otherwise would be impossible to see. You can see a person's predictions of the future and all the new space-age technology, if you look in the right book.

— Heather Peterson
Mountain View Intermediate School
Beaverton, OR

The Writer's Craft Imagine writing about an issue you care about. Would you choose one of these examples as a model for your writing? Which one? Why does that piece stand out amongst the others and grab you? See if you can explain why you find your choice especially persuasive.

I try to live what I consider a "poetic existence." That means I take responsibility for the air I breathe and the space I take up. I try to be immediate, to be totally present for all my work.

– Maya Angelou poet and author

My responsibility as a writer is to be as good as I can be at my craft. So I study my craft. I don't simply write what I feel, let it all hang out. That's baloney. That's no craft at all. Learning the craft, understanding what language can do, gaining control of the language, enables one to make people weep, make them laugh, even make them go to war. You can do this by learning how to harness the power of the word. So studying my craft is one of my responsibilities. The other is to be as good a human being as I possibly can be so that once I have achieved control of the language, I don't force my weaknesses on a public who might then pick them up and abuse themselves.

— Maya Angelou
from *Black Women Writers at Work*

Be proud of your ethnicity and language. Don't be afraid to use it. Don't give in to the stupidity of those know-nothings who insist that one language is better than two or three. You should know, and be proud, that in the Western Hemisphere more people speak Spanish than English; that Español was the language of the hemisphere's first university—the Santo Tomás de Aquino University in the Dominican Republic, founded in 1538—and of the books in its first library. When you discover the long and honorable tradition to which you belong, your pride will soar.

So do not lose the language of your parents, which is also yours. Instead, refine your skill in it. If you're having trouble with grammar or writing, take courses in Spanish. Go to the library and read Cervantes' *Don Quixote*, the first full-fledged novel, or the works of the hundreds of great modern Hispanic authors, such as Gabriel García Márquez, Lola Rodriguez de Tío, Carlos Fuentes, Mario Vargas Llosa, Octavio Paz, Jorge Luis Borges and Oscar Hijuelos, the 1990 Pulitzer Prize-winner in fiction (who writes in English). Read them in both languages; note the strength of both. This is the treasure that no one can ever steal.

— José Torres
from "A Letter to a Child Like Me"

Mapping Your Plans

Persuasive writing:
- *expresses an opinion or a point of view and tries to persuade the reader.*
- *uses well-chosen, powerful words to win the reader over.*
- *can be conversational in tone, as in a letter to a friend, or more formal, as in an editorial.*

Stop! Think of an issue you feel strongly about—just one, for now. It might be a concern facing you personally, your neighborhood community, the entire nation, or the world at large.

Look! Do some "close-up" thinking about why you feel that way. You could also think about the times that you feel most interested in that issue—for example, when you see a report on TV or when you and your friends are talking.

Listen! Take the next step by talking to yourself. (It doesn't have to be out loud!) Try asking yourself, "What change would I like to see happen? How do others feel about this issue? What could I write that might get them to see things my way?"

Brainstorm: Purpose and Audience Some writers find it helpful to talk through their ideas with friends; others like to think on their own. Either strategy can help you make decisions about your purpose and audience.

Then try visualizing your audience. Many writers find that this technique helps give their writing direction. Keeping in mind the needs of your audience will help you persuade them more effectively. See page 216 for more about visualizing.

You may know your own opinion on an issue. How clearly can you share it with others?

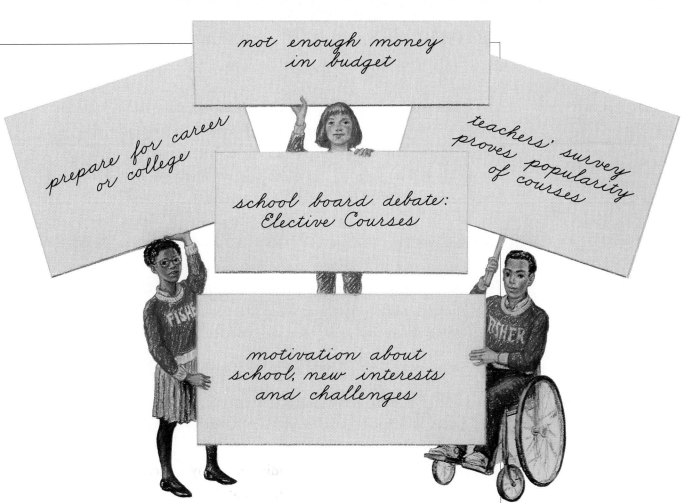

not enough money in budget

prepare for career or college

teachers' survey proves popularity of courses

school board debate: Elective Courses

motivation about school, new interests and challenges

A diagram or chart can help you to map out an editorial or another form of persuasive writing. It can help you to see your ideas and opinions more clearly and to think through aspects of an issue. This diagram helped one writer to plan an editorial. You may want to try another planning method, such as jotting down ideas in a list or freewriting. If you want to know more about making and using diagrams, turn to page 221.

IN YOUR JOURNAL In this unit you'll see a newspaper editorial take shape. Maybe you'd like to write an editorial, too. If you'd rather work on a different form of persuasive writing, see the Writer's Project File on page 158 for ideas.

If you haven't decided on a topic, now is the time to do it. Use your Journal to work out your thoughts. Drawing diagrams, making lists, or jotting down key words can put you on the right track. Use whatever method helps you to put your opinions on paper and to organize your ideas for writing. See your own piece of persuasive writing take shape as you begin to plan in your Journal.

FOR MORE HELP

For more help in:
- *choosing a topic,* turn to pages 213–215.
- *selecting a planning strategy,* turn to pages 216–224.
- *self-selecting,* turn to the **Writer's Project File** on page 158.

Hitting the Road

With your purpose and audience clear in your mind, you can begin drafting. Use the plans in your Journal as a road map. They'll keep you on course and help you remember the points you want to make. If you make good use of *Policies of Persuasion,* you'll soon have a powerfully persuasive piece of writing.

Policies of Persuasion

- Persuasive writing tries to convince the reader of something. Stay on track about your purpose and audience. Why is it so important to do something about this issue? Who could do something about this issue? How can you reach this audience?

- Make sure your opinion is clearly stated.

- Sort out your arguments. Try to think of logical reasons and facts to support your opinion. Complete this list:
  1. I think we should _____.
  2. One reason is that _____.
  3. The facts show _____. My source is _____.
  4. The most important reason is that _____.
  5. For all these reasons, we should _____.

- Use forceful, persuasive language. Ask yourself, "What words can I use to clarify my point of view and to draw my readers over to my way of thinking?"

- Think about using a more formal and objective tone. You want your audience to know that you are serious about your subject. You will probably hit a good balance if you avoid using slang and the latest expressions. In addition, contractions tend to sound informal, so you may want to think twice before using them.

Talk About Drafting Look over this draft with your partner for a few minutes. Compare it to the planning diagram the writer used on page 149. Is every item in the diagram included in the draft? Which reason seems strongest to you? Do you think the editorial might convince the school board? Does the tone of the editorial help to make it persuasive?

The Student Council Speaks

The school board is debating the funding of elective courses for our school. It is said by some members of the board that there isn't enough money in the budget for elective courses. Many students have been talking about wanting to take elective courses that are not required, such as Cultural Comparisons or Advanced Computer Literacy. Perhaps the board members could try to save some money from other parts of the budget in order to fund elective courses.

Electives lead students to think about the future. In addition, the Teachers' association published a survey that had said eighty percent of students who took an elective course during the first year of junior high school took an elective course each following year. The classes may open doors to new career interests in many fields, including nutrition, electronics, and computer technology. So, elective courses are both useful and popular.

The members of the Student Council would like the school board to look closly at the budget and to find money to fund elective courses. We believe that elective courses can contribute to our success and to the success of future students.

— Sonia Cruz

Student Council President

Fisher Junior High

CRITICAL THINKING

In persuasive writing you offer your own opinion. Would you ever use other people's opinions to support your position?

Solid facts are the best support for an argument. Sometimes, though, you could quote experts and other sources, such as magazine articles, to support your opinion. See **Information Resources** *on page 371 for more about developing research skills.*

Compare the examples in **Writers at Work** *on pages 146–147. How many facts can you find? How many supporting opinions?*

ON YOUR OWN Use your plans to write your own persuasive piece. Keeping your purpose in mind, just start writing. You may discover that putting your first ideas in writing gives you new ideas. It's all right to make mistakes at this stage. Your main concern now is developing your ideas on paper. You can make changes and corrections later.

At the Crossroads

You've finished your draft of a persuasive writing project. Now step back and take a break. Every writer must decide just how long the break should be—maybe an hour, maybe a day, maybe a week! The result, however, is the same. When you take some time out before revising, you are able to return to your writing with a fresh eye.

Before you begin revising any persuasive draft, you may want to look back over your original plans for the piece. Are there any important points that you forgot to include in the draft? Then ask yourself these questions:

- Is my work going in the right direction? Do I make a strong presentation of my opinion?

- If I read my draft aloud—to myself or to a partner—does the piece flow smoothly from one point to the next? Where can I utilize transition words and phrases in the piece? (To learn more about transition words and phrases, turn to page 245.)

- Did I include all of the most important reasons why I feel the way I do about this topic? Are my ideas expressed as clearly as possible? Which ideas can I further clarify?

- Have I supported my opinions with facts and logical reasons? What magazines, newspapers, and other resources can I read for more information? Will a quote from one of these resources give my opinion more weight?

- Is my concluding sentence strong?

- What will my audience think of my persuasive piece? Will it be able to persuade them to agree with my point of view?

Talk About Revising With a partner, discuss the revisions in the editorial about elective courses shown on page 153. Why did the writer make those changes? Do you both agree with the writer's choices? What changes do you disagree with? Toss around ideas for other changes you might have made, too.

REVISING STRATEGIES

When you revise persuasive writing:
- *Make sure you've stated your opinion clearly. Does your point of view jump out at the reader?*
- *Ask yourself if you've expressed your ideas in the most convincing way. Look for places where you could add persuasive words to strengthen the points you make.*
- *Check the language. Is the tone right for your audience? (See page 279.)*

The Student Council Speaks

The school board is debating the funding of elective courses for our school. It is said by some members of the board that there isn't enough money in the budget for elective courses. *Offering such courses would improve our school.* Many students have been talking about wanting to take elective courses that ~~are not required~~, such as Cultural Comparisons or Advanced Computer Literacy. Perhaps the board members could try to save some money from other parts of the budget in order to fund elective courses.

Electives lead students to think about the future. In addition, the Teachers' association published a survey that had said eighty percent of students who took an elective course during the first year of junior high school took an elective course each following year. The classes may open doors to new career interests in many fields, including nutrition, electronics, and computer technology. So, elective courses are both useful and popular.

The members of the Student Council ~~would like~~ *strongly urge* the school board to look closly at the budget and to find money to fund elective courses. We believe that elective courses can contribute to our success and to the success of future students.

— Sonia Cruz

Student Council President

Fisher Junior High

ON YOUR OWN Decisions, decisions! What changes do you want to make in your writing? Does your partner think the piece is convincing? Does the tone reflect the fact that you take your subject seriously? Did you include support for your opinions? Would a quotation from an expert or other source help strengthen your writing? Work with your draft until it says just what you want it to say.

FAST FOCUS

Is this a clearer statement of point of view?

This phrase is redundant: <u>elective</u> means "based on the principle of choice."

This presents the point of view more formally. How does it strengthen the persuasive tone of the piece?

CONFERENCING STRATEGIES

When you and your partner discuss persuasive writing, you may want to say things such as:
- *Are you persuading your audience to _____?*
- *You wrote a really powerful piece! Maybe if you said _____ instead of _____, the reader would follow you more easily.*

For more advice about conferencing, see page 229.

Clear Road Ahead

Does your persuasive writing now say what you want it to say? Good! Maybe you're thinking about publishing it. Is it ready for your audience?

When writers publish their work, they must check it over to be sure there are no mistakes. You really want to persuade your audience to agree with your point of view, and even small errors can be jarring to readers. They may find themselves focusing on the mistakes rather than on your arguments. Then their attention will wander, and it will be much harder to persuade them.

Talk About Proofreading With a partner, spend a few minutes discussing the proofreading corrections in this draft. Which grammar, spelling, or punctuation errors were corrected? Why was each change made?

The Student Council Speaks

The school board is debating the funding of elective courses for our school. ~~It is said by some members of the board~~ *Some members of the board say* that there isn't enough money in the budget for elective courses. *Offering such courses would improve our school.* Many students have been talking about wanting to take elective courses ~~that are not required~~, such as Cultural Comparisons or Advanced Computer Literacy. Perhaps the board members could try to save some money from other parts of the budget in order to fund elective courses.

Electives lead students to think about the future. In addition, the Teachers' association published a survey that ~~had~~ said eighty percent of students who took an elective course during the first year of junior high school took an elective course each following year. The classes may open doors to new career interests in many fields, including nutrition, electronics, and computer technology. So, elective courses are both useful and popular.

The members of the Student Council ~~would like~~ *strongly urge* the school board to look (closly) *closely* at the budget and to find money to fund elective courses. We believe that elective courses can contribute to our success and to the success of future students.

— Sonia Cruz

Student Council President

Fisher Junior High

Proofreader's Marks

∧	Add.
ℓ	Take out.
≡	Make a capital letter.
/	Make a lower-case letter.
¶	Indent the paragraph.
◯	Check the spelling.
⊙	Add a period.
∧	Add a comma.
˅˅	Add quotation marks.
∽	Reverse the order.

• Check your capitalization and punctuation by using the **Mechanics Handbook** on page 353.
• Are you having any verb problems? Check page 325.
• Circle misspelled words. Use the **Word Finder** on page 368 or your dictionary.

ON YOUR OWN If you would like to publish your work, think about how to do it. In your Journal, write down a few possible ways to publish your piece that might help you to reach your target audience. Then proofread your work.

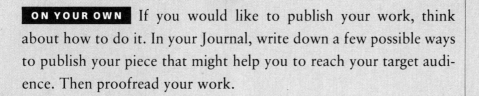

Reaching Your Destination

For more help in:
· *deciding how to publish your work,* turn to page 237.

What is the best way to publish your work? Thinking about your target audience can help you to decide. How can you reach the greatest number of people in that audience? Maybe you can persuade some other people, too, if they have a chance to read your published work. The reactions of your audience might even give you some new ideas about your topic to consider.

Talk About Publishing Talk about the newspaper editorial shown below with your partner. It was published in the local newspaper. What audience will the editorial reach? Do you think it will persuade its audience? Why or why not? Discuss your opinions.

THE STUDENT COUNCIL SPEAKS

The school board is debating the funding of elective courses for our school. Some members of the board say that there isn't enough money in the budget for elective courses. Offering such courses would improve our school. Many students have been talking about wanting to take elective courses, such as Cultural Comparisons or Advanced Computer Literacy. Perhaps the board members could try to save some money from other parts of the budget in order to fund elective courses.

Electives lead students to think about the future. The classes may open doors to new career interests in many fields, including nutrition, electronics, and computer technology. In addition, the Teachers' Association published a survey that said eighty percent of students who took an elective course during the first year of junior high school took an elective course each following year. So, elective courses are both useful and popular.

The members of the Student Council strongly urge the school board to look closely at the budget and to find money to fund elective courses. We believe that elective courses can contribute to our success and to the success of future students.

— Sonia Cruz
Student Council President
Fisher Junior High

ON YOUR OWN Now that your piece of persuasive writing is looking and sounding its best, what ideas do you have about how to publish it? If you wrote an editorial, you could submit it to a newspaper or a magazine, of course. You can consider many other options. One is to publish it as a leaflet that you yourself distribute to friends and family. Remember, your opinion is important! You can make a difference by sharing it with others.

SELF-CHECK

*How does your finished work compare with the **Model for Self-Evaluation** on page 290?*

Here are some ideas for projects that use persuasive writing. Take some time to read them and choose one that interests you. Remember, your opinion really counts!

Great Moments in History

Think about an important moment in world history. What issues would the people of that time be considering? For example, in the 1700s, colonists argued whether or not to revolt against British rule. Choose a country and an issue. Write a persuasive essay expressing your opinion.

A Jazzy School Offering

Your school is giving a concert to honor great jazz musicians. Research the different styles of jazz, how they developed, and who was famous for playing in each style. Then write an advertising brochure, urging the public to attend the concert.

Save Our Library!

If your local library closed due to a lack of funds, where would you borrow books? Write a letter that someone facing library closings could send to town officials. Persuade them to find a different solution to the town's money problems. Be sure to compare and contrast the possibilities before you begin writing.

Media Watch

Conduct a media watch for examples of unfairness in product ads. Look for misleading claims or illogical thinking. Will a certain running shoe really turn the wearer into a hero? Write the results of your media watch in an editorial.

I lined up for the one-hundred-yard dash with the other runners—the finest athletes from every corner of the country. As I hunkered down and fitted my spiked shoes into the ground so as to get a good start, a sharp pain ran down my back. But I didn't give it any thought. I was only thinking of the race that would start in a second.

"Runners, take your marks," the starter said.
We all fidgeted nervously.

"Get set," said the starter.
I felt my body lifting slowly into the air as it had hundreds and hundreds of times before. All my weight was on the tips of my fingers now. My feet were waiting to push me out as hard as they could. Out of the corner of my eye, I saw the starter point his gun up toward the sky. Then he pulled the trigger. The sound shot through the stadium like a crash of thunder.

But even before that sound had died away, we were all up and out, our feet dance-pounding over the cinders.

—Jesse Owens
   with Paul G. Neimark
   from *The Jesse Owens Story*

I'll Never Forget the Time . . .

Special moments come in little sizes and big sizes. They're tear-jerkers. They're hilarious. They're touching. You can work very hard planning them, or they can take you totally by surprise. Sharing one of your special moments with others is a gift only you can give.

IN YOUR JOURNAL Think about some of the most important events in your life. Perhaps exciting events come to your mind first—like winning a contest or saving the game during the last seconds of play. What are some quieter times that you treasure? Could they include such memories as making up with your best friend after a big argument or welcoming the arrival of a new brother or sister? Make a list in your Journal of some of the events in your life that you think you'll never forget. Which ones would you like to tell others about?

- *What are some stories about myself that I would like to tell other people?*
- *Which moments really stand out in my memory as the happiest and saddest times of my life?*
- *What kinds of stories do I most enjoy when older people talk about their lives in "the good old days"?*

Meet Tanya Achmetov

Why should people write? Tanya Achmetov responds with enthusiasm, "I think people should write for their own enjoyment. They should look for and find one part of writing that they like."

She continues, "I like writing; it's like a hobby. It's a way to express myself. I also have a diary, but I don't show it to anyone else. It's just for my personal enjoyment."

Tanya lives in Falls Church, Virginia, and attends Longfellow Intermediate School. Tanya loves to read, especially fantasy books. She enjoys seeing new places and traveling through the countryside.

Tanya wrote "A Special Birthday," the autobiographical poem on page 162, "both for myself, because I just wanted to express the feelings, and to share with other people. Hopefully, people of all places can relate to it and remember a happy moment they had."

WRITERS'
GALLERY

*For more examples
of writing that
entertains, turn to
page 201.*

Writers at Work

Writers can entertain you in many ways. They can make you laugh or cry, keep you in suspense, frighten you, or make you cheer for a character. As you read these excerpts, think about what makes each piece entertaining. How does each writer's work capture your interest? What are your feelings when you read each piece?

A Special Birthday

Shiny.
New.
Bright racy red.
I got it for my birthday,
A gift from Mom and Dad.
Envious looks,
From neighborhood playmates.
A grin, ear to ear,
On my six-year-old face.
A twinkle of light,
Seemed to gleam,
From my dark excited eyes.
I touched it. The cold metal.
A shock of electricity went up my arm.
It was all mine and I loved it.
My Bike.

—Tanya Achmetov
Longfellow Intermediate School
Falls Church, Virginia

Lost

I know not of my forefathers
nor of their beliefs
For I was brought up in the city.
Our home seemed smothered and surrounded
as were other homes on city sites.
When the rain came
I would slush my way to school
as though the street were a wading pool.
Those streets were always crowded.
I brushed by people with every step,
Covered my nose once in awhile,
Gasping against the smell of perspiration on humid days.
Lights flashed everywhere
until my head became a signal, flashing on and off.
Noise so unbearable
I wished the whole place would come to a standstill,
leaving only peace and quiet

And still, would I like this kind of life? . . .
The life of my forefathers
who wandered, not knowing where they were going,
but just moving, further and further
from where they had been,
To be in quiet,
to kind of be lost in their dreams and wishing,
as I have been to this day,
I awake.

Then I recalled this trail
    Swept away by the north wind,
It wasn't for me to follow,
    The trail of the Long Walk.

Deciding between two cultures,
    I gave a second thought,
Reluctantly I took the new one,
    The paved rainbow highway.
I had found a new direction.

—Bruce Ignacio

The Writer's Craft Each of these excerpts is autobiographical; each deals with a special moment in the life of the writer. Did you feel a part of that moment as you read the excerpt? If so, you left your own world, just for a few minutes, and became a part of the writer's world. How could you make a reader feel that way about an episode in your life?

I suppose there were about a dozen Indian children in the school —which contained perhaps forty children in all—and four of them were in my class. They were all sitting at the back of the room, and I went to join them. I sat next to a small, solemn girl who didn't smile at me. She had long, glossy-black braids and wore a cotton dress, but she still kept on her Indian jewelry—a gold chain around her neck, thin gold bracelets, and tiny ruby studs in her ears. Like most Indian children, she had a rim of black kohl around her eyes. The cotton dress should have looked strange, but all I could think of was that I should ask my mother if I couldn't wear a dress to school, too, instead of my Indian clothes.

I can't remember too much about the proceedings in class that day, except for the beginning. The teacher pointed to me and asked me to stand up. "Now, dear, tell the class your name."

I said nothing.

"Come along," she said, frowning slightly. "What's your name, dear?"

"I don't know," I said, finally.

—Santha Rama Rau
from *Gifts of Passage*

It was the first day of my apprenticeship. My mother had let me wear a new pair of *waraji,* or straw sandals. The toolbox was crushing my shoulder bone, while the stiff thongs of the *waraji* scraped my bare skin. We passed many unfamiliar houses, stone walls, fences, and gates, but I saw them all through only the corner of my eye. In spite of the pain, I hurried to keep up with my master. When we finally arrived at the customer's house, the owner greeted us with a "good morning" and a "thank you for coming." Immediately I looked for a place to put the toolbox down.

—Toshio Ōdate
from "The Soul of the Tool"

To me, my life has seemed ordinary enough, not usual perhaps as lives go but satisfactory to my needs. Yet I know that there are many people, including some of my best friends, who consider it odd, peculiar, even a little mad. Or exotic. So it occurred to me that it would be amusing to weld together these very personal stories—each of which has a basis in a true happening—with autobiographical comment. This I have done, prefacing each story with such details of my wandering life as seemed relevant.

*–Santha Rama Rau
author*

Planning the Entertainment

If you were planning an evening of entertainment for some friends, what kind of party would it be—a large, crowded gathering filled with music and laughter, or a quiet gathering of a few close friends?

Just as there are different kinds of parties you can give to entertain people, there are different ways you can entertain people with words and ideas. Perhaps your imagination takes flight into the future as you create things fanciful, strange, or funny. It could be that you prefer to write about things close to home—family and friends, for example—or about yourself. Nearly any form of writing is entertaining if it captures the readers' interest and involves them in the world the writer creates. Now you can involve readers in a world of your own creation.

Brainstorm: Purpose and Audience As you explore ideas for writing a piece that would entertain others, talk about your purpose and audience with a classmate. Do you want to make your audience laugh? Do you want to thrill your readers with an adventure? Do you want them to share a time in your life that has special meaning for you? Talk about your audience. Who will enjoy entering your world?

Writing that entertains, such as an autobiography:
- *captures the readers' interest, carrying them from their own world into the one the writer creates.*
- *focuses on important events that readers react to with feelings that could include amusement, excitement, or delight.*
- *is organized in any way that is effective in engaging and holding the readers' attention.*

WHO are the important people in this episode?
     me, Paw Paw (my Grandma), Mr. Wu

WHEN did it take place?
     6 years ago, on Paw Paw's 50th birthday

WHAT are the most important details?
     preparing dessert, recipe blew out the
     window, Mr. Wu found it, Paw
     Paw's discovery at end

WHY did this mean a lot to me?
     turned a near-disaster into something
     special; gave Paw Paw an unexpected
     gift

HOW did I feel about the events?
     excited at first, then worried about
     the results of my cooking, then happy at
     the end

If you plan to write about an episode in your life, you can draw a few sketches of the event to help you remember the details you want to include. You may want to ask yourself focusing questions like the ones on page 164. The questions and answers remind you to include all of the important details as you write. Even if these details may not seem to add up now, it's helpful to get them down in the heat of the moment because you may want to use them later. If you'd like to learn more about focusing questions, see page 218.

IN YOUR JOURNAL In this unit you'll see how one episode from a writer's life developed into an autobiographical story. Look at the list of important events you made in your Journal. You may want to use one of those episodes to write an autobiography. If not, glance through the Writer's Project File on page 174 for some other ideas for writing that entertains. One of those suggestions may appeal to you.

Once you've decided on your topic, let your memory and imagination roam for a while. Then begin shaping the images and ideas that come into your mind by asking focusing questions or using some other planning technique that helps you to organize your thoughts. Write your plans in your Journal.

FOR MORE HELP

For more help in:
• *choosing a topic,* turn to pages 213–215.
• *selecting a planning strategy, turn to pages 216–224.*
• *self-selecting, turn to the Writer's Project File on page 174.*

◼ Discovering Yourself

Telling a story about yourself is a wonderful way to entertain others. It's also a good way to discover new insights about yourself. You can look back at a part of your life that might have gone by so quickly that you didn't realize how much it meant to you. You may be surprised by what you learn about yourself as you put a part of your world down on paper. Let *The Art of Autobiography* be your guide as you explore your past.

The Art of Autobiography

◼ Before you begin, have a clear idea of your purpose and audience. To clarify them for yourself, complete these sentences:
- By writing about this episode of my life, I hope to _____.
- _____ will enjoy reading my story.

◼ Make sure your readers understand why the episode was important to you. Think about what you learned from the episode. How did the episode make you feel? How did it affect you?

◼ Help your readers experience the episode just as you did by using words and language that involve your audience in the emotions of that moment. Describe specific details. Include dialog if spoken words were part of the episode. (See page 247.)

◼ Develop the mood. Will the mood be somber, lighthearted, or suspenseful? See page 281 for more about mood.

◼ Think about different ways to organize your writing effectively. Would the story be most effective if you start with the exciting part and then tell the beginning? What do you want your audience to see or to understand right away?

◼ Keep yourself at the center of the episode. Other people are important, but you're writing about you—your experiences, your feelings, and your reactions to the world around you.

Talk About Drafting With a partner, talk about this draft of an entertaining autobiography. Did you become a part of the writer's world as you read it? How does the writer capture your interest?

CRITICAL THINKING

One of the most important decisions a writer must make is how best to organize the piece. Time order and spatial order are techniques used to organize writing. (See pages 250–251.) Experiment with the organization of your piece. Have you ever opened a story with the climax?

How are the **Writers at Work** *pieces on pages 162–163 organized? Does the organization affect your interest in the piece?*

My Favorite Disaster

Sometimes a little thing can really make a difference. It was my grandmother's birthday, and she still tells this story.

I was going to surprise Paw Paw by making her favorite dessert, Four Color Rice Pudding. My mother invited all the relatives to celebrate Paw Paw's fiftieth birthday and her twenty-fifth year (to the exact day) in this country.

I propped the recipe card up against the window to look at it while cooking. I turned around to check how much milk to add when poof! a sudden breeze took the card right out the window. That open window turned out to be more important than I ever imagined. I didn't go down right away to look for it, though. I couldn't leave the ingredients half-mixed. Besides, I figured that I'd made the recipe so many times I couldn't go wrong.

The whole family sat down to eat. Then the doorbell rang. It was Mr. Wu from the first floor. ''Is this yours?'' he asked. He had seen the recipe flutter down from our fourth-floor window. Then I panicked! I forgot the cornstarch!

Everyone were talking all at once, but I couldn't pay attention. I was to worried about my poor rice pudding. All of a sudden I heard Paw Paw say, ''You knew Lee Wai Jong?'' It seems Mr. Wu moved here not long ago from Hexian, where Paw Paw's childhood friend lives. Paw Paw had'nt heard any news about Wai Jong for more than 25 years. I started to apologize for my pudding, but I stopped. It was Paw Paw's birthday. I saw the faraway look in Paw Paw's eyes. I knew I had given her a birthday surprise that couldn't have turned out more better.

The writer uses parentheses in the second paragraph. Writers sometimes use parentheses to signal an explanation or an additional thought. For more about using parentheses, check page 357. Writers use some punctuation marks, such as exclamation marks and dashes, to give their writing a certain style or tone.

ON YOUR OWN Are you ready to entertain? Enjoy yourself as you write your draft. Concentrate on putting your ideas down on paper rather than making sure you include every detail.

Stepping Back a Moment

How did your draft turn out? Did you write about all of your ideas? Step back from your piece and take a long, cool break. Then go back to the piece and reread it. Did your story come out the way you intended? Are you satisfied that you captured your characters' personality traits, actions, and speech? Did you set the right mood and convey the feelings you wanted to get across?

Talk About Revising The draft about the birthday dinner is shown on the opposite page. As you look over the changes the writer made, talk about them with a partner. Do you think the changes helped the piece? Why do you think they were made? Would you have handled any of these corrections differently? What suggestions for additional changes would you give the writer?

ON YOUR OWN Think about ways you can make your writing clearer, more entertaining, or more effective. Try reading your draft aloud. Often you can hear changes that are needed by reading a draft aloud at different points in its development. Jot down some ideas for changes right on your draft. If you want to make major changes, such as reorganizing, make those changes first. Then you can go back and look at each sentence to check on structure and choice of words. Don't miss a chance to make a sentence sparkle!

My Favorite Disaster

An open window can make a big difference in someone's life. 🖎

~~Sometimes a little thing can really make a difference.~~ It was my grandmother's birthday, and she still tells this story.

I was going to surprise Paw Paw by making her favorite dessert, Four Color Rice Pudding. My mother invited all the relatives to celebrate Paw Paw's fiftieth birthday and her twenty-fifth year (to the exact day) in this country.

I propped the recipe card up against the window to look at it while cooking. I turned around to check how much milk to add when poof! a sudden breeze *sucked* ~~took~~ the card right out the window. ~~That open window turned out to be more important than I ever imagined.~~ I didn't go down right away to look for it, though. I couldn't leave the ingredients half-mixed. Besides, I figured that I'd made the recipe so many times I couldn't go wrong.

I couldn't wait for the big moment to bring out dessert.
The whole family sat down to eat. Then the doorbell rang. It was Mr. Wu from the first floor. ''Is this yours?'' he asked. He had seen the recipe flutter down from our fourth-floor window. Then I panicked! I forgot the cornstarch!

Everyone were talking all at once, but I couldn't pay attention. I was to worried about my poor rice pudding. All of a sudden I heard Paw Paw say, ''You knew Lee Wai Jong?'' It seems Mr. Wu moved here not long ago from Hexian, where Paw Paw's childhood friend lives. Paw Paw had'nt heard any news about Wai Jong for more than 25 years. I started to apologize for my pudding, but I stopped. ~~It was Paw Paw's birthday.~~ I saw the faraway look in Paw Paw's eyes. I knew I had given her a birthday surprise that couldn't have turned out more better.

Does the phrase <u>an open window</u> give a more concrete picture than <u>a little thing</u>? How does the new sentence get you interested right away?

The writer thought this sentence was repetitious. What do you think— should it have been removed?

How does knowing that the writer felt a keen sense of anticipation make you feel, especially when the writer tells you about Mr. Wu arriving with the recipe card?

Last-Minute Details

You always have a few last-minute things to check on before the guests arrive at your party. In the same way, you will need to make a final check of your writing before you invite others to read it— especially if you are sharing a part of your personal life. You will need to look for errors of all kinds to correct. A couple of mistakes won't ruin your entertainment for your audience, but errors won't improve it, either. You want to make sure that nothing distracts your audience from enjoying your work.

Talk About Proofreading Read this part of the proofread draft about the birthday celebration. Examine the proofreading corrections that the writer made. Discuss with your partner the reasons for each change. Have you ever had to make similar corrections?

ON YOUR OWN Proofread your writing before you make a clean copy for publishing. If you wrote a piece that has several paragraphs, make sure each paragraph begins and ends where you want it to. Do you have pet mistakes—errors in spelling or grammar that you seem to make again and again, despite knowing better? Track them down and get rid of them. Don't let anything spoil your good work!

My Favorite Disaster

An open window can make a big difference in someone's lif
∧ Sometimes a little thing can really make a differenc~~e~~

was my grandmother's birthday, and she still tells this st

I was going to surprise Paw Paw by making her favorite

sert, Four Color Rice Pudding. My mother invited all the

tives to celebrate Paw Paw's fiftieth birthday and

twenty-fifth year (to the exact day) in this country. ∧

I propped the recipe card up against the window to lo

it while cooking. I turned around to check how much milk t
sucked
when poof! a sudden breeze ~~took~~ the card right out the wi

~~That open window turned out to be more important than I~~

~~imagined.~~ I didn't go down right away to look for it, though. I

couldn't leave the ingredients half-mixed. Besides, I figured

that I'd made the recipe so many times I couldn't go wrong.

I couldn't wait for the big moment to bring out dessert.

The whole family sat down to eat ∧ Then the doorbell rang.

It was Mr. Wu from the first floor. ''Is this yours?'' he asked.

He had seen the recipe flutter down from our fourth-floor win-

dow. Then I panicked! I forgot the cornstarch!
was
Everyone ~~were~~ talking all at once, but I couldn't pay at-
too
tention. I was (to) worried about my poor rice pudding. All of a

sudden I heard Paw Paw say, ''You knew Lee Wai Jong?'' It seems

Mr. Wu moved here not long ago from Hexian, where Paw Paw's

childhood friend lives. Paw Paw had'n't heard any news about Wai

Jong for more than 25 years. I started to apologize for my pud-

ding, but I stopped. ~~It was Paw Paw's birthday.~~ I saw the far-

away look in Paw Paw's eyes. I knew I had given her a birthday

surprise that couldn't have turned out ~~more~~ better.

Proofreader's Marks

∧	Add.
ℓ	Take out.
≡	Make a capital letter.
/	Make a lower-case letter.
⌐⌐	Indent the paragraph.
◯	Check the spelling.
⊙	Add a period.
⋏	Add a comma.
ᵛᵛ ᵛᵛ	Add quotation marks.
∽	Reverse the order.

PROOFREADING CHECK-UP

- *Check your capitalization and punctuation by using the* **Mechanics Handbook** *on page 353.*
- *Are you having any verb problems? Check page 318.*
- *Circle misspelled words. Use the* **Word Finder** *on page 368 or your dictionary.*

Welcome to My World

For more help in:
• *deciding how to publish your work, turn to page 237.*

SELF-CHECK

How does your finished work compare with the Model for Self-Evaluation on page 291?

Through the years, you've discovered some new things about yourself and about how you see the world. You've chosen to share, through writing, a bit of you with others. With your work in final form, you are ready to share it with your audience. They will enter your world through the entertaining writing you've prepared for them. How will you publish your work for this eager audience?

Talk About Publishing Read the published version of "My Favorite Disaster" on page 173. The author included the piece, along with the Four Color Rice Pudding recipe, in a book of favorite recipes made for a friend. What do you think of the publishing method used by the author? How would you have published the piece? Talk about your reactions with a partner.

ON YOUR OWN Decide whether or not you'd like to publish your writing. If so, you may have thought about different ways to publish your work. You may want to submit your piece for publication in a magazine. Think about making your piece of writing the first page in an album about yourself. You could illustrate it with photos and add both writing and pictures to it as time goes on. Then you could share it with family and friends someday or look back on it yourself and remember what you were like in the seventh grade.

My Favorite Disaster

An open window can make a big difference in someone's life. It was my grandmother's birthday, and she still tells this story.

My mother invited all the relatives to celebrate Paw Paw's fiftieth birthday and her twenty-fifth year (to the exact day) in this country. I was going to surprise Paw Paw by making her favorite dessert, Four Color Rice Pudding.

I propped the recipe card up against the window to look at it while cooking. I turned around to check how much milk to add when poof! a sudden breeze sucked the card right out the window. I didn't go down right away to look for it, though. I couldn't leave the ingredients half-mixed. Besides, I figured that I'd made the recipe so many times I couldn't go wrong.

The whole family sat down to eat. I couldn't wait for the big moment to bring out dessert. Then the doorbell rang. It was Mr. Wu from the first floor. "Is this yours?" he asked. He had seen the recipe flutter down from our fourth-floor window. Then I panicked! I forgot the cornstarch!

Everyone was talking all at once, but I couldn't pay attention. I was too worried about my poor rice pudding. All of a sudden I heard Paw Paw say, "You knew Lee Wai Jong?" It seems Mr. Wu moved here not long ago from Hexian, where Paw Paw's childhood friend lives. Paw Paw hadn't heard any news about Wai Jong for more than 25 years. I started to apologize for my pudding, but I stopped. I saw the faraway look in Paw Paw's eyes. I knew I had given her a birthday surprise that couldn't have turned out better.

Writing about an event in your life is only one of many exciting ways to entertain others. Let one of these projects bring out your talent as an entertainer. Use the writing form that works best for your piece.

A Nobel Prize-Winning Mistake

Imagine that you've accidentally made an amazing discovery. For example, a mistake you made in preparing a recipe led to an instant cure for the common cold. You have won the Nobel Prize in Science and Medicine. Write an acceptance statement explaining your discovery.

News Reports: The Whole Truth?

Should news reporters stick to the facts, or should they make their reports dramatic and exciting? Write two accounts of the same event. Make the first one factual and informative. Write the second account accurately, but as though your main purpose were to entertain.

Heroic Tales

History includes a lot more than names and dates. It's the story of people who have risked their lives exploring the unknown or fighting for political freedom. Who is one of your heroes from history? Write a dramatic episode from that person's life. Make your audience feel that they are sharing that moment in history.

Animal Lessons

You probably heard many make-believe stories as you were growing up. Remember the story about the race between the tortoise and the hare? "The Tortoise and the Hare" entertains while teaching the readers a lesson. Write an entertaining story in which animals with different characteristics learn a lesson about life. Imagine that your audience is a group of seven-year-olds.

On January 8, 1985, five Argentine climbers were forging a new route to the 22,834-foot summit of Cerro Aconcagua, the highest mountain in the Western Hemisphere, when they stumbled upon a semicircular pile of stones containing a bundled human body, with the top of the skull partly exposed. The discoverers had the good judgment to leave the site intact, taking only photographs and some loose samples of cloth. These later served to identify the site as a pre-Columbian high-mountain sanctuary, a legacy of the far-flung Inca empire, which at its height extended from northern Ecuador to central Chile and Argentina.

— Juan Schobinger
from *Natural History* magazine

Tell Me About . . .

- *Which do I enjoy learning about—different countries, scientific theories, or historical events?*
- *Have I read or seen anything recently that taught me something about one of these subjects? What did I learn?*
- *How can I find out more about a subject that interests me?*

Suppose you could board a time machine and become a part of any period of history. Would you choose to be the first to climb Mount Everest, to ride to freedom on the Underground Railroad, or to sail with Cleopatra along the Nile? What sights and sounds would you experience? What aspects of your trip would you relate to others when you returned to the present?

Now you can take those kinds of journeys. By researching different cultures and civilizations, you can become an explorer. You can share with others the exciting information you discover by writing a social studies report. Your journey can begin right now.

IN YOUR JOURNAL Jot down a list of topics in your Journal that you would like to know more about. Think about anything at all that has captured your interest—something you learned in school, a situation in the world today, an event from the past. Then suppose you could meet someone who has seen and remembered everything since history began. What three questions would you want to ask that person?

Meet Jennifer Duda

''What really catches the reader's eye is your own personal input,'' says Jennifer Duda. Jennifer lives in Glenwood, Illinois, and attends Brookwood Junior High School. She likes dancing—jazz, ballet, and tap—as well as cheerleading, singing, and art. Jennifer thinks about being a fashion designer.

An excerpt from Jennifer's report ''Women's Rights in Professional Baseball'' appears on page 178. She talks about a few roadblocks she faced. ''I went to the library and there weren't any books on my subject, and there were probably only two magazine articles. I got the name of the All American Girls Professional Baseball League Association president. I called her, she gave me names, and I got interviews. I took notes on my telephone interviews and taped the personal ones.

''Before I started writing, I read my notes and listened to the tapes. Then I organized my notes in an outline using time order: when and how the league first started, how it progressed, and why it ended. I used bits and pieces of my interviews. I also wrote to the Indiana Historical Society that did a display on the league. I went to one of the league reunions, and the players still write me. I have all their names, a scrapbook, and a baseball that all the league women signed.''

Writers at Work

How could you find out more about life on Earth five thousand years ago or five thousand years from now? You can find the answers to these questions by reading. Writers have produced millions of books, articles, stories, and even poems and letters that inform readers about every aspect of the world. As you read these selections, think about the way each author organized information. What facts tell you about the subject?

WRITERS ON

" "

WRITING

What really helps with research papers is if you just take things bit by bit. If you just look at it like "I have to do this paper—it's due in two weeks," you're not going to get it done. If you say instead, "By Thursday I'm going to have my notes done, and I'm going to have my bibliography done by Saturday," you really will get the paper done.

– Jennifer Duda writer and student

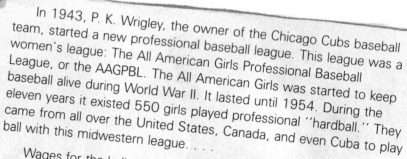

In 1943, P. K. Wrigley, the owner of the Chicago Cubs baseball team, started a new professional baseball league. This league was a women's league: The All American Girls Professional Baseball League, or the AAGPBL. The All American Girls was started to keep baseball alive during World War II. It lasted until 1954. During the eleven years it existed 550 girls played professional "hardball." They came from all over the United States, Canada, and even Cuba to play ball with this midwestern league. . . .

Wages for the ladies of the All American Girls players seemed good—wages were usually about $50.00 a week and even higher for some of the really special players. And these were great compared to what some of the girls were making at other jobs. Lib MaHon, who played for the South Bend Blue Sox, recalls, "I made $90.00 a month teaching 8th grade girls. Making $50.00 a week seemed like a fortune." However, this was nothing compared to what the men playing professional baseball made. The men of yesterday made almost more than twice what the highest-paid woman player made. . . .

The death of the league was a slow one. World War II ended, and the men returning home wanted their families together at home and their women in the traditional roles again. Television came into play and was an excuse to stay at home for entertainment. With fewer people coming out to watch the baseball games, income to the teams went down, and the All American Girls Professional Baseball League had money problems. In 1954, the league folded.

—Jennifer Duda
Brookwood Junior High School
Glenwood, Illinois

Nameless, Tennessee, was a town of maybe ninety people if you pushed it, a dozen houses along the road, a couple of barns, same number of churches, a general merchandise store selling Fire Chief gasoline, and a community center with a lighted volleyball court.

— William Least Heat-Moon
from *Blue Highways: A Journey into America*

The Writer's Craft The writers of these selections are similar to guides in a museum. Some guides take you to several displays and point out the main features of each one. Other guides spend most of the time on one display. Writers can choose to illuminate many issues or to explore one issue in depth. Which of these writers do you think is the most informative guide? How would you go about guiding an audience through the information you would present?

WRITERS'
GALLERY

For more examples of informative writing, turn to page 202.

Your heart weighs well under a pound. It is only a little larger than your fist. But it is a powerful, long working, hard working organ. Its job is to pump blood to the lungs and to all the body tissues. . . .

The heart is really a double pump. One pump (the right heart) receives blood which has just come from the body after taking nutrients and oxygen to the body tissues. It pumps this dark, red-blue blood to the lungs. Here the blood gets rid of a waste gas (carbon dioxide) and picks up a fresh supply of oxygen. It turns a bright red again. The second pump (the left heart) receives this blood from the lungs and pumps it out through the great trunk-artery (aorta). It will then be carried by smaller arteries to all parts of the body.

— American Heart Association
from "Your Heart and How It Works"

The four astronauts now moved into a large office together. They would spend the next year working with each other and training for their mission.

Training for one flight was even harder than studying the parts of the Space Transportation System. Instead of learning about space experiments in general, Sally Ride and John Fabian studied in detail all the experiments of STS-7. They also learned about the three satellites that would be launched from the orbiter during the mission.

One of the most important things that the crew members studied was a timeline of the flight. The timeline was the list of all the jobs to be done and when to do them. The astronauts practiced each job many times on the ground so that they wouldn't waste time getting it done in space.

Sally worked hard on her part of the timeline. During much of the mission, she would be performing experiments or using the remote manipulator arm. After a while, she had practiced her jobs so much that she felt she could do them in her sleep.

— Carolyn Blacknall from *Sally Ride: America's First Woman in Space*

Planning the Exhibit

When planning a new exhibit, a museum curator naturally must first decide on the subject of the exhibit. Then the curator must decide what items to include in the exhibit. When you write an informative piece, you also need to decide on your subject and on what facts and details to include.

What would you most like to know about in greater depth? Think about a general topic. A good way to explore your topic and to decide what facts you will need is to use the reliable 5 *W*'s and *H*— *Who? What? Where? When? Why?* and *How?* Planning your work is easier when you begin to think as a curious anthropologist would. Digging to find answers to questions can enrich your store of knowledge and assure you of an accurate and clear finished product.

Brainstorm: Purpose and Audience The audience for your informative writing will probably be any reader who has interest in or is curious about the topic that you have chosen. Your purpose will be to inform, to enlighten, and perhaps even to instruct your audience. What are the main questions that you would like to answer? You and a partner can exchange ideas about what your audience would want to know about your topics.

As you research your topic, you may find it helpful to jot down facts and details on note cards.

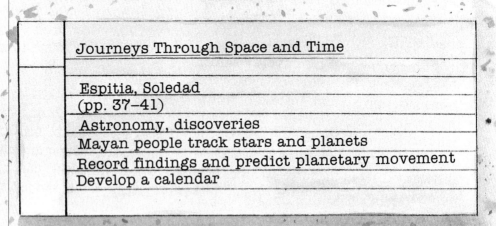

Journeys Through Space and Time

Espitia, Soledad
(pp. 37–41)
Astronomy, discoveries
Mayan people track stars and planets
Record findings and predict planetary movement
Develop a calendar

A writer used index cards, such as the one above, to write research notes. Then the writer organized the cards according to topic and used them to develop an outline for a report on the Maya.

MAKE CONNECTIONS

Where will you begin looking for information about your topic? Some sources, such as encyclopedias, can give you a quick overview. You could then look for specific articles and books about your topic. For help in finding research materials, turn to **Information Resources,** *which begins on page 371. When doing research, keep some index cards handy. Index cards are great places to record information.*

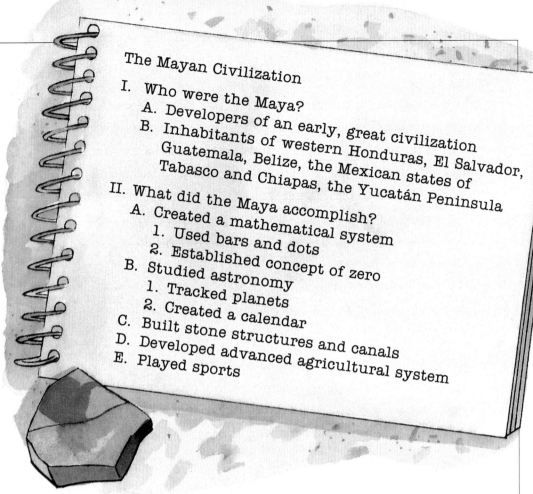

The Mayan Civilization

I. Who were the Maya?
  A. Developers of an early, great civilization
  B. Inhabitants of western Honduras, El Salvador, Guatemala, Belize, the Mexican states of Tabasco and Chiapas, the Yucatán Peninsula

II. What did the Maya accomplish?
  A. Created a mathematical system
    1. Used bars and dots
    2. Established concept of zero
  B. Studied astronomy
    1. Tracked planets
    2. Created a calendar
  C. Built stone structures and canals
  D. Developed advanced agricultural system
  E. Played sports

This outline shows some of a writer's detailed plans for a social studies report. The writer can write the report by following the outline. How do you think that starting each section with a question can help the writer? Have you ever used an outline as a checklist to sort out notes you made while doing research or thinking about your topic? See page 221 for more information about outlines. Charts or diagrams can help you to organize information, too.

IN YOUR JOURNAL   In this unit you'll observe the development of a social studies report about a civilization that flourished long ago. Look over the topics you listed in your Journal. Which of them piques your interest enough to make you want to write a report? If you'd like to try another form of informative writing, turn to the suggestions in the Writer's Project File on page 190.

After you choose a topic and do some research about it, begin an outline or some other kind of plan in your Journal. Determine the method of planning you feel most comfortable with and begin to plot out your piece of writing.

WHAT'S THE POINT?

Writing that informs:
- presents information about a well-defined topic.
- includes accurate, clear statements of fact.
- organizes information according to relationships, such as cause and effect.

FOR MORE HELP

For more help in:
- *choosing a topic,* turn to pages 213–215.
- *selecting a planning strategy,* turn to pages 216–224.
- *self-selecting,* turn to the *Writer's Project File* on page 190.

Setting Up the Displays

Once the items for a museum exhibit have been collected, the curator must begin to set up the exhibit. In your research you may unearth more information than you think you can use. It's better to have more information than not enough. As you write, include any facts and details you find intriguing. Think about which pieces of information you will need to use to help you make your points. Then take a few minutes to look at *The Intrigue of Informing*.

The Intrigue of Informing

- Keep your purpose and audience in mind to help you define and focus your topic.

- Choose a topic that is well enough defined to treat effectively. If your topic is too broad to be covered in a piece of reasonable length, narrow it. Try to focus on a key aspect of your topic. For more about exploring and narrowing topics, see pages 213–214.

- Each paragraph of your writing should make a point. Think about how to introduce your topic and what you will cover in each paragraph. How will you conclude your report?

- Remember that people who read reports want information. Even if you have strong opinions about your topic, rely only on the facts. Make sure every fact is accurate and clear.

- Compile a bibliography, a list of the books and articles you used, which will enable you to keep track of your sources.

- You can help readers to understand your points by organizing your facts in certain ways. Think about using these methods of organization: cause and effect, time order, and order of importance. To learn more about organizational strategies, see pages 248–254.

Talk About Drafting Talk about the draft on page 183 with your partner. Did the writer focus on a few key aspects of the Mayan civilization? What method of organization did the writer use? What questions would you want answered about the Maya?

CRITICAL THINKING

How can demonstrating cause-and-effect relationships help to clarify your points for a reader?

In the report on the Maya, the writer linked a sport played (cause) to the suitable kinds of playing courts (effect). The relationship helped researchers determine what kind of sport was popular among the Maya. See page 254 to learn more about cause and effect.

*Look at the **Writers at Work** excerpt from Sally Ride: America's First Woman in Space on page 179. The astronauts practiced each job again and again. What was the cause? the effect?*

An Extraordinary Civilization

The ancient world saw great civilizations, including those developed by the Egyptians, the Chinese, and the Greeks. Among the earliest civilizations was that of the Maya. The Mayan civilization was in what today is western Honduras, El Salvador, Guatemala, Belize, the Mexican states of Tabasco and Chiapas, and the entire Yucatán Peninsula. Historians date the Maya to 2000 B.C., and their descendants still live in the area today.

They developed a mathematical system based on 20, used the concept of zero, and could calculate in numbers greater than one million. The accomplishments of the ancient Maya were many. They were fine astronomers who tracked the movements of Venus and accurately predicted eclipses. Their predictions weren't hardly never wrong. The Maya developed a precise calendar based on the movement of the sun.

The Maya were sophisticated engineers and arckitecks who used stone and cement to erect buildings. They constructed a series of canals and practiced terrace farming. Maize, beans, manioc, cotton and cacao were some of the crops the Maya cultivated. A sport played with a rubber ball was popular, since many courts are evident among the old Mayan ruins.

The ancient Maya still influence the modern world. Miguel Angel Asturias, Nobel Prize winner at literature in 1967, noted in <u>Monuments of Civilization Maya</u>, "The Mayan spirit still lives among the peoples currently living in the same territories." We feel their influence today.

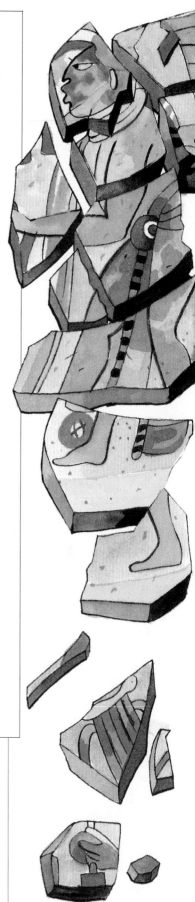

ON YOUR OWN Refer to your outline or other plans as you write your draft. If you sense that you're not fully explaining a fact or that you're not making a connection between ideas clearly enough, you can make a note in the margin to adjust your writing later. Try thinking of each idea and fact you have as part of a seamless story that you're about to tell.

Rearranging and Replacing

When you and your partner discuss informative writing, you may want to say:

• *These facts are interesting, but can you explain how they relate to your topic?*

For more advice about conferencing, see page 229.

REVISING STRATEGIES

When you review writing that informs:

• *Make sure that your topic is well defined and that your readers can identify it immediately.*

• *Check your facts for accuracy. Present information as clearly as you can.*

• *Clarify any factual relationships, such as cause-and-effect or time-order relationships.*

Once an exhibit has been set up, the museum curator needs to stand away from it and evaluate the overall display. The curator often rearranges parts of the display or even replaces one or two items. In a similar way, the information that you've gathered and arranged is ready to be evaluated. You can take your work apart and put it together again as many times as you want until it looks right to you.

Talk About Revising Discuss with a partner the revised report on page 185. How do you think the changes improved the report? Has the writer included any information that strays from the main idea? Examine the way in which the writer has presented the facts. Would you have used other methods of organization? Why or why not?

An Extraordinary Civilization

The ancient world saw great civilizations, including those developed by the Egyptians, the Chinese, and the Greeks. Among the earliest civilizations was that of the Maya. The Mayan civilization ~~was~~ *flourished* in what today is western Honduras, El Salvador, Guatemala, Belize, the Mexican states of Tabasco and Chiapas, and the entire Yucatán Peninsula. Historians date the Maya to 2000 B.C., and their descendants still live in the area today.

They developed a mathematical system based on 20, used the concept of zero, and could calculate in numbers greater than one million. The accomplishments of the ancient Maya were many. They were fine astronomers who tracked the movements of Venus and accurately predicted eclipses. Their predictions weren't hardly never wrong. The Maya developed a precise calendar based on the movement of the sun.

The Maya were sophisticated engineers and arckitecks who used stone and cement to erect buildings *that still stand today*. They constructed a series of canals and practiced terrace farming. Maize, beans, manioc, cotton and cacao were some of the crops the Maya cultivated. A sport played with a rubber ball was popular, since many courts are evident among the old Mayan ruins.

The ancient Maya still influence the modern world. Miguel Angel Asturias, Nobel Prize winner at literature in 1967, noted in <u>Monuments of Civilization Maya</u>, "The Mayan spirit still lives among the peoples currently living in the same territories." ~~We feel their influence today.~~

F A S T F O C U S

Why is this sentence now in a better position in the paragraph?

How does this addition help to emphasize the significance of this Mayan feat?

The writer felt that this idea had already been stated and illustrated with a quotation. Do you agree that this sentence is unnecessary?

ON YOUR OWN Reread your draft and fix major organizational problems first. How are your facts related? What cause-and-effect and time-order relationships can you highlight? Can you add a transition word or phrase to help your readers to grasp a sequence of events more easily? How can you polish your piece?

Last-Minute Details

When an exhibit is finally ready to be viewed, a dedicated curator takes one last look. Are all the display cases dusted, polished, and labeled correctly? Is the lighting perfect? You must do the same thing with a finished piece of writing before you publish it. Is your grammar correct? Are all marks of punctuation placed appropriately? Have you double-checked your spelling?

Talk About Proofreading With your partner, look at this report about the Maya. Discuss the grammar, punctuation, and spelling errors and how they were corrected. Notice how the correction of even minor errors improves the finished product.

An Extraordinary Civilization

The ancient world saw great civilizations, incl[uding] those developed by the Egyptians, the Chinese, and [the] Greeks. Among the earliest civilizations was that of the [Maya.] The Mayan civilization ~~was~~ *flourished* in what today is western Hond[uras,] El Salvador, Guatemala, Belize, the Mexican states of T[abas]co and Chiapas, and the entire Yucatán Peninsula. Histo[rians] date the Maya to 2000 B.C., and their descendants still li[ve in] the area today.

They developed a mathematical system based on 20, use[d the] concept of zero, and could calculate in numbers greater [than] one million. The accomplishments of the ancient Maya were many. They were fine astronomers who tracked the movements of Venus and accurately predicted eclipses. Their predictions *were*~~weren't~~ hardly ~~never~~ *ever* wrong. The Maya developed a precise calendar based on the movement of the sun.

The Maya were sophisticated engineers and ~~arkitecks~~ *architects* who used stone and cement to erect buildings *that still stand today*. They constructed a series of canals and practiced terrace farming. Maize, beans, manioc, cotton, and cacao were some of the crops the Maya cultivated. A sport played with a rubber ball was popular, since many courts are evident among the old Mayan ruins.

The ancient Maya still influence the modern world. Miguel Angel Asturias, Nobel Prize winner ~~at~~ *for* literature in 1967, noted in <u>Monuments of Civilization Maya</u>, "The Mayan spirit still lives among the peoples currently living in the same territories." ~~We feel their influence today.~~

Proofreader's Marks

∧ Add.

℮ Take out.

≡ Make a capital letter.

/ Make a lower-case letter.

¶ Indent the paragraph.

○ Check the spelling.

⊙ Add a period.

⋏ Add a comma.

ᵛᵛ Add quotation marks.

↻ Reverse the order.

PROOFREADING CHECK-UP

- *Check your capitalization and punctuation by using the* **Mechanics Handbook** *on page 353.*
- *Are you having any problems with double negatives? Check page 344.*
- *Circle misspelled words. Use the* **Word Finder** *on page 368 or your dictionary.*

ON YOUR OWN Think about whether or not you'd like to publish your piece. If you decide to publish, proofread your work carefully. Have you misspelled any words? Go over your punctuation and check for any inaccurate grammar. Make sure your facts are effective; errors in grammar and punctuation will make them seem less so.

Opening Day

*The writer of this report used someone else's words to conclude the piece. If you want to quote directly from a book or an article, remember to quote the exact words, to use quotation marks, and to identify the writer and the source. For more information about quoting sources, see the **Mechanics Handbook**, page 353.*

For more help in:
*• **deciding how to publish your work**, turn to page 237.*

When every detail is in place, a curator can proudly open the exhibit to the public. When your piece of informative writing is as nearly perfect as you can make it, you can proudly share it with others. By publishing your work, you can help others to discover a new interest or to probe a subject about which they've always been curious.

Talk About Publishing The writer of this report read it aloud on a cable television documentary program about ancient civilizations. Can you think of any other methods of publishing that would be interesting? Discuss the published report with a partner. How does knowing something about the Maya make you wonder about the fate of your own civilization? What aspects of the Mayan culture would you like to explore in more detail?

ON YOUR OWN Dozens of magazines publish articles about numerous subjects—animals, computers, history, music, sports. Some magazines are written especially for students. Do you think you could publish your work as a magazine article? Maybe you and your classmates could start a unique interclass newsletter about subjects that interest seventh-graders. You could include pieces that you write, as well as newspaper and magazine articles that you find. How can you turn your writing into an exhibit that others could enjoy?

How does your finished work compare with the Model for Self-Evaluation on page 292?

An Extraordinary Civilization

The ancient world saw great civilizations, including those developed by the Egyptians, the Chinese, and the Greeks. Among the earliest civilizations was that of the Maya. The Mayan civilization flourished in what today is western Honduras, El Salvador, Guatemala, Belize, the Mexican states of Tabasco and Chiapas, and the entire Yucatán Peninsula. Historians date the Maya to 2000 B.C., and their descendants still live in the area today.

The accomplishments of the ancient Maya were many. They developed a mathematical system based on 20, used the concept of zero, and could calculate in numbers greater than one million. They were fine astronomers who tracked the movements of Venus and accurately predicted eclipses. Their predictions were hardly ever wrong. The Maya developed a precise calendar based on the movement of the sun.

The Maya were sophisticated engineers and architects who used stone and cement to erect buildings that still stand today. They constructed a series of canals and practiced terrace farming. Maize, beans, manioc, cotton, and cacao were some of the crops the Maya cultivated. A sport played with a rubber ball was popular, since many courts are evident among the old Mayan ruins.

The ancient Maya still influence the modern world. Miguel Angel Asturias, Nobel Prize winner for literature in 1967, noted in <u>Monuments of Civilization Maya</u>, "The Mayan spirit still lives among the peoples currently living in the same territories."

Think about topics for writing that informs. Are you the local expert on any topic? Whichever project you choose, remember to let the facts tell the story. Here are a few suggestions.

Questions and Answers

Interview a relative or friend who has lived in another country. Ask about different customs, holidays, and any unusual experiences the person had. Write an informative piece about the interview results. Include a biographical sketch of your subject.

Cause and Effect

What happens when an underwater volcano erupts or a glacier moves? Choose a scientific topic in which you can identify a cause. Write an article that informs the reader of all the effects.

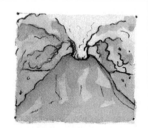

Fact-Based Fiction

Some writers combine their knowledge of history with a talent for entertaining. They write historical fiction—stories or novels based on events in the lives of real people. Think about a person in history you admire. Write a story or a scene from a novel based on an actual episode in that person's life. Plan to read a section of your work aloud to friends or family.

News That's Fit to Print

People write editorials to present their opinions. Find an editorial in a newspaper or a magazine. Search behind the writer's interpretation of the facts to find out what the actual facts are. Write an informative article explaining the factual background of the issues.

straightening fact: I thought Mrs. Bates the gonest: six feet tall, thin, with pretty teeth that shone when she did that slow pull back of her thick lips to the laugh lines at the sides of her mouth. She had mixed gray hair, bunned at her neck; always wore two-piece outfits of soft wool, in different colors, which seemed made to fit her long, lanky frame. And she always wore one strand of pearls. My name for her from the first: El-e-gant. I had a picture of her eyes drawn in my head: two pools of melted tar, beneath which the sun had sunk. I never looked straight into them.

— Rosa Guy
from *Edith Jackson*

i had never been in this part of Tokyo, and the shabbiness of the neighborhood depressed me. The dead-end street was full of cracks and puddles, and the two-storied office building in front of me looked more like a run-down barracks than a place of business. I looked blankly at the rain-soaked side shingles and thought of rows and rows of decaying teeth stacked on top of one another. The place just didn't seem like the home of the great man I'd come to meet.

Suddenly a deafening noise exploded, and the screeching sound of electricity drowned me. The large speaker of a nearby movie theater began to blast away the theme music, announcing the start of the first afternoon show. I looked back toward the bustling train station where I'd gotten off a train only a few minutes before, and wondered if I should go back.

— Allen Say
from *The Ink-Keeper's Apprentice*

— Jim Davis from *Garfield food for thought.* GARFIELD reprinted by permission of UFS, Inc.

If There Be Sorrow

If there be sorrow

let it be

for things undone . . .

undreamed

  unrealized

    unattained

to these add one:

Love withheld . . .

. . . restrained

—Mari Evans

Starry Night by Vincent Van Gogh, 1889

I think
if you flew
up to the sky
beside the moon,
you would
twinkle
like a star.

— Li Po
from ''The Firefly''

SERENITY

When I am singing to you,
on earth all evil ends:
as smooth as your forehead
are the gulch and the bramble.

When I am singing to you,
for me all cruel things end:
as gentle as your eyelids,
the lion with the jackal.

SUAVIDADES

*Cuando yo te estoy cantando,
en la Tierra acaba el mal:
todo es dulcé por tus sienes:
la barranca, el espinar.*

*Cuando yo te estoy cantando,
se me acaba la crueldad:
suaves son, como tus párpados,
¡la leona y el chacal!*

— Gabriela Mistral

ou get a little dry moss, some wood shavings, a flat board, and a round piece of wood. You make a small round hole in the flat board and stuff in moss and chips or shavings of dry wood. With a pointed piece of twig between the palms of your hands, rolled back and forth, you press the pointed end into the hole. In no time, this causes friction and the moss catches the heat and smolders into embers. The shavings catch fire. You add more shavings, then little twigs, and the fire will grow bigger and bigger until you can put it under the logs. It's really easy."

— Piri Thomas from *Stories from El Barrio*

CURRIED RED SNAPPER
with Vegetables

1 ¾ cups water
1 medium-size tomato, finely chopped
2 tablespoons curry powder, preferably Jamaican
1 teaspoon chopped fresh thyme or
   ½ teaspoon dried thyme
¼ teaspoon salt (optional)
¼ teaspoon ground black pepper

Two ½-pound red snappers, pan-dressed
   with head and tail intact
1 medium-size onion, chopped
1 small green bell pepper, seeded, cut into strips
1 small red bell pepper, seeded, cut into strips
½ bunch broccoli, cut into florets
   with short portion of stem attached

In large 12-inch skillet or fish poacher over medium heat, BRING *water to simmer;* STIR *in tomato, curry, thyme, salt (if desired) and black pepper.* ADD *snappers, onion, bell peppers and broccoli. Cover;* SIMMER *until fish is cooked through and flakes when tested with tip of table knife, about 8 minutes. Using wide spatula,* REMOVE *fish to dinner plates;* SPOON *with vegetables and sauce. Makes 2 servings.*

— Donald Campbell from *Essence* magazine

I who am blind can give one hint to those who see—one admonition to those who would make full use of the gift of sight: Use your eyes as if tomorrow you would be stricken blind. And the same method can be applied to the other senses. HEAR the music of voices, the song of a bird, the mighty strains of an orchestra, as if you would be stricken deaf tomorrow. TOUCH each object you want to touch as if tomorrow your tactile sense would fail. SMELL the perfume of flowers, TASTE with relish each morsel, as if tomorrow you could never smell and taste again. Make the most of every sense; glory in all the facets of pleasure and beauty which the world reveals to you through the several means of contact which Nature provides. But of all the senses, I am sure that sight must be the most delightful.

— Helen Keller
  from "Three Days to See"

THE LAST WOLF

the last wolf hurried toward me
through the ruined city
and I heard his baying echoes
down the steep smashed warrens
of Montgomery Street and past
the few ruby-crowned highrises
left standing
their lighted elevators useless

passing the flicking red and green
of traffic signals
baying his way eastward
in the mystery of his wild loping gait
closer the sounds in the deadly night
through clutter and rubble of quiet blocks

I heard his voice ascending the hill
and at last his low whine as he came
floor by empty floor to the room
where I sat
in my narrow bed looking west, waiting
I heard him snuffle at the door and
I watched
he trotted across the floor

he laid his long gray muzzle
on the spare white spread
and his eyes burned yellow
his small dotted eyebrows quivered

Yes, I said.
I know what they have done.

— Mary TallMountain

Mexican Wolf
by John Nieto,
1991

A sharp crack and the boat shook. Alec was thrown flat on his face, stunned. Slowly he regained consciousness. He was lying on his stomach; his face felt hot and sticky. He raised his hand, and withdrew it covered with blood. Then he became conscious of feet stepping on him. The passengers, yelling and screaming, were climbing, crawling over him! The Drake was still—its engines dead.

— Walter Farley from The Black Stallion

At the word "marbles," she sat up. "That's it. Maybe I could be good at playing marbles." She hopped out of bed and rummaged through the closet until she found a can full of her brother's marbles. She poured the rich glass treasure on her bed and picked five of the most beautiful marbles.

She smoothed her bedspread and practiced shooting, softly at first so that her aim would be accurate. The marble rolled from her thumb and clicked against the targeted marble. But the target wouldn't budge. She tried again and again. Her aim became accurate, but the power from her thumb made the marble move only an inch or two. Then she realized that the bedspread was slowing the marbles. She also had to admit that her thumb was weaker than the neck of a newborn chick.

— Gary Soto
from "The Marble Champ"

n Monday, Ligaya and I couldn't go out to play after school. It was a gloomy day with dark, heavy clouds covering the sun. Flashes of lightning appeared in the sky, and we could hear the occasional rumbling of thunder in the far distance. Scared, we stayed indoors. Soon it started to rain lightly, then stopped. A while later we heard soft footsteps outside as if someone was walking in the yard, followed by a loud urgent "Quack!"

At first we thought Father had come home early from work. He sometimes imitated Babba as a joke. But it was Monday, and on Mondays Father seldom, if ever, arrived home early. So I stood up and went to look out the window. Surprised, I saw a tall, slightly built boy, wearing short pants and a ragged shirt; he had no hat and was barefooted. His back turned to the window; he was holding what appeared to be a rice sack. I could see that he had something alive inside the sack, because the material was bulging and straining as the creature inside struggled to break free.

Suddenly I thought of the loud Quack I had heard.

— Antonio E. Santa Elena
from Mahinhin: A Tale of the Philippines

— Charles M. Schulz from *You're You, Charlie Brown.* PEANUTS reprinted by permission of UFS, Inc.

Living in a Solar House

I live in a solar house. It is not that different from other homes except that you don't have blackouts. It is run on batteries. When the sun hits the roof of the house, the solar panels collect the sun's rays. Our lights are the same as other lights and work just as well. Our heat is run by windows on the south side and a wood stove. Having solar electricity makes me feel as though I am helping to save our planet.

Cynthia Boston
Ravenswood, West Virginia

P.S. I wrote this letter on a home computer that uses electricity made by the sun!

—from *Cobblestone*

Bee! I'm expecting you!
Was saying Yesterday
To Somebody you know
That you were due —

The Frogs got Home last Week —
Are settled, and at work —
Birds, mostly back —
The Clover warm and thick —

You'll get my Letter by
The seventeenth; Reply
Or better, be with me —
Yours, Fly.

Emily Dickinson

Here's a very interesting thing about light. Light that looks white to you really has all the colors of the rainbow in it. You can split white light into its separate colors with a piece of glass or with water. The complete range of rainbow colors is called the *spectrum.*

Does this mean that you can make white paint by mixing together all the colors in your paintbox? No—you'll get something closer to black. It's confusing, but mixing colors of light is not the same thing as mixing colors of paint.

Simultaneous Contrasts: Sun and Moon
by Robert Delaunay, 1913

When you paint a picture of a green apple, it looks green because the paint is letting green light escape from it. It is absorbing (taking in) all the other colors of light. In a funny way, the green apple you painted has every color *but* green in it! A blob of all your paints mixed together will hardly let any light escape. So it will look almost black.

— **David Suzuki**
from *Looking at Senses*

MAKING EYES

People have always suspected that you can read love in a person's eyes, but only recently, scientists discovered just what it is about eyes that can convey the message. Humans dilate their pupils when they gaze at people of whom they are very fond. They contract their pupils when they glance toward those they dislike. This gesture is not under anyone's control; and it can't be hidden. It may account for the fact that, no matter what certain people say to you, or how well they control their voices and gestures, you can often sense with certainty that they are really unfriendly to you.

— Sara Stein
from *The Science Book*

The Nucleus of a Cell

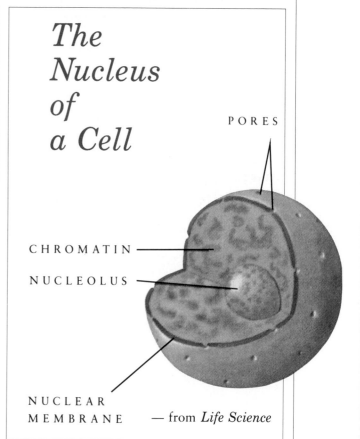

PORES

CHROMATIN

NUCLEOLUS

NUCLEAR
MEMBRANE

— from *Life Science*

The voices of the 17 women whose works make up this collection speak of the sacred traditions that weave the fabric of their tribal identity, of the spirit beings with whom they coexist, of the importance of "right kinship," and of the connection of all creatures to each other and to the land. They also tell of the war, captivity, separation and loss that have pervaded the lives of their people for five centuries.

> — review of *Spider Woman's Granddaughters*
> by Paula Gunn Allen

To the dauntless Issei whose "blood, sweat and tears," against impossible odds helped build America strong. . . .

In 1897, a young Japanese traveler shipped out from Seattle as cabin boy on a ship bound for Skagway. The job was short-lived, but his impulsive excursion stretched to five years in the Alaskan interior. One of a handful of Japanese prospectors and adventurers, he found both hardship and intoxicating freedom. Neither the caste system of Japan nor the segregation of Seattle's Japantown followed him to the frontier. For the first time he felt judged on his own worth as a man.

> — summary of *Sushi and Sourdough*
> by Tooru J. Kanazawa

"Ev'ry Time I Feel the Spirit" illustrates William Dawson's sensitive feeling in preserving the characteristics of spirituals in his choral arrangements.

William Dawson, born at the turn of the century, has arranged many African American spirituals. By creating arrangements, he has made it possible for choirs to perform this exciting and expressive music. As choir director at Tuskeegee Institute in Alabama, Dawson has shared his arrangements with people throughout the United States and Europe.

"Ev'ry Time I Feel the Spirit" is one of William Dawson's best-known choral arrangements. He uses strongly syncopated rhythms, contrasts between group and solo singing, and the improvised quality of the choral parts to create an exciting musical setting.

> — review from *Music and You*

Don't ever say you just don't care;
The chances you take will take you as
    far as you dare.
Don't be afraid! Hold your head high!
There's strength in your soul—you
    never know till you try.
    When your life is low—hold on.
    And you want to let go—be strong,
    hold on!

Remember the dream we had
    When there was nothing else.
Remember the light that shines,
    And find it in yourself.
Remember the dream is yours,
    So let it guide your way
    And keep it alive with you each day.

> — Stephanie Tyrell, Joe Sample, and
> Steve Tyrell
> from "Remember the Dream"

To
Whom
It
May
Concern: Last year we studied
what our English teacher called "personal" writing. Mainly they were
diaries and journals, stuff like that. One
of the reasons people write that way,
she said, is that the writing helps them
bring things together, to see where
they fit in life. Right now that seems
like a good idea. The English teacher
said that I write well, and I know I
need to get some things together in
my own head, so I figured a journal
would be cool.

> — Walter Dean Myers
> from Won't Know
> Till I Get There

ENERGY OF THE FUTURE

I think that in the future, the world will rely on solar and hydro-electric energy because it is safe, there is an endless supply of sunlight and water, and it does not produce harmful wastes. I also believe that in years to come, Americans won't have a choice; there will be marked garbage bins for glass, aluminum, paper, plastic, and so on, and we will *have* to recycle. I think these changes should be made along with other attempts to care for the environment. If we preserve the earth, the earth will preserve us. Even little things can help. We can use less water, stop using aerosol cans, and turn on lights only when necessary.

> Jean Cannon
> Statesville, North Carolina
>
> —from *Cobblestone*

THE SUN WAS OUT
IN ITS FULL APRIL GLORY.
THE AIR AROUND MY FACE WAS FRESH,
THE SIDEWALK UNDERFOOT WAS SMOOTH. I FELT LIKE BURSTING OUT IN SONG.

I was at the trolley stop, but it was so pleasant that I decided to continue walking and explore the route. To my right, there was no steady sound-shadow of a wall or a fence to guide me along the sidewalk; there was just empty, undifferentiated space. To my left, there was a steady stream of cars going both ways at about forty miles an hour, with an occasional large vehicle whose passing sounded like the roar of an airplane and temporarily paralyzed my facial vision. But my facial vision—or whatever it is that enables the blind to perceive obstacles—soon got more or less adjusted to the noise of the traffic echoing in that undifferentiated space. Happily, I imagined that I was by the sea listening to the waves breaking at high tide.

— Ved Mehta from *Sound-Shadows of the New World*

Papá parked the car out in front and left the motor running. "Listo," he yelled. Without saying a word, Roberto and I began to carry the boxes out to the car. Roberto carried the two big boxes and I carried the two smaller ones. Papá then threw the mattress on top of the car roof and tied it with ropes to the front and rear bumpers.

Flower Day
by Diego Rivera, 1925

Everything was packed except Mamá's pot. It was an old large galvanized pot she had picked up at an army surplus store in Santa María the year I was born. The pot had many dents and nicks, and the more dents and nicks it acquired the more Mamá liked it. "Mi olla," she used to say proudly.

I held the front door open as Mamá carefully carried out her pot by both handles, making sure not to spill the cooked beans. When she got to the car, Papá reached out to help her with it. Roberto opened the rear car door and Papá gently placed it on the floor behind the front seat. All of us then climbed in. Papá sighed, wiped the sweat off his forehead with his sleeve, and said wearily: "Es todo."

As we drove away, I felt a lump in my throat. I turned around and looked at our little shack for the last time.

— Francisco Jiménez from "The Circuit"

IN 1987, THERE WAS a great movement throughout the East. From Georgia to Long Island and westward to Illinois, the Rip van Winkles of the insect world emerged from their subterranean bedrooms for the first time in 17 years.

Not since 1970 had the shrill, buzzing mating call of Brood 10, by far the largest population of the 17-year cicada, drowned out conversations in those parts. Not since 1970 did pedestrians have to skip like schoolchildren to avoid crunching the large locust-like insects that can drop by the hundreds from their arboreal perches. And not since 1970 did these countless billions of burrowing cicadas have the chance to emerge and lay their eggs.

— Jane Brody
from "After 17 Years, Cicadas Prepare for Their Roaring Return"

In 1940 a desperate call came from across the Atlantic Ocean. Human blood was being spilled from the wounded bodies of men fighting World War II. Soldiers in the battlefield and in hospitals lay close to death. Many lives were saved because fresh blood plasma from America was passed into the bodies of the injured men. This happened because of shipments of preserved plasma that were flown to the foreign battlefields.

It was Dr. Charles R. Drew, a black American medical scientist, who made possible the availability of stored blood plasma for blood transfusions. He did this by finding a way to preserve blood plasma for long periods of time. When the wartime need for blood arose, Dr. Drew had already set up a successful experimental blood bank to test his ideas about blood preservation. Before Dr. Drew's time there was no efficient way to store large amounts of blood for long periods of time.

— Robert C. Hayden from *Seven Black American Scientists*

PART 2

Writer's Workshop

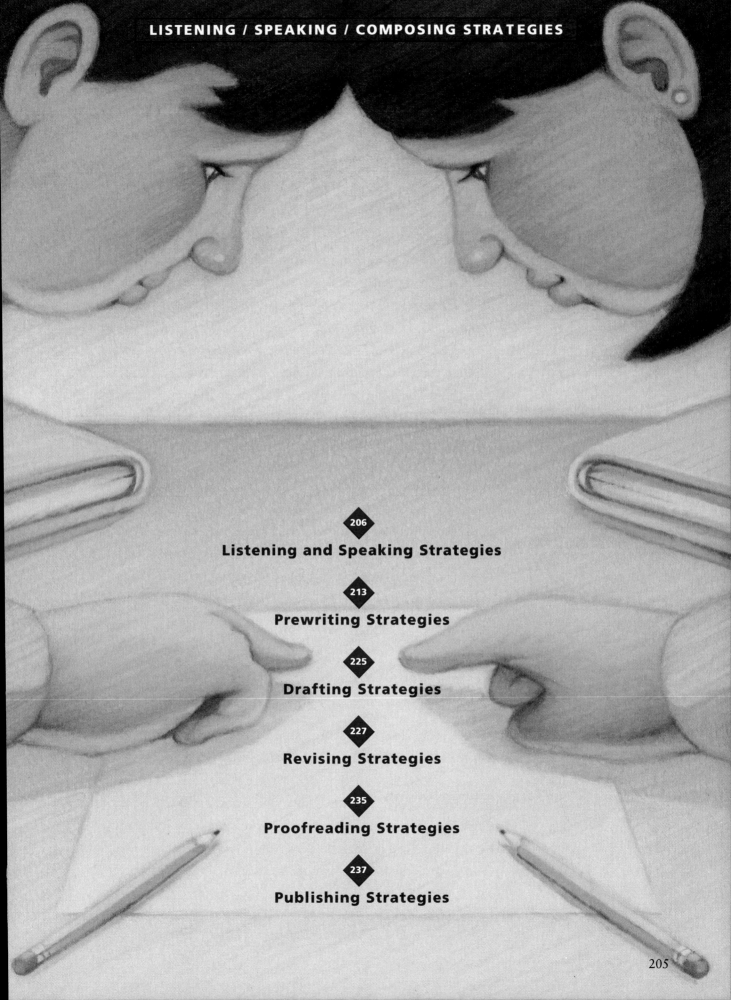

Are You Listening?

Have you ever listened closely for directions to a place? Have you found yourself hanging on every word of a special song? If you have, you already know what good listening requires: paying attention and knowing what to listen for. Here are some strategies to help you to focus your listening:

■ Main Idea and Details

- Focus first on the main idea, the details that support the main idea, and the transition words that lead up to the main idea.

   I consider this an honor. Being nominated for such a high position is something I'll always cherish. At this time, however, I need to devote my energies elsewhere. In short, I do not accept the nomination for chairperson.

   Listener: The main point is that the nomination is being turned down. Details explain that the nomination is an honor. The transition words *however* and *in short* point out the main idea.

■ Style and Tone

- Once you have determined the main idea, focus on style, mood, and the kind of picture the piece creates in your mind.

   On a full stomach, layered with the proper clothes, the cold's amusing. But for a working man . . . what grief! Men are twice as poor in such cold. Thieves are craftier and robbers fiercer.

   —Anton Chekhov, on the Russian winter

   Listener: The passage has a sad but funny tone; rhythmic, poetic language; and dramatic, exaggerated images.

Make sure you understand your partner's comments and the reasons for them. Ask your partner's opinion on new ideas.

IN YOUR JOURNAL The next time you hear a speaker, take notes. Jot down such things as the main idea, the speaker's style, and the images that the speaker creates. What new ideas does active listening help you to understand? Record observations in your Journal.

Strategies to Build Your Audience Awareness

The mockingbird changes its song according to the company it keeps. It might play one melody when an oriole is around and a completely different melody for the red-winged blackbird.

As a writer, you, too, need to be able to change your message according to your audience. In order to know what song to sing, you need to know something about your audience.

■ Who Is My Audience?

Your audience might seem like a faceless group when you begin, but it really isn't. Audiences are composed of actual individuals just like you. The secret to identifying your audience is to ask yourself a simple question: For whom am I writing or speaking? From there, branch off to other questions about your audience, such as:

- How old is my audience?
- What kinds of values and experiences do I share with my audience?
- Does my audience already have an opinion of my topic?
- What kinds of things interest my audience? What excites or bores them? What touches their hearts? What makes them laugh?
- What will influence my audience most?

By the time you finish answering these questions or questions of your own about your audience, you should be able to picture one or more people who will be reading your work. Then you can direct your writing or speaking to that person or group of people.

■ What Is My Relationship to My Audience?

This is a question of how well you and your audience know each other. If you and your audience aren't on familiar terms, you should be as formal as possible. Use your best manners. Assume nothing and explain everything. If, however, you and your audience are friends, you can loosen up a little, as long as you don't get sloppy!

■ How Much Does My Audience Know?

This is a critical question. It tells you what you can take for granted. If your audience is familiar with your topic, you can "speak in shorthand." You don't need to spell everything out or explain every detail. If your audience is unfamiliar with your topic, you need to explain your concepts thoroughly and, maybe, provide a few definitions. You need to go slowly and lay out the information in a clear, easy-to-follow manner.

Here are some situations involving different audiences for whom you may choose to write or speak:

- Your best friend is spending the year with a cousin in Mexico. You speak to her on the phone about school and your family and friends.
- Your best friend's cousin is interested in American films. You plan to write to her or to speak to her about your favorite movies. You must keep in mind that she is just learning the English language.
- You are submitting some of your writing to *Space-Laugh*. *Space-Laugh* is a fantasy and humor magazine that prides itself on being wild and crazy. It's written especially for teenagers—no adults allowed!
- Your aunt is recovering in the hospital. You want to cheer her up by writing her a get-well note or calling her on the phone.
- Beings from another planet have made radio contact with Earth. They want to know what life is like for a typical earthling like you. You relay a written or spoken response on behalf of the planet Earth.

ON YOUR OWN Write or speak as one of the audiences on the list above. Consider what you, the audience, might say in reply. Jot down some thoughts on your experience of switching roles with your audience.

Persuasive Speaking Strategies and Techniques

Most people rely on clear arguments, facts, and logic to get their point across—but sometimes more subtle or unfair methods are used. Once you become aware of how writers use persuasive techniques, you will be better equipped to decide for yourself where the truth lies. You can also apply these techniques to influence others with your opinions.

■ When You Listen

- *Distinguish between fact and opinion.* Watch out for opinions that are cloaked in facts. You can prove a fact to be true. Opinions are beliefs or judgments. Slanted facts express a point of view by leaving out selected details or by mixing fact and opinion.

    If Nolan Ryan isn't the greatest pitcher of all time, I don't know who is. Ryan has won over 300 games. His fast ball and curve are the best in history. He has thrown more strikeouts than anyone in the major leagues.

    The speaker includes opinion and only certain facts. For example, no one has ever measured the quality of a curve ball. So the third sentence sounds like a fact but is actually an opinion. Ryan did win over 300 games—that's a fact—but many pitchers have won more games than Ryan. The speaker slants the facts by omitting certain ones. What opinions did the speaker state?

- *Be on guard for loaded language.* Loaded words make value judgments that appeal to your emotions rather than to your sense of fairness or of logic. Look for loaded words, such as *dingy,* in this paragraph:

    The downstairs of the house was cramped and dingy with sickly green walls and broken-down furniture. The upstairs, on the other hand, was sunny and bright, with warm wooden paneling and soft, luxurious carpeting.

DID YOU NOTICE?

The Nolan Ryan paragraph presented Ryan's pitching ability as an either-or question. Either you agreed that Nolan Ryan was the greatest ever, or you were wrong. Either-or setups make things seem simple when they are really more complicated. The discussion following the paragraph about Ryan shows that the situation is not as simple and clear-cut as the writer wants to make it seem.

• *Beware of jumping on a bandwagon.* Just because someone else does something, it doesn't mean that you need to do it, too.

Anyone who knows anything about cameras would buy the ZX-50. More professionals own ZX-50s than any other model. For the past five years, every winner of the Lux Award in photography has used a ZX-50.

• *Don't be snared by charged words.* Sometimes a speaker bypasses logic and reason and appeals to an audience's emotional side. Consider an ad that proclaims, "Buy Healthy Juice—good health is priceless." The ad uses the charged phrase *good health* and doesn't give you any nutritional information about the juice.

■ When You Try to Persuade

• *Be fair.* Tricks such as loaded language, slanted facts, the bandwagon appeal, and opinions posing as facts are exactly that—tricks! Once your audience catches on, it becomes suspicious of everything you say—even when you aren't using any tricks.
• *Honesty is the best policy.* Search for facts and use them to convince others that your logic and conclusions are correct.
• *Organization is the key.* Structure your argument. What facts persuaded you to form your own opinion on the matter? Hunt them down! Use those facts to build your case. Will you save the most persuasive argument you have for last, or will you capture your audience's attention by presenting the strongest argument first? Remember to summarize, listing reasons why your audience should agree with you.

ON YOUR OWN Go through a newspaper editorial. Underline and label persuasive techniques such as loaded language, the bandwagon effect, and slanted facts. Then read between the lines of the editorial. Decide where you think the truth of the matter really lies.

Interviewing Techniques and Strategies

Good interviewers and good interview subjects approach their interviews with a purpose. Beyond the questions and answers involved, each side has goals it wants to achieve. To achieve your goals in an interview, think about the following points.

■ When You Are the Interviewer

- *Do a background check.* Find out everything you can about your subject. The more preparation work you do digging up facts, the easier your actual interview will be.
- *Ask yourself some questions.* What is the purpose of your interview? Try to structure your questions so that you will get the information you need. Think about the relationship between yourself and your subject. Is the interview friendly or formal?
- *Prepare your questions in advance.* Write your questions and design them so they get to the heart of the important issues. During the interview, you can always choose not to use a certain question or to change track in order to follow up on an unexpected possibility.
- *Be polite.* Do everything you can to make your subject feel comfortable. Explain the purpose of the interview. Ask questions simply and directly. Listen carefully to the answers. If you become confused, ask a follow-up question to clarify the point.

■ When You Are Being Interviewed

- *Do some homework.* Try to anticipate the questions that the interviewer will ask. If you like, write down some questions and rehearse giving your answers with a friend.
- *Relax and open up.* Concentrate on answering the questions as thoroughly as you can. Listen carefully to each question. Feel free to pause and to think about your answer before saying anything. Make sure you fully understand each question before you answer it, and ask the interviewer to clarify it if you need to.
- *Speak clearly and support your statements with facts and details.* Give examples to clarify your thoughts. Take your own notes if you feel the need to!

MAKE CONNECTIONS

The next time you watch an interview, ask yourself these questions:

Do the interviewer and the subject seem prepared? How can you tell?

Is the interview informal or formal?

Are subject and interviewer being fair to one another?

• *If you are the subject of a school admissions interview or a job interview, show your interest.* Do some research in advance about the school or the company. Prepare any questions that you may have about the position. Dress appropriately and arrive on time. State clearly what you think you can contribute to the school or organization.

■ **Sharpen Your Interviewing Techniques**

Try one of the following situations:

• *Interview a parent or an older relative about his or her childhood.* Learn about experiences you have in common that neither of you were aware of.

• *Interview a performer.* After a school play, interview the director or one of the actors. After a musical performance, interview one of the musicians. After a game, interview an athlete.

• *Interview a government official.* Schedule an interview with someone in your local government. You'll really need to do your homework!

• *Be interviewed by a classmate.* Have a classmate ask you questions about one of these topics: your childhood, your future occupation, a performance you gave, or your political opinions.

ON YOUR OWN Use a videotape or audiotape to record an interview. Analyze the questions and answers to help you to develop interview skills. Use your analysis to make a checklist for future interviews.

Choosing, Exploring, and Narrowing Topics

Imagine that you've decided to take a trip. Before you go, there are things you'll need to do. First, you have to decide where you're going. How will you make the best choice? Will it be a place by the ocean or a place in the mountains? Will the weather be warm or cool? Then, imagine being there. Think about the sights you want to see. Will you need to buy any tickets or to make any reservations in advance? What clothes will you need to bring? Do you have such things as a camera, a map, and a passport? Okay, now you're ready to go, but wait! How will you get there? Who will deliver the newspapers on your route while you're gone? Are there any other arrangements you need to make before you go?

A writing project can be like a trip. It's important to know where you want to go, that is, your purpose for writing and your audience. Your writing journey will be easier if you make some plans in advance. Prewriting and planning strategies help by pointing out different ways to look at your destination before you get there.

■ What Strategy Will I Use?

There are many strategies you can choose from. Some planning strategies suit particular kinds of writing. For example, try visualizing your subject before you begin to write a description. Visualizing can help bring to mind sensory details about how your subject looks, smells, feels, tastes, and sounds. Graphic organizers are helpful as you begin to plan a piece of persuasive writing. Outlines, charts, and diagrams can help you organize your ideas in the most convincing sequence. Try writing down some focusing questions when you're telling a story. Questions such as "What will happen in my story? When, where, why, to whom, and how will it happen?" can help you to organize a narrative.

You'll find that all the strategies in this section can work for almost any type of writing project. So, choose the method or methods that appeal to you each time you begin a new project.

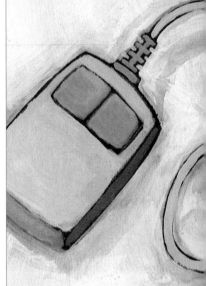

WRITERS ON WRITING

My ideas come from everywhere—from things I read, from things people tell me about, from things I see about me, from things I experience. The important aspect is that they must interest me very much, because then I want to share them with other people and so I write about them.

– Patricia Lauber author and editor

■ How Will I Explore?

Choosing a topic to write about is a little like buying a new car. It helps to shop around, especially when you don't know exactly what you want. Think about your own experiences—favorite activities, memories, hobbies, and vacations.

Once you have a topic you like, look it over. Explore your topic to see what aspects of it interest you most. Slam the doors. Kick the tires. See how solid it seems. Then take it for a spin in your imagination. Ask yourself questions such as "Where does this topic take me?" or "What would happen if I . . ." The more you ask questions, the more you focus your choices toward a final topic.

■ How Will I Narrow a Topic?

Try to limit your general topic so that you can write about it adequately in a brief composition, say, of from three to five paragraphs. Narrowing your topic will help you focus your writing.

When narrowing a topic, start with a general subject that interests you, then further refine it, step by step. Work from the general to the specific. For example, if you were interested in computers, you might proceed like this:

GENERAL TOPIC: Computers
SOMEWHAT SPECIFIC TOPIC: Computer Art
MORE SPECIFIC TOPIC: Computer Photography
SPECIFIC TOPIC: How computers are used to enhance photography
VERY SPECIFIC TOPIC: How computers can make a photograph of an apple look like a photograph of an orange

IN YOUR JOURNAL In your Journal, explore a subject that interests you by writing notes, listing ideas, and organizing details about the topic. Then narrow it down to find a specific topic that you could use for a brief composition. What aspect of your subject would be general enough to require a few paragraphs but specific enough to provide a focus for your writing? You may want to test-drive your topic by sharing your ideas with a partner and asking for reactions.

Talking About Purpose and Audience

Writing is a voyage with a destination. You begin the voyage with a desire to get somewhere. Your writing destination, or purpose, may be to gain a clearer understanding of your subject or to entertain your friends with a story. To reach your destination, focus on fulfilling your purpose and reaching your audience. Just remember, writing without a clear purpose is like taking a voyage without a destination.

■ Remember Your Purpose

- Your purpose is the reason or reasons you are writing. What do you hope to accomplish? Purposes for writing include to describe, to explain, to inform, to persuade, or a combination of these.
- Try to state your purpose for writing in a single sentence. If you can't, your purpose is probably too vague or too complicated.
- Your purpose can be simple. A worthwhile purpose does not need to contain any earthshaking ideas.
- Purposes for writing are not written in stone. You can change your purpose later if you like.
- Make sure your purpose is achievable. If you have an impossible goal, you'll feel lost and discouraged during the writing process.

■ Remember Your Audience

- Who will your readers be? What is their age group?
- Respect your audience. They are giving you something extremely valuable—their time.
- Plan your work with your audience in mind. Try to determine what they know and what they don't know. Don't state what they already know: Give them something new to consider.
- Anticipate your readers' reactions or opinions. Make sure you address their possible arguments.

ON YOUR OWN Take out a recent piece of your writing. Write a profile of a possible member of the audience who may read the piece. How might this person view your subject? What would be new information or a new perspective for your audience?

Visualizing, Drawing, and Dramatizing

A bird lifts its wings. Feathers curve. Muscles brace. Tail extends. Wings rotate as the legs push off, and suddenly the bird is falling. . . .

Did you know that birds fall before they fly? As a writer you will find that noticing things like this can be very valuable. The observing habit can help you later when you might want to visualize your subject before writing about it. Visualization is the process of picturing your subject in your mind's eye. You might picture a bird's flight or a scene from your past.

Visualization is especially useful at the beginning of the writing process. Even before you select your final topic, you can start visualizing. It can help you decide whether or not a subject is appropriate for your piece. Turn your imagination into a camera. Take a look at how your topic might appear after it is developed. Try to see beyond the obvious, beneath the surface. Writers extend their powers of observation into the past, the present, and the future. You can even visualize things you've never seen before!

Drawing your subject is another way of thinking about a writing topic and gathering information before you write. A sketch can help you to see your subject more clearly and can remind you of unique details you'll want to include.

Dramatizing—acting out—aspects of your subject, such as the particular steps in a process, can also help you plan your writing.

IN YOUR JOURNAL If you're like most people, your mental camera isn't always reliable. The images you see are faint, flickering, and often fade before you have a chance to examine them closely.

To organize those images so that you can use them, it is helpful to get the images down into some concrete form. Think of a process you are familiar with. For example, you may choose the process of making a paper airplane or building a sand castle. In your Journal, write the steps involved in one process. To help you, you can visualize, draw, or dramatize the steps. You may find that drawing a sketch helps in examining some processes, like setting a table, while acting the process out is helpful in examining a process like a baseball pitch.

MAKE CONNECTIONS

Film and television scriptwriters often use storyboards to plan how a story will proceed. A storyboard is a series of drawings showing the setting and action of each scene in the story.

You may want to use storyboards to plan some or all of the action in a story that you write. Sketch out the action. Don't worry about making life-like drawings. Use stick figures if you wish.

Brainstorming and Listing

Brainstorming is a form of thinking, a spontaneous flow of thoughts about a subject. One idea gives birth to another. You can brainstorm alone or in a group. Gather several people in a room, and the ideas start rolling.

How does brainstorming work? It works because your mind is already full of connected ideas or associations. When a word or a thought comes to mind, it sparks another thought that has some connection (no matter how loose a connection) with the first thought. By continuing to build on thoughts, a brainstormer can generate ideas about a subject. A group of brainstormers can think of ideas that no single member of the group would have come up with.

For example, suppose you invented a new pineapple-flavored breakfast cereal. Everything about it seems perfect except the name, *Tasty Pineapple Circles*. To come up with a new name, you and your partners try brainstorming and listing ideas.

Key Words	Name	Score
pineapple	Tasty Pineapple Circles	clumsy
pineapple→Hawaii	Tasty Hawaiian Circles	reject
Hawaii→island	Hawaiian Island Circles	dull
island→hopper	Hawaiian Island Hoppers	silly
hopper→dancer→hula	Hawaiian Hula Hoppers	better
hula→hoop	Hawaiian Hula Hoops	bingo!

Is *Hawaiian Hula Hoops* a good name for a breakfast cereal? For your own brainstorming sessions, let your ideas flow freely. Play off previous ideas and try to stay on track by keeping your purpose in mind. Be flexible: turn ideas upside down and inside out to get a fresh view. Save all of your ideas for future reference.

ON YOUR OWN Practice your brainstorming skills with a partner. Each of you could write the word *earth* at the top of a sheet of paper. Silently brainstorm ideas for a piece of writing on that topic by making a list. Then compare lists. Now continue your lists by orally brainstorming with each other. Which process led to the best ideas? Do you think you brainstorm better alone or with a partner?

Focusing Questions and Techniques

WRITERS ON

WRITING

I'm a character writer. Some writers are plot writers. . .

I have to begin with people. I always know my characters, exactly what they look like, their birthdays, what they like for breakfast. It doesn't matter if these things appear in the book. I still have to know.

– S. E. Hinton author

Imagine that you're writing a story about a father taking his son to meet the boy's grandfather for the first time. The boy has heard a lot about his grandfather and feels proud of him but is kind of afraid to meet him. How should the story proceed? To make a decision, ask yourself some focusing questions like the following:

- Why is the boy afraid? What has he heard about his grandfather?
- Does he let his father know the problem?
- What could the father do to help?
- Who will present a solution?

Focusing questions usually begin with the words *who, what, where, when, why,* or *how.* These questions can be used with any type of writing to help you clarify and focus your plans. When you write a story, for example, focusing questions zero in on who the characters are and what the story is really about.

In your writing you can ask questions to focus on the important elements that you want to remember as you're writing. Questions you may want to ask yourself include:

- Who are my characters, and what are they really like?
- What is the setting?
- What do my characters really want?
- What is my story about? What message am I trying to communicate?
- What is my purpose? Who is my audience?
- What are the main events in my story?
- How do I want the story to end? Will this be consistent with the rest of my story?
- What is my main idea? What information needs to be added or removed to help make the main idea clear?
- What idea or feeling do I want to leave my audience with?

ON YOUR OWN Freeze time at a key moment in one of your favorite stories. Imagine you are the author. Ask yourself focusing questions to decide on a new direction the story should take. List your focusing questions. Use this strategy when you need to decide on the direction your own writing should take.

Graphic Organizers — Clusters, Charts, Outlines, and Diagrams

An illustration can contain a great deal of information. With a single illustration you can often grasp at a glance an idea that might take hours to absorb by listening or reading. Visual devices can also help you generate ideas and organize information for your writing. Here are a few graphic organizers you can use to plan your writing.

■ A Cluster

Suppose you are writing a description of your favorite place to go to "get away from it all." The first thing you might do is create a cluster that shows some of the details about the place.

To create your own cluster, think of the central theme, such as the pier. Write it in the center of the cluster. Add categories, such as memories, view of the bay, and peacefulness. Then add examples of each category. Feel free to change your categories and to add or re-move examples. Just remember to keep it simple.

■ A Chart

A chart can help you organize details for your writing. Charts can take many forms. Here is part of a story chart.

Character A	Character B	Setting	Plot

■ A Flowchart

A flowchart shows the steps in a process. This flowchart shows the steps in the publication of a book.

The information in a flowchart can be similar to that given in an outline. When is the best time to use each?

Flowcharts work best to explain steps in a process: how something works, cause and effect, a system of organization, or how to create something.

Outlines work best with information that can be organized around main ideas and supporting details.

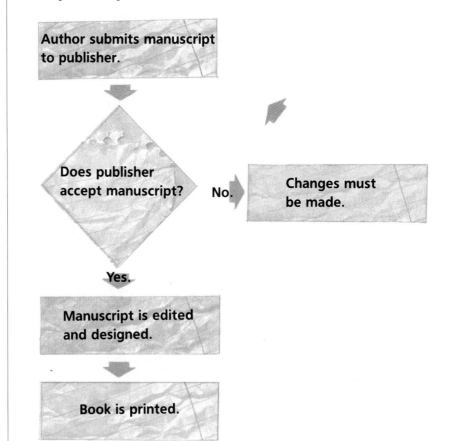

To create your own flowchart, make a series of boxes that represent the steps in the process. Move the first step to the top position. Continue with each step in order until the last step is in the bottom box. Connect the boxes with arrows. Show where choices or decisions need to be made by using a diamond-shape box. "Talk through" your flowchart; that is, check its accuracy by summarizing the ideas with words.

A Topic Outline

An outline shows the main ideas and important supporting details for a piece of writing. Use Roman numerals to list major categories. Use letters to list subcategories and Arabic numbers to list subcategory items. Include two or more items for a category or subcategory. Here is an outline for a report on the Underground Railroad.

I. Helping enslaved people escape
   A. Secrecy
      1. Night travel
      2. Code language
   B. Breaking the law
      1. Enslaved people legally owned in some states
      2. Strict fugitive slave laws
II. Conductors
   A. Harriet Tubman
   B. Levi Coffin
III. Stations

A Diagram

Use a diagram to visually plan and organize information. Here is a Venn diagram, which compares and contrasts two subjects. Each circle lists details of one subject. The section where the circles overlap lists details that fall into both categories.

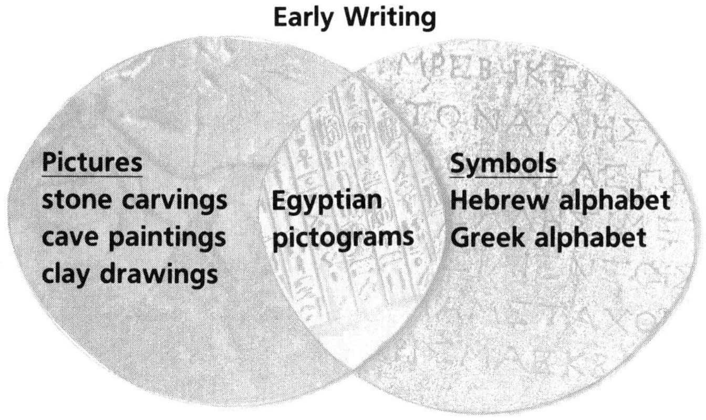

Early Writing

Pictures
stone carvings
cave paintings
clay drawings

Egyptian
pictograms

Symbols
Hebrew alphabet
Greek alphabet

To create your own diagram, draw simple lines. Don't worry if you're not the world's greatest artist. Keep the diagram clear. Label all parts. Show the important features; avoid a lot of details.

ON YOUR OWN Use an aspect of your school as a topic for making a cluster, a flowchart, an outline, or a diagram.

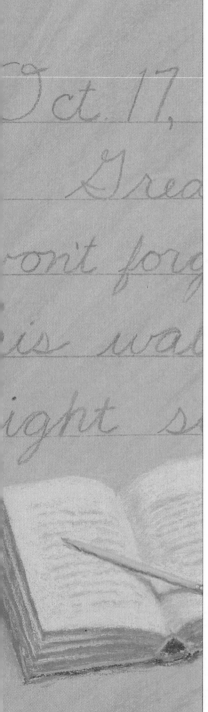

Keeping Notes, Drawings, and Freewriting in a Journal

Would you like to start an idea collection? It's more fun than baseball cards, easier to take care of than priceless paintings, and best of all, it doesn't cost you a thing because you make the collection yourself. How do you start one? There's a simple way. Just get a journal, which is a book or notebook with blank pages, and start filling it up with ideas. Arrange it in any way you like. Your Journal is a place for all of your thoughts, notes, quotations, dreams, memories, observations, plans—anything that strikes you as worth keeping.

One thing your everyday Journal isn't really designed for is finished work. If you want to write out six drafts of something, your Journal probably isn't the place to do it. Use your Journal for plans, ponderings, and possibilities.

You can also make drawings and sketches in your Journal. What details do you remember most about a person, place, or thing? Your drawings may give you ideas for writing projects.

Freewriting is a method of exploring and discovering ideas in which you are completely free of normal writing rules. The goal of freewriting is to transfer your thoughts, feelings, or ideas directly onto the page in a completely unrestricted manner. Here a student freewrites about keeping a journal.

Great! a perfect place to store my thoughts at night so I won't forget them like the change tray where my Dad puts his wallet and keys and if I wake up in the middle of the night with a good dream I can lean over and write it all down while it's still fresh and I can write the way I like because nobody but me will ever look at this. I'm free to experiment!

IN YOUR JOURNAL Begin a freewriting exercise on a topic of your choice. As in the passage above, you may want to freewrite about keeping a journal or about writing as a means of exploration and discovery. What memory, wish, or dream stands out in your mind? What problem is troubling you most? Writing about it may be a step toward a solution.

Working with a Partner — Peer Conferencing

Working together with a partner or in a small group is a chance to test your ideas before you put a lot of work into them. A successful partnership of writers keeps the following points in mind.

■ **What partners are:**

- Partners are members of a cooperative team.
- Partners are responsible for helping to improve each other's writing.
- Partners are sympathetic readers and listeners.
- Partners are constructive critics.
- Partners are polite and respectful of each other's feelings.
- Partners are honest with one another.

■ **What partners do:**

- Partners suggest improvements.
- Partners test out ideas together.
- Partners ask focusing questions about each other's work. (See page 218 to learn more about focusing questions.)
- Partners work as alternate sets of eyes and ears for each other.
- Partners work through ideas for plots, characters, or settings.
- Partners encourage each other.
- Partners listen carefully to each other's comments.
- Partners point out which ideas are clearly expressed and which need more work.
- Partners make comments about each other's ideas in terms of what is effective and ineffective, not in terms of good and bad.
- Partners brainstorm together to improve ideas or come up with new ideas. (See page 217 for more on brainstorming.)

ON YOUR OWN Find a partner. Look through a student or local newspaper for an interesting article. As a team, decide on ways that the article might be improved. Ask each other questions about the effectiveness of the article's content, organization, style, clarity, introduction, conclusion, and so on. Perhaps one of you could take on the role of author and answer questions about the article.

Interviewing

An interview is an opportunity for you to ask a person a series of questions. The person's answers may provide you with just the information you're looking for. Perhaps you're interested in the person and want to find out more about his or her personal experiences. Your purpose may be more specific: to gather information from an expert resource and use quotations in a report.

Before you conduct an interview, the first person you need to question is yourself. What is the purpose of your interview? Who will be the audience? What will they find most interesting about your subject? What is your subject's background? Finally, what style of interview will you conduct—formal or informal? light and friendly or challenging and in-depth?

Now it's time to prepare questions for the interview.

- Even in an informal interview, it is useful to be prepared with questions for your subject. If the interview itself stimulates new questions, you can always ask them at the appropriate time.
- Write down your questions. Leave space to write your subject's responses next to your questions. If you write questions on index cards, use the backs of the cards for responses. You may want to tape-record or videotape the interview.
- Arrange your questions so that they progress smoothly from topic to topic.
- Ask *what* questions first. Ask *why* questions later.

Here are some special considerations to keep in mind for tough interview subjects. Subjects who don't say enough may be ill at ease. Phrase your questions to make them feel relaxed. The subjects may also be uncertain. Move on to questions that get them talking. Subjects who say too much may need guidance. Design your questions to keep them focused on a single topic. Politely remind them of any time restrictions you may have.

IN YOUR JOURNAL You never know when you're going to run into someone famous. Be prepared. Imagine you have an opportunity to interview your favorite celebrity. What would you ask that person?

Have you read an interview in a magazine lately? Do you think the interviewer did a good job? What questions would you have asked the subject?

Writing Rehearsals

Have you ever been in a play? If you have, you know the value of a rehearsal. A rehearsal is a practice performance that helps you see the problems before opening night.

In a writing rehearsal, you try to picture in advance what you are going to write. You might jot some notes or sketch out what you plan to do. This gives you the opportunity to anticipate your writing needs. Here are some general points and questions to ask during your writing rehearsal.

■ Visualize Your Story

Picture its organization and estimate its length. Will it consist of several paragraphs or several chapters?

■ Think About Your Story Structure

Do you have ideas for:

- the beginning or introduction?
- a climax?
- one or two plot developments?
- a conclusion?

■ Review Your Notes, Outlines, and Plans

With a partner, go over your plans. Talk about:

- your purpose and intended audience.
- potential problem areas.
- characters, plot, and setting.

■ Talk Your Story Out Loud

With a partner, brainstorm in order to:

- eliminate ideas that don't seem to fit the story.
- develop good ideas that need more thought.
- find out more about your characters.
- determine if your story is appropriate for its intended audience.

ON YOUR OWN To practice rehearsing, think of a story someone has recently told you. Visualize the incident and write some notes to develop it into a written story. Then brainstorm with a friend. How many characters will there be? Where will it take place? How long will it be? How will you handle the structure of your story?

Freewriting

A blank page can be intimidating for a writer. You know what your piece will be about, but you don't yet know how to tell it.

Should you introduce the characters first or the setting? Should you tell the story in the past or the present tense? What should the tone be, the mood . . .

One method to make these decisions easier is freewriting. Freewriting lets you put technical matters aside and focus on the story. Just let your ideas spill out onto the page. Don't worry about form or grammar. You'll take care of those concerns later.

Talk About Freewriting When you freewrite, all you need to do is the following:

- loosen up.
- forget all the rules.
- work fast.
- enjoy yourself.

The "Max and Maxine" exercise is written in run-on sentences (sentences without proper starting and stopping points) and incomplete sentences (sentences without subjects and predicates). Freewriting is one of the very few kinds of writing in which an ungrammatical style is appropriate. In freewriting, speed and looseness are your top priorities.

Here is an example of freewriting for a story about a writer. It will be entitled "Max and Maxine." Discuss it with a partner. Does it lay out the main idea and include usable details?

> Maxine Fishbein, a very successful novelist whose writing is serious and respected by literary critics secretly loves horror stories . . . one day she writes one under the name Max Savage and of course, it's a big success, everyone loves it. except literary critics who think Max Savage's books are "disgusting, horrible." they invite Maxine to debate Max Savage and his crude books, of course, there is no Max so Maxine must decide what to do.

ON YOUR OWN Freewrite an ending for "Max and Maxine." If you prefer, freewrite a story entirely of your own making. For ideas, you could look at a newspaper, think about a party you recently attended, or recall a character in a story that you have always admired.

Taking Time Out

There is a popular expression, "You can't see the forest for the trees." Sometimes writers get so close to their work that they lose their perspective. They can't see the overall picture because they have been looking so hard at the details. One way for you to regain your perspective is to take time out. Gain some distance from your work.

■ How Can I Distance Myself from My Rough Draft?

Set your draft aside. When you work on something for too long, you tend to lose your objectivity. Your work becomes a part of you, so it is difficult to see the work for what it really is.

■ How Long Should I Stay Away from My Work?

The answer to that depends upon you and upon the complexity of the work. Sometimes several hours away can give you a new perspective. Other times, several days may be more useful.

■ Is There Anything Special I Should Do?

Not really, but perhaps the best thing to do is to involve your mind in an activity other than writing. Take a walk or run an errand.

■ What Is the Benefit of Staying Away from My Work?

When you come back to your work, you should be able to read it objectively—as if it were written by someone else. With that fresh perspective, it will be easier to identify and to fix problem spots. You will also be able to see more clearly where you are going.

■ What Else Can I Do to Increase My Objectivity?

Develop what some writers call a third eye. Focus on what the words *actually* say, rather than on what you *intended* them to say.

IN YOUR JOURNAL Compare something you wrote more than six months ago with your most recent piece of writing. How objective are you as you reread each piece? How effective is the piece in accomplishing its purpose and reaching your intended audience? Write your impressions in your Journal.

Looking at the Big Picture

Like football coaches, writers go into their work with a game plan, or a set of strategies to achieve their goals. Once you have finished a first draft, it is often a good idea to review your original game plan. Stand back and look at the big picture. See how well your plan is working, and adjust those parts that need to be changed. Remember to always keep your audience in mind.

■ Reevaluate Your Purpose

Now that you've been through a draft, think about your purpose again. Through the process of writing, has your purpose changed at all? Does your original purpose still seem worthwhile? Do you still think you can fulfill your purpose? In a few short sentences, state the purpose of your writing as you now see it.

■ Think About Your Audience

Does your draft seem appropriate for your intended audience? Did you assume things about your readers that you must reevaluate? Does your draft still address the needs and interests of your audience?

■ Think About Your Main Idea

Has your main idea changed? If the process of writing turned your attention to a new main idea, feel free to change it. Write a summary of the main idea as you now see it before you begin revising.

■ Reevaluate Form

Did you stick with the form—for example, story, report, or editorial—that you originally planned? If not, list reasons why you changed it. If you did stick with your originally planned form, list reasons why the form you chose works best for the message you want to communicate.

IN YOUR JOURNAL For future writing projects, make a chart for keeping track of purpose, audience, main idea, and form. Jot down comments as you reach each stage of the writing process. See if you can discover trends that will help you plan for future projects.

WRITERS ON WRITING

Most people seem interested in turning their dreams into reality. Then there are those who turn reality into dreams. I belong to the latter group.
–Allen Say
author, illustrator, and photographer

Working with a Partner and Peer Conferencing

Criticism is like medicine—it's hard to take, but if it's wisely prescribed, it can be good for you. As a partner, you need to be able to give criticism as well as take it. The secret to most successful partnerships is teamwork and a cooperative attitude.

■ Treat Your Partner's Work with Respect

Be positive. Treat others as you would like to be treated. If you are not enthusiastic about your partner's work, focus on the parts that work for you. Your goal is to help to improve each other's writing.

> You put the line *All roads lead to Rome* in the wrong place, where it gets completely lost.

> This line *All roads lead to Rome* is the real key for me. I think it would be terrific at the end.

■ Remember the Purpose and Audience

Your own likes and dislikes are not the issue. Your goal is to improve the writing so that it fulfills its purpose and will reach its audience.

> I think you should get rid of the long technical part about computers. That subject is very boring.

> Was your purpose to include so many facts about computers? Will your audience be interested?

■ Think of What Is Effective or Ineffective, Not Good or Bad

Value judgments have no place in a partnership. Think about what works and what doesn't work. Don't waste time and risk hurting your partner's feelings by being negative.

> This image *underneath the pearly moon* is really corny. What could you possibly have had in mind?

> The *pearly moon* image doesn't really work here. How about saving it for a different situation?

◼ Make Specific Suggestions

Whether your opinions are positive or negative, back them up with reasons. It's not enough just to say you like or dislike something. Explain yourself. Support your explanations with examples.

> It was great. I loved it.

> The overall mood really captured the feel of the cave. Laird was a convincing guide. The bear was truly menacing. I was scared out of my wits.

◼ Be Flexible

While it's good to feel proud of your writing, try to resist the temptation to defend your work when it is criticized. Have enough confidence in yourself to listen to suggestions objectively. Sort through them, and take advantage of the helpful suggestions you receive. Why is the second statement more flexible than the first?

> That's the best part of my story. I can't change that.

> I'm not sure I would want to change that. But let's try your suggestion, just to see how it sounds.

◼ Help Your Partner

If your partner resists your criticism, try to find out why. Are you truly being constructive? How can you improve your methods? Remember, your opinions are valuable, and you'd like to help improve your partner's writing. The choice here is clear:

> If you don't like my criticism, fine! Don't take it!

> If you have any suggestions about how I could change the way I criticize, I'd like to hear them.

IN YOUR JOURNAL In the next conference that you take part in, take notes in your Journal on the comments your partner made that were most helpful to you. Analyze these comments. Why were they effective? How will you use your partner's comments to improve your work?

Focusing on Elaboration

Good ideas deserve to be fully developed. Every time you make a point, you also need to ask yourself, "Have I explained too much or too little?" The art of elaboration is a balancing act. Saying just the right amount about a particular point will help your work to be perfectly understood. Ask yourself questions like these:

■ Do I Need All of This?

Each sentence you write should serve a purpose. If it sounds good but isn't really necessary, get rid of it. Why is the second sentence in this example unnecessary?

> Walking up a ramp is a good form of exercise. The grocery store has a ramp. Climbing a ramp requires the same amount of work as going straight up. You just climb gradually instead of all at once.

■ Have I Forgotten Any Key Details?

The flip side of too much is not enough. Details can clarify the ideas you want to express. Details can make an idea more specific. Explain why the second description is an improvement over the first.

> An ax is a good example of a wedge.

> An ax is a good example of a wedge. The wedge-shaped ax head moves downward. This downward movement creates a sideways force that splits apart the wood.

■ How Can I Use Elaboration in My Stories?

In stories a common error is to tell too much. Let the characters' words and actions do the talking for you. The second description makes Molly seem a more interesting character.

> Molly was extremely intelligent for a two-year-old. She seemed much more advanced than the other children.

> When Molly saw a toy that interested her, she would examine it closely. The more complicated the toy, the more intrigued Molly seemed.

■ Are My Descriptions Complete?

In descriptions a common error is to leave out key details. Give your readers all the information they need. Why does the second description succeed better than the first one?

> The final score was 6–4, 6–2, 6–4. Pete had lost decisively. Still, he had to feel good about his game.

> The final score was 6–4, 6–2, 6–4. Pete had lost decisively. Still, since he was only 13 and his opponent was 18, he had to feel good about his game.

■ Is My Persuasive Writing Effective?

In persuasive writing a common error is to tell too little. You want to persuade your readers; give them every strong argument you know. Which of these two paragraphs is more persuasive?

> Benson did not play a role in the scandal. He should be re-elected this term.

> Benson did not play a role in the scandal. In fact, he helped to expose those who were involved. He appointed the commission that brought the culprits to justice. Benson should be re-elected this term because he will not tolerate injustice.

ON YOUR OWN Find the owner's manual to a household appliance such as a washing machine, a TV, or a portable heater. Read through the instructions. Find instances in which the manual leaves out important details or gives too much information. Rewrite a page of the manual to make it easier to understand. Then show your page and the original page to a friend. Does she or he think you succeeded in writing clearer instructions?

WRITERS ON WRITING

The beautiful part of writing is that you don't have to get it right the first time, unlike, say, a brain surgeon. You can always do it better, find the exact word, the apt phrase, the leaping simile.

— *Robert Cormier author*

Creating Checklists

A checklist helps a writer to keep track of goals, performance, and points that will need to be addressed during the revision process. You can make your own customized checklist to cover points similar to the ones below.

■ Do I Need to Reorder or Rearrange My Work?

- Do the ideas that I present follow one another in a logical sequence?
- Do any of the ideas seem out of place?
- Do any of the ideas just seem thrown in?
- Do I find myself wondering why a paragraph or a sentence appears where it does?

■ Do I Need to Do Any Cutting?

- Are there any sentences or paragraphs that I just can't get to sound right?
- Are there any sentences that aren't relevant to the topic?
- Could any part of my writing be simplified?
- Are there examples where the text (a) explains too much? (b) describes too much? (c) gives unnecessary facts or examples? (d) includes unnecessary quotations? (e) seems long-winded?

■ Do I Need to Add Passages to My Writing?

- Are there instances in which I brought up a topic but failed to develop it fully?
- Are all my topic sentences supported by necessary details?
- Are there any characters, ideas, or descriptions that seem incomplete in some way?

■ Do I Need to Rewrite Parts of My Story?

- Are there passages that just don't make sense?
- Does my story contain any clunkers—that is, images or descriptions that sound clumsy and inappropriate?
- Do the ideas that I present create the impact I want?
- Are there any characters, ideas, or descriptions that seem lifeless or meaningless?

MAKE CONNECTIONS

Making checklists can help you to organize other things in your life besides writing. For example, you can use checklists for activities like:

- *preparing for a trip.*
- *completing homework assignments.*
- *fixing or taking care of your bike, sports or stereo equipment, and pets.*
- *planning work such as yard work, housework, or paper routes.*

■ Do I Need to Clarify Parts of My Writing?

- Are there points in my writing that seem unclear?
- Did I forget to define any key terms?
- Are there instances where two or more ideas get tangled up together?
- Do my most important ideas really stand out in the text?

■ Are There Points That Need to Be Refined?

- Were there instances in which I was too blunt?
- Should I have been more sensitive in the way I presented specific ideas in my writing?
- Did I focus so much on the big ideas that I neglected some subtle points I could have made?

■ Should I Make Style Changes in My Writing?

- Does the overall style seem appropriate to my topic? How would I characterize it?
- Does the style communicate my own personality? (Do I want it to communicate my own personality?)
- Is there anything I can do to make the style a little more distinct —perhaps vary my sentences more?

■ Should I Add More Imagery Where Appropriate?

- Have I used figurative language effectively? Should I include more similes and metaphors in my writing?
- If a formal style is required, have I used formal language consistently throughout my piece? If an informal style is more appropriate, have I included informal language?

IN YOUR JOURNAL What special topics would you include in a checklist for your own writing? Choose two checklist topics such as those listed above and on page 233. In your Journal, write three or more checklist questions for each. You can use these checklist topics the next time you go over a rough draft.

Eyeing Details

Have you ever gone bird-watching? A bird can be perched right in front of your eyes, but sometimes you still can't see it. Proofreading is a lot like bird-watching. Errors can be staring you in the face, but sometimes you still don't notice them.

Proofreading may not seem as important as drafting or revising, but it is a valuable step in the writing process. If you don't proofread your work, errors in spelling, grammar, or punctuation can become big distractions for your reader. Submit a mistake-free final copy of your work, so that your readers can focus on its content.

■ Proofread Your Final Draft

Proofreading is a cleanup process. When you proofread, you should be looking for technical errors, not changes in content. While proofreading, if you see that you need to change your text, go back in and do revisions. Then resume proofreading.

■ Keep Your Eyes Open

Good proofreaders have a sixth sense for spotting mistakes. For example, have you ever looked at a word and thought that it just didn't look right? Very likely, you found that the word was misspelled. Focus on developing your proofreading sixth sense. With a little practice, most people find that their ability to spot mistakes improves.

■ Read Your Work Out Loud

If you don't see your errors, perhaps you will hear them when you read your work out loud. Even better, get a classmate to read your work. Listen for things to correct.

■ Exchange Papers with a Classmate

Professional writers often have someone else give their work a final proofreading. A reader who has a little distance from the writing can sometimes spot mistakes better than the author.

■ Check for Only One Type of Mistake at a Time

This method is especially recommended if you have trouble with proofreading. Break the process down. For example, look for spelling errors the first time around. In your second round, look for punctuation errors. In your third round, look for grammar errors. Finally, check for capitalization errors. That way you'll be sure to catch every proofreading error.

■ Use Reference Sources

For spelling, use the Word Finder on page 368 or a dictionary. If you aren't sure how to spell a word, look it up. Take a little time now to avoid problems later.

Consult the Mechanics Handbook on page 353 for answers to questions such as "Do I need a comma here?" or "Should this word be *who* or *whom*?" Questions like these can be tough. You may also want to consult an expert, such as a teacher or an older student. If no expert is available, get the opinion of a classmate.

■ Know Your Proofreader's Marks

Each proofreading mark has its own specific meaning and use. The advantage to using proofreader's marks is that it can simplify and speed up your proofreading. Here are some of the proofreader's marks used in this book:

∧	Add.	◯	Check the spelling.
ℓ	Take out.	⊙	Add a period.
≡	Make a capital letter.	∧	Add a comma.
/	Make a lower-case letter.	ᵛ ᵛ	Add quotation marks.
¶	Indent the paragraph.	∽	Reverse the order.

ON YOUR OWN To see the effectiveness of proofreading, try an experiment. Type out two versions of a short essay or story. You can copy a paragraph from a magazine or newspaper or write your own short work. Make the first version of the piece letter-perfect. Insert several proofreading errors into the second version.

Then make several copies of each version and ask friends, classmates, or family members to read your piece. Give each person one version or the other. Which version receives more positive response?

Presenting Your Work

There is almost no limit to the ways in which you can publish your writing. You can read your work to friends or reach the whole town by publishing in the local newspaper. Take the time to find the publishing method that is right for your piece. Choose the publishing method that will most appeal to your audience and help you to accomplish your purpose. Use one of the suggestions listed below, or think of your own way to publish.

■ Assemble an Anthology

Collect stories, poems, personal narratives, and nonfiction works under one cover. You may want to coordinate your anthology so that it has a single theme or sections with different themes. Possible themes include "Growing Up" and "Justice for All."

■ Publish a Magazine

Look over the format of your favorite magazine with a few classmates. Then decide how you would like to organize your own magazine. Encourage others to submit writing in various categories, such as essays, cartoons, and poetry.

■ Create an Encyclopedia

Compile nonfiction pieces in alphabetical order by topic. You can make this an ongoing project as students in your class complete pieces. Over the school year, your encyclopedia can become a substantial reference source for the entire class.

■ Present a Reading

Make this a "classy" class event. Create posters to publicize the authors who will appear on the program. Invite parents and guests.

■ Give a Performance

Write dialog for your story or poem and have a few friends act it out. Read your story while actors give a dramatic interpretation of the action. Try recording the performance, and add music, sound effects, and commercial breaks if you choose!

■ Shoot a Video

Turn your story, essay, or poem into a multimedia event. Flash images on the screen while a narrator reads your work aloud. You could use music to enhance the drama.

■ Make a Poster

Create a poster for the film version of your poem, short story, or personal narrative. Include pictures of the starring actors.

■ Create a Cartoon Strip

Turn your story or personal narrative into a cartoon. Draw several panels, each showing an action that takes place in your writing.

■ Submit Your Work to Magazines

Many magazines, such as *Merlyn's Pen, Stone Soup, Cricket, Scholastic Scope,* and *Icarus,* publish student writing. Read one of these magazines, and decide if your writing seems suitable for it. Submit your work in the form indicated by the publisher.

■ Write to the Editor of a Newspaper

Look through the editorial sections of the weekly and daily newspapers in your area. Some newspapers encourage people of all ages and backgrounds to share their views through a column. Does your editorial or essay address a topic that might be of interest to your community at large? Consider sending your editorial to the Editor's Desk and voicing your concerns.

IN YOUR JOURNAL   In your Journal, jot down some ideas you have for publishing some of your completed writing projects. Then put one of your plans to work! Write an announcement that publicizes the upcoming publication of your work. Send the announcement to friends and family.

WRITERS ON

WRITING

Mainly I think of myself as a story-teller, though using today's medium (radio, television, stage, picture books, song, music, drama, etc.) to carry out the once-upon-a-time profession.
–Arthur Scholey
author and
playwright

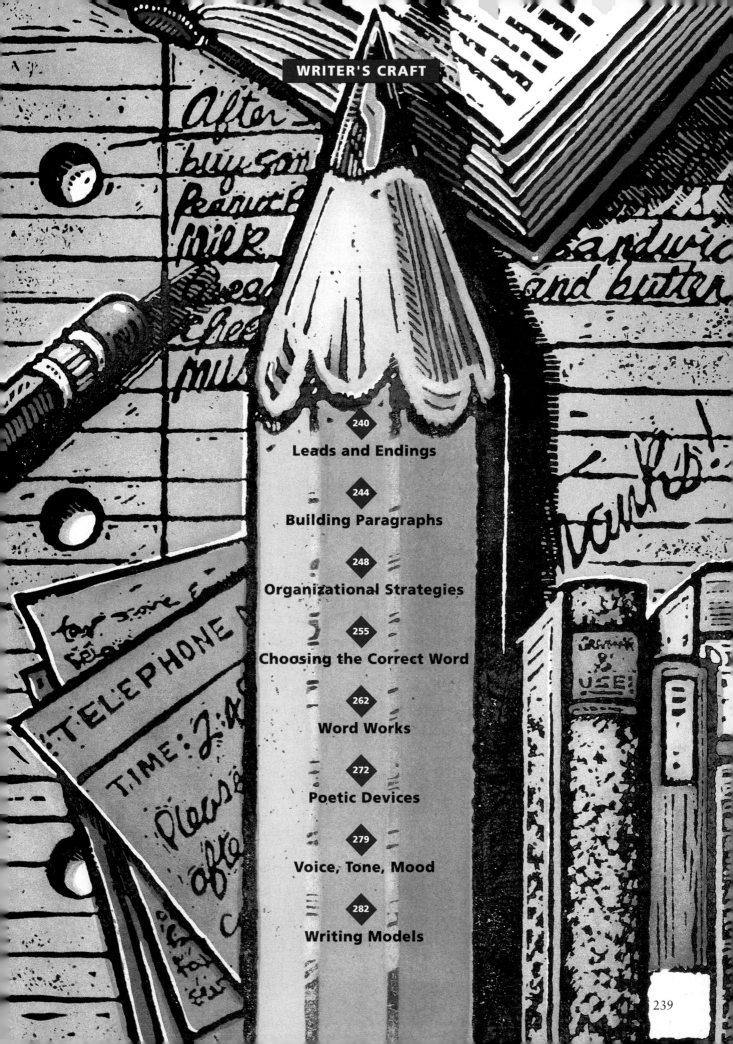

WRITER'S CRAFT

Leads and Endings

Get the Point! How would you start an opening paragraph in order to grab your readers' interest? Have you ever closed a piece with a provocative question?

Alert! Remember to indent your paragraphs.

The Writer's Eye Compare these news articles.

*Which paragraph in **The Writer's Eye** grabs your interest at the start? Which paragraph feels as though it has a satisfying ending? What makes the ending strong?*

"I still can't believe it!" exclaimed Rocio Santos. Our very own Norwood Middle School seventh grader won the citywide prize for best student poem. The contest was open to all students in grades 7 to 12. Congratulations, Rocio! You're an inspiration!

There was a citywide contest for best student poem. The contest was open to all students in grades 7 to 12. The contest was won by Rocio Santos, a seventh grader here at Norwood Middle School.

Key Ideas

- A *lead* is the opening part of a piece of writing, particularly a news story. Its function is to hook the readers' interest so that they'll go on to read more. A question, a piece of dialog, or a strong, intriguing statement can make a good lead.
- An *ending* is the last part, or conclusion, of a piece of writing. A good ending leaves the reader thinking about the writer's main point. It also leaves the reader feeling satisfied and clear about the writer's intention. Restating a topic sentence, making a joke, or choosing a strong quotation can make an effective ending.

Try It Out Write a second paragraph for the first article in The Writer's Eye. Discuss what Rocio's poem is about. Use a strong lead to begin your paragraph and close with a powerful ending.

New News Choose a serious or humorous topic for a good news story. Write a paragraph that begins with an interesting lead and ends with a satisfying conclusion. Share your paragraph with friends.

Sentence Sense

Get the Point! First, is there any question that an *interrogative* sentence is a question? Second, think about *imperative* sentences for a few moments. Next, if you know what an *exclamatory* sentence is, shout it out now! Finally, you are left with the simple fact that a *declarative* sentence makes a statement.

Alert! Remember that a sentence is a group of words that expresses a complete thought.

The Writer's Eye Reflect on these proverbs and famous quotes.

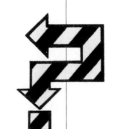

> I think; therefore, I am.
> Don't look back; something might be gaining on you.
> I have a dream!
> Am I my brother's keeper?

Key Ideas

- *Declarative* sentences make statements.
- *Imperative* sentences give commands. Sometimes the subject isn't named. The subject is an understood *you*.
- *Interrogative* sentences ask questions.
- *Exclamatory* sentences express ideas or give commands in a forceful way.

Try It Out Can you think of a way to change any of the sayings and quotes in The Writer's Eye to a different type of sentence? For example, can you change *I think; therefore, I am* to a question? Try this with two or three of the sentences.

Quick! You can be a philosopher, too. Think of advice you might share with others. What age-old truths have you observed or learned from your life? Write four proverbs based on your own thoughts and experiences. Edit your proverbs to make sure they are clear and concise. What types of sentences did you write?

PARTNER TALK

Which saying in **The Writer's Eye** *asks a question? Which gives an order? Which makes a statement? Which expresses an idea in a forceful way?*

Sentence Style

Get the Point! Sentence style can make a difference in your writing. Without style, you can make an interesting topic dull. With style, you can make a dull topic interesting.

Alert! Remember to use a comma between the two clauses that form a compound sentence.

The Writer's Eye Read these two versions of Archimedes's story.

> King Hiero was worried. Was his crown pure gold? Even Archimedes did not know what to do. He took a bath. The water spilled out of the tub and gave him the solution.

> King Hiero anxiously drummed his fingers on the table top. Was his crown pure gold—or wasn't it? Wait! He could call Archimedes! However, Archimedes, the brilliant scientist, was stumped. He thought of one thing, then of another, but no solution seemed to fit the puzzle. Later, as Archimedes stepped into his bath, he cried, "Eureka!"

Key Ideas

- Writing with *style* lets you say what you want to say in a graceful and interesting way.
- Every writer has his or her own personal style. Word choice, rhythm, use of images, variety of sentence length and type, and many other factors all go into putting *you* in your writing.
- An effective writing style draws the reader in and makes him or her want to read more.

Try It Out Write a few sentences to continue the second paragraph in The Writer's Eye. Tell what happened when Archimedes tried to measure the volume of the king's crown. Was the crown pure gold after all? Reread your paragraph. Does it seem to flow together?

Eureka Revisited Look up the story of Archimedes in an encyclopedia. Devise an experiment to test his ideas. Write a description of your experiment results.

PARTNER TALK

*Which paragraph in **The Writer's Eye** reads more smoothly? Which paragraph is more interesting? Which style appeals more to you? Why? How would you describe this style?*

Sentence Variety

Get the Point! Variety is the spice of life. Some sentences are short. Others are long because they express more complicated ideas. Try to include both types of sentences in your writing.

Alert! Remember to avoid run-ons and sentence fragments as you vary your sentences.

The Writer's Eye Read these reports on hieroglyphics.

The Maya had a sophisticated picture-writing system. The system was first studied in the sixteenth century. Scientists were baffled. A recent discovery showed that Mayan hieroglyphics represent single syllables. This was a breakthrough for experts. They have deciphered much of the Mayan language.

The sophisticated picture-writing system of the Maya has baffled scientists since the sixteenth century, when it was first studied. Recently, Mayan hieroglyphics were found to represent single syllables. This was a major breakthrough. Using it, experts have deciphered much of the Mayan language.

Key Ideas

- Effective writing includes a *variety of sentences*—long, short, and medium-length.
- For sentence variety, write simple, compound, complex, and compound-complex sentences. Use introductory phrases and descriptive adjective and adverb phrases.

Try It Out Write a few sentences to continue a paragraph in The Writer's Eye. What types of sentences did you use?

A Picture Worth a Thousand Words Create your own picture-writing system. Compile a dictionary of your picture characters. Then write a short paragraph using your system, and exchange paragraphs with a classmate. Use your dictionaries to decipher each other's hieroglyphic paragraphs.

PARTNER TALK

*Which paragraph in **The Writer's Eye** contains more sentence variety? Which paragraph sounds more natural to you?*

DID YOU NOTICE?

Read the excerpt from Thomas Mills's book review of Ransom *(page 132). How does sentence variety add to the writing?*

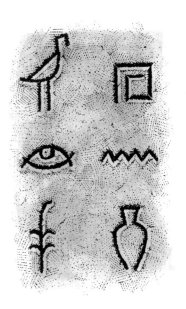

Topic Sentence and Details

Get the Point! Have you ever read a piece of writing two or three times, looking for the main point? If so, you know how frustrating it can be when a paragraph doesn't have a clear topic sentence. A topic sentence pulls the rest of the paragraph's details into place around it. When a topic sentence is unclear (or missing), the details are like a forest of closely planted trees, with no clear path between them.

Alert! Remember to indent at the beginning of every paragraph.

The Writer's Eye Read these adventuresome paragraphs.

The most exciting sport I know is parasailing! It's the closest thing to flying I've ever tried, and believe me, I've tried a lot. I've ridden roller coasters. I've gone whitewater rafting and water-skiing. Parasailing has a thrill like no other sport.

I've ridden roller coasters. I've gone whitewater rafting. Parasailing is very scary. I've even gone water-skiing. Those other sports were like flying, too, but not as much as parasailing was. Actually, parasailing is safer than you'd think.

Key Ideas

- A *paragraph* is a group of sentences that develops one main idea.
- The main idea of a paragraph is stated in the *topic sentence*. It can appear anywhere in a paragraph.
- *Detail sentences* support the topic sentence.

Try It Out Write two or three detail sentences to add to the first paragraph in The Writer's Eye. How do they support the main idea?

Phony Facts Write a paragraph with a topic sentence and supporting detail sentences. Include accurate facts. Now make up a nonsense topic sentence and invent a few inaccurate detail sentences to support it. Ask a friend to identify the phony.

*Which paragraph in **The Writer's Eye** has a clear main idea? What is the main idea? How do the detail sentences support the main idea?*

Take a look at the excerpt from "Undercover" by Heather Peterson on page 146. What details does the writer use to support the topic sentence?

Transition Words and Phrases

Get the Point! *In my opinion,* making statements can be easy. *For example,* that statement was a snap. *On the other hand,* connecting statements in a paragraph can be tricky. *Most important,* you need transition words and phrases to make these connections clear.

Alert! Be sure to use a comma after introductory words and phrases if you need to do so.

The Writer's Eye Read these two paragraphs.

In my opinion, democracy means that everyone has the right to vote. In the United States of America, however, only adults can vote. As a result, teenagers are left out of the democratic process until they are eighteen. I think this is unfair. Furthermore, it turns people under eighteen into second-class citizens. Is this democracy?

Democracy means that everyone has the right to vote. In the United States of America, only adults can vote. Teenagers cannot vote until they are eighteen. This is unfair. It turns people under eighteen into second-class citizens. Is this democracy?

Key Ideas
- *Transition words and phrases* connect one idea to another.
- To present facts, use transition words and phrases such as *first, furthermore,* and *as a result.* To state opinions, use transition phrases such as *I believe, I think,* and *I feel.* To show the other side of an issue, use transition words and phrases such as *on the other hand* and *however.*

Try It Out Think of another sentence you could add to the first paragraph in The Writer's Eye. What transition word or phrase would you use to connect it to the other ideas in the paragraph?

Quick! Should teenagers have the right to vote? Write a paragraph explaining how you feel. Reread your paragraph. Where might you add transition words to help to connect your ideas?

PARTNER TALK

*Which paragraph in **The Writer's Eye** uses transition words and phrases to connect ideas? What are the transition words and phrases used in this paragraph?*

Conjunctions

Get the Point! Conjunctions join words *or* groups of words together. Most writers avoid beginning sentences with conjunctions *but* do not hesitate to use them in the middle of a sentence.

Alert! Remember to use a comma after the conjunction *however*.

The Writer's Eye Read these whimsical paragraphs.

What would happen if words came in a box? Short nouns would come in small sizes. Long nouns would come in large sizes. There wouldn't be many conjunctions in the box. They would be important. They would be the little connectors that you use to stick other pieces together.

What would happen if words came in a box? Short and long nouns would come in small and large sizes. There wouldn't be many conjunctions in the box, but they would be important. They would be the little connectors that you use to stick other pieces together.

Key Ideas

- *Conjunctions* are words that join other words or groups of words together.
- Commonly used conjunctions include *and, but, or,* and *yet.* Some conjunctions, like *either . . . or* or *both . . . and,* work in pairs. Other conjunctions include *as, since, while, because, if, however, though,* and *unless.*

Try It Out Add two more sentences to the second paragraph in The Writer's Eye. Reread your work. Did you use conjunctions? Would using conjunctions help make your writing flow more smoothly?

The Building Blocks of Language What if language did come in a box, like a big building-block set, with a word on each block? Design a basic building-block set. Cut paper into squares. Identify words you want to include, and write one on each piece of paper. Then construct sentences using your building blocks.

*Which paragraph in **The Writer's Eye** reads better and makes more sense? Which paragraph makes use of conjunctions such as <u>and</u>, <u>or</u>, and <u>but</u>? What function do they serve in the paragraph?*

Dialog

Get the Point! "Dialog for sale. Get your red-hot dialog!"

"How much is your dialog?" I asked.

"Fifty cents a quote," she answered.

"That's outrageous!" I exclaimed. "Is the dialog even real?"

"Of course it's real," she said. "It's just two people talking. A few quotation marks. Nothing else. How much d'you want?"

"I'll take three dollars' worth," I said.

"Fine," she said. "Will that be regular or extra-clever?"

Alert! Always use quotation marks before and after dialog.

The Writer's Eye Read these two versions of a joke.

"Did you give the goldfish fresh water?" I asked Phil.

Phil shrugged, "I didn't see any reason to. They didn't finish the water I gave them yesterday."

I asked Phil if he had changed the water in the goldfish tank. He hadn't. I wanted to know why. His reason was that the fish had not made use of the water he had given to them the day before.

Key Ideas

- *Dialog* is a recording of the exact words that characters speak. Quotation marks indicate that dialog is being spoken.
- Dialog should sound natural. Normal rules for writing can be loosened a little. People do not need to speak perfect sentences, but what they say should make sense.

Try It Out Extend the dialog in The Writer's Eye. What will the narrator say next? Make sure the dialog you write is in character.

Quick! Have you ever wondered what things would say if they could talk? Bring two inanimate objects, such as a comb and a brush, to life. Write a conversation between the two objects which gives clues as to their identities. Then read it to friends, and ask them to identify the objects.

Which version of the goldfish joke in **The Writer's Eye** *is more fun to read? Which has a better punch line? Which gives you a better feel for the characters—Phil and the narrator?*

Beginning, Middle, and End

Get the Point! Most stories have a Who, Where, What, and How pattern. The beginning tells who the characters are and where the story takes place. The middle gives the conflict and how the characters plan to resolve it. The end of the story tells how the conflict is resolved and what happens to the characters.

Alert! Remember that transition words and phrases can connect the ideas in a story.

The Writer's Eye Read this playful story.

There was once a story with no middle or end. The whole story consisted of a beginning. Since there was no plot, there was no way to resolve the plot. The story was doomed to repeat itself forever. One day the story with no middle or end met a storyteller and asked her, "Will you help me?" The story offered all it had—a beginning. The storyteller took the beginning and gave it a fine middle and a clever end. The story and storyteller lived happily ever after.

Key Ideas

- The *plot* is the series of events in a story.
- The *beginning* of a story introduces the characters, the setting, and the plot.
- The *middle* of a story develops the plot.
- The *end* of a story comes when the events of the story are resolved. The end can give the reader something to think about.

Try It Out Can you think of some ways to expand on the story in The Writer's Eye? What title would you give it? Round out the story by adding a few sentences to its beginning, middle, or end.

Mix and Match Write Mix-and-Match stories with two friends. Each of you writes the ending of a story. Exchange papers. Write the beginning of that story. Exchange papers again, and write the middle of that story. How well does each story flow?

Does the story in **The Writer's Eye** *with no middle or end really have no middle? Think about this for a while before you come to a conclusion.*

How is the story summary of Ryan White: My Own Story *from* Publishers Weekly *on page 133 organized? Would you include the beginning, middle, and end in a story summary? Why?*

Story Structure

Get the Point! "Why did the cow cross the road?" asked Denise.
"I don't know," said Ernesto. "Why did it?"
"I don't know either," said Denise. "I just wondered."

If you're wondering what the point of Denise's question was, then you already understand something basic about story structure. A story needs to be *about* something, and it needs to reach a climax that makes clear what its point was—like the punch line of a joke.

Alert! Remember that the plot is the series of events in a story.

The Writer's Eye Take a look at this outline.

> I. Meg asks Sandra to pass her the answers to the next test. If Meg fails it, she must leave the school.
> II. Sandra talks to Aunt Clara about cheating and to Uncle Lou about helping friends.
> III. On test day Meg pats the seat next to her.
> IV. Sandra takes a seat at the other side of the room.

Key Ideas

- Stories are often structured around a *conflict*—a clash between two opposing forces. A conflict can be *external*—between two people or between a person and an object. A conflict can be *internal*—when a person is torn between two choices.
- The *climax* is where one force or the other wins out. It leads to a *resolution* of the story.

Try It Out How else might the conflict in the story in The Writer's Eye have been worked out? Write your own version of the outline.

Quick! Try your hand at your own story outline. First, decide on the conflict, the climax, and the resolution in your story. Next, write an outline in which the first point introduces the conflict, the next points show the conflict getting stronger, and the last two points show the climax of the conflict and then the resolution.

PARTNER TALK

*What is the conflict in the story outlined in **The Writer's Eye?** What is the most exciting or intense moment? Where does the conflict get resolved?*

Time Order

Get the Point! In the real world, time only moves in one direction —forward. This means first things come first, and last things go last. As a writer, you can put the end before the beginning, good-bye before hello. Just remember, once you turn back the clock, it starts moving forward again, unless you say otherwise.

Alert! Be sure to use commas after introductory words such as *first, second,* and *finally.*

The Writer's Eye Read these timely paragraphs.

I passed ancient civilizations and all recorded history. Staring me in the eye was a tyrannosaurus. I selected the date May 8, 95 million B.C., on the time machine. Then, there was a clonk. Back I went, past wars, floods, and famines. I jumped in and pushed ON.

I selected the date May 8, 95 million B.C., on the time machine. I jumped in and pushed ON. Back I went, past wars, floods, and famines. I passed ancient civilizations and all recorded history. Then, there was a clonk. Staring me in the eye was a tyrannosaurus.

Key Ideas

■ Keep the *time sequence* in stories logical. A good time sequence helps the reader to see how one event leads to the next.

■ Generally, you shouldn't tamper with time in your writing unless you have a good reason. For example, one reason may be that a character is thinking of something that happened in the past.

Try It Out Add details to one of the paragraphs in The Writer's Eye. Stay consistent with the time pattern that is already established. For example, what other events did the time traveler pass on the way to the year 95 million B.C.?

Back to the Future If you had a time machine, to what time would you travel? Write an account of your imaginary trip. Be sure to make any flashbacks in your story clear.

PARTNER TALK

Which paragraph in The Writer's Eye seems better arranged with respect to time? Which paragraph makes more sense? In the paragraph that makes better sense, how would you describe the way events are ordered in time?

DID YOU NOTICE?

Compare the excerpts from Julia Child and Company by Julia Child (page 54) and Anno's Sundial by Mitsumasa Anno (page 116). What differences do you notice in the writers' presentations of time?

Spatial Order

Get the Point! Creating spatial order in your writing is like cleaning your room. Socks go in a drawer. Pillows go on the bed. In your writing you can put things in the wrong places, but only at the risk of confusing the reader. Readers want things described in an order they can follow easily. For example, you might describe a room from left to right. Remember to stick to an order that makes sense to you.

Alert! Remember to use commas to separate items in a series.

The Writer's Eye Read these moving paragraphs.

The axle turns the wheels, which make the car go. The gas explodes and pushes down on the crank. The flywheel turns the drive shaft, which is connected to the axle. A spark plug ignites gas in the cylinder. The crank turns the flywheel around.

A spark plug ignites the gas in the cylinder. The gas explodes and pushes down on the crank. The crank turns the flywheel around. The flywheel turns the drive shaft, which is connected to the axle. The axle turns the wheels, which make the car go.

Key Ideas
- *Spatial order* involves arranging things in space according to size, function, position, appearance, and so on.
- The most important thing is that your arrangement have some kind of pattern that the reader can recognize.

Try It Out Add a few simple sentences to one of the paragraphs in The Writer's Eye. If you don't know how a car works, add some sentences that describe what the car does after the wheels make it go.

Quick! Think of things that are arranged in space, such as players on a field or furniture in a room. Write a detailed description of one arrangement. Read your description to a friend, and ask him or her to draw the arrangement. Does the picture accurately portray the arrangement you had in mind?

Which description in The Writer's Eye makes more sense to you? How would you describe the order in which it is arranged? How would you describe the order of the other paragraph?

Comparison and Contrast

Get the Point! Your brain constantly compares and contrasts—even when you don't know it. Picture this. You see a face. Your brain compares this face to the hundreds of other faces it has stored in its memory. Finally, a match! Something is wrong, however. You turn up the contrast to find differences. It's the hair. The person you are looking at is you—staring in the mirror at your new haircut.

Alert! When comparing and contrasting in your writing, remember to use commas in compound sentences.

The Writer's Eye Read these two unusual travel brochures!

A stay at Camp Forlorn, Arizona, is just as good as a Paris, France, vacation. In Paris you eat ten-course meals and stay at world-class hotels. At Camp Forlorn it's the mosquitoes that are world-class. If you don't cover up, they'll make *you* a ten-course meal!

Both Paris, France, and Camp Forlorn, Arizona, overlook water —Paris is located on the Seine river, and Camp Forlorn is on Skunk Creek. Both have famous towers—Paris's Eiffel Tower and the broken clock tower at Camp Forlorn. Best of all, admission is free to visit both places, although parking is up to $3.00 a day at Camp Forlorn.

Key Ideas
- *Comparison* shows the similarities between subjects.
- *Contrast* shows the differences between subjects.
- Sometimes both similarities and differences are used to describe one subject's relationship to another.

Try It Out Add one example of comparison and one that shows contrast to either of the paragraphs in The Writer's Eye. Use your imagination to supply the details in your sentences.

Vive la Différence! Compare and contrast your hometown with another place. Make your writing entertaining; choose a place that is wildly different from your town and find similarities between them.

*Which two places are compared and contrasted in **The Writer's Eye**? Which paragraph focuses more on comparison? Which focuses more on contrast? Can you find a sentence that describes both similarities and differences between the two subjects?*

Order of Importance

Get the Point! Learn *order of importance* and construct your arguments like a pro! That's right, with *order of importance,* you can learn how to organize supporting details, arrange facts, save your best points for last, and get maximum audience impact! Read on!

Alert! When ideas are arranged in a series within a sentence, be sure to use commas or semicolons to separate them.

The Writer's Eye Read these two versions of a film review.

The new film *Beach Commando* takes place in Texas. The star, Arnold Potato, speaks with a German accent. Get real, Arnold! Arnold stars as the 12-year-old boy who commands the famous Beach Patrol. The film is a real dud! Dressed as the 12-year-old, Arnold looks ridiculous. What 12-year-old has a mustache?

Arnold Potato stars in *Beach Commando,* the new film about a 12-year-old boy who commands the famous Beach Patrol. The film takes place in Texas, but Arnold speaks with a German accent! Even worse, Arnold looks ridiculous. What 12-year-old has a mustache? Get real, Arnold! All in all, the film is a real dud.

Key Ideas
- Use *order of importance* to arrange facts or arguments so they will have the maximum impact on your audience.
- First, decide what your key fact or argument is. Then, decide whether you want to place it first or last. Organize the other facts to support the key fact.

Try It Out Think of some imaginary details to add to either of the reviews in The Writer's Eye. Where would you place them to make the review even more persuasive?

Quick! Your assignment is to persuade a friend to see a film he or she hasn't seen before. List arguments for going to the film. Circle the key argument. Then, write a persuasive letter to your friend.

Which film review in **The Writer's Eye** *do you prefer? Which of the author's statements do you find most persuasive?*

Read "In My Spare Time" by Tamara Thomas on page 70. Which words signal the organization of ideas?

Cause and Effect

Get the Point! You wake up and see snow on the driveway. Be careful with cause and effect. Perhaps it snowed last night. Perhaps a wind blew snow from the trees or a truck accidentally dumped a load of snow. Perhaps . . .

Alert! Remember to use a semicolon before words like *therefore* and *however* in compound sentences.

The Writer's Eye Look at these two writing drafts.

A plague called *malaria* ravished the countryside. Some people got sick; some didn't. Those who didn't get malaria stayed home at night. Those who got it went out in the dark night air. It was especially bad near swamps, where the air was the dampest. The only protection against the dark air was a torch.

As time passed, people noticed things. Some people who never went out at night still got malaria. They lived near swamps. Also, when the mosquitoes were numerous, more people got malaria. When mosquito populations decreased, fewer people got the disease. Finally, all victims of malaria had at least one mosquito bite.

Key Ideas

- All *effects* are caused by something. Sometimes, though, the *cause* cannot be determined. Similarly, the full effect of a certain action may never be known.
- Causes may have multiple effects, and effects may have multiple causes. One effect may also be the cause of another.

Try It Out Make a chart listing the possible causes of malaria and the effects of damp night air and mosquitoes. Use the chart to analyze the situation presented in the paragraphs in The Writer's Eye.

The Big Chill What is the cause of the common cold or the flu? Write a report about the causes and effects of a topic you are interested in. Make sure the causes and the effects are clear.

PARTNER TALK

*What does each paragraph in **The Writer's Eye** tell you about the cause of malaria? Does either paragraph tell you in all certainty what factors cause malaria?*

Specific Nouns

Get the Point! Specific nouns get right down to business. A *bunch* of *flowers* may look pretty on the table, but a *bouquet* of *snapdragons* and *chrysanthemums* brings to mind a more specific image. Specific nouns can add a splash of color to your writing.

Alert! A noun names a person, a place, a thing, a feeling, or an idea.

The Writer's Eye Look at the draft and revision of each sentence.

I took my *pet* for a walk in the woods.
I took my *dalmatian* for a walk in the woods.

The smell of *flowers* perfumed the air.
The smell of *honeysuckle* perfumed the air.

My dog barked at a noisy *bird*.
My dog barked at a noisy *blue jay*.

Key Ideas

■ Using *specific nouns* makes your writing more interesting and helps the reader to picture exactly what you want to convey.

■ Using specific nouns can also help you to focus your thoughts and to state your ideas clearly on paper.

Try It Out What other specific nouns could you have used in The Writer's Eye sentences? Create three new sentences by substituting other specific nouns for *dalmatian, honeysuckle,* and *blue jay.*

Quick! Look at a picture in a magazine and name the first thing you see. Try to find a specific noun that identifies the object more precisely. Next, find a third noun that is even more specific. For example, the first picture you see might include *furniture.* A more specific noun is a *chair.* Finally, that chair is an *armchair.*

*Which sentences in **The Writer's Eye** use specific nouns? How do they change the sentences?*

Reread the excerpt from "A Worn Path" by Eudora Welty (page 24). How does the author's choice of nouns help to create a picture in your mind?

Vivid Verbs

Reread The Writer's Eye. Do the sentences in each pair differ from one another? Which sentences are most effective? Why?

Get the Point! Vivid verbs *command* attention. Dull verbs *snooze* on the page, but vivid verbs make sentences *ring*!

Alert! Remember that a verb is a word that expresses action or identifies the subject.

The Writer's Eye Compare these scary sentences.

We *went* into the old haunted house yesterday.
We *sneaked* into the old haunted house yesterday.

A bat *flew* down from the rafters and *scared* us.
A bat *swooped* down from the rafters and *terrified* us.

We *ran* out of there as fast as our legs could carry us.
We *dashed* out of there as fast as our legs could carry us.

Key Ideas
■ *Vivid verbs* express actions precisely and clearly.
■ Vivid verbs help to make actions come alive, helping the reader to picture exactly what's happening.

Try It Out What other verbs could you have used in the sentences in The Writer's Eye? Revise the sentences, substituting new vivid verbs for the ones that are already there.

Verb Exchange! Create a partner-story. The first player makes up the first sentence of a story. The other player repeats the first sentence but substitutes a vivid verb—and then offers the second sentence of the story. Continue taking turns substituting new vivid verbs. Then think of a believable ending to the story. Here's an example:

First player: Carlos was walking down the road.

Second player: Carlos was strolling down the road. Suddenly, he saw something he had never seen before.

Effective Adjectives and Adverbs

Get the Point! Are your adjectives *bright, shiny,* and *colorful,* or do they seem *dull, dreary,* and *dismal*? Do your adverbs make your readers sit up *sharply* and look at your work *intently,* or do they cause readers to yawn *sleepily* and *gently* shake their heads?

Alert! Remember that adjectives modify nouns, while adverbs modify verbs, adjectives, and other adverbs.

The Writer's Eye Compare these two story excerpts.

The children approached the meadow. The picnic cloth was laid out on the moss, with a basket of rolls, a bowl of salad, and a pitcher of lemonade. Blue jays sang as the children sank down to rest on the ground.

The *hot, tired* children *eagerly* approached the *fragrant, shady* meadow. The *red-and-black-checked* picnic cloth was *carefully* laid out on the *springy, green* moss, with a basket of *crusty, hot* rolls, a bowl of *crisp* salad, and an *icy* pitcher of *tart, sweet* lemonade. Blue jays sang as the children sank *slowly* down to rest on the *cool* ground.

Key Ideas

- *Adjectives* and *adverbs* can add sensory details to your writing. Sensory details refer to one or more of the five senses—sight, hearing, touch, taste, or smell.
- *Sensory words* make your writing more effective. Readers use their senses to re-create the experience you describe.

Try It Out Rewrite the first excerpt in The Writer's Eye, using adjectives and adverbs of your own. How does your choice of sensory words change the overall mood or impression of the description?

Quick! Choose a paragraph from a favorite story. Read it aloud, leaving out the adjectives and adverbs. Does the feeling change? Rewrite the paragraph, adding your own sensory words.

How are the two descriptions in **The Writer's Eye** *different? Which description seems more effective? Why?*

Effective Adjective Phrases and Adverb Phrases

Get the Point! Joanna began writing *with long, scratchy strokes.* She looked *at the bright blue ink* and laughed. Her list *of adjective and adverb phrases* would help her writing, but could she actually read her page *of smeared, messy words?*

Alert! Remember that adjective and adverb phrases are prepositional phrases. Each phrase begins with a preposition and ends with a noun or a pronoun.

The Writer's Eye These sentences are both similar and different.

The surface *of the blue lake* rippled *in the fragrant breeze.*

The surface *of the murky green lake* rippled *in the wind.*

The surface *of the choppy lake* rippled *in the snowstorm.*

Key Ideas

- An *adjective phrase* modifies a noun or a pronoun. An *adverb phrase* modifies a verb, an adjective, or another adverb.
- Adjective phrases and adverb phrases add vivid details to your writing and help to make your writing more precise.
- Use adverb phrases and adjective phrases that appeal to the five senses to add texture and depth to your writing.

Try It Out Substitute adjective and adverb phrases of your own for the description of the lake in The Writer's Eye. See if you can create a different image of the lake.

Phrase Builders! Play this game with a classmate. One player writes a simple statement using an adjective phrase or an adverb phrase. Players take turns adding phrases to make the sentence more detailed and specific. See how long and interesting a sentence you can construct before you run out of ideas.

*How do the words in italics in **The Writer's Eye** affect the mood and image of each sentence? How do the words in each phrase appeal to the reader's senses?*

Synonyms

PARTNER TALK

What do the words in italics in each sentence group in **The Writer's Eye** *have in common? How are the italicized words different?*

Get the Point! If you want to *know, understand, grasp,* or *comprehend* how using synonyms can make your writing more *interesting,* more *absorbing,* or more *entertaining,* read on!

Alert! Be careful about using too many synonyms in the same sentence. It may make your writing seem redundant.

The Writer's Eye Compare these similar sentences.

The night was *humid.*
The night was *steamy.*
The night was *sultry.*

    The musicians played *well.*
    The musicians played *superbly.*
    The musicians played *brilliantly.*

        Everyone was *pleased* with the performance.
        Everyone was *happy* with the performance.
        Everyone was *content* with the performance.

Key Ideas

■ A *synonym* is a word that has the same, or nearly the same, meaning as another word.

■ Sometimes there are subtle differences in meaning among synonyms. Choose the synonym that best expresses your meaning.

■ Synonyms are often used to avoid repeating the same word.

Try It Out What other synonyms could have been used in the sentences in The Writer's Eye? Substitute other synonyms for *humid, well,* and *pleased.* How do the new synonyms affect the meaning of the sentences?

The Same but Different! Write a brief report on a book, a movie, or a television program you've recently enjoyed. Then revise each sentence by replacing as many words as possible with synonyms. For extra fun, try it a third time. Use the Thesaurus on pages 382–397 to help you. How did your use of synonyms affect the report?

Antonyms

Get the Point! Two words that are very *different* in meaning often work well together in the *same* sentence. Do you find that *easy* or *hard* to understand? For the *long* and the *short* of it, check out antonyms. They can make your writing fun to read.

Alert! Sometimes two words have different meanings but are not antonyms. If you want to use an antonym, carefully consider the meaning of the word you select.

The Writer's Eye Read about these two seventh-graders.

> Carla was the *loudest* person in the class, and Rosa was the *quietest*. Rosa was sometimes *reluctant* to speak up, but Carla was always *eager* to voice her opinions. Although the girls sometimes acted like *worst enemies,* they were really *best friends*.

Key Ideas
- *Antonyms* are words with opposite meanings.
- You can use antonyms to contrast ideas in your writing.

Try It Out Rewrite the sentences in The Writer's Eye. Replace the antonyms with different pairs of antonyms. Try to find the wildest contrasts that you can. Then think about any two people you know who have very different personalities. Write an entertaining paragraph which compares and contrasts the two. You may want to use exaggeration. Let your imagination run free!

Quick! Think of two people you know well or create two fantasy characters in your mind. Then write a few sentences using antonyms to compare and contrast the two characters. Here is an example:

> Alice has curly hair, but Sam's hair is straight.
> Alice loves beets, and Sam hates them.

PARTNER
TALK

*How are antonyms used in each sentence in **The Writer's Eye**? What effect can the use of antonyms have on a piece of writing?*

Denotation and Connotation

Get the Point! What makes one person's writing *powerful* while another's is only *strong* and a third person's is *overwhelming*? The denotation may be similar while the connotation is not.

Alert! A word may have a connotation that is different from its exact definition. Use a dictionary to check a word's meaning.

The Writer's Eye Compare these cool comparisons.

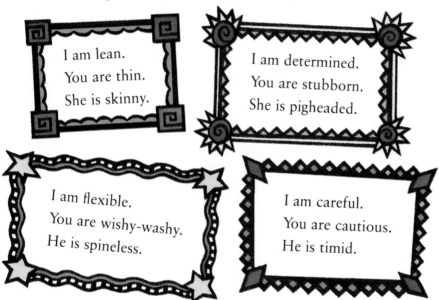

I am lean.
You are thin.
She is skinny.

I am determined.
You are stubborn.
She is pigheaded.

I am flexible.
You are wishy-washy.
He is spineless.

I am careful.
You are cautious.
He is timid.

*Do the three sentences in each group in **The Writer's Eye** mean the same thing, or are their meanings different? Which person has the best qualities: he, she, you, or I? Which people have the worst qualities? How do you know?*

Key Ideas

- The *denotation* of a word is its exact definition—the thing it *denotes,* or refers to.
- The *connotation* of a word is the impression it conveys—the image it *connotes,* or suggests.
- Words can have similar meanings and yet convey very different thoughts, feelings, images, or opinions.

Try It Out Write a few of your own I-you-she-he sentences like those in The Writer's Eye. Then share them with a partner.

Connotations Unlimited Write a description of a place in which you use words with positive connotations. Rewrite the piece, replacing the words with positive connotations with synonyms that have negative connotations. How do the pieces compare?

Homophones

*How are the words in italics in **The Writer's Eye** alike? How are they different? What can happen if they get mixed up?*

Get the Point! Are you a person *who's* sometimes confused by words that sound alike but *whose* meanings are different? Homophones are easy to understand if *you're* willing to take *your* time.

Alert! Be especially careful not to spell one homophone when you mean to use another. Check a dictionary when in doubt.

The Writer's Eye Compare these sound-alike sentences.

Are you coming to the *fair* with us?
Do you have the *fare* for the bus?

My father was going to drive us, but the car had *brake* trouble.
I wonder what will *break* next?

I rode a *horse* at the fair last year.
I shouted until my voice was *hoarse*.

Key Ideas

- *Homophones* are words that sound alike but have different spellings and different meanings.
- A dictionary can help you spell a homophone correctly.

Reread the excerpt from Always to Remember by Brent Ashabranner (page 55). What homophones do you know for the words hangar and site? If you were listening to a reading of this excerpt, how would you understand the author's meaning?

Try It Out Think of some other words that sound alike but have different meanings. Then write some sentences using your homophone pairs. For example:

The wind blew across the blue lake.

Sound Versus Sense! Write a humorous dialog between two characters who confuse each other by using homophones. Try to use several pairs of homophones. Don't be afraid to get silly. Homophones can be a lot of fun! Here is an example:

Edna: I went to a bridal party last week.

Fred: A bridle party? Were you on a horse?

Edna: Why would I be hoarse?

Homographs

Get the Point! Homographs are easy to confuse, but don't worry. You should be *close* to clarity by the *close* of this lesson, and you'll get *wind* of the differences by the time this lesson starts to *wind* down.

Alert! A dictionary can usually help you to determine the correct pronunciation of a homograph.

The Writer's Eye Compare these slippery sentences.

> I bought a *pound* of potato salad.
> I ran so fast my heart started to *pound*.
>
> Alma described the *content* of the story.
> Are you *content* with the results of your efforts?
>
> I *saw* the workers repairing the building.
> They used a *saw* to cut the lumber.

Key Ideas

- *Homographs* are words that are spelled the same but have different meanings and sometimes different pronunciations.
- You can usually tell the correct meaning of a homograph by the context in which it appears.

Try It Out Think of several homograph pairs. See if you can write a few sentences using the homographs. For example:

I couldn't lead my horse over the huge lead pipe.

Quick! List as many homograph pairs and triplets as you can. Then write a nonsense poem with your homographs. Try to make your poem as entertaining as possible. Then have a friend read your poem out loud. Were the homographs pronounced the way you intended them to be?

*How are the words in italics in each pair of **The Writer's Eye** sentences the same? How are they different? How can you tell what the italicized words really mean?*

Multiple Meanings

Get the Point! Once you get to the *heart* of the matter, do you also find blood and arteries? When you feel *funny,* do you tell jokes or just sit and rest awhile? Multiple meanings can be a lot of fun!

Alert! Use your dictionary to double-check the spelling of a word with multiple meanings.

The Writer's Eye Compare these shifty sentences.

We went for a two-mile *run.*
I had a *run* in my stocking.
Our team scored a *run* in the last inning.

She has a good *eye* for judging distances.
He poked the thread through the *eye* of the needle.
Winds whirled around the *eye* of the hurricane.

Summer ended, and *fall* began.
The leaves began to *fall* off the trees.
I saw his face *fall* when he heard the bad news.

Key Ideas

- Many words have *more than one meaning*.
- You can usually tell which meaning the writer had in mind by checking the context in which the word is used.
- When you use a word with more than one meaning in your writing, make sure your meaning is clear from the context.

*How are the words in italics in each group of sentences in **The Writer's Eye** alike? How are they different? How can you tell the meaning of the words in italics?*

Try It Out Can you think of any other meanings for the words in italics in The Writer's Eye? Make up at least one sentence of your own using a different meaning for one of these words.

It's a Funny World! When a joke takes advantage of a word's double meaning, it's called a *pun.* Write about someone's adventures in a funny world. For example, a person wonders if a road is safe—and sees a huge safe come hurtling through the sky!

Prefixes

Get the Point! Question: What do a university, a submarine, a foreword, and an intergalactic spaceship all have in common? Answer: They all begin with prefixes!

Alert! Adding a prefix to a word sometimes changes its spelling.

The Writer's Eye Look at these examples of words with prefixes.

Prefix	Meanings	Examples
uni-	one	unicycle, universe
fore-	to the front	foreword, forearm
inter-	between	intermission, intermediate
micro-	small	microscopic, microorganism
anti-	opposed to	antifreeze, antidote
over-	too much, above, on top	overload, overcoat
out-	outside, more than	outcry, outshine

Key Ideas

- A *prefix* is a word part added at the beginning of a word. Each prefix has a meaning that affects the meaning of the word to which it's added.

- Some common prefixes are *a-, ab-, ad-, an-, ante-, be-, co-, contra-, en-, im-, macro-,* and *tele-.*

- Learning about prefixes and their meanings can expand your vocabulary by helping you to figure out the meaning of new words.

Try It Out Think about how the prefixes affect the meanings of the words in The Writer's Eye. For example, *inter-,* which means "between," is part of *intermission,* the time between two parts of a play. Try to deduce the definitions of a few words in The Writer's Eye. Then check with a dictionary.

Shifting Prefixes Play this game with a partner. The first player thinks of a word with a prefix. The second player must think of another word starting with the same prefix. Continue until someone draws a blank. Start again with a new word.

What does each group of words in **The Writer's Eye** *have in common? What other words can you think of that have those prefixes?*

Suffixes

Get the Point! Luisa is an *optimist* who's always looking *forward* to more *happiness* and *celebration*. Her *optimistic* attitude has often helped her out of a difficult position.

Alert! Adding a suffix to a word can change what part of speech it is. Be sure you are using each word with a suffix correctly.

The Writer's Eye Look at these examples of words with suffixes.

Suffix	Meanings	Examples
-ity	the state, condition, or quality of	inferiority, formality
-less	lacking, without	meaningless, loveless
-ness	the quality of	sadness, peacefulness
-ion	the action of, state of being	incubation, recognition
-ward	in the direction of	forward, backward

Key Ideas

- A *suffix* is a word part added to the end of a word. Each suffix has a meaning that affects the meaning of the word to which it's added.
- Some common suffixes are *-ant, -ent, -ance, -ence, -ation, -ten, -eous, -ous, -ious, -ie, -ible, -hood, -ian, -ic, -ish, -ist, -ure, -gram, -graph, -phone,* and *-some*.
- Learning about suffixes and their meanings can expand your vocabulary by helping you to use new words.

Try It Out How many more words can you think of using the suffixes in The Writer's Eye? Write a list as quickly as you can. Then check your list. If you're not sure whether a word you listed is really a word or whether you've spelled it correctly, look it up in a dictionary.

Happy Endings! Write a word, such as *happy*. Challenge a partner to change the word by adding a suffix and to use the new word in a sentence. For example, *Money doesn't bring happiness*. Take turns challenging each other to create new sentences.

PARTNER TALK

Look again at the suffixes in The Writer's Eye. What words can you think of that have different suffixes?

Base Words and Roots

Get the Point! You don't have to be a college *soph*omore or a *so-ph*isticated student of philo*soph*y to understand how words are put together. Base words and roots are often called the building blocks of our language. You can use them to build your own vocabulary.

Alert! If you know how to spell a base word or root, you can usually count on its being spelled the same way in every word of which it is a part. Sometimes the spelling changes. Check your dictionary.

The Writer's Eye Read these word cousins.

manicure, manipulate, manuscript, manual, manage
contract, tractor, extract
doctor, indoctrinate, document
sympathy, telepathy, pathology
paid, repaid, unpaid, underpaid, overpaid

Key Ideas

- A *base word* is a word that can be combined with prefixes and suffixes to form other words. A base word can also stand on its own as a word.

- A *root* is a part of a word used to form other words. A root cannot stand alone as a word.

- Expand your vocabulary by recognizing how base words and roots combine with prefixes and suffixes to form other words.

Try It Out Use a dictionary to look up any unfamiliar words and to figure out the roots or base words of the words in The Writer's Eye. For example, the words in the first group all contain *man,* from the Latin *manus,* meaning "hand." Can you see how the words in that cluster relate to hands?

Word Chains Work with a partner to list words based on one base word or root. One of you starts by naming a word. The other names another word with the same base word or root. Keep taking turns until neither of you can think of any more words. Then start again.

PARTNER TALK

How are the words in each group in **The Writer's Eye** *similar? How can you figure out the meanings of any unfamiliar words?*

Coined Words

Get the Point! The next time you ride an *escalator,* visit the *laundromat,* or watch a *videocassette,* you might pause to consider how new words enter the constantly changing English language.

Alert! Some coined words are compound words, and some are shortened forms of longer words. Check the spelling of coined words.

The Writer's Eye Read these up-to-date sentences.

Tyrone watched the *newscast* on television.
The surgeon used a *laser* to perform the operation.
After school, Cara took a *bus* to the park.
The *motel* was located near the highway.

Key Ideas

■ The English language is continually growing and changing. New words are formed in many different ways. The word *scuba* came from the acronym for *self-contained underwater breathing apparatus.*

■ *Coined words* are words that have been invented to describe a new idea or thing. The words *rayon* and *nylon* were invented to identify new products.

■ *Clipped words* are shortened forms of longer words. *Gymnasium,* for example, was clipped to form *gym.*

■ *Blends* are a type of coined words formed from parts of other words. For example, *smog* is a blend of *smoke* and *fog.*

Try It Out Use the dictionary to look up the words in italics in The Writer's Eye. What were their origins? Try to think of other words that were coined in similar ways.

Quick! Work with two or three classmates to coin some original words. Imagine a brand-new invention that you would like to see developed. Then write a description of your invention.

Do you think any of the words in italics in **The Writer's Eye** *existed a hundred years ago? Where do new words come from? How do new words become part of our language?*

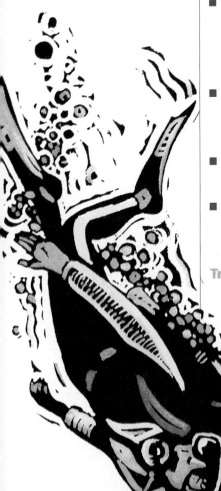

Colloquialisms

Get the Point! "Learning about colloquialisms often seems very difficult," said Michael.

"Yeah, learning about the way people really talk can *get on my nerves*," Mike agreed.

"However, it is important to persevere," said Michael. "That is the way to succeed."

"You bet!" Mike agreed. "The big thing is to *stick with it*. That's how to *make it*."

Alert! Remember to use quotation marks when punctuating direct quotes.

The Writer's Eye Compare these scintillating sentences.

I saw a program on television about a diner.
I saw a TV show about a *greasy spoon*.

Do you know that Anthony is still preparing for the test?
Guess what? Tony is still *cramming for the exam*!

She was irritated by the subject of their questions.
She was *fed up* with their *line of questioning*.

*How do the sentences in **The Writer's Eye** differ? How are they the same? What colloquialisms are used in your community?*

Key Ideas

- *Colloquialisms* are words and expressions that are considered standard, but informal, English.
- Colloquialisms are colorful words or phrases commonly used in informal speech and in informal writing, such as personal letters.

Try It Out Write another couple of lines of dialog for Michael and Mike. Make sure the two of them say the same thing, except that Michael speaks formally and Mike uses colloquialisms.

Quick! Summarize the plot of a favorite movie exactly as you would if you were talking to your best friend on the telephone. Use colloquialisms to express your views.

Jargon, Slang, and Dialect

Get the Point! "Our skills objective for this unit is to understand the functional implementation of jargon," said Jermaine.

"That's cool," responded Sam. He nodded, "We've got to get the word on slang, right?"

"Why, I just don't know what y'all are going on about," said Delia. "I surely thought we were going to be studying dialect."

Alert! Be sure to spell jargon, slang, and dialect correctly so that your reader can understand your intention.

The Writer's Eye Look at these fascinating groups of words.

skills level	What's happening?	stoop
employability	in the know	rap
hyperactive	get with it	sack

Key Ideas

- *Jargon* is the specialized language of a particular group or profession. Avoid using jargon when addressing an audience that is not in that field.
- *Slang* is very informal language that tends to change quickly with the times. Slang is mainly used in informal speech.
- *Dialect* is the language and pronunciation used by people from a particular place or cultural background.

Try It Out Add two or three words of your own to each list in The Writer's Eye. Use one or two words from each list in a sentence.

Radio Station WJSD Pretend that you work for a radio station that only broadcasts in jargon, slang, or dialect. Write an advertisement, a news report, or a weather report in jargon, slang, or dialect. Be as realistic as possible to avoid stereotyping regions, cultures, and peoples. Share your broadcasts with the class.

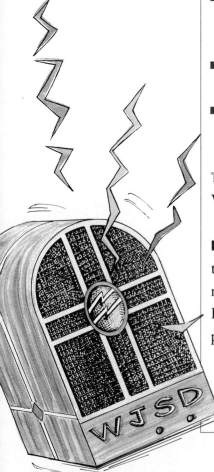

What do the words in each column in **The Writer's Eye** *have in common? Have you ever read or used any of these terms? Where would you be likely to see or hear them?*

Idioms

Get the Point! Do politicians have to wear sneakers when they *run for office?* Do you have to run fast to *catch a cold?* Are you feeling a little *at sea?* When you *get a handle on* idioms, you'll be *in on the joke.* Read on.

Alert! Getting even one word wrong can turn an idiom into nonsense. Make sure you get your idioms exactly right!

The Writer's Eye Read these snappy sentences.

I *ran across* an old friend yesterday.
We *hit it off* right away.
She seemed to be a little too *full of herself.*
I told her not to *lose her head.*
A *slip of the tongue* almost gave me away.

Key Ideas

- An *idiom* is an expression whose meaning cannot be grasped from the meaning of the individual words composing it.
- Many idioms are not slang or colloquialisms but are considered part of standard English and perfectly appropriate for formal writing. Other idioms are considered more appropriate for informal speech and writing.

Try It Out Add two or three sentences with idioms to the list in The Writer's Eye. Would you use these expressions in formal writing? Why or why not?

Quick! Work with two or three classmates. Make a list of idioms. Then write a humorous story about a robot that always takes idioms literally. For example, what would such a robot do if you said, "Step on it!" or "Shake a leg"?

What possible double meanings can you find in the words in italics in **The Writer's Eye?** *How do you know whether to take the phrases literally or as idioms?*

Rhythm and Rhyme

How do rhythm and rhyme make the poems in **The Writer's Eye** fun to read? Try reading the poems in different ways. How does the rhythm of your reading affect the way the words rhyme?

Get the Point!

Rhythm and rhyme
Are something to remember.
The two go together
Like *No* and *vember*.

Like *Satur* and *day,*
Like *lemon* and *lime,*
Like *Milky* and *Way,*
It's rhythm and rhyme.

You can dance to rhythm
'Cause it's got a good beat.
It makes you want to move
And get off your feet.

You can climb on a rhyme,
Even one that sounds dumb,
'Cause it sticks to your mind
Like a piece of bubble gum.

Alert! Punctuation and capitalization may vary in poetry. Choose your own style—and then be consistent!

The Writer's Eye Read these unusual pieces of poetry.

Is our reliance
On Electronics, Technology,
And Science
Simply a phase?

For a grilled cheese sandwich
It takes about a minute,
Depending how it's made
And exactly what's in it.

Key Ideas

- *Rhythm* is the beat of the poem or the pattern of its sounds. This pattern is also called meter.
- *Rhyme* is the effect of certain words ending in the same sound.
- To be effective, rhymes must fit in with a poem's overall rhythm.

Try It Out Add a few lines or a verse to either of the poems in The Writer's Eye. Don't worry about meaning. Just be faithful to the rhythm and rhyme scheme that is already established.

A Lot of Nonsense With a partner, write a nonsense poem—a poem with rhythm, rhyme, and a lot of nonsense words. Just start a rhyme and rhythm scheme and fill it in with nonsense. If you get stuck, remember, you can always just invent a new nonsense word.

Rhyming Patterns

Get the Point!

The King of Silesia had a strange dream
That took place inside a rhyming scheme.
Within the dream they made it a crime
To utter a statement that wasn't a rhyme.

> The king arose and said, "I protest!"
> His minister said, "It's all for the best."
> The king said, "This is quite outrageous."
> "Yes," came the answer, "and it may be contagious."

Alert! Remember to use quotation marks for direct quotes.

The Writer's Eye The story of the King of Silesia continues.

The king said, "There must be some way to escape,"
So they pushed rewind and played back the tape.
Amazed that a dream could be rewound,
The king then announced that he had found

That what they had to do to stop all the rhyming—
if they really wanted to break the spell—
Was to disrupt the pattern and spoil its timing,
And if they did so, then all would be well.

Key Idea

■ Poems may have *rhyming patterns*. The first line is given a letter. Each line that rhymes with it is given the same letter. The first line that doesn't rhyme with it is assigned a new letter, and so on. There are any number of rhyming patterns possible. In The Writer's Eye, the rhyme scheme in the first stanza is *a-a-b-b* and in the second is *a-b-a-b*.

Try It Out Write another verse for the poem in The Writer's Eye. Follow one of the rhyming patterns already used in the poem.

The King and I With a small group, write a poem about the Queen of Silesia. Talk about an idea and brainstorm the poem. Each person adds one line to the poem. A person can revise an earlier line.

*What rhyming patterns does the poem in **Get the Point!** follow? Use letters (a, b, and so on) to describe the rhyming pattern. If you were the king, how would you choose to disrupt the rhyming pattern of the poem?*

Take another look at the poem by Jesse Russon on page 40. How would you describe the rhyming pattern of this poem?

Repetition and Alliteration

Get the Point!
Repetition repeats the words
Again and again, again and again.
Alliteration repeats the letter
Neatly, nicely, now and then.

Alert! Alliterative words begin with the same sounds but not necessarily the same letters. For example *kn, gn,* and *n* make the *n* sound. Use a dictionary to check the spelling of alliterative words.

The Writer's Eye Read these menus.

◆ CHICK CHILSON'S CHICKEN, CHIP, AND CHILI-CHEESE CHOWDER HOUSE
◆ CHICK'S CHUNKY CHILI-CHEESE CHOWDER • • • • • • • • $ 3.95
◆ CHICK'S CHICKEN, CHICKEN, AND MORE CHICKEN DINNER • • • $ 7.95

CHICK'S IS CHEAP! CHEAP! CHEAP!

◆ AL CHILSON'S FRIED CHICKEN, FRENCH-FRY, AND CHOWDER HOUSE
◆ AL'S SUPER-THICK CHILI WITH CHEESE • • • • • • • $ 3.95
◆ AL'S ALL-YOU-CAN-EAT CHICKEN DINNER • • • • • • • • • $ 7.95

AL'S WILL SAVE YOU MONEY!

PARTNER TALK

Which menu in The Writer's Eye uses alliteration and repetition? How does this menu help the owner get his message out to his customers?

Key Ideas

- *Alliteration* is the repetition of the same initial sound, usually of a consonant, in a series of words. *Repetition* involves repeating words, phrases, or even whole lines.
- Both devices make writing musical and catchy, and they help the piece to stand out in the reader's mind.

Try It Out Add a few dishes to Chick Chilson's menu in The Writer's Eye. Use alliteration and repetition.

Quick! Write an ad for a product—real or imaginary—of your own choosing. Drive home your message by using alliteration and repetition.

Onomatopoeia

Get the Point! The world *hums* with the sound of onomatopoeia. Just look outside your window. Bees *buzz*. A squirrel *crunches* a nut. A dog *yawns*. A cat *purrs*. The dog spots the cat and *zips* after it.

Alert! Many onomatopoeic words have standard spellings. Check your dictionary before inventing an onomatopoeic word.

The Writer's Eye Read these musical paragraphs.

The tugboat chugged across the bay. Above, gulls soared and dove, waiting for garbage time. Finally, the mate appeared. Clang! went the metal garbage can. Splash! went the leftover food into the water. Whoosh! came the gulls, swooping and swerving in the churning wake of the boat, picking and pecking at their tasty plunder.

The tugboat cruised across the bay. Above, gulls flew around, waiting for garbage time. Finally, the mate appeared. She opened the metal can with the day's leftover food and dropped it into the water. The gulls came in fast, attacking the garbage in the wake of the boat. They battled each other for their tasty plunder.

Key Idea

■ *Onomatopoeia* is the use of words that sound like the thing they describe. For example, the word *ring* sounds a bit like a bell.

Try It Out Write a few sentences that continue the description of the tugboat scene in The Writer's Eye. For example, try to describe sounds made by foghorns and by the birds themselves. Reread your paragraph. Did you find yourself using onomatopoeia?

Quick! Invent some onomatopoetic words of your own to describe these sounds:
- drinking the last drops of a milkshake through a straw
- a dot-matrix printer for a computer printing a draft
- a person in high heels running across a tile floor

*Which paragraph in **The Writer's Eye** seems more colorful? Which gives you a more vivid picture of the scene being described? Find each example of onomatopoeia in the paragraphs. How does onomatopoeia make the writing seem more lively?*

Imagery

Get the Point! Imagery is the visual portion of what you write—the pictures, the action, the video. With imagery, your words come alive, leap off the page, and blossom like bright flowers for your readers.

Alert! When using more than one adjective to describe an image, be sure to separate the adjectives with commas whenever necessary.

The Writer's Eye Read these imagined paragraphs.

At World Park, an exact replica of the globe, I went for a run. I went halfway through the entire park. I started in the middle and hopped over some rocks to a sandy area that was very hot. From there I went through a woods, swam across a large pool of water, and came up on the other side of the park. As I looked around, I was much bigger than the things on the ground. It felt strange to be so big and out-of-place.

At World Park, an exact replica of the globe, I ran halfway around the world! I started in Italy, which was about the size of a boot-shaped bedroom. I hopped over some islands no bigger than boulders to the blazing sands of Egypt. I trudged over the African underbrush and swam across the Atlantic Ocean, coming up in New York City. As I towered over the tiny skyscrapers, I suddenly knew how King Kong must have felt.

Key Idea

- *Imagery* is the use of words to create pictures, or images, in the reader's mind.

Try It Out Write a few sentences that add to one of the descriptions of World Park in The Writer's Eye. Try to create vivid visual images with the sentences you write.

Quick! What part of the world would you visit if you could go to World Park? Write about an adventure you might have there. Illustrate your adventure and share it with a classmate.

PARTNER TALK

What vivid pictures are created in the paragraphs in The Writer's Eye?

Personification and Hyperbole

Get the Point! Personification has a mind of its own. If it starts to exaggerate, you can't stop it. Personification does what it wants.

Alert! Decide whether the image you are using to personify something is a *he,* a *she,* an *it,* or a *they.* Then be consistent!

The Writer's Eye Read these two accounts of a lawn mower experience.

I take care of my lawn mower. I oil and sharpen it. Every night I store it in a clean garage. So how can I explain why it suddenly broke down for no apparent reason? It sputtered and wouldn't start. I almost purchased a new ride-around model like the big one my neighbors bought, when suddenly my mower started working again. I can't explain it.

I'm good to Fritz, my lawn mower. I oil and sharpen him. Every night I put him to bed in a cozy garage. Then the neighbors bought a new MXT4 ride-around mower. Fritz went on strike! I pulled his rope about five hundred times, but he just coughed. It stayed this way until the MXT4 broke. Suddenly, Fritz was better.

Key Ideas

■ *Personification* is a comparison in which human traits are given to objects, ideas, or animals.

■ *Hyperbole* is exaggeration. Writers use hyperbole to stretch the truth about their subjects in order to entertain their audiences.

Try It Out If Fritz had remained on strike, what tactics might the narrator have used to get him back to work? Write a few suggestions. Don't worry if they are far-fetched.

Frankenstein Revisited Are there any machines or animals in your life that seem almost human? Write a character sketch of one. Then show it to some classmates. Give the object or animal a name. If it already has a name, think of a title, such as Hector the Protector.

*Which paragraph in **The Writer's Eye** is more fun to read? What makes it more fun? What things is the lawn mower compared to? How would you describe its personality? What exaggerations can you find in these paragraphs? By how much do they exaggerate?*

Compare "The North Wind and the Sun" from Aesop's Fables (page 71) to "The City Is So Big" by Richard García (page 25). How does each author use personification?

Simile and Metaphor

Get the Point!

For similes and metaphors
Here's the basic scoop,
Using a simple example
Of creamy mushroom soup.

For a simile you could say:
"This soup is just like cream."
A metaphor could change it to
"This soup is just a dream."

Alert! Remember that when the word *like* is followed by a pronoun, use *me, her, him, us,* or *them.*

The Writer's Eye Read these two versions of a personal essay.

> Before the pancake-eating contest, I was very hungry. I told myself to try to eat as much as I could. My sixth pancake didn't taste so good. My tenth pancake tasted even worse. My fifteenth and twentieth pancakes tasted worse yet. I stopped at twenty-two.

> Before the pancake-eating contest, I was hungry as a bear. "I'm an eating machine," I told myself. After six pancakes, the machine clogged. My tenth pancake tasted like starch; my fifteenth like sand; my twentieth like a shag rug. I stopped at twenty-two.

Key Ideas

- A *simile* uses the word *like* or *as* to compare one thing (person, animal, idea, and so on) to another.
- A *metaphor* is a comparison in which one of two things is said to be the other.

Try It Out Which paragraph in The Writer's Eye did you enjoy reading more? Add two sentences to the paragraph, using a simile and a metaphor.

Simile Fever Play Simile Fever with a few friends. Have each player write the beginning of a simile on a card, for example, *The first day of school is like* . . . Mix the cards. Each player takes a turn picking a card. Players have two minutes to complete the simile out loud.

*Which paragraph in **The Writer's Eye** gives you a more distinct picture of the pancake-eating contest? Find all the similes and metaphors in the paragraphs. What two things are being compared in each simile or metaphor?*

Read the excerpt from Sweetwater by Laurence Yep (page 25). Why do you think the author chose to compare eyes and stars?

Formal and Informal Language

Get the Point! Formal language is like a black-tie affair: polite and sometimes a little stuffy. Informal language is like getting together with friends: cool and easy, casual and breezy.

Alert! Remember to use formal language in a business letter.

The Writer's Eye Read these excerpts from two different letters.

Dear Ms. Merola:

Your assistant, Jeff Omache, told me that you often speak at schools. I would like to invite you to speak to the Jasper Junior High newspaper staff about your experiences in the newspaper world. Please let me know if this is possible. We look forward to seeing you.

Dear Jeff,

Thanks a zillion for telling me about Monica Merola. She's the best, you know. She's been my idol since fifth grade. Please encourage her to come. Use your charm! And remember, I owe you one.

Key Ideas

- *Formal language* is appropriate in formal situations, such as when writing business letters, job applications, and letters to people you don't know. Formal language is polite in tone and correct in grammar. Avoid using slang. You want to make the best impression possible.
- *Informal language* is reserved for people you know. Here, you can loosen up your language and say what you really mean.

Try It Out Write a P.S., a postscript, for either of the letters in The Writer's Eye. Be sure to be faithful to the tone of the letter.

Quick! Think about the most recent school holiday. How did you spend your time? Write an informal letter to a friend about your experiences. Then share your letter with a classmate.

PARTNER TALK

*Compare the tones set in the two **The Writer's Eye** letter excerpts. How do they differ? Can you explain why the letters are written in different styles?*

Point of View

*Which paragraph in **The Writer's Eye** is written from the first-person point of view? the limited third-person point of view? the all-knowing third-person point of view? What is the relationship of each narrator to the action?*

Get the Point! Different narrators can tell the same story in different ways, depending on their points of view. The observer has one truth to tell, and the person being observed may have a different truth. Which is the real truth? It depends on your point of view.

Alert! First-person narrative uses quotation marks only for actual dialog, not for thoughts that the narrator shares with the reader.

The Writer's Eye Read these sporty paragraphs.

Gina Stein felt great. Boom! went her serve. Whack! went her forehand. Her usually unreliable backhand was giving her opponent a fit. Maggie Curtis wondered what she was doing wrong.

I can't believe it. The one match I thought would be easy is against Gina, and Gina's on fire. She can't miss. It's a nightmare!

Stein and Curtis played a spirited tennis match. The key seemed to be Stein's backhand, knocking in winners from every angle.

Key Ideas

- From the *first-person point of view,* the reader sees and knows only what one person sees and knows. *I* is used to tell the story.
- With the *third-person limited point of view,* a narrator tells the story through a character, but the character is referred to using the pronouns *he* or *she.* This point of view is limited to what that character experiences.
- The *third-person omniscient point of view* is told by an all-knowing narrator, who knows the thoughts and feelings of all the characters. *He* and *she* are used.

Read the excerpt from The Tosa Diary by Ki no Tsurayuki on page 15. Which point of view has the author used? Do you think it's the most effective choice?

Try It Out Add a few sentences to a paragraph in The Writer's Eye. Be consistent with the point of view established by the narrator.

Quick! Describe a sporting event you have been involved in, from your own point of view, the point of view of your opponent, and the point of view of a sportswriter who covered the event.

Mood

Get the Point! Mood is the feeling that flows beneath the surface. Mood affects how characters think and what they do and say. Mood also affects the audience reaction and involvement in a piece.

Alert! Remember that using synonyms throughout a paragraph can help reinforce a particular mood.

The Writer's Eye Read these descriptions.

As Dane settled in the hammock, she smelled smoke and smiled. It was a wonderful smell—burning hickory on an open fire. Perhaps the guys were cooking something. Who knew—maybe they'd even caught some salmon. Dane sighed sleepily as she thought of how good that would taste.

As Roger came to the clearing, the smell of hickory smoke entered his nostrils. "Doggone it," he muttered. He needed one more shot of the grizzly with a wide-angle lens. Smoke meant people, and grizzlies avoided people. The whole project might be ruined.

Key Ideas
- *Mood* is a feeling that exists beneath the surface of a story.
- Different moods include happy, sad, gloomy, tense, silly, spooky, unsettled, and contented.
- Word choice, imagery, similes, metaphors, and rhythm all help to create mood in a piece of writing.

Try It Out Think of a sentence or two that would add to the mood of either paragraph in The Writer's Eye. For example, you could describe Roger's first encounter with the bear. Be sure the sentences you add are in keeping with the mood of the paragraph.

Mood Piece Look through magazines for a photograph that captures a mood for you. Write a poem about your feelings. Does the scene conjure up a particular mood? What memories does it provoke? What action can you imagine taking place here?

*How would you describe the mood of each paragraph in **The Writer's Eye**? What event or events occurred to establish this mood?*

Character Sketch

My Friend Ward

From head to toe, my friend Ward is one of the most amazing people I know. He grows his red hair long and ties it back behind his neck. That way you can really see his mischievous eyes, which usually make him look like he's thinking up a new practical joke. He probably is. I still remember the time he convinced me that I could grow a tree by planting a clothespin. He doesn't laugh when he tricks you. He just smiles his signature smile, which is sort of a crooked cross between a smirk and a grin.

His neck and shoulders are impressively muscular. They got that way from practicing for his races. He competes every year in the local Special Olympics wheelchair races. Last year he won a silver medal. This year he wants to win gold, so he's practicing every day. During a race, his hands move so fast on the rims of his wheelchair that they practically disappear.

His legs are less developed than his upper body. He lost the use of them after an auto accident when he was seven. At first, he had quite a struggle to learn how to live without using his legs. Now he says that he just thinks of the wheels on his chair as his legs. They let him do everything he wants. He likes to keep his chair in tip-top condition, so it usually gleams as he glides to classes. It's extra quiet. He sometimes sneaks up behind me, and I don't even know he's there until he blows his horn. It makes me jump, but I'm always happy to see my friend Ward.

This writer used a poem to express an intense personal feeling.

The writer uses a metaphor to describe the brain.

Vivid and expressive words help the reader understand how the writer feels.

Stage Fright

I'm backstage waiting for the play to start.
I've memorized the lines I need to know.
In just a minute I'll begin my part
The lights will rise and we'll begin our show.

I've practiced till I know it all by heart
The words, the moves, the gestures and the cues
So why is it when we're gonna start
My brain feels like it blew its only fuse?

There's nothing else that makes me feel this way —
Excited, nervous, worried, and extreme.
I'd almost like to scream and run away.
So I could just relax and blow off steam.

But then the lights come up and I go on
And the pounding in my heart becomes a song.

A Lakota Nation Game

"Stop" is a dance-step game originally played by Native American children of the Lakota nation. The game is easy to organize, and it needs little preparation and few materials. It can be played in large or small groups and by people of all ages.

To play, you will need one or more drums. If a ready-made drum is not available, you can easily make one. Find a large, empty aluminum can or any large cylinder, like an oatmeal container, and make sure one end is open. Turn the cylinder upside down, and you have your drum. You can also use an upside-down pail. Cans and pails of different sizes will make different musical tones when struck with your hand: the greater number of different sounds, the more interesting the game.

Gather together the game players and choose one player to beat the drums. The drummer creates a steady rhythm, fast or slow, and all the other players must dance or perform exaggerated leg and arm movements to the beat of the music. At any moment the drummer may suddenly stop beating the drums. When this happens, all the dancers must "freeze" positions. Those who cannot hold their positions must sit down, and they are eliminated from the game. The drummer resumes drumming the beat, and the dancing continues. The last dancer left standing wins the game and becomes the next drummer.

Essay

An Ideal Choice

I believe that the old schoolhouse should become our town's first shelter for the homeless and needy.

The need for such a shelter in Monte Sereno is obvious. A recent article in the <u>Monte Sereno Gazette</u> reported a steady decline in affordable housing in town. Some people are having a hard time making ends meet. No one should have to live in the park.

The old schoolhouse is an ideal choice for the shelter. It has not been used since Pony Express School was built 13 years ago. It is a solid brick building, needing little in the way of repairs. It also has a kitchen area where hot meals can be made and a small cafeteria for eating. Shower facilities are available in the gym locker rooms.

The project might be a good way to bring together the townspeople for a cause that is worthy. It is important to acknowledge that we are "our brother's keeper."

The writer has stated a point of view in the first paragraph.

This writer seeks to persuade others to share his point of view.

The writer concludes with an appeal to the reader's ethics.

Story

This writer wanted to convey a mood of mystery at the beginning of the story.

This writer has used colorful and descriptive language.

The writer makes her characters clear to the reader.

The writer concludes the story with a twist.

Only a Shadow?

Elena and Pilar carefully checked their scuba gear, and then, in coordinated dives from the deck of the *Explorer,* entered the warm, clear, Caribbean waters. The twins' aunt, Dr. Marisa Salazar, headed a team of marine biologists who were studying coral in the area. Both of the sisters considered themselves lucky to be taken on the expedition by their aunt. It was a team rule to dive with at least one partner, so the twins usually went diving together.

After descending about 80 feet, Elena and Pilar suddenly saw the remains of a sunken ship. Pilar waved to Elena and indicated that she wanted to take a closer look. Together they swam up to a broken and jagged porthole and gazed into a cabin of the ship. There, on a rotted wooden table, sat an ancient, crumbling treasure chest filled with what looked like sparkling gold coins.

Although they were excited, Pilar and Elena ascended slowly, since they knew it would be dangerous to return to the surface too quickly. They called to their aunt, who stood on the deck ready to dive. "Tía Marisa, Tía Marisa, you must follow us! We've found a sunken treasure."

"Calm down, you two," answered Dr. Salazar. "Rest for a few minutes, and then I'll follow you." Soon all three divers returned to the sunken ship. It looked exactly the same, but the treasure chest was gone.

When they had returned to the deck of the *Explorer,* Dr. Salazar said, "Don't feel too bad. I know you both think you saw a treasure chest, but it was probably just a shadow caused by your torch lights. Now, stop thinking about imaginary treasure and concentrate on our scientific work."

"Okay, Tía Marisa," agreed Elena. "Your explanation sounds reasonable. Only, how do you explain this?" Just then Pilar held out in her hand the one shiny gold Spanish coin she had taken from the chest on their first dive.

Business Letter

3675 Rossen Street ◄ Heading
Caxton, Arizona 83269
March 15, 1993

Ms. Alison Wagner ◄ Inside Address
Superintendent of Schools
903 Oakdale Road
Caxton, Arizona 83627

Dear Ms. Wagner: ◄ Greeting

    I am writing to you on behalf of the Madison ◄ Body
School seventh grade students. We would like to
tell you about our World Culture Day on Saturday,
May 8, from 11:00 A.M. to 4:00 P.M. (Rain date:
Saturday, May 15), and invite you to attend. The
activities will be held in the Madison School
auditorium and playground. Admission is $1; arts,
crafts, and food will be available for purchase.
All proceeds will be donated to the Madison
School Sports Equipment Fund.
    Many diverse cultures will be represented on
this day. Among the artistic offerings is a booth
that will give lessons in origami, the Japanese
art of paper folding. A demonstration of Navajo
weaving will be presented at another booth. Early
American quiltmaking will also be demonstrated.
    Multicultural games will be played throughout
the day. A Choctaw stick game is one of the games
that will be played.
    Food booths will serve foods from many
nations. A chili relleno dish from Mexico, a
mushroom crepe dish from France, and a Cajun-
style chicken dish from the Louisiana Bayou are
just some of the delicious selections we are
planning.
    The students of Madison School understand how
busy you must be with your many responsibilities
as school superintendent. However, we do hope you
can spend some time with us on World Culture Day.

Closing ► Sincerely yours,

Signature ► *Tomas Ramos*

Tomas Ramos, President
Madison Student Council

A business letter has six parts: heading, inside address, greeting, body, closing, and signature.

This writer has used a formal tone, which is appropriate for a business letter.

The writer has used logical order and clear language to provide information to the reader.

Science Report

Wish Upon a Falling Star

Have you ever looked up at the sky at night hoping to make a wish upon a falling star? Do you think falling stars are things that fairy tales are made of? a figment of the imagination? an optical illusion?

Astronomers confirm that falling stars do exist. A falling star is the bright streak seen in the sky when a meteor strikes the Earth's atmosphere. A meteor is made of tiny grains of sand or other debris. Each grain of sand or piece of debris might have less than one gram of mass. As the meteor strikes the Earth's atmosphere at a tremendous speed, these particles burn with the heat of the intense friction. The energy given off creates the light we see as the meteor burns and falls through the atmosphere.

Scientists report that we are more likely to see a falling star after midnight. Studies have shown that before midnight there may be only three falling stars in the sky and after midnight there may be up to fifteen per hour. One falling star per minute has been recorded after midnight at certain times of the year. One reason for this difference in number is that the frequency of meteors colliding with our atmosphere depends on the Earth's orbit direction. Before midnight, Earth is traveling in the same direction that meteors travel. After midnight, the Earth is traveling at an angle against the tide of meteors. This is when we see the greatest number of falling stars.

A falling star is one of the many wonderful things that draws our eyes and imagination to the sky. Since we know that a falling star is actually a meteor striking and entering our atmosphere, we can turn to other natural phenomena we observe or hear about. Astronomy, the study of the universe, can help to open these wonders to us.

FAST FOCUS

The writer begins the report by asking some questions.

The writer goes on to define the subject.

The writer quotes authorities in the field.

The writer concludes by restating the definition that was introduced earlier.

Story Summary

"Raymond's Run"
by Toni Cade Bambara

"Raymond's Run," by Toni Cade Bambara, is a story about a champion runner who learns that there are more important things than winning a race. The main character is a young girl named Squeaky. Other story characters include her older brother, Raymond, and a new girl in the neighborhood, Gretchen.

The story begins with Squeaky preparing for a big race. She is practicing her breathing techniques, and Raymond, whom she takes care of, tags along. They meet a few of Squeaky's classmates who taunt her about Raymond not being "quite right." The classmates also say the new girl Gretchen will beat Squeaky at the race. Squeaky defends Raymond and continues training.

During the race Squeaky decides two important things. She gains respect for Gretchen, who takes running as seriously as Squeaky does. Squeaky also notices that Raymond runs very fast. She decides to retire as a runner and train her brother to become a champion. Then Raymond can have ribbons, medals, and respect of his own. As Squeaky and Gretchen wait for the race results, they smile at each other in friendship.

The writer presents an overview of the story in the opening paragraph.

The writer describes the main events of the plot.

Editorial

This writer begins stating an opinion and supporting it with three reasons.

The writer then goes on to elaborate on each of the reasons.

The writer concludes by responding to anticipated arguments by those who might oppose his or her point of view.

Buses for Ross County

Ross County needs mass transit; Proposition A needs your support! Bus service will help lessen air pollution and traffic congestion, save commuters money, and enable nondrivers to travel about independently.

Air pollution and traffic congestion have become problems in our county. During the last two years, Ross County's population has more than doubled. With that growth has come twice as many cars and exhaust pollution. Stop-and-go rush-hour traffic has developed in all five towns in the county.

A mass transit system would be a welcome financial alternative for drivers. Nondrivers would also benefit. Students who are too young to drive, the elderly who prefer not to drive, and the physically challenged who cannot drive would be able to travel about more independently.

Opponents of Proposition A state that mass transit is too costly and that few would use it. Studies have shown, however, that within the first 18 months of service, bus fares will repay the initial cost of the buses. On the second point, a recent poll conducted by the Ross County Daily shows that 70 percent of the county would like bus service.

As the county grows, the need to institute mass transit will grow. Contribute to a cleaner, less congested environment for us all! Invest in the future of your county! Vote YES on Proposition A!

Autobiography

A Day in November

My leg reached across the finish line like thousands had before me, and just like the thousands that would follow me, on that second day in November. A final "aargh," arms raised, and I slowed to a walk down the ribbon-lined chutes, as moisture filled my eyes. Did I really do it?

I remember that first spring morning. Walking briskly to wake myself up, my white breath looked a strange contrast to the deep red and orange of the rising sun and the lightening dark of the sky. When I reached the track by the river, I thought ten minutes would never end, but I finished that mile. Every morning I ran just a few minutes longer than the last, and as the days lengthened and warmed, I became but one of many who were improving themselves around that river track.

Almost three months of telling myself "just five more minutes" passed before I attempted a two-digit run. Like that first day, I thought ten miles would never end. I thought of the Aikeden runners who might have been my ancestors, long before my grandparents were born in Japan's Aichi farming province. To tell you the truth, I thought of anything--but <u>anything</u>--just so I wouldn't think of the ten miles. On my first twenty-mile run, I wondered why in the world anyone would ever do this anyway.

Today was such a great feeling. And it was just me--doing a little bit each morning for me. I can't believe I ran 26.2 miles: my first marathon.

The writer has chosen an autobiographical moment to share with the reader.

The writer shares the feelings involved with preparing for the moment.

Through divulging these feelings, the writer lets the reader know the person whose life is being shared.

Social Studies Report

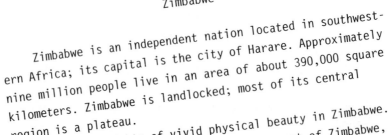

Zimbabwe

Zimbabwe is an independent nation located in southwestern Africa; its capital is the city of Harare. Approximately nine million people live in an area of about 390,000 square kilometers. Zimbabwe is landlocked; most of its central region is a plateau.

There are sights of vivid physical beauty in Zimbabwe. Victoria Falls, located in the northwest part of Zimbabwe, between Zimbabwe and its neighbor, Zambia, is one of the most breathtaking waterfalls in the world. Several Zimbabwe wildlife reserves are havens for elephants, zebras, leopards, and lions.

In 1980 the Zimbabwean people won majority rule of their country, and every adult citizen was given the right to vote. The country is governed by a Parliament that consists of a House of Assembly and a Senate. A prime minister serves as the chief executive.

Farming is a major industry in Zimbabwe. The country is rich in many natural resources, such as gold, copper, coal, iron, and nickel. However, Zimbabwe must import petroleum.

As the multifaceted nation of Zimbabwe moves toward the twenty-first century, the Zimbabwean people continue to build their new country.

The writer begins by stating the subject of the report.

The writer arranges the information about the country in logical order.

The writer concludes with a statement about the future of the country.

Invitation

5440 Dewes Road North
Brainerd, Minnesota 56400
June 10, 1994

Dear Kiyok,

My family and I are going on a camping trip the week after school ends. If I remember correctly, school is over for you the same week it is over for me. If that is the case, would you like to come camping with us?

We are going to Itasca State Park on June 22 and staying for one week. Please write or call me (555-9356) to let me know if you can join us. I really hope you can.

Your friend,

Tom

The purpose of an invitation is to ask someone to come somewhere with you.

Saying when and where the event will be is very important.

It is a good idea to give your phone number, in case the person you're inviting needs more information.

Thank-You Note

18 Richardson Avenue
Arlington, Massachusetts 02174
July 30, 1993

Dear Aunt Clarice,

Thank you so much for taking me to see <u>Romeo and Juliet</u>. I was always a little afraid that I wouldn't like Shakespeare, but I've been proven wrong! Also, seeing it in the park is a wonderful experience. Watching a play while sitting under a starry sky--what could be better?!
Thank you so much again.

Love,

Tony

A thank-you letter is written to thank someone for a gift he or she gave you, or for taking you somewhere.

Thank-you letters mention the gift that was given.

Friendly Letter

1610 East Boston Terrace
Seattle, Washington 98112
April 26, 1993

Dear Renu,

It was so nice to receive your letter. I haven't heard from you in too long a time. Naturally, I had to write back to you immediately. For once, I actually have a lot of news.

First things first. Do you remember my beagle, Lefty? Well, she had puppies — four of them! Two are almost all brown, with little patches of black and grey. There's another one that looks a lot like Lefty. Last, there's my personal favorite. She's mostly white, with brown speckles on her back and sides. I know it's corny, but I couldn't resist calling her Spot.

The other big news is that I was elected vice-president of the seventh grade. I had stiff competition from Joseph Parks, and I have to admit that it was a very close race. I just hope I can be a good V.P.

How's everything in your new school? Mr. Tanabe's English class really misses you. You wrote better limericks than anyone else. I hope you can come back for a visit sometime soon.

Your friend,
Rick

Rick Diehl
1610 East Boston Terrace
Seattle, WA 98112

Renu Nahata
5316 Dorchester Avenue
Chicago, IL 60615

A friendly letter often shares news and other information.

Friendly letters are written in informal language.

Friendly letters are exchanged between relatives and friends.

Job Application

280 S.E. 23rd Street,
Apt. 4E
Ft. Lauderdale, FL 33316
June 2, 1995

Lauderdale Recreation Center
1720 S.E. 17th Street
Ft. Lauderdale, FL 33316

Dear Ms. Torres,

I am writing to inquire about positions available for tennis court attendant. Summer is almost here, and I know that you usually hire students to be caretakers of the town tennis courts.

I am very interested in this job. I used to sweep the junior high school courts after phys. ed. class. I am a very responsible person. I also have a bicycle, so I would be able to ride to the courts early in the morning.

I hope you will consider me for this position. If you would like to arrange an interview, you can call me at home. My number is 555-0187. Thank you for your time.

Sincerely,

Kiyoshi Isa

Kiyoshi Isa

A job application letter is usually written to get information about a job and to find out whether or not the job is available.

A job application letter always names what the job is.

A letter of application tells the employer something about the candidate's qualifications.

Scene

You can set the stage by including the cast of characters and the time and place of action.

Before each line of dialog, write the name of the character in capital letters, followed by a colon. This shows which character is speaking.

Place stage directions in parentheses to show they are not spoken lines.

The sequence of events is made clear through the dialog and stage directions.

The mystery is resolved in this scene.

The stage directions tell what the characters are doing as the scene ends.

Cast of Characters:
Jamila, a seventh-grade girl
Aaron, her best friend
Several more seventh-grade boys and girls
Mrs. Wanatee, their math teacher

Scene: Morning. Jamila and Aaron are outside the door to Mrs. Wanatee's classroom.

AARON: I can't believe I have to go to school on my birthday.

JAMILA: Yeah, that's too bad. Mine's in the summer, so I never have to.

AARON: *(sighing)* Oh well, let's just go to class.

(They enter the classroom. It is dark and empty.)

AARON: Where *is* everybody?

JAMILA: *(a little nervous)* Gee, um, *I* don't know.

AARON: We're not early, are we?

JAMILA: *(looking at her watch)* No, we're right on time.

(All of a sudden, the classroom door flings open.)

SEVENTH-GRADERS AND MRS. WANATEE: Surprise!

(Everybody marches into the room. Mrs. Wanatee is carrying a cake with candles.)

JAMILA: Happy Birthday, best friend!

(JAMILA, the SEVENTH-GRADERS, and MRS. WANATEE gather around AARON and begin singing "Happy Birthday.")

Biography

Father of India

Mohandas Karamchand Gandhi, also known as Mahatma Gandhi, is considered by the people of India to be the father of their nation. He helped to free India from control by the British by using an unusual form of nonviolent protest and resistance. He was also responsible for many social and economic reforms in India. His life was ended by an Indian assassin.

Gandhi was born in 1869, the son of a merchant. In 1888, after being educated in India, he went to England to study law. In 1891 he returned to India to practice law but had a hard time earning a living. In 1893 he went to South Africa to do some work with an Indian law firm. Gandhi soon became a successful lawyer and worked for the rights of Indians in South Africa. He had only planned to stay one year but remained for twenty-one.

In South Africa Gandhi experimented with forms of civil disobedience and nonviolent action. When he returned to India, he again used nonviolent techniques to help Indian peasants and mill workers. Within five years of his return to India, Gandhi became the leader of the Indian nationalist movement.

Gandhi worked hard all his life to help India gain independence from Britain. One method he used was to fast until changes he wanted were made. He also led a fight against "untouchability" and promoted women's rights, basic education, village and home industries, and Hindu-Moslem unity. Gandhi was often jailed for his efforts. Finally, in 1947 Great Britain granted freedom to India. Less than a year later Gandhi was shot to death by a member of India's upper class.

His people had called Gandhi the Mahatma, which means Great Soul. Gandhi searched all his life for truth. He spent his life struggling to gain rights for the oppressed and promoting peace and unity among all races and religions.

F A S T F O C U S

Important facts and events are highlighted by being placed in the opening paragraph.

It is important to include some specific details.

The events in a biography are usually organized in chronological order.

The closing paragraph works to summarize the story of Gandhi's life.

Announcement

COME ON DOWN Y'ALL

to the 4th Annual Roosevelt Junior High
HAYRIDE AND SQUARE DANCE

Hop on the Hay Wagon!
WHERE: at the Newtown Lane Elementary School
WHEN: Saturday, October 27th at 4:00 P.M. sharp

We'll ride to Roosevelt Junior High, and square
dance 'til the cows come home!
Refreshments will be served until 9:00 P.M.
Admission is $4.00.

Wear your best square dance clothes!

This writer wanted to announce a square dance.

An announcement should always include what the event is, who is involved, and where and when it will take place.

Important information is highlighted.

Form

Application for Garage/Yard Sale Permit

Name: Chung Tsiang

Address: 1044 Island Drive Court, Ann Arbor, MI 48105

Closest Cross Street: Lakeview Highway

Phone Number: (313) 555-5667

Sale Date Desired, 1st Choice: July 2, 1992

2nd Choice: July 9, 1992

Proposed Hours of Sale: 9:00 AM to 4:00 PM

Where will sale be held? garage and front yard

Type of items to be sold: clothes, furniture, toys

Chung Tsiang
signature

4/12/91
date

When you fill out any kind of form, make sure to print legibly.

Always give accurate information.

Response to a Literary Selection

M.C. Higgins, the Great
by Virginia Hamilton

This is the story of a young man, M.C. Higgins, who must learn how to face important challenges. He learns many lessons about himself as he struggles to protect the home he loves on Sarah's mountain.

As I read this book, I was reminded of the various new things I have had to learn in my life--maybe not to protect my home, but in school or in my after-school activities. When I have been faced with hardships, I did the same thing this character did--I relied on myself and my inner strength to help me through. I guess all human beings do that.

The writer begins with an overall summary of the story.

The writer includes a personal response to the story by relating events in it to his or her life.

Directions to a Place

Be sure to be clear and complete when you give directions.

Use accurate details.

Name the steps in chronological order.

Don't include any unnecessary information.

To get from my mother's office at 866 Third Avenue to my grandmother's apartment building on West 96th Street, you'll probably want to take the Number 57 Bus. First, walk north on the west side of Third Avenue to 57th Street. Cross over to the north side of 57th Street. You will see a bus shelter there. Wait for the #57, and take it across town to Sixth Avenue. (Don't get on the #5.) Get off the bus at the northwest corner of 57th Street and Sixth Avenue. Cross back over Sixth Avenue so you are on the northeast corner of 57th and Sixth. On this corner, wait for the #7 bus uptown. Take the #7 to 96th Street. Across the street from the bus stop is my grandmother's building, 209 West 96th Street.

Making Sentences That Make Sense

Learn more about using the four different types of sentences in your writing. See "Sentence Sense" on page 241 in the Writer's Craft.

Apply what you've learned about sentences to your work. Look at some of your recent writing projects. Have you made sure all your sentences are complete?

Quick! Choose four different animals you like. List them in your Journal. Next to each animal, write a word or two describing something about the way it looks or sounds.

rhinoceros   horns
giraffe   long neck
lion   roar
zebra   stripes

Focus on Sentences

- A *sentence* is a group of words that expresses a complete thought.

- A *declarative* sentence makes a statement and ends with a period. An *interrogative sentence* asks a question and ends with a question mark. An *exclamatory sentence* expresses strong feeling and ends with an exclamation mark. An *imperative sentence* gives a command or makes a request and ends with a period.

Examples:
A rhinoceros can have one or two horns.
How do giraffes use their long necks?
The lion's mighty roar is awesome!
Take a photo of a zebra with wide stripes.

Animal Safari Exchange **Quick!** lists with a partner. Use each animal- and-description pair to make up a sentence. Make sure each sentence expresses a complete thought. Then take turns reading your sentences aloud and identifying the types of sentences written.

Write Home Do some research on the topic of animals in the wild. Then imagine that you are touring a wildlife preserve with a friend. Write a short postcard to your family. Describe some of the fascinating animals you've seen. Here's an example sentence:

Did you know that the gorilla is the largest ape in the world?

Fixing Fragments and Run-Ons

Quick! Think about your room at home. Does it look the same as it did five years ago? In your Journal, list three phrases that tell how your room looks now. Then write three phrases that tell how it looked five years ago.

How My Room Looks	How My Room Used To Look
is painted green	was painted yellow
neat and orderly	a real mess!
has posters on walls	had drawings on walls

Focus on Sentence Fragments and Run-Ons

- A *sentence fragment* is a group of words that is only part of a sentence. It does not express a complete thought.
- A *run-on sentence* joins two or more sentences that should be written separately.
- Correct a run-on sentence by joining the two ideas with a comma and *and, but,* or *or.*
- Correct a run-on sentence by splitting it into two separate sentences.

Fragments:
Hung the new picture in the corner.
The curtains in Raynell's room.

Complete Sentences:
Rufo hung the new picture in the corner.
The curtains in Raynell's room were light blue.

Run-On Sentences:
I wanted to paint the room beige my sister wanted purple.
Wilson could buy a new poster he could buy a new map.
Alesta was disappointed she didn't have enough fabric for drapes.

Corrected Sentences:
I wanted to paint the room beige, but my sister wanted purple.
Wilson could buy a new poster, or he could buy a new map.
Alesta was disappointed. She didn't have enough fabric for drapes.

Today and Yesterday! Read your **Quick!** list again. Now turn each of your notes into a complete sentence. Each sentence should describe your room today or how it looked five years ago. Make sure your sentences are complete. Use commas and *and, but,* or *or.* Here's an example:

> Today my room is painted green, but five years ago my room was yellow.

A Room of My Own Use your **Quick!** list to make game cards. For each today-and-yesterday pair of phrases, write a run-on sentence on a separate card. For example, you could write, "I used to drape my clothes on the chair now I put them away." Pool game cards with several classmates. Take turns picking cards and suggesting different ways to correct each run-on sentence you pick.

Rewrite That Clue! Join with a small group of classmates. Look through old newspapers and magazines to find a crossword puzzle. Try to solve some of the clues in the puzzle and write in the answers. Then take turns rewriting clues that are sentence fragments as complete sentences. For example, if a clue reads *teacher's headquarters* and the answer is *desk,* your sentence might read: *A desk is a teacher's headquarters.*

Run-On Clinic Describe a famous building. Use the almanac to find out facts about the building, such as when it was built and how tall it is. Write a description of the building. Do so in the form of one big run-on sentence, with no capital letters or punctuation. Then trade papers with a classmate and correct each other's run-on sentence. Talk about the corrected paragraphs. Would you have corrected the run-on sentences differently?

Communication Write a brief letter to a relative. Then rewrite the body of the letter as one long run-on sentence. Give both versions of the letter to a friend and talk about which will best communicate your message.

Look at some of your recent writing projects. Apply what you've learned about fragments and run-ons to your work. Correct any incomplete or run-on sentences.

Speaking of Sentences

Quick! Think of four different musical instruments. Write a sentence in your Journal about each one. You can describe how the instrument looks or sounds, or how you feel when you hear it played.

Trumpets are cheerful and loud.
The sound of a flute makes me sad.
Listen to the thunderous drums.
Do you like the blare of tubas?

Complete and Simple Subjects:
The prize-winning <u>orchestra</u> played for the visitors.
Didn't *José's <u>brother</u>* buy a ticket?

Complete and Simple Predicates:
The audience *<u>appreciates</u>* the music.
<u>Hear</u> the applause.

The Subject Is Band Meet with a partner and exchange your **Quick!** sentences. Underline the complete subjects. Then take turns making up new complete predicates for each complete subject. Here's an example:

Trumpets greeted the king's entrance.

Apply what you've learned to your work. Look at some of your recent writing projects. Can you identify the subjects and predicates?

Focus on Subjects and Predicates

- The *complete subject* includes all the words that tell whom or what the sentence is about.
- The *simple subject* is the main word or words in the complete subject.
- The *complete predicate* includes all the words that tell what the subject does or is.
- The *simple predicate* is the main word or words in the complete predicate.
- The subject of an imperative sentence is understood to be *you.* For example: *Begin the test now.*

Sounding Off Play this game with two classmates. Imagine that you are calling in to a radio music program. Take turns making up sentences about your favorite performers. Say your sentences out loud. Make sure each of the sentences has a subject and a predicate.

Calling All Combinations

Quick! Think of four ways you like to listen to music and list them in your Journal. Don't spend more than five minutes.

Focus on Combining Sentences
- A *sentence* expresses a complete thought. A *simple sentence* has one complete subject and one complete predicate.
- *And, but, or,* and *nor* are *coordinating conjunctions. Correlative conjunctions,* such as *both . . . and, not only . . . but also,* and *either . . . or,* are sets of words that connect parts of sentences. Conjunctions can join two or more simple subjects to form *compound subjects.* Conjunctions also join simple predicates to form *compound predicates.*
- A *compound sentence* contains two or more simple sentences called independent clauses, which are usually joined by *and, or,* or *but.*
- An *expanded sentence* is one to which greater descriptive detail, such as adjectives, adverbs, and prepositional phrases, has been added.

Look at some of your recent writing projects. Apply what you've learned about combined and expanded sentences to your work. Have you made sure that you have expanded your sentences with enough detail to help the reader picture what you have in mind?

Combining Subjects:
James plays the guitar. Marisa plays the guitar.
James *and* Marisa play the guitar.

Combining Predicates:
Luis studies the violin. Luis plays the piano.
Luis *not only* studies the violin *but also* plays the piano.

Forming a Compound Sentence:
I put on a CD. I didn't really hear the music.
I put on a CD, *but* I didn't really hear the music.

Expanding Sentences:
Before sentence is expanded: The stew bubbled.
With adjectives and adverbs: The *spicy* stew bubbled *noisily.*
With prepositional phrases: *With a noisy popping sound,* the stew bubbled *in the pot.*

Musical Times Share your **Quick!** list with one or two friends. Take turns making up sentences about ways you like to listen to music. Then talk about any compound subjects, compound predicates, or compound sentences used to express thoughts.

People Notes Write four sentences about ways that you connect music with people you know. Then revise your sentences to include compound subjects, compound predicates, or a compound sentence to express your thoughts. Here are two examples:

> Lou and Molly remind me of lively music.
> Jazz makes me think of my brother, but rock makes me think of my sister.

Signs and Signals Get together with a couple of friends and describe what colors to paint your ideal community center. Then work together to revise the sentences so that your description includes a few expanded sentences. Here is an example:

> If people feel sad, they can play in a soft yellow room.

Color Codes Suppose you wanted to send a friend a message using only color and images, not words. Write three or four sentences describing the card, the picture, or the collage you would make. Reread your description. Can you use expanded sentences to help the reader to picture exactly what you are trying to convey? Here is an example:

> I missed my friend very much when she moved away.
> To express this, I would color the paper a dark, gloomy gray.

Musical Colors You and your friends are forming a band called The Purple Complex. You're going to perform at the Fall Festival, and you plan to hand out lyrics to a song that you've composed. Write your song. Then combine sentences to form compound sentences. Here is an example of one line from a song:

> I didn't know what a good time was, but then I came to the Fall Festival.

More About Combining Sentences

Quick! Think about some traditional crafts that are still popular today. List a few of these crafts in your Journal.

Crafts
basket making   pottery
wood carving   macrame

Focus on Combining Sentences

- *Subordinating conjunctions,* such as *because, after, before, since, although,* and *when,* can join two simple sentences into a *complex sentence.*
- *Coordinating conjunctions,* such as *and, but,* and *or,* can join a simple sentence and a complex sentence into a *compound-complex sentence.*
- Sentences can also be expanded by using *appositives.* An appositive is a word or group of words that immediately follows a noun and identifies or explains it. Use commas to set off most appositives.

Forming a Complex Sentence:
I turned 13.
I became interested in quilting.
When I turned 13, I became interested in quilting.

Forming a Compound-Complex Sentence:
Colonial quilts are national treasures.
You can often see quilts displayed when you visit museums.
Colonial quilts are national treasures, and you can often see quilts displayed when you visit museums.

Expanded Sentence Using an Appositive:
Jim Watson is my uncle.
He teaches jewelry making.
Jim Watson, my uncle, teaches jewelry making.

My New Hobby Share your **Quick!** list with a few friends. How many different crafts did your group think of? Choose one of the crafts and write a few sentences about the materials you would need to practice the craft. Exchange papers with one other member of your group. Can you combine two sentences to form a complex sentence? Share your results with the whole group.

Spare Time How do you like to spend your spare time? Write a brief letter to an imaginary pen pal. Tell your pen pal about your favorite pastime. Reread your letter. Are there any sentences that can be combined by using appositives? Here's an example:

> Ms. Lopez is my drama coach. She says I have talent.
> Ms. Lopez, my drama coach, says I have talent.

My New Business Join with a few friends to create advertising slogans for a new craft business. Try to combine your ideas and write complex and compound-complex sentences.

Tell a Story With two friends, tell a story about a craft club. One of you says a sentence about a person performing an activity at the club. The second person identifies who the person is. The third person combines the two sentences using an appositive. Keep going until each of you has a chance being the third person. Here's an example:

> First Person: Norah completed a silk-screening project.
> Second Person: Norah is the club's president.
> Third Person: Norah, the club's president, completed a silk-screening project.

Historical Crafts Are you interested in the origins of quilt making? Or perhaps you would like to learn more about the history of metalworking, pottery making, or weaving? Do some research about the origins of a craft and present a short report to your class. Check your report. Are there any sentences you can combine to form complex sentences or compound-complex sentences?

Apply what you've learned about complex and compound-complex sentences to your work. Look at some of your recent writing projects. Did you correctly use subordinating conjunctions in any complex and compound-complex sentences?

Use what you've learned about combining sentences to add greater sentence variety to your writing. See "Sentence Variety" on page 243.

Is It More Than One?

Quick! Design the house of the future. Here's your chance! Choose features that an ideal house of the future might have. List them in your Journal.

```
dishes washed by robots
self-cleaning carpets
remote control-operated windows
```

Focus on Singular and Plural Nouns

- A *noun* names a person, place, thing, or idea.
- A *singular noun* names one person, place, thing, or idea.
- A *plural noun* names more than one.

Singular Nouns	To Form Plural	Examples		
most singular nouns	add *s*	home homes	clue clues	chair chairs
nouns ending with *s, ss, x, zz, ch, sh*	add *es*	class classes	box boxes	sandwich sandwiches
nouns ending with a *consonant* and *y*	change *y* to *i* and add *es*	pantry pantries	baby babies	activity activities
nouns ending with a *vowel* and *y*	add *s*	day days	key keys	tray trays
nouns ending with *f* or *fe*	most add *s;* some change *f* to *v* and add *es*	belief beliefs	shelf shelves	life lives
nouns ending with a *vowel* and *o*	add *s*	radio radios	ratio ratios	video videos
nouns ending with a *consonant* and *o*	most add *es;* some add *s*	potato potatoes	veto vetoes	piano pianos
some irregular nouns	change spelling	woman women	goose geese	ox oxen
a few irregular nouns	keep the same spelling	deer deer	salmon salmon	sheep sheep

Kitchen Patrol Do you help your family in the kitchen? Reread your **Quick!** list. For each feature on your list, write a sentence telling how the kitchen of the future will be kept clean. Then rewrite each sentence changing the form of the nouns. Here's an example:

A robot will wash and dry all the dishes.

Design Contest! Get together with a group of two or three classmates. Share your **Quick!** lists. Choose the best features for a dream house of the future. Then write a paragraph describing this house. If possible, draw exterior and interior sketches of the house to illustrate your paragraph. Then underline the plural nouns. Share your paragraph and sketches with other groups of classmates.

Pioneers in Space You've been whisked ahead to the next century! You are part of a group that sets out to found a new colony in space. Write a paragraph of five sentences identifying objects and possessions you've brought with you on the journey. Then go back to your paragraph and insert a few plural nouns that end in *es*.

Transport to the Future Think about what transportation may be like in the future. Will you ride a flying skateboard to school? Ponder the possibilities with a friend. Then write about the ways in which the two of you spend time together would be different.

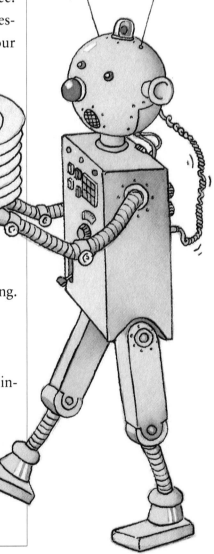

Home Job Bank Play this challenger with three classmates. Think about careers that involve houses or some form of housing. For example:

- a carpenter
- an infant caretaker, working in the home

Each student writes down as many careers as possible. After ten minutes, the person with the greatest number of careers related to the home wins the game. Exchange lists with each other and write a sentence describing each career on the list. Then underline any plural nouns used in the sentences.

Look at some of your recent writing projects. Apply what you've learned about plural nouns to your work. Have you used plural nouns correctly?

Who Does This Belong To?

Quick! What three people or groups have you seen today? Make a chart in your Journal. In the left column, list the people. In the right column, write an article of clothing that each one was wearing.

People	Clothes They Wore
Mr. Vasquez, in grocery store	tie
my brothers, at breakfast	shoes
children, in playground	jeans

Focus on Possessive Nouns

- A *possessive noun* is a noun that names who or what has something.
- Use an *apostrophe* and *s* ('s) to form the possessive of most singular nouns and of plural nouns that do not end with *s*.
- Use only an *apostrophe* (') to form the possessive of plural nouns that end with *s*.

Noun	To Form Possessive	Example
most singular nouns	add *apostrophe* and *s* ('s)	Mr. Vasquez wore a tie. Mr. Vasquez's tie . . .
plural nouns not ending with *s*	add *apostrophe* and *s* ('s)	The children had on jeans. The children's jeans . . .
plural nouns ending with *s*	add *apostrophe* (')	My brothers wore shoes. My brothers' shoes . . .

What's That Person Doing? Play this game with three classmates. Begin by making game cards. Write the name of each person or group of people listed in **Quick!** on a card. Shuffle the cards and place them face down in a pile on a table. The first player picks a card and has two minutes to use the person or group as the subject of a complete sentence. The sentence must have a possessive noun. Take turns until all cards have been used. You may want to try another round!

Rap It Out! Reread your **Quick!** chart. Try making up rap rhymes about each person and article of clothing you listed. Use a possessive noun in each of your rhymes. For example, you might write the following about your brothers' shoes:

My brothers' shoes would make you cry.

Purple like that is fit to dye.

Read your rhymes aloud to a group of classmates.

Classroom Possession Challenge a classmate to play this possession game. Look around your classroom and list five inanimate objects you see. Exchange lists with your partner. Write the answer to "Whose is it?" for each item on your partner's list.

Sale! You are running a garage sale of used items. With a small group of classmates, write an ad that mentions some of the items. Identify the former owner or owners of each item. Use possessive nouns correctly. For example:

Buy the Tuckers' used kitchen table.

The table's finish is just like new!

Travel Destinations Look carefully at a globe. Identify three cities in foreign countries you would like to visit. Write the name of each city on a flash card. Show your partner a card and ask, "Whose city is this?" Your partner may use the globe to write the answers on a piece of paper. Answers should take the form of possessive nouns, such as *Japan's* for Tokyo. Then allow your partner a chance to name some cities.

Apply what you've learned about possessive nouns to your work. Look at some of your recent writing projects. Have you used possessive nouns correctly?

Do your readers know exactly what's on your mind? Try focusing on the use of specific nouns in your writing. See page 255 in the **Writer's Craft.**

Joined Forever

Quick! How will you find out about events in the world today? There are so many ways to keep on top of current events, sometimes it's hard to decide. In your Journal, make a list of some of the ways you can stay on top of what's happening.

Focus on Compound Words

- A *closed compound* is two or more words joined together as one word.
- An *open compound* is two or more words that function as one word without being joined.
- Some compounds are formed by joining two or more words with a hyphen.

Take a look at some of your recent writing projects. Apply what you've learned about compound words. Do you notice any open compounds in your work?

Nose for News Look at the **Quick!** list you wrote. Which do you think informs you best? Write a paragraph or two that explains why you feel this way. Be sure to give some specific examples. Ask a friend to look over your work. Can your reviewer see how many news-related compounds you've used?

Get the Scoop You have just started as teen reporter for your local newspaper. Before you can go on your first assignment, your editor wants to be sure you know enough about newspapers. To show your knowledge, make a chart of newspaper terms and phrases and explain what each means. You'll probably find that many of the terms—such as *headline, city desk,* and *four-star edition*—are compounds.

Taking Action with Verbs

Quick! What are some of your family's achievements? In your Journal, jot down a list of family members. Beside each name, write one thing that the person is proud of accomplishing.

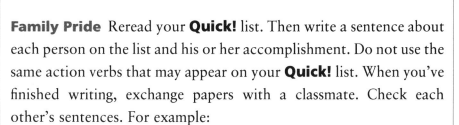

Family Members	Accomplishments
Uncle Roger	volunteers as a community firefighter
Aunt Bess	learned Spanish
Rudy	teaches Little League
Mom	won a chess tournament

Focus on Action Verbs

■ An *action verb* is a word that expresses action. The action can be physical or mental.

Examples:

Dad *grows* tomatoes in the garden.
Cousin Celia *thought* about her decision.
Grandmother *swims* twenty laps a day.
Marisa *loves* her new hobby.

Family Pride Reread your **Quick!** list. Then write a sentence about each person on the list and his or her accomplishment. Do not use the same action verbs that may appear on your **Quick!** list. When you've finished writing, exchange papers with a classmate. Check each other's sentences. For example:

> Uncle Roger joined the volunteer fire department last year.
> Aunt Bess studied Spanish at night school.
> Rudy helps Little Leaguers to hit home runs.
> Mom participates in chess tournaments.

Sportscast Tape-record a brief sportscast made by a radio or television reporter. Then play the recording and jot down all the action verbs you hear. Play the recording to a small group of your classmates and see if they can identify the same verbs that you listed.

EDITOR'S DESK

Apply what you've learned about action verbs to your work. Look at some of your recent writing projects. Do all your sentences have verbs? Can you find all the action verbs in your own writing?

How to Help a Verb

Quick! What people do you admire? Take a couple of minutes to choose four of your heroes and list them in your Journal.

Heroes

my brothers   Barbara Jordan
my grandmother   Cesar Chavez

Vivid verbs help to bring your characters and their actions to life! See page 256 in the **Writer's Craft** *for more about "Vivid Verbs."*

Focus on Main and Helping Verbs

- A *verb phrase* consists of a main verb and its helping verbs.
- A *main verb* is the last word in a verb phrase. It tells what the subject does or did or what it is or was.
- A *helping verb* helps the main verb to show an action or to make a statement. Common helping verbs are forms of the verbs *be, have,* and *do,* as well as *will, shall, would, should, can, could, may, might,* and *must.*
- The forms of the verbs *be, do,* and *have* can be used either as main verbs or as helping verbs.

Look at some of your recent writing projects. Apply what you've learned about main and helping verbs to your work. Can you identify the main verbs and the helping verbs in your own writing?

Examples:

My brothers *have entered* law school.
Law *has fascinated* them since childhood.
Must Jim *pack* all his books?
A friend of theirs *will be driving* them to school.

Verb Switch! Look over your **Quick!** list of heroes. Choose one person on your list. Write a paragraph describing this person. Include the qualities your hero has which you would like to have. Then exchange papers with a partner. Identify the verb phrases, main verbs, and helping verbs in each other's paragraphs.

Birthday Surprise! Think of three friends. What birthday gift would you like to give each one? Write a sentence explaining why each present you've chosen is appropriate for that friend. Exchange papers with a classmate. Underline all the verb phrases in each other's sentences and identify the main verbs and the helping verbs.

Linking Parts of a Sentence

Quick! Imagine that you want to describe your home to a pen pal in a foreign country. In your Journal make a list of rooms or objects at home. Next to each item, write a phrase that describes it.

kitchen   bright yellow wallpaper
Dad's chair   soft and comfortable
bookshelf   crowded with knick-knacks

Apply what you've learned about linking verbs to your work. Look at some of your recent writing projects. Have you used many linking verbs in your own writing?

Focus on Linking Verbs

- A *linking verb* connects the subject of a sentence with a predicate noun or a predicate adjective. Linking verbs do not express actions. Forms of the verb *be* are common linking verbs.
- A *predicate noun* renames or identifies the subject. A *predicate adjective* describes the subject.
- The verbs *seem, appear, look, become, taste, feel, smell,* and *grow* are often used as linking verbs. These verbs are linking verbs when no action is performed.

Examples:
Shawna's room *is* next to mine.
Mother's flower garden *smells* wonderful.

Keeping in Touch Using your **Quick!** list for reference, write a letter to a pen pal in a foreign country. Describe the place where you live. When you've finished, exchange letters with a partner. Underline all the linking verbs in each other's letter.

Menu Game Play this game with two classmates. Each player lists three favorite fruits or vegetables. Players take turns saying a sentence that uses a linking verb to describe the fruit or vegetable. Other players guess the favorite item. Award points for the most imaginative clues and for correct answers. Here's an example:

This fruit looks round and is yellowish red. (a peach)

Subject and Verb Must Work Together

Quick! In your Journal, name three careers that interest you. Next to each career, write a phrase telling what a person does in that job. Don't take more than five minutes.

Career	Activity
doctor	helps sick people
singer	entertains people
chef	cooks delicious dishes

Focus on Subject-Verb Agreement

- Use a verb that *agrees* in number with its subject. Use a singular verb with a singular subject and a plural verb with a plural subject.
- Use a verb that agrees with its subject even if the verb comes before the subject or if the verb is separated from the subject.

Singular Subject and Singular Verb:

Juanita works for a fabric manufacturer.

She creates the new designs.

There *is* a *nurse.*

Here *is* the *flute.*

The *chef* with the tall, white hat *sautés* pecans.

Plural Subject and Plural Verb:

The soccer *players practice* for long months.

They play many games in a season.

There *are patients* in the hospital.

Here *are* your *sheets* of music.

The *dishes* with aluminum covers *sit* on the table.

Career Focus Think about the careers on your **Quick!** list. Then write some sentences describing each career. Explain the reasons why you are interested in that area of work. Exchange papers with a partner and underline any singular and plural subjects. Make sure the subjects and verbs of the sentences agree!

Guess Who Play this game with a classmate. Think of a few musical performers and groups you admire. Write a few sentences describing the performers, without mentioning their names. Then exchange papers. Check the subject-verb agreement in each other's sentences. Then guess the group described.

Biographical Sketch Read about a famous U.S. scientist who worked in this century, such as Dr. Charles Richard Drew, who began his pioneering medical research during the 1930s. Prepare a short report of a few sentences and check them for correct subject-verb agreement. Then read it aloud to a small group.

Can You Cook This? Imagine that you are the new chef at a restaurant. Write a menu describing unusual dishes you will create. Write a brief description of each dish. Exchange menus with a partner and check for subject-verb agreement. For example:

> Super-Special Sandwich—Served on Saturday, the super-special sandwich has sardines, Swiss cheese, and salad dressing. Sesame seeds are added for crunch.

Invent! Invent! Sketch a picture of an imaginary but useful invention! Write a short explanation of how the invention works. Make sure you have written sentences where subjects and verbs agree. Here's one invention:

> My new invention is a window-cleaning robot. Glass cleaner fluid is stored in the robot's arms. Sponges are attached to the robot's hands.

EDITOR'S DESK

Look at some of your recent writing projects. Apply what you've learned about subject-verb agreement to your work. Have you used singular verbs with singular subjects and plural verbs with plural subjects?

The Verb Agrees

Quick! Imagine that you and your classmates are putting on a play. The play's setting is a campsite in a forest. In your Journal, list some props you'll need for the play.

Props for the Play

tent   canteens
wood   lanterns
knapsacks   compass
binoculars   sleeping bags

Focus on Verb Agreement with Compound Subjects and with Collective Nouns

- A *compound subject* must agree with the verb. When two or more subjects are joined by *and* or by *both . . . and,* use the plural form of the verb. When two or more subjects are joined by *or, either . . . or,* or *neither . . . nor,* the verb agrees with the subject that is closest to it.

- A *collective noun* names a group of people or things. With collective-noun subjects, use the singular form of a verb when the group is acting as a unit. When the members of a group are thought of as acting as separate individuals, use the plural form of a verb. Some examples of collective nouns are *family, team, club, band, staff, army, public,* and *company.*

Compound Subjects:
<u>Rose and I</u> *play* two sisters in the first act of the play.
<u>Either the drama coach or our teachers</u> *choose* the performance dates.

Collective Nouns:
The <u>drama club</u> *receives* the profits.
(one group, singular form of verb)
The <u>class</u> *disagree* about the ending.
(individuals, plural form of verb)

EDITOR'S DESK

Apply what you have learned about subject-verb agreement to your work. Look at some of your recent writing projects. Have you made sure that all of your subjects and predicates agree?

Get the Props! Combine your **Quick!** list with a partner's list. Work together to write three or four sentences telling where you would borrow or buy secondhand the props for this play. When you use compound subjects or collective nouns in your sentences, make sure the verbs agree with their subjects. Here is an example:

The bird watchers' club lends us the binoculars.

Story Dialog Form a group of four students. Create a short scene that takes place in the forest. You are four hikers who are lost; your only compass is broken. How will you get home? Write some dialog that includes a few compound subjects and collective nouns. Present your scene to the rest of the class. Ask the class to listen for correct subject-verb agreement.

Write an Ad! With a partner, design an ad for a school play. Include more than just the details about date, time, and place! Highlight the students' efforts in costume and lighting design, as well as set production. Use compound subjects and collective nouns when appropriate.

Calling On Wardrobe Imagine that the drama club has named you to head the wardrobe department. You must decide what everyone will wear in the play, which is set at a campsite. Make a few notes to yourself. Include compound subjects. Here's an example item:

Neither the drama coach nor the actors like the color navy.

What a Play! What would your review for the school newspaper be like for *Lost in the Forest,* a play performed by the eighth-grade class? In a short review, explain why you thought the play was terrible but the actors were great! Make sure verbs agree with compound subjects and collective nouns. Here's part of one review:

Then the army rescues the campers during a tidal wave! Who ever heard of a tidal wave in a forest? At least Len Greene and Sarah Winkle are convincing as the army lieutenants.

Everyone Agrees

Quick! Do you have a favorite pastime? What do your friends and family like to do in their spare time? Jot down a short list of pastimes in your Journal.

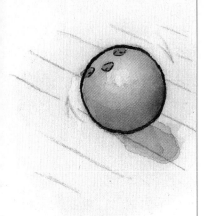

play softball

play computer games

play chess

go bowling

Focus on Verb Agreement with
Indefinite Pronoun Subjects

■ *Indefinite pronouns* do not refer to particular people, places, things, or ideas.

■ Use a singular verb with a singular indefinite pronoun. Use a plural verb with a plural indefinite pronoun.

■ Some indefinite pronouns can be singular or plural. Look at the phrase that follows the pronoun to decide whether to use a singular or plural verb.

Indefinite Pronouns

Singular	another	each	everyone	neither	one
	anybody	either	everything	nobody	somebody
	anyone	everybody	much	no one	someone
	anything			nothing	something
Plural	both	few	many	others	several
Singular or Plural	all	any	most	none	some

Examples:

Everyone has a favorite pastime.

Each of my friends is interested in physical fitness.

Several of the players are fine athletes.

Most of the softball game was exciting.

Most of the fans were on the edge of their seats.

Stay Fit! Use your **Quick!** list to write four sentences about the favorite pastimes of people you know. Exchange sentences with a partner. Make sure the verb in each sentence agrees with its subject. Include several indefinite pronoun subjects. Here are two examples:

All my cousins like to jog. Each runs three times a week.

Indefinite Pronoun Game Organize an even number of teams; each team should have four students. Each team prepares four cards, with one indefinite pronoun written on each card. The first team displays a card. A second team uses the indefinite pronoun as a subject in a sentence within ten seconds. Check all sentences for subject-verb agreement. Award one point for each correct sentence. Continue playing until all cards have been used up by all the teams.

Telephone Call Work with a partner to make up a telephone conversation about a contest one of you attended. Include a few indefinite pronouns as subjects of sentences. The students below attended a chess tournament.

First Student: Everybody was very quiet in the audience.
Second Student: Did some of the chess players look nervous?
First Student: Well, a few were a little tense.

Apply what you have learned about indefinite pronouns to your work. Look at some of your recent writing projects. Have you made sure all your indefinite pronoun subjects agree with their predicates?

Rules of the Game With a partner, create your own board game. Sketch a rough layout for the game's playing board. Then write the rules of the game. Try to use a few singular and plural indefinite pronouns in the rules. Explain the game to the rest of the class.

Covering the Game Compose a radio or TV report about a sports event in progress. Use indefinite pronouns now and again throughout your play-by-play report. Present the report to the class. Here's part of one report:

No one believes Smith hit that home run! All of the fans are on their feet! Some of Smith's teammates are congratulating her at home plate.

More About Verbs

Quick! Jot down a few notes in your Journal about ways to keep your neighborhood safe and clean. Name ways to prevent safety hazards and to clean up the environment.

> enforce the speed limit
> place a stop sign at Vineland and Lark avenues
> recycle old newspapers and bottles

Focus on the Verbs *Be, Do,* and *Have*

- Use *is, was, does,* and *has* to tell about one person or thing. Use these verbs with the pronouns *he, she,* and *it.*
- Use *are, were, do,* and *have* to tell about more than one person or thing. Use these verbs with the pronouns *we, they,* and *you.*

Singular Subject and Verb:

Mr. Ruiz <u>is</u> our community organization leader.

He <u>has</u> the minutes of our last meeting.

This *letter* to the city council <u>is</u> well written, and *it* <u>has</u> all the facts.

Plural Subject and Verb:

The used aluminum *cans* in the recycling bin <u>were</u> mine.

They <u>are</u> members of the clean-up team.

<u>Do</u> you <u>have</u> the mops and brooms?

Bumper Slogans Reread the notes you made for **Quick!** Think up two or three bumper sticker slogans that address your environment and safety concerns. Each slogan should be brief and catchy. Use a form of *be, do,* or *have* in each slogan. Design bumper stickers using your slogans. Here are two examples:

Clean Neighborhoods Have More Fun! Recycling? Do It!

Mood Music Think of some of your favorite songs or pieces of music. Write a sentence about each musical selection. Describe the mood of that piece or your feelings when you listen to it. Underline any forms of *be, do,* or *have* that you used in your sentences.

EDITOR'S DESK

Look at some of your recent writing projects. Apply what you've learned about the verbs <u>be</u>, <u>do</u>, *and* <u>have</u> *to your work. Have you made sure that you used singular verbs with singular subjects and plural verbs with plural subjects?*

Speaking in the Active and Passive Voices

Quick! Imagine that your family is about to go on vacation. In your Journal, jot down four preparations that you and your family would need to make.

Preparing for Vacation
plan the route
pack the car
arrange for mail to be held
bring the pets to the kennel

Active Voice:

Polly *made* the cheese sandwiches for the trip.

The postal clerk *takes* all the information.

Someone *left* a leash at the kennel.

Passive Voice:

The cheese sandwiches for the trip *were made* by Polly.

All the information *is taken* by the postal clerk.

A leash *was left* at the kennel by someone.

Vacation Diary Reread your **Quick!** list. Write a sentence telling which family member took care of each item on the list. Then exchange papers with a partner. Change the voice, from passive to active or from active to passive, in each sentence. Here is an example:

> The car was packed by Miya and Daniel.
>
> Miya and Daniel packed the car.

Headliners! Look through current newspapers and magazines. Copy six headlines from articles that interest you. Exchange papers with a partner. Identify the verbs in each headline as active voice or passive voice. Then experiment with changing the active voice to passive voice, and vice versa. Read your new headlines aloud and discuss them with your classmates. Do you think the verbs in the active voice make the statements seem stronger than the verbs in the passive voice do?

Focus on Active and Passive Voices

- A verb is in the *active voice* when the subject of the sentence performs the action.
- A verb is in the *passive voice* when the subject receives the action of the verb.

Look at some of your recent writing projects. Apply what you've learned about active voice and passive voice to your work. Remember that using verbs in the active voice makes your writing stronger.

Tours of Yesterday, Today, and Tomorrow

Quick! Think of different places you would like to visit. Choose three cities and list them in your Journal. Next to each destination, write a few words that come to mind when you think about that city.

Los Angeles   *movies and Hollywood*
New Orleans   *Dixieland jazz*
San Diego   *the zoo and beaches*

Focus on Present, Past, and Future Tenses

- An *action verb* is a word that expresses physical or mental action.
- A *linking verb* connects the subject of a sentence with a noun or an adjective in the predicate.
- Change verb *tense* forms to show changes in the time of an action.
- The *present tense* tells that something is happening now.
- The *past tense* shows an action that has already happened.
- The *future tense* shows an action that will take place in the future.

Present Tense:
It *is* snowing.
Tim and Cathy *visit* San Diego.

Past Tense:
It *snowed* yesterday.
Tim and Cathy *visited* San Diego.

Future Tense:
It *will snow* tomorrow.
Tim and Cathy *will visit* San Diego later.

Cities in Song Share your **Quick!** list with a partner. Work together to write a brief song about two of the cities. After completing your song, change all of the verb forms to the present tense. Talk about the two versions of your song. Which do you prefer?

Tense Test Play this game with a partner. Agree on a location that interests you both, such as a country or a city. The first player thinks of a sentence about the location and says it out loud. The other player has one minute to rephrase the sentence in another tense.

Look at some of your recent writing projects. Apply what you've learned about present, past, and future verb tenses to your work. Have you used the verb tenses that show the correct time of the actions?

Express an Action in Perfect Tense

Quick! Choose three topics about the earth's environment that interest you. List your topics in your Journal.

> **Topics About the Environment**
> soil erosion
> the greenhouse effect
> waste disposal

Present Perfect Tense:
I *have learned* about recycling.
We *have checked* the erosion every week for two months.

Past Perfect Tense:
Aiko *had read* the report in the paper before she went to the library. Before the friends ate lunch, they *had returned* the aluminum cans.

Future Perfect Tense:
By the year 2020 our garbage problems *will have increased*. Global warming *will have worsened* by the time the show is aired.

Focus on Perfect Tenses

- The *perfect tenses* are made up of two parts: a form of the helping verb *have* and the past participle of a verb.
- The *present perfect tense* expresses an action that happened at an indefinite time in the past or that started in the past and is still happening in the present.
- The *past perfect tense* expresses an action that happened before another action in the past.
- The *future perfect tense* expresses an action that will be completed before another action in the future.

Planet Earth Share **Quick!** lists with a partner. Choose a topic that interests you and read an article about it. Write down verbs in the perfect tenses that you find.

Up, Up, and Away! Play this game in groups of three. Your group has been invited to ride in a hot air balloon. Take turns making up sentences about the sights you see—on board and outside—as well as your reactions. Use a variety of verbs in your sentences.

Apply what you've learned about perfect tenses. Look at your recent writing projects. Have you used verb tenses correctly?

We Are Using Our Time Well

Quick! What did you do last weekend? In your Journal, jot down a list of three specific things you did or made.

1. helped make lunch on Saturday
2. watched a ball game on television
3. went bike riding with friends

Focus on Progressive Forms of Verbs

■ *Progressive forms* are made up of a form of *be* and the present participle of a verb.

■ The *present progressive form* of a verb expresses action that is continuing now.

■ The *past progressive form* of a verb expresses action that continued for some time in the past.

Present Progressive Form:

Max *is playing* football with great enthusiasm.

Today the players *are practicing* for the championship.

Past Progressive Form:

Last week people *were waiting* to buy tickets.

No one *was supporting* the team last year.

Weekend Relaxations Team up with a friend and compare the activities on your **Quick!** lists. Decide who was doing what when. Then take turns making up sentences that compare how the two of you spent the weekend. Here are two examples:

While you were raking leaves, I was making lunch.

We both were riding our bikes on Sunday afternoon.

Lend a Hand Think of three people you know who spend time helping others. Write a sentence about each person. Then exchange papers with a classmate. Underline any present progressive verb forms. Here is an example:

Rita is donating clothes to the thrift shop.

Look at some of your recent writing projects. Apply what you've learned about the progressive verb form to your work. Did you correctly use present progressive and past progressive forms of verbs?

How Special Is That Verb?

Quick! If you could be famous in one field, what would it be? Choose four areas or fields in which you think it would be exciting to achieve fame. List the four fields in your Journal.

the arts   movies
journalism   sports

Examples:

Verb	Past	Past Participle
be	was, were	(have, has, had) been
do	did	(have, has, had) done
have	had	(have, has, had) had
come	came	(have, has, had) come
break	broke	(have, has, had) broken
know	knew	(have, has, had) known
think	thought	(have, has, had) thought
leave	left	(have, has, had) left
run	ran	(have, has, had) run
write	wrote	(have, has, had) written
eat	ate	(have, has, had) eaten
throw	threw	(have, has, had) thrown
see	saw	(have, has, had) seen
sing	sang	(have, has, had) sung
drink	drank	(have, has, had) drunk
spring	sprang	(have, has, had) sprung

Starstruck! Reread your **Quick!** list. Select one field in which you would like to star. Imagine that you are now about seventy years old. Write a paragraph telling your grandchildren what you have achieved in your chosen field. Then go back to your piece and revise it, using a variety of past and past participle forms of irregular verbs.

Horror Show! Play this game with a classmate. Each of you should write about a scary experience. Then rewrite your story using the past or past participle forms of verbs. Read your stories to each other.

Focus on Irregular Verbs
- To form the past and the past participle forms of regular verbs, add *ed*.
- The past and the past participle forms of *irregular verbs* are formed in various ways.

Apply what you've learned to your work. Look at a recent writing project. Did you use irregular verbs correctly?

*The English language uses many irregular verbs. **Information Instantly** lists more on page 362.*

Irregular Form

Quick! You've just won a contest. The prize is 15 minutes of free shopping at the mall. Write down the types of stores you'd like to race through in order to collect your prize merchandise.

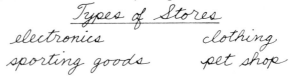

Types of Stores

electronics   clothing
sporting goods   pet shop

Focus on Irregular Verbs II

■ For regular verbs, you add *ed* or *d* to form the past and the past participle. For *irregular verbs,* you do not.

■ To form the past participle of *irregular verbs,* add *have, has,* or *had.*

Examples:

Verb	Past	Past Participle
blow	blew	(have, has, had) blown
burst	burst	(have, has, had) burst
choose	chose	(have, has, had) chosen
draw	drew	(have, has, had) drawn
fly	flew	(have, has, had) flown
freeze	froze	(have, has, had) frozen
set	set	(have, has, had) set
wear	wore	(have, has, had) worn

All Shopped Up Look over your **Quick!** list and choose one of the stores from it. Imagine that you are the manager of one of the stores that a prize-winning shopper has just raced through. Write a report for your supervisor that explains why the store looks the way it does. Underline any irregular verbs in your report, and remember to use *have, has,* or *had* with the past participle.

Fireworks It's the hundredth anniversary of your town. Write a letter to a friend about the fireworks display that was held during the celebration. Make sure that your subjects and verbs agree.

Apply what you've learned about irregular verbs to your work. Look at some of your recent writing projects. Have you used the correct past and past participle forms of irregular verbs?

*There are many irregular verbs in the English language. More are listed in **Information Instantly** on page 362.*

I'd Know Them Anywhere

Quick! Write down your favorite places to spend time, either by yourself or with friends. They can be enjoyable or serious.

Places I Like to Be

beach	science museum
movies	mall

Apply what you've learned about contractions to your work. Look at some of your recent writing projects. Have you used contractions correctly?

Focus on Contractions

- A *contraction* is a shortened form of two words. Some contractions are formed from a pronoun and a verb.
- Form contractions by adding an apostrophe and *s* to stand for *is* or *has* and an apostrophe and *d* for *had* or *would*. Also use an apostrophe with *m* for *am*, with *ve* for *have*, with *ll* for *will*, and with *re* for *are*.

Contraction	Meaning	Contraction	Meaning
I'm	I am	we're	we are
I've	I have	we've	we have
I'd	I had/would	we'd	we had/would
I'll	I will	we'll	we will
he's	he is/has	you're	you are
she's	she is/has	you've	you have
it's	it is/has	you'd	you had/would
he'd	he had/would	you'll	you will
she'd	she had/would	they're	they are
he'll	he will	they've	they have
she'll	she will	they'd	they had/would
it'll	it will	they'll	they will

Tour Guide Choose a place from your **Quick!** list and plan a guided tour for your best friend. Point out the highlights in your written plan. Then revise your piece to include three contractions.

Songwriter Write down the lyrics to your favorite song. Change the pronouns and verbs to contractions throughout the song. Show your new song to a friend.

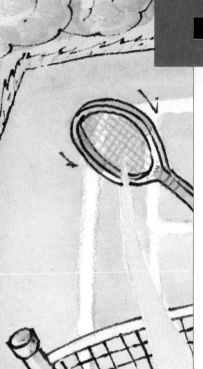

You and I, Pronouns Together

Quick! Think of people you know, such as friends or relatives. Choose a few of these people and list their names in your Journal.

Focus on Pronouns

- A *pronoun* is a word that takes the place of one or more nouns.
- A *personal pronoun* is a pronoun that usually refers to a person, thing, or group of people.
- A *subject pronoun* is used as the subject of a sentence. An *object pronoun* is used as the object of a verb or preposition.

Subject Pronouns		Object Pronouns	
Singular	**Plural**	**Singular**	**Plural**
I	we	me	us
you	you	you	you
she, he, it	they	him, her, it	them

Examples:

I played tennis yesterday with Uncle Alvin.

Did *you* see *us?*

Uncle Alvin won, but *he* told *me* that *I* am improving.

Among Friends Read your **Quick!** list again. Write two sentences about each person on your list, describing some of the person's likes and dislikes. Here is an example:

My sister bakes carrot cake. It's her favorite cake.

Code Breakers Write four sentences. Then write your sentences, using all capital letters, with no punctuation or extra space between words or sentences. Exchange papers with a partner and break the code. Then circle all of the pronouns. Here's an example:

IMSUREYOUCANREADTHISAMIRIGHT

Apply what you've learned about pronouns to your work. Look at some of your recent writing projects. Are you using pronouns correctly?

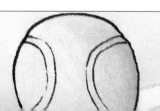

That's My Job!

Quick! Reflect on some careers or jobs in which people help other people. Choose a few of the careers that interest you and list them in your Journal. Next to each, write an object or possession that you associate with each job.

doctor	stethoscope
teacher	book
coach	whistle

Focus on Possessive Pronouns

- A *possessive pronoun* shows who or what owns something.
- Possessive pronouns used before nouns are *my, our, your, his, her, its,* and *their.*
- Possessive pronouns used alone are *mine, ours, yours, his, hers, its,* and *theirs.*

Examples:
You can't judge a book by *its* cover.
The new job is *hers.*
Look at these photos! They're *ours!*

Lost and Found Get together with a classmate and reread your **Quick!** lists. Write a sentence using each career-and-object pair on your list. Here are examples:

The coach lost her whistle.
The teacher found his book.

Then take turns revising each sentence so that the subject is plural.

The coaches lost their whistles.
The teachers found their books.

Workers, Unite! Form a group with three other classmates. Take turns telling facts or stories about jobs you've had. For example, you could tell an interesting anecdote about working as a yard worker, a car washer, or a baby-sitter. You can also discuss jobs you'd like to have. Try to use a variety of possessive pronouns.

Look at some of your recent writing projects. Apply what you've learned about possessive pronouns to your work. Did you use the correct pronoun form before a noun?

Possessive pronouns never use apostrophes. For example, <u>its</u> is a possessive pronoun. <u>It's</u> is the contraction for <u>it is</u>.

Our Pronouns and Their Antecedents

Quick! What are your three favorite songs? Who sings them? List your favorites in your Journal. Next to each title, write the name of the singer. Don't take more than five minutes.

Favorite Song	Performer
"First in Line"	Paul Wing
"Shout About It"	Kids U Know
"Not the Easy Way"	Stacey Butler

Focus on Pronouns and Antecedents

- A *pronoun* is a word that takes the place of one or more nouns.
- An *antecedent* is a word or group of words—one or more nouns—that a pronoun refers to or replaces.
- Pronouns and antecedents must agree in *person* (first, second, or third), *number* (singular or plural), and *gender* (male, female, or thing).
- Use a *subject pronoun* in a compound subject and an *object pronoun* in a compound object.

Antecedents:
Sal played the guitar.
Carlos and *I* left.
Sandy and *Mavis* sang solos.

Pronouns:
He played beautifully.
We left by the side door.
They sang for an hour.

Antecedents and Pronouns:
Will heard that *tape*, and *he* enjoyed *it*.
Maria and *I* knew *Al* and *Sandy*, and *we* greeted *them*.

Singers and Songs Reread your **Quick!** list. Choose one of the songs on the list and write a brief review of it. In your review, describe the performance given by the singer. Then take a few minutes to reread the review. Make sure each of your pronouns clearly refers to an antecedent. Here's an example:

Paul Wing sings beautifully, and he also plays the flute.

At the Movies Get together with a partner. Look through current issues of newspapers and magazines for movie reviews. Locate two reviews and read them carefully. Then challenge each other to circle the pronouns in a review. Draw an arrow from each pronoun to its antecedent.

Today and Yesterday How have the methods of recording music changed since the 1800s? How has the technology improved? With a partner, prepare an oral report about the changes through the years. Include recent technological developments in your report, such as the advent of compact discs in the record industry. Check all pronouns in your report; be sure they agree with their antecedents. Then present the report with your partner to a group of classmates.

My Famous Interview Think of several questions that you would like to ask your favorite singer about his or her career. Then write an imaginary interview in which your favorite singer answers your questions. Exchange interviews with a classmate. Correct any mistakes, including any involving pronoun agreement with antecedents.

Buy This Record With a couple of friends, make a poster that advertises a new record by a popular rap group. Include your personal opinions about the rap group. Check that all pronouns agree with their antecedents. Here is an example:

> Jacob and Tom listen to this record, and they think it sounds great!

Apply what you've learned about pronouns and antecedents to your writing. Look at a few of your recent writing projects. Does each pronoun agree with its antecedent in your own writing?

When using I in a compound subject or me in a compound object, always put I or me last.

Buying and Selling

Quick! You're spending the day at a flea market. You've brought some things to sell. Also, you want to buy some things for people you like. In your Journal, list three things you'd like to sell and three things you'd like to buy.

Sell	Buy
sailboat model	red sweater
transistor radio	headlight for bicycle
old compass	pair of headphones

Focus on Direct and Indirect Objects

- A *direct object* is a noun or pronoun in the predicate that receives the action of the verb. It answers the question *Whom?* or *What?* after an action verb.

- An *indirect object* is a noun or pronoun in the predicate that answers the question *to whom? for whom? to what?* or *for what?* after an action verb.

- A *transitive verb* is a verb that has a direct object. An *intransitive verb* does not have a direct object. Transitive verbs may take both a direct object and an indirect object.

Direct Objects:
Francine sold a *lamp*.
Santos gave *directions*.
Yang helped *us*.

Direct Objects and Indirect Objects:
George made *them* a *bookcase*.
Louisa showed *me* your *pottery*.
Jaime offered *Janice* the *tickets*.

Flea Market Bargains Working with your **Quick!** list, write sentences describing your sales and your purchases at the flea market. Then exchange papers with a classmate. Circle the direct objects and underline the indirect objects.

Advertising Objects Play an advertising game with two or three classmates. Look through a pile of old magazines and look at the slogans in the advertisements. If a slogan contains a direct or an indirect object that is a pronoun, write it down. The first person to identify a total of ten direct and indirect objects that are pronouns wins.

Look at some of your recent writing projects. Apply what you've learned about direct and indirect objects to your work. How have you used direct objects to help you clarify the action in your writing?

You're Not All by Yourself!

Quick! Think of four friends. Then try to remember where you met them. Write a list of names in your Journal. Next to each name, describe the place where you met one another.

Friend	*Where We Met*
Kyle	in the library
Juanita	at camp
Arlon	at Sue's party
Mace	at the bike shop

Reflexive Pronouns:
I found *myself* in the kitchen.
Barb gave *herself* an early birthday present.
The members discussed the idea among *themselves*.

Intensive Pronouns:
The mayor *himself* introduced us.
We *ourselves* organized the party.
Did you *yourself* say hello?

> **Focus on Reflexive and Intensive Pronouns**
> - A *reflexive pronoun* is a special pronoun used as a direct object, an indirect object, or an object of a preposition. It points the action of the verb back to the subject.
> - An *intensive pronoun* adds emphasis to a noun or pronoun already named.

Introductions Look over your **Quick!** list. Using the entries on your lists as a springboard, write four sentences telling how and where you met your friends. Then revise your sentences. Use reflexive pronouns in two sentences and intensive pronouns in the other two sentences. Here are two examples:

> For three days I found myself sitting across a library table from Kyle MacGruder.
> I asked Sue herself to introduce me to Arlon.

Calling All Volunteers! Think of a party you gave or attended where you met a new friend. Make notes about who helped to organize the party. Write a short description of the event. Then read your description to a group of classmates. Ask them to identify any reflexive and intensive pronouns you may have used in the report.

Look at some of your recent writing projects. Apply what you've learned about reflexive and intensive pronouns to your work. Has using them added variety to your sentences?

Pronouns on the Horizon

Quick! Have you ever wanted to be a set designer? Here's your chance! Imagine the set you would design for a new mystery that will appear in the theater. In your Journal, write a phrase that summarizes the setting. Then list four objects that are essential to your set.

Setting: A quaint hotel nestled in the mountains near Denver
My set needs: a door that squeaks when opened
                a portrait of the princess
                diamond earrings
                several heavy draperies

Focus on Demonstrative and Relative Pronouns

- A *demonstrative pronoun* replaces a noun and points out something. *This, that, these,* and *those* are demonstrative pronouns.
- A *relative pronoun* relates a clause to the word or words that the clause modifies. *Who, whom, whose, which,* and *that* are relative pronouns.

Demonstrative Pronouns:
This is a squeaky door.
These are cotton drapes; *those* are wool drapes.
Relative Pronouns:
The guests *who* objected were angry.
The vase *which* held the roses fell.

Get Set Reread your **Quick!** list. Then write a paragraph describing your theater set. When you've finished, read your paragraph to a classmate. Challenge your classmate to identify and classify the demonstrative and relative pronouns.

Look at some of your recent writing projects. Apply what you've learned about pronouns to your work. Did you use pronouns correctly?

Travel Poster Get together with two partners. Decide on a travel destination you think would be fun to visit. Brainstorm with the group about the attractions of the place you've chosen. Then design a poster advertising a special vacation package bargain. Be sure to give details about the bargain in your poster. Try to use some demonstrative and relative pronouns in your vacation ad. When you've finished, display your poster on the class bulletin board.

Bright and Beautiful Creatures

Quick! List in your Journal three or four creatures you might see at an aquarium.

At the Aquarium

porpoise   sting ray
squid   penguin

Focus on Adjectives

- An *adjective* is a word that modifies, or describes, a noun or a pronoun. Adjectives tell which one, what kind, or how many. A *predicate adjective* follows a linking verb and describes the subject.
- *This*, *that*, *these*, and *those* may be used as *demonstrative adjectives*, which point out people, places, or things.
- An *article* is a special kind of adjective. *The* is the *definite* article. *A* and *an* are the *indefinite* articles.

Examples:
Several penguins just waddled by.
The spotted fish swam in *a large* tank.
That porpoise is *young*.
This squid has *ten* tentacles.
An octopus eats fish.

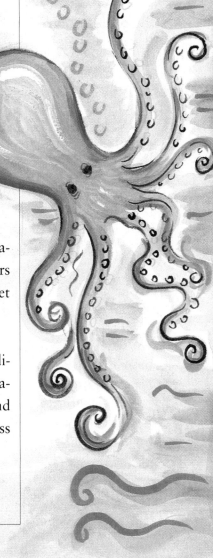

Ocean Inhabitants Refer to your **Quick!** list. Choose one creature and write a few descriptive sentences about it. Exchange papers with a partner. Underline all the adjectives you can find. Don't forget to underline the articles and the demonstrative adjectives.

My New Aquarium Imagine that you have been appointed the director of a new aquarium in your town. Decide what colorful creatures you want to house in the aquarium. Describe the aquarium and the creatures for your class. Use details that will convince the class that you are planning a wonderful aquarium.

Look at some of your recent writing projects. Apply what you have learned about adjectives to your work. Did you use adjectives to add colorful details to your writing?

The Best Lunch in Town

Quick! Pick four foods or beverages. List them in your Journal.

chicken sandwich   lemonade
bananas   grapes

Grab your readers' attention and pull them into your writing with a thoughtful choice of descriptive words. See "Effective Adjectives and Adverbs" on page 257.

Focus on Comparative and Superlative Adjectives

- A *comparative adjective* compares two things and is formed by adding either *er* or the words *more* or *less*. Do not use *er* and *more* together.

- A *superlative adjective* compares more than two things and is formed by adding either *est* or the words *most* or *least*. Do not use *est* and *most* together.

- Some comparative and superlative forms are irregular.

Comparative Adjectives:
This blue pot is *fuller* than that orange one.
The grapes are *less plentiful* than the strawberries.

Superlative Adjectives:
The green pot is the *fullest* pot.
Her menus are the *most creative* I've ever seen!

Irregular Forms:
The carrots were *worse* than the potatoes.
"That was the *worst* food I've ever tasted!" Luis exclaimed.

Taste Test Get together with another classmate and combine your **Quick!** lists to play this game. The first player asks a question about a food item on the lists. The other player answers the question with a sentence using a comparative or a superlative adjective.

Question: How is the lemonade?
Answer: It could be colder.

Dining Around You're a food critic who travels around the world, eating wonderful meals. Write a letter to a friend. Share your culinary opinions and experiences by comparing the food of one location to that of another.

Look at some of your recent writing projects. Apply what you've learned about adjectives to your work. Did you use the comparative form to compare two things and the superlative form to compare more than two things?

Soaring Words

Quick! Think of a few types of birds that inhabit the United States. List a few of your favorites in your Journal. You may also want to include you own state's bird.

Birds of the United States

robin	quail
mockingbird	finch
meadow lark	cardinal

Focus on Adverbs

- An *adverb* is a word that modifies a verb, an adjective, or another adverb.
- Adverbs tell how, when, where, or to what extent.

Examples:

Gulls glided *swiftly* through the mist.
(modifies the verb *glided*)

A *very* small hummingbird flew to the flower.
(modifies the adjective *small*)

Ostriches run *surprisingly* quickly.
(modifies the adverb *quickly*)

Birds of a Feather Combine your **Quick!** list with a partner's list. Read the name of one bird from the combined list. Then have your partner think of a sentence that describes how that bird flies. Identify any adverbs your partner may have used in the sentence. Your turn is next. Continue until you complete the list. Here's an example:

The eagle soared majestically amid the clouds.

Our Wildlife Have you ever visited a wildlife refuge? There are hundreds in the United States that are owned and operated by the federal government. In these areas, birds and other wildlife are protected. Do some research on a rare bird that lives in this hemisphere. Include in a short report to your class the efforts being made to protect this bird.

Look at some of your recent writing projects. Apply what you've learned about adverbs to your work. Did you use adverbs effectively to tell how, when, where, or to what extent?

Playing Better Than Ever

Quick! Make believe you're watching an important game. Write a few verbs that describe different actions you are watching. Then think of an adverb that gives more information about each verb.

Verb	Adverb
run	fast
throw	far
leap	high

Focus on Comparative and Superlative Adverbs

- A *comparative adverb* compares two actions. Add *er* or use *more* or *less* with the adverb. Do not use *er* and *more* together.
- A *superlative adverb* compares more than two actions. Add *est* or use *most* or *least* with the adverb. Do not use *est* with *most*.
- Some comparative and superlative forms are irregular.

Comparative Adverbs:

Paul runs *faster* than Lee.

Our team plays *more eagerly* than our opponents.

Superlative Adverbs:

Stacy runs *fastest* of all.

Who does push-ups the *least enthusiastically?*

Irregular Forms:

The contestant who played *best* was Lisa.

After practicing, Hector complains the *least*.

Animal Audio Exchange **Quick!** lists with a partner. Use the verbs and adverbs on the lists to make up a radio script. Describe the game or match in vivid detail by using comparative and superlative adverbs.

Olympic Games Imagine you have won an Olympic Medal. Make up four sentences about the event. Exchange papers with a partner and underline the comparative and superlative adverbs.

A Million, Modified

Quick! In your Journal, write three sentences that describe the action on a television show you watched recently.

The woman was running wildly and almost lost her shoes.

The child huddled with the thin, frightened cat.

Reaching the child at the same time, the woman and the police officer were relieved.

> ### Focus on Misplaced Modifiers
> - A *modifier* can be a single adjective or adverb, or it can be a phrase, such as a prepositional phrase.
> - A modifier should be as close as possible to the word it modifies. A misplaced modifier can result in a confusing or misleading sentence.

What Really Happened? Rewrite your **Quick!** sentences so the modifiers are misplaced. What's the result? Does it change what really happened in the show you watched? Try sketching a picture of the new episode.

Running wildly, the shoes almost came off.

Thin and frightened, the child huddled with the cat.

The woman and the police officer were relieved, reaching and hugging her child.

Modify My Lines Work with a group of friends to write the plot for a television drama. As you develop the story and the stage directions for the actors, notice how and where you place your modifiers.

Apply what you've learned about misplaced modifiers to some of your recent writing. Take a look at some of your recent writing projects. Are your modifiers where they should be? Are your sentences clear?

DIRECTOR

Liking the Unlikely

Quick! Think about stories or biographies you have read. In your Journal, write the names of four characters you have enjoyed reading about. Next to each name, think of one way that you and the character are different from one another.

Look at some of your recent writing projects. Have you made sure that your sentences are free of double negatives?

Character	How We're Different
Chalene	She plays the guitar; I play the piano.
Felipe	He's two years older than I am.
Ray	He plays baseball. I play basketball.
Mamie	We don't like the same foods.

Double Negative:

We *didn't* have *no* books in common.

Nobody never plans a friendship like ours.

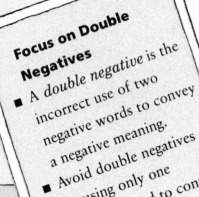

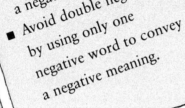

Focus on Double Negatives

- A *double negative* is the incorrect use of two negative words to convey a negative meaning.

- Avoid double negatives by using only one negative word to convey a negative meaning.

Corrected Sentences:

We didn't have any books in common.

We had no books in common.

Nobody ever plans a friendship like ours.

A person never plans a friendship like ours.

Friendly Contrast Look over your **Quick!** list. Then write a paragraph about the characters you listed. Describe the differences from your list. Be sure to avoid double negatives! Here is an example:

No one plays the guitar like Chalene. The guitar is an instrument I've never played.

Rules of the Game Get together with a classmate. Decide on your favorite board game. Then imagine you want to teach the rules of this game to a new friend who has never played it. Take turns making up sentences that tell your new friend some mistakes he or she should avoid. Check your sentences to make sure you've used negative verb forms correctly.

Thinking About Home

Quick! Imagine that you have to give a friend directions to travel from your school to your home. Choose four landmarks you would use in giving directions. Write a list of your landmarks in your Journal.

Old Oak Hill
the Multiplex Cinema
town hall
the post office

Focus on Prepositions and Prepositional Phrases

■ A *preposition* relates a noun or a pronoun to another word in a sentence. Common prepositions include *at, before, of, under,* and *with.*

■ A *prepositional phrase* is a group of words that begins with a preposition and ends with a noun or pronoun. The *object of a preposition* is the noun or pronoun that follows the preposition in a prepositional phrase.

■ An *adjective phrase* is a prepositional phrase that modifies, or describes, a noun or pronoun.

■ An *adverb phrase* is a prepositional phrase that modifies, or tells more about, a verb, an adjective, or an adverb.

Examples:
Tell me *about your route.*
We laughed *during our walk.*
Classes *for most students* end early.

Traveler's Aid Using the landmarks on your **Quick!** list, write a paragraph describing how to travel from your home to your school. Exchange papers with a classmate, and see how many prepositions and prepositional phrases you can identify in each other's sentences.

Dream Room Suppose you could arrange a dream bedroom any way you wanted. Write a paragraph describing your ideas. Reread your paragraph and underline all the prepositional phrases.

Apply what you've learned about prepositions to your writing. Look at some of your recent writing projects. Use prepositional phrases in your work to add precise details to your writing.

Learn more about using adjective phrases and adverb phrases effectively in your writing. See page 258 in the Writer's Craft.

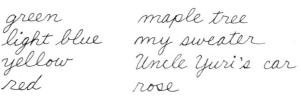

Colors of Conjunctions

Quick! Choose four colors. Beside each color, write the name of an object you are reminded of when you think of that color.

> green   maple tree
> light blue   my sweater
> yellow   Uncle Yuri's car
> red   rose

Focus on Conjunctions

■ *Conjunctions* join words or groups of words.

■ *Coordinating conjunctions,* such as *and, or,* and *but,* connect parts of a sentence or two sentences.

■ *Correlative conjunctions* are pairs of words used to connect parts of a sentence or two sentences. Some common correlative conjunctions are: *both . . . and, neither . . . nor, either . . . or,* and *not only . . . but also.*

Coordinating Conjunctions:
We drew *and* painted in the garden.
Seth looked carefully, *but* he did not find the red squirrel.

Correlative Conjunctions:
Either Emma will frame the pictures, *or* Hussein will do it.
They disturbed *neither* Carla *nor* us.

Tell It to a Friend Share your **Quick!** list with a friend. Take turns making up sentences about colors and objects. Then underline the conjunctions in each of your sentences.

Art Class Sit in a circle with two friends. You've agreed to teach an art class together! Your class might be about sculpting, painting, or weaving. Take turns making up sentences about your class. Use a coordinating conjunction or correlative conjunctions in each sentence. Here is an example:

> Pay equal attention to the color and texture of your work.

Look at some of your recent writing projects. Apply what you've learned about conjunctions to your work. Did you use a comma before a coordinating conjunction when combining two sentences? You can check the **Mechanics Handbook** *on pages 354–355 for more comma rules.*

To learn more about using conjunctions in your writing, see "Conjunctions" on page 246 in the Writer's Craft.

Hooray! An Interjection!

Quick! Think about the people you've seen during the last two days. Who has brightened up your life by giving you a compliment, a smile, or a kind word? In your Journal, list four of these people.

People Who Have Made Me Happy
Mom
my big sister
Mr. Tapper, the bus driver
Diego Cruz

Examples:
Aha! I think I've got the answer.
Wow! Wasn't that concert awesome?
Gee, where did you get the new radio?
My goodness, it's already time to leave.

Songfest Here's your chance to be a poet! Choose one of the people from your **Quick!** list and write a short poem about him or her. Tell what the person did to make you feel happy and how you feel about the person. Your words do not need to rhyme. Try to use at least three different interjections in your poem. Then see if you can fit the poem to a tune, either choosing a melody you like or humming your own original music.

Telephone Trouble Join with two classmates to play this game. Think about situations in which you might urgently need to communicate with someone over the telephone. For instance, you might need to leave a message before boarding a train or call a doctor when a family member is unwell. Decide on a situation and three characters whom it involves. Then choose parts and take turns making up a dialog that would be spoken over the telephone. Use interjections whenever they seem appropriate. Remember, phone messages can become garbled!

> **Focus on Interjections**
> - An *interjection* is a word or group of words that expresses strong feeling.
> - An interjection that stands alone is followed by an exclamation mark. An interjection that comes at the beginning of a sentence is followed by a comma.

Look at some of your recent writing projects. Apply what you've learned about interjections. Are they punctuated correctly?

Something Borrowed

Quick! Imagine that you've been given 15 minutes to choose as many items as you like from your local department store. In your Journal, write a list of some of the items you might choose.

pajamas   moccasins   boomerang

Focus on Borrowed Words

- *Etymology* is the study of words and their histories.
- Words from many languages have become part of the English language.
- These words are often more accurate than English words or phrases would be.

French: *potpourri*   English: mixture of dried flower petals

Chinese: *ketchup*   English: condiment sauce usually made from tomatoes

German: *sauerkraut*   English: chopped cabbage in brine

Arabic: *cotton*   English: soft, white fiber; plants of genus *Gossypium*

Japanese: *kimono*   English: loose robe with wide sleeves and a sash

Our society is continually growing and changing. Everything—from new technology to new types of music—affects society. In turn (and to keep up!), our language is constantly evolving, too. Turn to pages 268–271 to learn more about coined words, colloquialisms, jargon, slang, dialect, and idioms.

Shopping Spree! Uh, oh! Before you can leave the store with your shopping prizes you have to tell how the items got their names. Hurry to the book department and look in the dictionary to check out the items on your **Quick!** list. Jot the information in your Journal.

pajamas: Hindi

moccasins: Algonquin

boomerang: Native Australian

Look at some of your recent writing projects. Apply what you've learned about borrowed words. Do you notice them in your writing?

Mail Order You and some friends are creating an international meal. You've decided to order the ingredients for each dish from a store in the country the dish represents. Write a letter to a store in each country. For example, if you decide to make enchiladas, you might order tortillas, beans, and peppers from a store in Jalisco, Mexico. See how far and wide your letters will travel.

These Are My Roots

Quick! Now's the time to clean out that bookbag. Take out five items. Then make a chart in your Journal and write the bookbag items in the chart.

book   paper   ruler   pen   eraser

Focus on Language History
- Many words in the English language have developed from words in other languages, such as Latin, Greek, French, and German.
- Knowing the history of language can help you to understand the meanings of words.

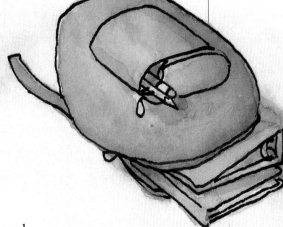

Examples:
student, Latin: *studere,* to study
desk, Latin: *desca,* a table
class, French: *classe,* a division of people

What's in a Name? Take a look at your **Quick!** items and grab a dictionary. Did you ever wonder how these things got their names? Check out the entries for each item, and find out the origin of each name. Add this information to your chart.

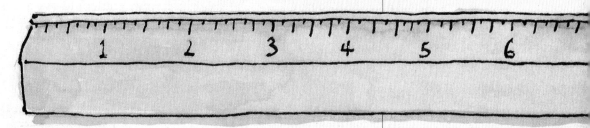

Where to Next? With a partner, choose three of the classes you attend together on one day of the week. Write a summary of the topics you have studied and the materials you may have used in those classes. After you have finished your writing, see if you can figure out where the names of some of these things originated. Then check a dictionary to see how close your guesses were.

Look at some of your recent writing projects. Apply what you have learned about language history to some of your recent writing. Can you see how some of the words developed?

Poster Parody Imagine that your class is planning a special event that will take place in a special area of the school. Work with a group of friends to make a poster for the event. Instead of using the "real" name of the area, use the definition of the name based on the original word. For example, on a poster for a buffet in the cafeteria, you might write: Don't miss the great food in the coffee store. Show your poster to some other friends, and see if they know where to go.

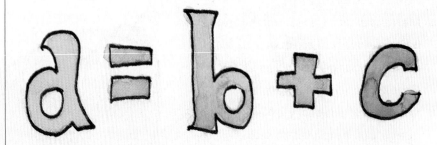

Math Masters What's going on in math this year? Have you learned about *algebraic equations*? How about *theorems*—heard any good ones lately? Write a paragraph about the concepts you've studied in math this year. After you've finished your writing, add a paragraph about the languages from which these concepts developed.

Art History Put on your beret, grab your palette, and interview your art teacher about the materials used to create paintings. In your interview, you could ask about the history of the names of the different colors and tints. Consider publishing your interview in your school yearbook.

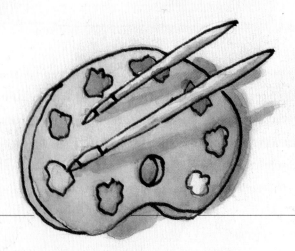

3

Information
Instantly

> *This **Grammar, Mechanics, and Usage Handbook** is a good reference for writers. It contains rules about capitalization and punctuation. It also contains some information about verb forms, adjective forms, and noun spellings. You'll find the U.S. Postal Service state abbreviations in this handbook, too.*

Punctuation Guide

End Punctuation Use end punctuation at the end of a sentence. A **period** ends a declarative sentence. A declarative sentence makes a statement.

> Charlie plays badminton and tennis.

A **period** is used at the end of a sentence that asks a polite question.

> Will you kindly give this ticket to the attendant.

A **period** ends an imperative sentence. An imperative sentence makes a command or a request.

> Fold the laundry. (command)   Please walk the dog. (request)

A **question mark** ends an interrogative sentence. An interrogative sentence asks a question.

> Why did Maria leave?   Did she go to the library?

An **exclamation mark** ends an exclamatory sentence. An exclamatory sentence expresses strong emotion. It also follows an interjection, a word or group of words that expresses strong feeling such as surprise or anger.

> You're the greatest!   Oh, no! Try it again.

Periods Use a **period** at the end of an abbreviation (in informal writing).

> Highway—Hwy.   Fort—Ft.   Park—Pk.
> Wednesday—Wed.   October—Oct.
> Mr. Jim Ober (Mister)   Evelyn Quiñones, V.P. (Vice President)

Use a **period** in abbreviations for time (in both formal and informal writing). Note that B.C. (before the birth of Christ) follows the date and that A.D. (after the birth of Christ) precedes the date.

2:30 P.M.   4:00 A.M.   40 B.C.   A.D. 301

Use a **period** after initials.

Dorrie K. Berkowitz   E. C. Higgins

Use a **period** after numerals and letters in outlines.

I. Languages
   A. Swahili
   B. Spanish

Commas Use a **comma** between the name of a city and a state in an address.

San Antonio, Texas   Albany, NY

Use a **comma** before and after the name of a state or a country when it is used with the name of a city in a sentence.

We located Tempe, Arizona, on the map in our classroom.

Use a **comma** between the day and year in a date.

December 26, 1933

Use a **comma** before and after the year when it is used with both the month and the day in a sentence. Do not use a comma if only the month and the year are given.

Classes will start on September 3, 1991, on the North Campus.
We return to school in September 1991.

Use **commas** to separate three or more items in a series.

George describes stars, moons, leaves, and clouds.

Use a **comma** before *and, but,* or *or* when they join simple sentences.

Bert cooked dinner, and Martha set the table.

Use a **comma** or a **pair of commas** to set off an adjective clause that is nonessential to the meaning of the sentence.

The cat, which had four white paws, was very friendly.

Do not use a **comma** or a **pair of commas** to set off an adjective clause that is essential to the meaning of the sentence.

The cat that has four white paws is the friendliest.

Use a **comma** to set off an adverb clause if it begins a sentence.

After mixing the dough, Greg rolled and cut the biscuits.

Do not use a **comma** to set off an adverb clause if it ends a sentence.

Greg rolled and cut the biscuits after mixing the dough.

Use a **comma** or **a pair of commas** to set off nouns of direct address.

Carolyn, your room is chilly.

Your room, Carolyn, is chilly.

Your room is chilly, Carolyn.

Use **commas** to set off introductory words, appositives that are not essential to the meaning of a sentence, and words or phrases that interrupt the flow of thought in a sentence.

Yes, I will drive you to the store.

Mrs. Rosenthal, our art teacher, showed us how to design our own jewelry.

David Ross, as we thought, got the lead in the school play.

Use a **comma** after an introductory participial phrase.

Covered with thick fur, the animals stayed warm throughout the long winter.

Use a **comma** after two or more introductory prepositional phrases.

At that stage in our negotiations, an agreement had not been reached.

Use a **comma** after the greeting in a friendly letter and after the closing in all letters.

Dear Tyrone,   As ever,

Use a **comma** to set off the word *too* when it is used to mean *also.*

I want to read your new book, too.

Use a **comma** or a **pair of commas** to set off an abbreviated title or degree following a person's name.

Jerry Weinfield, C.P.A., will prepare our income taxes.

Use a **comma** to set off a direct quotation.

"Karen and Mary will meet us at the station," Cheryl said.

"Their car," Jennifer commented, "is a green station wagon."

Use a **comma** to prevent misreading.

Turning to Mother Dad smiled his thanks.

Turning to Mother, Dad smiled his thanks.

Semicolons Use a **semicolon** to join the parts of a compound sentence when a coordinating conjunction such as *and, or, nor,* or *but* is not used.

Beth saddled up her pony; she rode him most of the afternoon.

Use a **semicolon** before words such as *consequently, furthermore, however, moreover, nevertheless,* or *therefore* when it joins two independent clauses. Be sure to use a comma after a conjunctive adverb.

Sarah has never been to Italy; nevertheless, she speaks Italian very well.

Colons Use a **colon** to separate the hour and the minute when you write the time of day.

We will be home before 7:00 this evening.

Use a **colon** after the salutation of a business letter.

Dear Ms. Ronson: To Whom It May Concern:

Use a **colon** to introduce a list of items that ends a sentence. Use a phrase such as *the following* or *as follows* before the list.

Our class schedule is as follows: English, social studies, mathematics, and
science.

Quotation Marks Use **quotation marks** before and after a direct quotation.

"I need some help in the yard," Aunt Ruth remarked.

Use a **comma** or **a pair of commas** to separate a phrase such as *he said* from the quotation itself. Place the commas outside the opening quotation marks but inside the closing quotation marks.

"I'll mow the lawn," Troy explained, "when it stops raining."

Place a **period** inside closing quotation marks.

Tricia said, "I have to start my homework now."

Place a **question mark** or an **exclamation mark** inside the quotation marks when it is part of the quotation.

Uncle Mike asked, "Who will drive me to the airport?"

Terry exclaimed, "What a great bicycle!"

Place a **question mark** or an **exclamation mark** outside the quotation marks when it is part of the entire sentence but not part of the quotation.

Did Mark say, "Bring the groceries into the kitchen"?

I heard Tanya say, "The new library has just opened"!

Use **quotation marks** to identify the title of a short story, an essay, a song, a short poem, a book chapter, or a magazine or newspaper article.

Short story: "A Boy's Best Friend"   Book chapter: "Rome and Venice"

Essay: "To My Friend"   Magazine article: "Save Our Planet"

Song: "Heart and Soul"   Newspaper article: "Weather and You"

Poem: "Who Am I"

Italics (Underlining) Use **italics** or **underlining** to set off the title of a book, a play, a film, a TV series, a magazine, or a newspaper.

Book: *The Incredible Journey*   Magazine: <u>Newsweek</u>

Newspaper: *The New York Times*   TV series: *Sesame Street*

Apostrophes Use an **apostrophe** and an *s* ('s) to form the possessive of a singular noun.

Fred's drum   the candle's wick

Use an **apostrophe** and an *s* ('s) to form the possessive of a plural noun that does not end in *s*.

the cattle's pasture   the mice's cage

Use an **apostrophe** alone to form the possessive of a plural noun that ends in *s*.

the tenants' meeting   the actors' workshop

Use an **apostrophe** and an *s* ('s) to form the possessive of an indefinite pronoun.

everybody's responsibility   someone's jacket

Use an **apostrophe** in a contraction to show where letters have been omitted.

would + not = wouldn't   he + will = he'll   that + is = that's

Hyphens Use a **hyphen** to show the division of a word at the end of a line. Divide the word between syllables.

On our recent class trip to the museum, we saw a collection of fine water-
color paintings.

Use a **hyphen** in compound numbers from twenty-one through ninety-nine.

thirty-two plates   seventy-eight books

Use a **hyphen** in a fraction that is used as a modifier. Do not use a hyphen in a fraction used as a noun.

We measured a one-third portion in the cup.

One third of our money was given to charity.

Use a **hyphen** or **hyphens** in certain compound nouns. Use the dictionary to determine which compound nouns need hyphens.

great-grandmother   Cuban American   sister-in-law

Use a **hyphen** in a compound modifier when it precedes the word it modifies.

She is a Cuban-American artist.   She is a Cuban American.

Use a **hyphen** after the prefixes *all-*, *ex-* (meaning former), and *self-*. Use a hyphen to separate a prefix from a word that begins with a capital letter.

all-inclusive   ex-treasurer   self-centered   pre-Incan

Dashes Use a **dash** to show that a thought is unfinished or interrupted. If the sentence continues, use a second dash to mark the end of the interruption.

Toni—you must buy that sweater.

Toni—as you may have guessed—picked the red sweater.

Parentheses Use **parentheses** for material that is not part of the main statement but is important to include.

Andy (the man on the right) grew up in Sharon, Vermont.

Punctuation in Bibliographic References Organize a bibliography—the list of sources that you used to prepare a report—alphabetically by the authors' last names. Note the punctuation.

> Baker, Horace, "Africa." *World Book,* Vol. 2, 1976 ed.
>
> Donner, Arnold, *Africa.* Berkeley, CA: Starfield Press, 1981.

Abbreviations In both informal and formal writing you may use abbreviations for certain organizations and government agencies.

> Association for the Prevention of Cruelty to Animals—ASPCA

In informal writing and on envelopes, you may use United States Postal Service abbreviations for the names of states.

Alabama AL	Montana MT
Alaska AK	Nebraska NE
Arizona AZ	Nevada NV
Arkansas AR	New Hampshire NH
California CA	New Jersey NJ
Colorado CO	New Mexico NM
Connecticut CT	New York NY
Delaware DE	North Carolina NC
District of Columbia DC	North Dakota ND
Florida FL	Ohio OH
Georgia GA	Oklahoma OK
Hawaii HI	Oregon OR
Idaho ID	Pennsylvania PA
Illinois IL	Rhode Island RI
Indiana IN	South Carolina SC
Iowa IA	South Dakota SD
Kansas KS	Tennessee TN
Kentucky KY	Texas TX
Louisiana LA	Utah UT
Maine ME	Vermont VT
Maryland MD	Virginia VA
Massachusetts MA	Washington WA
Michigan MI	West Virginia WV
Minnesota MN	Wisconsin WI
Mississippi MS	Wyoming WY
Missouri MO	

In scientific writing use abbreviations for units of measure. The abbreviation is the same for singular and plural units.

    inch—in.   pounds—lb.   kilometer—km   liter—L

Capitalization Guide

First Word in Sentences Capitalize the first word of a sentence.

    The violets spring to life with splendid color.

Capitalize the first word of a direct quotation. Do not capitalize the second part of an interrupted quotation unless it begins a new sentence.

    Kevin said, "The tennis courts will open at noon."

    "Come on," Ryan urged, "let's go swimming."

Capitalize the first word of each line of poetry unless the word is not capitalized in the original poem.

    O Kangaroo, O Kangaroo

    Be grateful that you're in the zoo

Capitalize the first word in the salutation and in the closing of a letter, and capitalize the title and name of the person addressed.

    Dear Ms. Carson: Best regards,

Proper Nouns: Names and Titles of People Capitalize the names and initials of specific persons or things.

    A. N. Horowitz   Lyndon B. Johnson

Capitalize titles of respect or abbreviations of titles when they come before the names of people.

    Mr. Jason Driver   Lt. Col. Yukio Yokoe

Capitalize the names and abbreviations of academic degrees that follow a person's name. Capitalize the abbreviations *Jr.* and *Sr.*

    Albert Lifton, M.D.   Darrel Roper, Jr.   Marilyn Dunn, C.S.W.

Capitalize words that show family relationships when used as titles or as substitutes for a person's name.

    On my birthday, Dad and Grandpa took me to a baseball game.

Do not capitalize words that show family relationships when they are preceded by a possessive noun or pronoun.

    Carol's mother writes clever articles for our local paper.

    My mother helped me with my homework.

Capitalize an official title when it appears before a person's name or when it is used in a direct address.

> When we had a problem in our city, we contacted Governor Hayes.

> "Thank you for responding to our concerns, Governor," Ms. Lee said.

Do not capitalize the title that follows or is a substitute for a person's name.

> Frances Bowdon, the mayor of a neighboring city, volunteered to help.

Capitalize the pronoun *I*.

> How shall I proceed?

Proper Nouns: Names of Places Capitalize the names of cities, states, countries, and continents.

> Schenectady   Kansas   Chile   Australia

Capitalize the names of bodies of water and geographical features.

> Indian Ocean   Grand Canyon   Colorado River

Capitalize the names of sections of the country.

> the Northeast   the Southwest

Capitalize compass points when they refer to a specific section of the country.

> the East   the North

Do not capitalize adjectives derived from words indicating direction.

> eastern Pennsylvania   the southbound turnpike

Capitalize the names of streets and highways.

> Central Street   New York Thruway   Interstate 691

Capitalize the names of buildings, bridges, and monuments.

> Chrysler Building   Tappan Zee Bridge   Mount Rushmore

Capitalize the names of celestial bodies.

> Mercury   Neptune

Capitalize *Earth* when it refers to the planet. Do not capitalize *earth* when preceded by *the*. Do not capitalize *sun* or *moon*.

> Astronauts have viewed Earth from outer space.

> The earth's natural satellite is the moon.

Other Proper Nouns and Adjectives Capitalize the names of clubs, organizations, businesses, institutions, and political parties.

> the Science Club   Lincoln High School

> National Brands Corporation   the Democratic Party

Capitalize brand (trade) names. Do not capitalize a common noun that follows a brand name.

> Corncrisps   Sparkles toothpaste

Capitalize the names of historic events, periods of time, and documents.

Prohibition   Emancipation Proclamation

Capitalize the names of the days of the week, months of the year, and holidays. Do not capitalize the names of seasons.

Monday   April   Martin Luther King Day   winter

Capitalize abbreviations.

Juliet C. Lee, R.N.   Tues.   Hwy.   Javier Santos, Jr.

Capitalize the first word and all important words in the titles of books, plays, short stories, poems, films, essays, articles, newspapers, magazines, TV series, chapters of books, and songs.

Book, play, short story: *Sweetwater, Hamlet,* "The Circuit"

Poem, film, essay: "The Dream Keeper," *E.T.,* "Our Pets"

Article, newspaper, magazine: "Rock's Finest Hour," *Boston Globe, Ebony*

TV Series, chapter of book, song: *Cheers,* "Oil Painting," "We Are the World"

Capitalize the names of ethnic groups, nationalities, and languages.

Native American   British   Italian

Capitalize the proper adjectives that are formed from the names of ethnic groups and nationalities.

Hungarian paprika   Polish sausages

Capitalize the first word of each main topic and subtopic in an outline.

I. Vacation ideas
  A. Scuba diving
  B. Deep-sea fishing

Usage Guide

Forming Noun Plurals You can use this chart when you want to spell plural nouns. Remember, some plural nouns have irregular spellings. Other plural nouns keep the same spelling as the singular form.

Singular Nouns	To Form Plural	Examples		
most singular nouns	add *s*	boy boys	friend friends	cat cats
nouns ending with *s, ss, x, z, ch, sh*	add *es*	box boxes	waltz waltzes	church churches

nouns ending with a consonant and *y*	change the *y* to *i* and add *es*	sky skies	city cities	baby babies
nouns ending with a vowel and *o*	add *s*	radio radios	studio studios	rodeo rodeos
nouns ending with a consonant and *o*	generally add *s* but sometimes *es*	piano pianos	cello cellos	tomato tomatoes
some nouns ending with a consonant and *o*	add either *s* or *es*	volcanos or volcanoes	mottos or mottoes	
nouns ending with *ff, f,* or *fe*	most add *s;* some change *f* to *ve;* add *s*	cuff cuffs	roof roofs	life lives
some irregular nouns	change their spelling	woman women	tooth teeth	foot feet
a few irregular nouns	keep the same spelling	moose	sheep	trout

Verb Forms Irregular verbs do not add *ed* or *d* to form the past or past participle.

Verb	Past	Past Participle
be	was	(have, has, or had) been
do	did	(have, has, or had) done
go	went	(have, has, or had) gone
begin	began	(have, has, or had) begun
come	came	(have, has, or had) come
drink	drank	(have, has, or had) drunk
ring	rang	(have, has, or had) rung
run	ran	(have, has, or had) run
sing	sang	(have, has, or had) sung

sink	sank	(have, has, or had) sunk
spring	sprang	(have, has, or had) sprung
swim	swam	(have, has, or had) swum
swing	swung	(have, has, or had) swung
break	broke	(have, has, or had) broken
choose	chose	(have, has, or had) chosen
drive	drove	(have, has, or had) driven
eat	ate	(have, has, or had) eaten
freeze	froze	(have, has, or had) frozen
give	gave	(have, has, or had) given
ride	rode	(have, has, or had) ridden
speak	spoke	(have, has, or had) spoken
take	took	(have, has, or had) taken
write	wrote	(have, has, or had) written
blow	blew	(have, has, or had) blown
draw	drew	(have, has, or had) drawn
fly	flew	(have, has, or had) flown
grow	grew	(have, has, or had) grown
know	knew	(have, has, or had) known
lie	lay	(have, has, or had) lain
see	saw	(have, has, or had) seen
tear	tore	(have, has, or had) torn
throw	threw	(have, has, or had) thrown
wear	wore	(have, has, or had) worn
bring	brought	(have, has, or had) brought
buy	bought	(have, has, or had) bought
catch	caught	(have, has, or had) caught
teach	taught	(have, has, or had) taught
think	thought	(have, has, or had) thought
feel	felt	(have, has, or had) felt
have	had	(have, has, or had) had
hold	held	(have, has, or had) held
lay	laid	(have, has, or had) laid
leave	left	(have, has, or had) left

lend	lent	(have, has, or had) lent
make	made	(have, has, or had) made
say	said	(have, has, or had) said
sit	sat	(have, has, or had) sat
burst	burst	(have, has, or had) burst
set	set	(have, has, or had) set

Adjective Forms You can use this chart when you need help with comparative and superlative adjective forms. Remember, some adjectives are irregular. They do not form their comparative or superlative forms in the usual way.

Adjective	Compares Two Things	Compares More Than Two Things
small	smaller	smallest
thin	thinner	thinnest
lengthy	lengthier	lengthiest
tiny	tinier	tiniest
gruesome	more gruesome	most gruesome
active	less active	least active
likable	more likable	most likable
energetic	less energetic	least energetic
much, many	more	most
little	less	least
good, well	better	best
bad	worse	worst
far	farther	farthest

> One of the most important things every writer does during the proofreading stage is to check that all of the words in a piece are correctly spelled. Poor spelling is more than an inconvenience to the reader. If even one or two words are spelled incorrectly, your writing may end up meaning something very different from what you wanted to say.

Strategies and Tips

Try spelling difficult words syllable by syllable, saying the word quietly to yourself as you write it. If you pronounce it correctly, your chances of spelling it correctly are improved. Also, try to picture what the word looks like. This will almost always help you to find the correct spelling. Always check your dictionary for any spellings you aren't sure of.

Spelling rules can help you to spell certain kinds of words correctly. Remember—these rules are only hints to help you to develop a sense of what's correct and what isn't. English is a tricky language; the following rules almost always have exceptions, so you can't depend on them in every case.

Words with *ie* and *ei* In most cases, a word is spelled with *ie* for the *e* sound, except when the *e* sound follows the letter *c:*

chief   belief   yield   niece
receipt   ceiling   perceive

In most cases, a word is spelled with *ei* when the sound is *not e,* especially if the sound is *a:*

eight   eighty   weight   neigh   sleigh

Be careful, however! These are common exceptions to this rule:

either   seize   weird

Adding s and es In most cases, *s* can be added to a word without any other change in the spelling:

> pet/pets   sign/signs   lock/locks

If the word ends in *ch, s, ss, sh, x,* or *z,* add *es:*

> inch/inches   wish/wishes   buzz/buzzes
>
> kiss/kisses   fix/fixes   chorus/choruses

For most nouns ending in a single *f,* change the *f* to *v* and add *es* to form the plural:

> elf/elves   scarf/scarves   loaf/loaves

Here are some exceptions to this rule:

> oaf/oafs   proof/proofs   chief/chiefs

Most words that end in *ff* simply add *s:*

> cliff/cliffs   stuff/stuffs   sniff/sniffs

Words ending in o Most words that end in a vowel followed by *o* add *s* to form the plural:

> rodeo/rodeos   folio/folios   studio/studios

Most words that end in a consonant followed by *o* add *es* to form the plural:

> hero/heroes   zero/zeroes   tomato/tomatoes

Some exceptions are words, mostly musical terms, borrowed from the Italian language. Their plurals are usually formed simply by adding *s:*

> piano/pianos   soprano/sopranos   cello/cellos

Sometimes, however, the original Italian plural form is used:

> concerto/concerti   libretto/libretti

Adding es, ed, ing, er, and est If a word ends in a consonant followed by *y,* change the *y* to *i* before adding any ending that does not begin with *i:*

> ruby/rubies   rely/relies   carry/carried

For most words that end in a vowel followed by *y,* keep the *y* when adding an ending:

> enjoy/enjoyed   stray/straying   obey/obeyed

Remember that some irregular verbs ignore this rule to form their past tenses:

> say/said   buy/bought   pay/paid

In most cases, if a one-syllable word ends in one vowel and one consonant, the consonant doubles when an ending that begins with a vowel is added:

> sag/sagged   trip/tripping   thin/thinnest

For most two-syllable words ending in one vowel and one consonant, the consonant doubles only if the accent falls on the second syllable:

trigger/triggered   bother/bothering

BUT: begin/beginning   prefer/preferred

If a word ends in a silent *e,* drop the *e* when adding an ending that begins with a vowel:

loose/looser   loose/loosest   large/largest

tape/taped   write/writing   breathe/breathing

Adding prefixes and suffixes When you add a prefix to a word, the spelling of the base word usually stays the same:

tie/untie   behave/misbehave   arm/disarm

When you add a suffix, the spelling of the base word may change. If the base word ends in silent *e,* drop the *e* before a suffix that begins with a vowel:

operate/operator   type/typist   love/lovable

For most words ending in silent *e,* keep the *e* when adding a suffix that begins with a consonant:

love/loveless   shame/shameful   elope/elopement

When you add the suffix *-ness* or *-ly,* the spelling of the base word usually does not change:

strange/strangely   fine/fineness   quick/quickly

Some exceptions are certain one-syllable words ending in two vowels or a vowel and *y:*

true/truly   due/duly   gay/gaily

If a word ends in *y* and has more than one syllable, change the *y* to *i* before adding *-ness* or *-ly:*

happy/happily/happiness   crazy/crazily/craziness

Homophones Homophones—words that sound alike but have different meanings and spellings—are responsible for a great many misspellings. Be sure you know the *meaning* of the homophone you want to use. That will usually help you to spell it correctly. Here are a few of those most often misspelled and misused:

rain/rein/reign   so/sew/sow   sheer/shear

chilly/chili/Chile   flare/flair   bough/bow

pair/pear/pare   forth/fourth   higher/hire

close/clothes   to/too/two   sea/see

piece/peace   hours/ours   real/reel

through/threw
won/one
pore/pour
stationary/stationery
principal/principle

Word Finder for Words Often Misspelled

As we pointed out at the beginning of this section, rules of spelling won't be enough to help you to spell correctly in every case. There are many words in the English language whose spelling seems to obey no rules at all or to contradict the rules you've taken so much trouble to learn. Some of them *do* follow the rules but are tricky to spell anyway. The only way to spell these "problem" words correctly every time is to memorize them.

To help you to do this, we've picked out some of the words that seem to give most people the most trouble most often—the words that you will see most frequently misspelled. Use this list or your dictionary often, whenever you are unsure of a word. The more often you see a word's correct spelling, the more likely you are to remember it for your own future use.

abdomen	assistant	cemetery	defenseless
absurd	athlete	certain	descendant
accommodate	authoritative	chasm	desolate
ache	auxiliary	chute	develop
acknowledge	awkward	cinnamon	diamond
acquire	bazaar	colossal	diaper
agile	bicycle	comparative	dilemma
aisle	boulevard	compatible	disappear
ally	breathe	complexion	disappoint
amateur	brilliant	congratulate	eerie
analyze	bruise	cough	elementary
answer	business	courteous	elephant
anxiety	canoe	crease	eligible
appearance	catastrophe	criticize	embarrass
appropriate	category	cylinder	enthusiasm
asbestos	caught	dandelion	especially

essential
exceed
excellent
familiar
fascinate
feminine
fiery
fluorescent
foliage
foreign
forfeit
forty
fourth
fragile
frighten
gauge
gaunt
genius
genuine
government
graduate
grammar
grudge
height
hideous
icicle
independent
indispensable
initiative
institution
intellectual
interrupt
irresistible
isolate
jealousy
jubilant
judgment
kiln

label
laboratory
lacquer
ladle
lapel
lavender
lieutenant
lightning
linoleum
lullaby
maneuver
marriage
matinee
measles
mediocre
meteor
miscellaneous
misspell
mobile
mosaic
municipal
murmur
mystery
nausea
necessary
necessity
nickel
niece
nineteenth
ninetieth
ninety
ninth
noticeable
obstacle
occasion
opportunity
orchid
pageant

parallel
particle
patent
peculiar
permissible
persuade
petal
pleasure
pliers
poison
prejudice
principal
principle
procedure
punctual
pyramid
realize
receive
reckless
recognize
recommend
relief
repetition
reservoir
responsible
restaurant
rhyme
rhythm
rhythmic
schedule
scissors
scour
secretary
seize
separate
similar
stationary
stationery

subdue
suburb
successful
sword
technical
tentacle
their
they're
throughout
tomorrow
toward
trapeze
treacherous
tread
treasure
trespass
truly
turbulent
typical
unique
utilize
variety
venom
vicinity
vise
waffle
wallet
weight
weird
we're
whether
whim
wretched
wring
yacht
you're

Handwriting Hints

Sometimes you will prepare your published writing in your personal handwriting. Just as you check your spelling at the proofreading stage, you will want to be sure that you use your best handwriting when you publish.

Everyone's handwriting is different. It is important, though, that your audience be able to read your writing. Your writing must be legible. Here are some questions that you can ask yourself about your handwriting. Review these questions when you look at your published work.

Self-Check Questions

- ☐ Is my handwriting smooth?
- ☐ Are my letters evenly spaced?
- ☐ Are my words evenly spaced?
- ☐ Are my letters shaped correctly?
- ☐ Are my letters the correct size?
- ☐ Do all of my letters sit on the baseline?
- ☐ Do my capital letters touch the top line?
- ☐ Do all of my letters slant in the same direction?

Handwriting Sample

*How can you make your handwriting legible?
Practice helps.*

Information Resources are books such as the dictionary, the encyclopedia, the atlas, and the almanac. These resources are very important to you as a writer. Understanding how to use the library and how to use the parts of a book are also very important. In this section of **Information Instantly** you will find out about many valuable resources.

Library Organization

Books and More Books As a writer, you will often need to support your work with general information or illustrations. Where will you go to get that support? Why, the library, of course! In fact, the library is so useful to a writer that it can sometimes seem like a second home.

Printed Material You will find that printed material in most libraries is organized in several main sections.

Fiction Works of **fiction**, such as novels and short stories, poems and plays, are in a section that is arranged alphabetically by authors' last names.

Nonfiction In another section you will find **nonfiction** books. These books contain factual information about real people, places, and events. Most libraries classify nonfiction books according to the Dewey Decimal System. This system uses call numbers between 000 and 999 to provide one thousand subject categories. Books are arranged on shelves according to these numbers, which are written on each book's spine below the title.

Reference The **reference section** is a very important part of any library. Here you will find general references such as encyclopedias, dictionaries, atlases, and almanacs.

Periodicals Newspapers and magazines, which are classified as **mass media** because they influence large numbers of people, are published periodically—daily, weekly, monthly, and so forth. In a library, such publications are called **periodicals**. The *Readers' Guide to Periodical Literature* will help you to find articles on particular subjects.

Nonprint Materials You might discover that your library has audiovisual aids and computerized reference sources. Tapes from the mass media of television and radio may also be available. Today many large libraries have computer labs where students can use word processors and laser printers. As more and more advances in technology occur, libraries will become filled with even more nonprint material.

On Your Own In what section of the library would you find the following:

- a tape of the TV program *Nature?*
- a map of Turkey?
- a book about Colin Powell?
- a copy of *Johnny Tremain?*
- a copy of *Time?*
- a book about lasers?

The Card Catalog Knowing how to use the **card catalog** will make your research efforts easier. The card catalog is a bank of drawers, with each drawer labeled with a range of letters. The cards inside each drawer are alphabetized according to the information presented on the top line of each card.

The card catalog usually has three cards for each nonfiction book: the author card, the title card, and the subject card. Each of these cards has a call number in the upper left-hand corner. The **call number** tells you how the book is classified and thus where it is found in the library. The card catalog has only two cards—an author card and a title card—for fiction books.

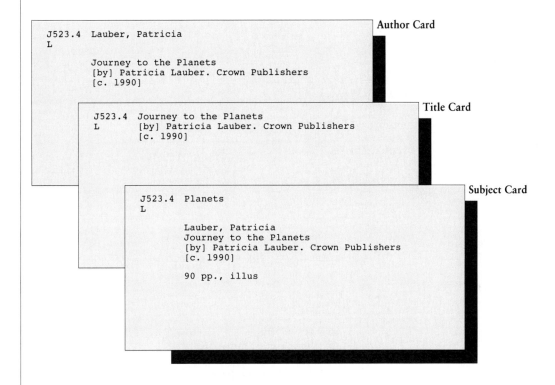

Author Card

```
J523.4  Lauber, Patricia
L

        Journey to the Planets
        [by] Patricia Lauber. Crown Publishers
        [c. 1990]
```

Title Card

```
J523.4  Journey to the Planets
L       [by] Patricia Lauber. Crown Publishers
        [c. 1990]
```

Subject Card

```
J523.4  Planets
L

        Lauber, Patricia
        Journey to the Planets
        [by] Patricia Lauber. Crown Publishers
        [c. 1990]

        90 pp., illus
```

On Your Own

- What is the title of this book?
- What is the author's name?
- What company published this book?
- In what year was it published?
- How many pages are in this book?
- What is the call number for this book?

Parts of a Book

What's Between the Covers? Books are one of a writer's most useful resources. Knowing how books are organized and how to use the different parts of a book efficiently can help you to get the most out of your research. Just by scanning the **title page, table of contents,** and **index** of a book, you can decide if it has information that will be helpful to you in your writing. When you look at the **copyright page,** which appears on the back of the title page, you can see how current the information in the book is.

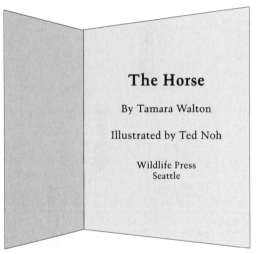

The Horse

By Tamara Walton

Illustrated by Ted Noh

Wildlife Press
Seattle

Title Page

Table of Contents

Table of Contents

Copyright Page

Index

Heavy breeds, 15–18
   Belgian, 15–16
   Clydesdale, 17
   Haflinger, 18
   See also Draft horses.
Horsemanship, 22–31
   saddles, 23–24
Light breeds, 19–21
   Arabian, 19
   Asian, 19–20
   Thoroughbred, 20–21
Saddles *See* Horsemanship.

Glossary Excerpt

equestrian (ĭ•qwĕs•trĭ•ăn)
relating to horses or the
riding of horses
gait (gāt) a horse's
movement, such as trot
or gallop

On Your Own Use your copy of *Write Idea!* to answer these questions:

- What is the name of the company that published this book?
- In what year was this book published?
- Use the table of contents. Find the page on which Unit 7 begins.
- Does this book have a thesaurus? a glossary?
- Look at the index. Find three main topics that contain subtopics.

Dictionary

Just What Does That Mean? A good **dictionary** is as important a tool for a writer as a pencil, a pen, or a computer keyboard. A dictionary contains **entry words,** listed in alphabetical order, and enough information to allow a writer to understand and use almost any word in the English language. With your dictionary by your side, you can be sure that you are using the right words in the right ways. That's confidence—the confidence it takes to be the best writer you can be!

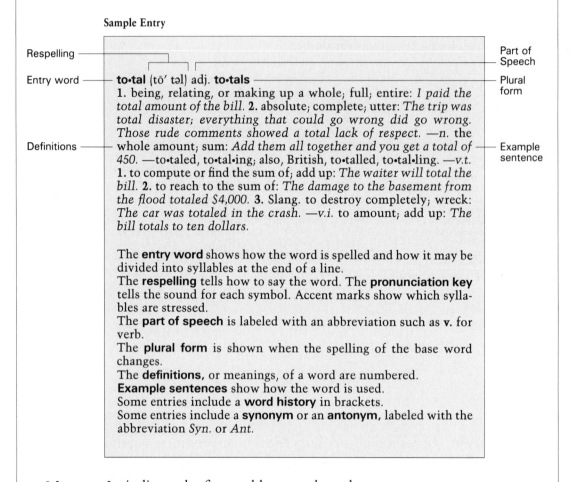

Sample Entry

Respelling — Part of Speech

Entry word — **to·tal** (tō′ təl) adj. **to·tals** — Plural form

Definitions — 1. being, relating, or making up a whole; full; entire: *I paid the total amount of the bill.* 2. absolute; complete; utter: *The trip was total disaster; everything that could go wrong did go wrong. Those rude comments showed a total lack of respect.* —n. the whole amount; sum: *Add them all together and you get a total of 450.* —to·taled, to·tal·ing; also, British, to·talled, to·tal·ling. —v.t. 1. to compute or find the sum of; add up: *The waiter will total the bill.* 2. to reach to the sum of: *The damage to the basement from the flood totaled $4,000.* 3. Slang. to destroy completely; wreck: *The car was totaled in the crash.* —v.i. to amount; add up: *The bill totals to ten dollars.* — Example sentence

The **entry word** shows how the word is spelled and how it may be divided into syllables at the end of a line.
The **respelling** tells how to say the word. The **pronunciation key** tells the sound for each symbol. Accent marks show which syllables are stressed.
The **part of speech** is labeled with an abbreviation such as **v.** for verb.
The **plural form** is shown when the spelling of the base word changes.
The **definitions**, or meanings, of a word are numbered.
Example sentences show how the word is used.
Some entries include a **word history** in brackets.
Some entries include a **synonym** or an **antonym**, labeled with the abbreviation *Syn.* or *Ant.*

guide words indicate the first and last word on the page

entry word shows how a word is spelled and how it can be divided into syllables

respelling shows how a word is pronounced (use the pronunciation key to determine the sound of each special letter or symbol)

accent marks show which syllables are stressed

part of speech shows which part (or parts) of speech a word may be used as; indicated by an abbreviation, such as *n.* for *noun* or *v.t.* for *verb, transitive*

plural form given when the plural is not formed in the regular way (by adding *-s* or *-es*)

past and present participle given when the spelling of the base word is changed when forming the past tense or the present participle

definitions explain the meaning or meanings of the word (each definition is numbered)

example sentence or phrase illustrates how the word is correctly used

word history tells the origin of the word; in brackets

synonym or antonym given for some words; labeled *syn.* or *ant.*

pronunciation key shows the pronunciation of special letters and symbols of the phonetic alphabet

---

T

torpedo boat / totem

tor•ren•tial (tô ren′ chəl) *adj.* of, resembling, or caused by a torrent: *a torrential rainfall.*

tor•rid (tôr′ id, tor′ id) *adj.* **1.** subjected to or parched by the intense heat of the sun: *the torrid regions of the world:* **2.** intensely hot or burning; scorching: *a torrid climate.* **3.** passionate; ardent: *a torrid love story.* —**tor•rid′ i•ty,** *n.*

Torrid Zone, a warm region between the Tropic of Cancer and the Tropic of Capricorn; tropics.

tor•sion (tôr′ shən) *n.* **1.** the act of twisting or the state of being twisted. **2.** a strain put on an object when one end is twisted in one direction while the other end is held firm or twisted in the opposite direction.

tor•so (tôr′ sō) *n., pl.* **tor•sos.** **1.** the trunk of the human body. **2.** a statue of this.

tort (tôrt) *n. Law.* any wrong or injury that does not involve breach of contract and for which the wronged person or party may sue in a civil court.

tor•til•la (tôr tē′ yə) *n.* a thin, round, unleavened cake made from water and cornmeal and baked on a griddle.

tor•toise (tôr′ təs) *n.* **1.** a turtle that lives on land.

tor•toise•shell (tôr′ təs shel′) *adj.* **1.** made of tortoise shell. **2.** having the mottled yellow and brown colors of tortoise shell.

tortoise shell **1.** the hard, mottled, yellow and brown material making up the outer shell of certain turtles. It is used especially to make combs, small decorative objects, and furniture inlay. **2.** any of a group of butterflies with mottled yellow, brown, and black coloration.

tor•tu•ous (tôr′ chü əs) *adj.* **1.** having many twists, turns, or bends; winding: *a tortuous road.* **2.** not direct, straightforward, or frank; devious: *a long, tortuous explanation for being late.* —**tor′ tu•ous•ly,** *adv.* **tor′ tu•ous•ness,** *n.*

tos•ta•da (tō stä′ də) *n.* a tortilla fried in deep fat, usually topped with a mixture of meat, beans, and raw vegetables. [From the Mexican Spanish word *tostada* meaning this food, from the word *tostado,* past participle of *tostar* "to toast, fry," going back to the Latin word *tostus,* past participle of *torrēre* "to make dry."]

tot (tot) *n.* **1.** a small child. **2.** a small amount of something, as an alcoholic beverage.

to•tal (tō′ təl) *adj.* **1.** being, relating to, or making up a whole; full; entire: *I paid the total amount of the bill.* **2.** absolute; complete; utter: *The trip was a total disaster; everything that could go wrong did go wrong. Those rude comments showed a total lack of respect.* —*n.* the whole amount; sum; *Add them all together and you get a total of 450.* —*v.,* **to•taled, to•tal•ing;** *also, British,* **to•talled, to•tal•ling.** —*v.t.* **1.** to compute or find the sum of; add up: *The waiter will total the bill.* **2.** to reach to the sum of: *The damage to the basement from the flood totaled $4,000.* **3.** *Slang.* to destroy completely; wreck: *The car was totaled in the crash.* —*v.i.* to amount; add up: *The bill totals to ten dollars.*

to•tal•i•tar•i•an (tō tal′i târ′ ē ən) *adj.* of or relating to totalitarianism. —*n.* a person who favors or supports totalitarianism.

to•tal•i•tar•i•an•ism (tō tal′i târ′ ē ə niz′əm) *n.* a system of government in which one political party aims at total control over the lives of the people under it, as by using a powerful secret police, restricting meetings and assemblies, and censoring or prohibiting books, newspapers, radio and televison broadcasts, and other forms of

to•tal•i•ty (tō tal′i tē) *n., pl.* **to•tal•i•ties.** **1.** the total amount; whole; sum. **2.** the state of being whole or complete.

to•tal•ly (tō tə lē) *adj.* completely; entirely; wholly: *We were totally unprepared for the May blizzard.*

tote (tōt) *v.t.,* **tot•ed, tot•ing.** *Informal.* to haul or carry: *to tote heavy packages home from the store.* —**tot′er,** *n.*

---

at; āpe; fär; câre; end; mĕ; it; īce; pîerce; hot; ōld; sông; fôrk; oil; out; up; ūse; rūle; pŭll; tûrn; chin; sing; shop; thin; this; hw in white; zh in treasure. The symbol ə stands for the unstressed vowel sound heard in about, taken, pencil, lemon, and circus.

On Your Own

- How many syllables are there in *totalitarianism?*
- How do the two meanings of *tot* differ?
- How is the last syllable of *totally* pronounced?
- What part of speech is the word *tote?*
- Why is the plural of *totality* given?
- From what language does the word *tostada* originally come?

Encyclopedia

Facts for the Taking What is the highest point on earth? Who was the first chief justice of the Supreme Court? What are comets made of? As a writer, you might need to answer these questions or others like them. Where should you turn first? Why, the **encyclopedia**, of course! The encyclopedia can be found in the reference section of the library. It is a collection of books, or volumes, arranged alphabetically. On the spine of each volume you will find a number and a guide letter. The **guide letter** shows the first letter of the subjects discussed in the volume.

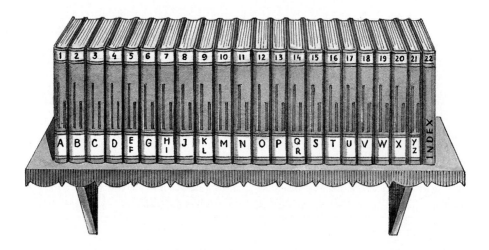

Tracking Down Your Topic Think about a word that sums up your topic. This important word will be your **key word**. Choose the volume that covers the first letter in your key word. For instance, imagine you want to write a report on the circulatory system. You may find information about your topic using key words such as *heart, blood, arteries,* or *veins.* Sometimes the encyclopedia will not have an article on the key word you look up but will refer you elsewhere. This is called a **cross-reference**. Most encyclopedias also have an **index volume**, which lists all of the topics in the encyclopedia and the volumes in which parts of a subject can be found.

Within each volume the articles are listed alphabetically. It is easiest to find what you want quickly if you use the **guide words**. These words are in dark print and name the first or the last topic on a page.

Next, look for the entry word that points out your topic. The article that follows the entry word provides you with information about your topic. At the end of the article you might find cross-references to articles with information related to your topic.

BLUE RIDGE. The eastern and southeastern part of the Appalachian Mountains system in the United States is called the Blue Ridge, or Blue Ridge Mountains. It extends southwestward 615 miles (990 kilometers), from Carlisle, Pa., through parts of Maryland, Virginia, North Carolina, South Carolina, and Tennessee, to Mount Oglethorpe in Georgia. A relatively narrow range, the Blue Ridge is 5 to 65 miles (8 to 105 kilometers) wide, with average heights of 2,000 to 4,000 feet (600 to 1,200 meters). The entire region is crisscrossed by many small streams, and three major Virginia rivers have cut gaps through the ridge—the Roanoke, the James, and the Potomac.

Within the Blue Ridge Mountains lie parts of seven national forests. More than 700 varieties of trees and plants have been catalogued there. Much of the region has remained culturally isolated, and traditional lifestyles prevail in many small villages and farms. Important farming activities include truck farming, tobacco production, and cattle raising.

Notable Blue Ridge peaks are Mount Rogers (5,729 feet; 1,746 meters), the highest point in Virginia; Sassafras Mountain (3,560 feet; 1,090 meters), the highest point in South Carolina; and Brasstown Bald (4,784 feet; 1,458 meters), the highest point in Georgia. (See also Appalachian Highlands.)

BLUES see **Jazz**.

BLY, Nellie (1867–1922). One day in 1885 an 18-year-old girl walked into the offices of the Pittsburgh Dispatch and introduced herself as Elizabeth Cochrane. She said she had written a letter, which the Dispatch had published, on more active life roles for women. On the basis of the letter she asked for a job. Miss Cochrane was hired and took as her pen name "Nellie Bly," from the song of the same name by American composer, Stephen Foster. She was to become famous for sensational, reform-oriented reporting.

On Your Own

- In which volume of the encyclopedia would you look if you wanted information on Chile?
- In what volume would you find information on the boa constrictor? How do you know?
- If you wanted more information on the Blue Ridge Mountains, under what topic would you look? How do you know?
- Where should you look to get information on the blues?
- How many national forests are found within the Blue Ridge Mountains?
- What is the tallest peak within the Blue Ridge Mountains? How tall is that peak?
- How long is the range in miles? in kilometers?

Information Resources

Atlas

Where in the World Am I? Suppose you were going to write a story about the faraway adventures of a character called Montana Feek. Montana loves to travel and never fails to get embroiled in capers filled with danger and suspense. You need a setting for Montana's latest adventure, but where in the world will it be?

An **atlas**, a book of maps, could help you to decide. Atlases offer abundant information about the world. Use the atlas's index to find the page with the map you need.

The **compass rose** on a map shows north, south, east, and west. Most maps also have a key, a small box containing facts about the map. The **key** usually includes a scale indicating the unit of measure that represents miles and kilometers (usually it's an inch).

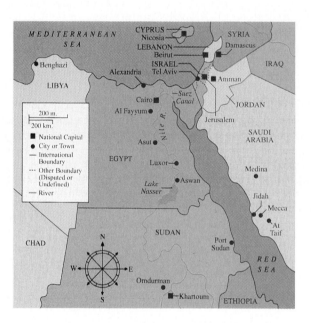

On Your Own

- If Montana were to go on a river trip in Egypt, on what river would she travel? On what lake might she go to fish?
- If Montana travels west from Egypt, in what neighboring country would she find herself?
- Montana might have to make a trip from Cairo to Aswan. If she does, about how many miles would she travel?
- Use an atlas to find some interesting places Montana might go on her next adventure.

Almanac

Quick and Easy—Just the Facts Imagine that you are a sports nut! You breathe, eat, and sleep sports. So is it any wonder that when your teacher tells you to write a report, you decide to do it on major league baseball?

Why not use the **almanac**, one of the writer's handiest tools? Almanacs are published every year, so they contain current information about a variety of subjects.

The almanac's complete index is usually in the front of the book. An abbreviated index may also be found in the back. Some almanacs place the complete index in the back, however. The complete index includes cross-references to topics you can look up to find information related to your subject.

MAJOR LEAGUE ALL-TIME PITCHING RECORDS
(through 1990)

Most Games Won - 511, Cy Young, Cleveland N.L., 1890–98, St. Louis N.L., 1899–90, Boston A.L., 1901–08, Cleveland A.L., 1909–11, Boston N.L., 1911

Most Games Won, Season - 60, Hoss Radbourne, Providence N.L., 1884. (Since 1900–41, Jack Chesbro, New York A.L., 1904.)

Most Consecutive Games Won - 24, Carl Hubbell, New York N.L., 1936 (16) and 1937 (8).

Most Consecutive Games Won, Season - 19, Tim Keefe, New York N.L., 1888; Rube Marquard, New York N.L., 1912.

Most Years Won 20 or More Games 16, Cy Young, Cleveland N.L., 1891–98, St. Louis N.L., 1899–1900, Boston A.L., 1901–04, 1907–08.

Most Strikeouts - 5,308, Nolan Ryan, New York N.L., California A.L., Houston N.L., 1968–1988 Texas, 1989–90 (still active).

Most Strikeouts, Season - 505, Matthew Kilroy, Baltimore A.A., 1886. (Since 1900 - 383, Nolan Ryan, California A.L., 1973.)

Most Strikeouts, Game - 21, Tom Cheney, Washington A.L., 1962, 16 innings. Nine innings: 20, Roger Clemens, Boston A.L., 1986; 19, Charles McSweeney, Providence N.L., 1884; Hugh Dailey, Chicago U.A., 1884. (Since 1900–19, Steve Carlton, St. Louis N.L. vs. New York, Sept. 15, 1969; Tom Seaver, New York N.L. vs. San Diego, April 22, 1970; Nolan Ryan, California A.L. vs. Boston, Aug. 12, 1974.)

On Your Own

- Imagine you are going to write a story about the pitcher who holds the record for the most games won. Whom would you write about?

- Who holds the record for the most strikeouts? How many did he have through 1990?

- Use an almanac to find other current data about major league baseball.

Thesaurus

A **thesaurus** is a writer's reference that provides synonyms for many common words. When you are looking for a more interesting or more exact word to use in your writing, look in your thesaurus.

The words in a thesaurus are listed in alphabetical order. The entries in a thesaurus will give you all sorts of information—part of speech, definition, and a sample sentence. In some entries you will also find antonyms—words with opposite meanings.

Sometimes you will find cross-references. For example, if you look up the word allow, you will find this cross-reference: "See let." This means that you should look up the word let; the word allow will be listed under let.

---

allow *See* let. — — — — — — — — — — — — — — — — — cross-reference

    — part of speech—verb

      — — — — — — — — — — — — — — — — — — definition

beg *v.* to ask for. He *begged* for mercy.

    appeal to make a strong request or call, especially for help. The homeless man *appealed* for affordable housing.   — entry

    plead to make a strong request or appeal. Triscina *pleaded* for an increase in her allowance. — sample sentence

    other synonyms: beseech, implore; *see also* ask. — — — — — — — cross-reference within an entry

A

ability *n.* the power to do or act; talent or skill. Dogs have the *ability* to bark.

>**knack** a special skill, ability, or method for doing something easily. Kitty has a *knack* for repairing old radios.
>
>**skill** the power or ability to do something, resulting from training, practice, knowledge, or experience. He showed great *skill* in writing poetry.
>
>**talent** a special natural ability or skill. Wilfred's classmates were amazed at his musical *talent*.

agree *v.* to have the same opinion or feeling. He asked a hundred people, and each one *agreed* with him.

>**assent** to express agreement. Six hours passed before Ms. Berstetta *assented* to the committee's plan.
>
>**comply** to act in agreement, usually with a request or rule. We will *comply* with the rule only if it's fair to everyone.
>
>**concur** to have the same opinion. Everyone in the group *concurred*.
>
>**other synonym:** consent
>**antonym:** disagree

allow *See* let.

angry *adj.* feeling or showing anger. Cal's lie made Fay *angry*.

>**enraged** filled with rage; angry beyond control. The *enraged* animal attacked the hunters.
>
>**furious** extremely angry. Dad was *furious* about my grades.
>
>**incensed** filled with anger. Leah was *incensed* by Barb's remark.
>
>**resentful** feeling bitter or indignant. Is he *resentful* about coming in second in the contest?

answer *v.* to speak or write in reply to. *Answer* any two of the questions.

>**reply** to answer; to respond in speech or writing. I *replied,* "Thanks for the car, but I don't need it today."
>
>**respond** to give an answer. Please *respond* immediately.
>
>**retort** to reply, usually in a quick, witty, or sharp way. "I suppose you don't want it then!" *retorted* Aunt Gina.
>
>**antonyms:** ask, inquire

ask *v.* to put a question to. *Ask* me anything you like.

>**demand** to ask forcefully. She *demanded* an immediate apology.
>
>**inquire** to seek knowledge or information by asking one or more questions. The mail carrier *inquired* about my dog.
>
>**query** to ask a question or questions of. Dad *queried* the singer about the words in her latest song.
>
>**other synonym:** question
>**antonyms:** *See* answer.

awful *adj.* causing fear, dread, or awe; terrible. The earthquake was *awful*.

>**dreadful** causing great fear or awe. I dreamed about a *dreadful* monster.

>**horrible** causing or tending to cause horror. What a *horrible* sight!

>**terrible** causing terror or awe. The movie was *terrible*.

>**unpleasant** offensive; not pleasant. Talking with her was an *unpleasant* experience.

>**other synonyms:** frightful, dire, shocking, ominous, horrifying

B

beautiful *adj.* having pleasant qualities. The rose is a *beautiful* flower.

>**attractive** having an appealing quality; pleasing. She is tall and *attractive*.

>**gorgeous** extremely beautiful or richly colored. The fireworks display was *gorgeous*.

>**handsome** having a pleasing appearance; good-looking. She fell in love with the *handsome* man.

>**other synonyms:** pretty, stunning, lovely, striking, appealing

>**antonyms:** ugly, hideous, unattractive

big *adj.* of great size or amount. Rajiv lives in a *big* house.

>**considerable** of great amount.

A college education costs a *considerable* amount of money.

>**enormous** much greater than the usual size or amount. Dinosaurs were *enormous* creatures.

>**gigantic** like or resembling a giant, especially in size. Joshua's boat is *gigantic*.

>**huge** of great size; extremely large. I ate a *huge* sandwich.

>**large** of great size, amount, or number; big. "Wow, this bedroom is so *large*!"

>**other synonyms:** monstrous, immense, massive, titanic

>**antonym:** little

brave *adj.* willing to face danger, pain, or difficulty; having or showing courage. The *brave* firefighter rescued all of the occupants.

>**bold** having courage; fearless. Police officers are *bold* people.

>**courageous** having or showing courage. Her *courageous* deed earned her everyone's respect.

>**fearless** showing or feeling no fear. Sister is a *fearless* pilot.

>**other synonyms:** heroic, unafraid

>**antonyms:** afraid, fearful, cowardly

bright *adj.* giving or reflecting much light; shining. The sunshine was *bright*.

>**brilliant** shining or sparkling with light. The North Star is *brilliant* in December.

shiny shining; bright. The stuffed bear had *shiny* black eyes.
other synonyms: luminous, vivid, sparkling
antonyms: dark, dull

C

cheap *adj.* low in price; inferior in quality or value. They bought *cheap* dresses for the party.
    gaudy tastelessly bright or ornate. He wore a *gaudy* red tie.
    inexpensive low in price. Fruit is *inexpensive* in the summer.
    antonym: expensive

clean *adj.* free from dirt. I like the smell of *clean* clothes.
    immaculate free from dirt or clutter. Our kitchen is always *immaculate.*
    pure not stained, spotted, or contaminated. Many coins are not *pure* silver.
    spotless absolutely clean. Her wedding gown was *spotless.*
    other synonyms: clear, stainless
    antonyms: dirty, filthy, messy

cook *v.* to prepare (food) for eating by using heat. Do you *cook* with a lot of spice?
    bake to cook in an oven. It is best to preheat the oven before you *bake.*
    broil to cook by flame or direct heat. Dad *broils* the best-tasting chicken in town.
    fry to cook something in hot fat, usually over direct heat. I like to *fry* potatoes.
    roast to cook without moisture, in an oven or over an open fire or hot coals. Theresa can *roast* a turkey better than anyone else.
    other synonyms: sauté, boil

D

different *adj.* not alike or similar; not the same. The man and the woman gave *different* descriptions.
    distinct not the same; not identical. Every car has a *distinct* identification number.
    varied consisting of different kinds, items, or parts. He put the car together from *varied* parts.

do *v.* to carry out or perform. What must we *do* now?
    achieve to do or reach successfully. Ms. Chang said, "You won't *achieve* your goals without hard work."
    perform to start and carry out to completion. The doctor *performed* the operation.
    other synonyms: contrive, execute

E

easy *adj.* needing little effort; not hard to do. Did you say math was *easy*?

effortless seeming to require little effort. For her it was an *effortless* task.

simple easily done, used, or understood. Reading is *simple* once you know your ABC's.

antonyms: difficult, hard

empty *adj.* having nothing or no one in it; lacking what is usually inside. Julius asked the teacher, "Sir, how can an *empty* barrel make noise?"

blank not written or printed upon; unmarked. One side of the dollar bill was *blank*.

vacant containing no one or nothing; unoccupied or empty. The parking lot is *vacant*.

other synonyms: barren, void, hollow

antonym: full

F

fast *adj.* acting, moving, or done with speed. Sharon is a *fast* thinker.

quick done or happening within a very short time. They are always *quick* to say they are sorry.

speedy moving rapidly. We started late, but a *speedy* taxi got us there on time.

swift moving with great speed. Only *swift* runners make the track team.

other synonyms: rapid, hasty

antonym: slow

friend *n.* a person one knows well and likes. My best *friend* lives next door.

buddy a close friend. Wayne has been my *buddy* for over six years.

companion a person who often goes along with another person. They were *companions* throughout kindergarten.

pal a close friend. Shayne said to Charlie, "You can't be my *pal* if you're going to tell lies."

other synonyms: mate, chum

antonym: enemy

funny *adj.* causing laughter or amusement. Bert has never said a *funny* word in his life.

hilarious extremely funny; very amusing. Some early television shows were *hilarious*.

humorous full of humor; funny. Aunt Lou told us a *humorous* story about Uncle Ned.

other synonyms: comical, amusing, entertaining

G

get *v.* to obtain possession of; receive or acquire. I'll *get* my diploma in the spring.

acquire to come into possession of; gain or obtain as one's own. His wealth was *acquired* through marriage.

earn to gain through effort. I need to *earn* more money.

obtain to get as one's own, especially as a result of effort. She told me to *obtain* written permission from the publisher before making the copies.

procure to get hold of through effort. He *procured* the supplies.

give *v.* to hand over to another as a present; to hand over or deliver. I can't believe they *gave* me a doll.

contribute to give along with others. They always *contribute* to worthy causes.

grant to give (something that is asked for). Sabra said, "Ms. Jones, can you *grant* us the rest of the day off?"

other synonyms: present, bestow, offer, donate, provide

antonyms: *See* take.

gloomy *adj.* dismal; depressing. Her finances are not as *gloomy* as she says.

bleak not cheerful; gloomy. She gave a *bleak* assessment of our team.

dismal dark and gloomy; bleak; dreary. The rain clouds made the afternoon *dismal.*

good *adj.* not bad or poor; above average in quality. I'm *good* at science.

appropriate suitable for an occasion; fitting. Naomi's dress was not *appropriate* for the wedding.

excellent remarkably good; superior. A grade of A+ in language arts is *excellent.*

other synonyms: fair, fine, decent

antonyms: bad, evil

great *adj.* unusual in ability or achievement. The *great* writer V. S. Naipaul was born in Trinidad.

distinguished famous for significant achievement or excellent qualities. From 1837 to 1901, the *distinguished* Victoria reigned as queen of Great Britain and Ireland.

famous very well known; having great fame. Aesop is *famous* for his fables.

outstanding so excellent as to stand out from others of its kind. Dr. Martin Luther King, Jr., was an *outstanding* defender of civil rights.

other synonyms: superb, remarkable, magnificent, sensational

antonym: ordinary

H

happy *adj.* having, showing, or bringing pleasure, joy, or contentment. Are you *happy* about your new assignment?

contented satisfied. She said she would be *contented* with a million dollars.

joyful very happy; feeling, showing, or causing joy. The choir sang a *joyful* tune.

pleased satisfied or content.

Dad said he was *pleased* with my grades.

other synonyms: delighted, merry, cheerful, contented, ecstatic

antonyms: *See* sad.

high *adj.* located or extending a great distance above the ground or other surface; tall. The clouds seemed to sit on the *high* mountains.

lofty extending high into the air; towering. The television station has two *lofty* towers.

tall of greater than average height; not short or low. Her mother is *tall,* but her father isn't.

towering very tall; lofty. She works on the top floor of the *towering* new building.

antonyms: low, short

hot *adj.* having a high temperature; having much warmth or heat. Yesterday was *hot,* but today is hotter.

fiery hot as fire; burning. The soup was *fiery.*

scorching intensely hot, enough to burn or cause drying. He burned his finger on the *scorching* engine.

tepid slightly warm; lukewarm. We bathed the wound in *tepid* water.

other synonyms: blistering, blazing, torrid, sizzling

antonym: cold

hurt *v.* to cause pain or injury. Marcia slipped on a banana peel and *hurt* her ankle very badly.

harm to do damage to; hurt. He screamed when they tried to *harm* him.

injure to do or cause physical damage to; harm. His neck was *injured* in the accident.

wound to injure by tearing, cutting, or piercing the skin. The report said no one was *wounded* in the fighting.

I

interesting *adj.* arousing or holding interest or attention. The *interesting* thing about this sentence is, it says nothing.

absorbing very interesting. Maya's speech was *absorbing* but quite long.

captivating capturing and holding attention by beauty or excellence. She wrote a *captivating* poem about ants.

fascinating very interesting or captivating; causing and holding interest through a special quality or charm. Many grandparents find computers *fascinating.*

antonyms: dull, boring

J

job *n.* anything one has to do. My *job* is to walk the president's dog.

chore a small routine task. Your *chore* on Mondays is dish washing.

Thesaurus

task a piece of work assigned to or demanded of a person; any piece of work. His *task* was easier.

large *See* big.

let *v.* to give permission or opportunity to. Did Wanda *let* Wendy walk away?

> **allow** to grant permission to or for; to let do or happen. Will you *allow* Matt to attend my party?
> **grant** to give what is asked for, such as permission. Sorry, I cannot *grant* your request.
> **permit** to allow. I'll *permit* you to go this time.
> **antonyms:** deny, refuse, forbid

look *v.* to make use of the sense of sight; to see with one's eyes. *Look* for the sign.

> **glance** to take a quick look. I saw you *glance* at her twice.
> **peer** to look closely. Ben's teacher *peered* at Marva's paper.
> **regard** to look at with a firm, steady gaze. The children *regarded* the new boy with curiosity.
> **stare** to look at steadily with eyes wide open, as in fear, admiration, or wonder. She hates it when people *stare* at her.
> **other synonyms:** behold, discern, inspect, scan; *see also* see.

loud *adj.* having a forceful sound. That's too *loud*!

> **deafening** having a sound that drowns out all others. My brother's car stereo is *deafening*.
> **resounding** having a loud, echoing, or ongoing sound. They gave him *resounding* applause.
> **other synonyms:** noisy, roaring
> **antonyms:** *See* quiet.

love *v.* to have a deep and tender feeling of affection for or attachment to. I think everyone *loves* a friendly person.

> **admire** to look at with wonder or delight. They *admired* my new dress.
> **adore** to love greatly or honor highly. My sister *adores* him.
> **cherish** to hold dear; to feel or show love for. You promised to *cherish* it forever.
> **other synonyms:** idolize, care for
> **antonym:** hate

many *adj.* consisting of a large number. Are there *many* people here?

> **numerous** consisting of many persons or things. Chandra made up *numerous* stories about them.
> **various** several or many. People from *various* countries live here.
> **antonym:** few

mean *adj.* bad-tempered; lacking in kindness or understanding. That was a *mean* thing to say to your best friend.

>**cruel** willing to cause pain or suffering to others. The boy was often *cruel* to smaller children.
>**nasty** very unpleasant; very harmful or troublesome. All he said was, "Don't you dare get *nasty* with me!"
>**spiteful** filled with ill feelings toward others. Are you being loud just to be *spiteful*?
>**antonyms:** *See* nice.

N

neat *adj.* clean and in good order. How can a living, breathing child keep a *neat* room?

>**meticulous** extremely concerned about detail. He is *meticulous* when he cleans his room.
>**well-groomed** clean and neat; carefully washed, combed, and dressed. Tom Sawyer was never a *well-groomed* boy.
>**other synonym:** tidy
>**antonyms:** messy, untidy, sloppy

new *adj.* never existing before; having just come into being, use, or possession. Guess how many *new* friends I met this summer.

>**innovative** newly introduced or changed. Terrence has an *innovative* pencil that also calculates.
>**modern** of the present or recent times; up-to-date. Everything he wears has to be *modern*.
>**novel** new and unusual. Henry is full of *novel* ideas.
>**antonyms:** *See* old.

nice *adj.* agreeable, pleasant, or delightful. It's a *nice* day to be outdoors.

>**agreeable** pleasing or pleasant; to one's liking. They became *agreeable* after I said it was a joke.
>**fine** excellent; very good. He has a *fine* personality.
>**pleasant** delightful; giving pleasure to. Don't expect me to be *pleasant* in the morning.
>**other synonyms:** kind, sweet, gratifying
>**antonyms:** *See* mean.

O

obtain *See* get.

odd *See* strange.

often *adv.* many times; again and again. They *often* visit relatives in the Midwest.

>**frequently** happening again and again, usually after a brief pause. Thunderstorms occur *frequently* in warm weather.
>**regularly** happening at fixed times. He visits *regularly*.
>**repeatedly** over and over again. She told him "no" *repeatedly*.
>**antonyms:** seldom, rarely

old *adj.* having lived or existed for a long time. I saw the *old* bed that the president slept on.

> **aged** having grown old. We visited our *aged* relative.
> **ancient** of great age; very old; of times long past. Kids often think people in their fifties are *ancient.*
> **elderly** somewhat old; past middle age. Sean says one becomes *elderly* at age 65.
> **other synonyms:** archaic, venerable, senior, antique
> **antonyms:** young; *see also* new.

P

plain *adj.* not distinguished from others in any way; ordinary. He got married in a *plain* blue suit.

> **common** not distinguished by anything special or outstanding; average or standard. It is now quite *common* for male athletes to complete a 100-meter dash in under 11 seconds.
> **homely** of a familiar or everyday nature. The room had a *homely* feeling to it.
> **ordinary** average; plain; common. His new car is an *ordinary* station wagon.
> **antonyms:** special; *see also* unusual.

proud *adj.* having a sense of one's personal worth or dignity. They were too *proud* to say they didn't know.

conceited having a very high opinion of oneself. She said she was the prettiest, and everyone shouted back, "How *conceited*!"

haughty having or showing much pride in oneself and dislike for others. A little money has made him *haughty.*

vain overly concerned with or proud of oneself. Everyone thinks Jimmy is *vain* because he likes to look in the mirror.

> **other synonyms:** gratified, pleased, egotistical, arrogant
> **antonym:** humble

Q

quiet *adj.* making little or no noise. When the children became *quiet,* we knew there would be trouble.

> **peaceful** calm; undisturbed. Babies are usually *peaceful* when they are asleep.
> **serene** peaceful; calm; not disturbed or troubled. We spent two *serene* days in the mountains.
> **silent** completely quiet; without sound. Her mom said, "Janet, just be *silent* when I'm talking."
> **still** without sound; silent. Be *still,* the president is about to speak.
> **tranquil** free from disturbance; calm; peaceful. I had a *tranquil* vacation in the country.
> **other synonyms:** calm, hushed
> **antonyms:** loud, noisy

R

really *adv.* in fact; in reality. I *really* like that book.

> **actually** in reality; in fact. He *actually* played himself in the movie.
>
> **indeed** really; truly. She was *indeed* pleased to see you.
>
> **truly** in fact; indeed; really. They *truly* believed every word.

reason *n.* an explanation or justification for an act or idea. She did not believe the *reason* I gave.

> **cause** a reason, motive, or ground for some action, feeling, and so on. What is the *cause* of your irrational behavior?
>
> **motive** some inner drive, impulse, or intention that causes a person to do something or act in a certain way; incentive. The police can find no *motive* for the crime.

rich *adj.* having great wealth. He has money, but I'm not sure he's *rich*.

> **affluent** having much money or property; wealthy; prosperous. Japan is among the most *affluent* nations.
>
> **prosperous** having success, wealth, or good fortune. The vice president comes from a *prosperous* family.
>
> **wealthy** having many material goods or riches. I'd rather be *wealthy* than have only a little money.
>
> **antonym:** poor

right *adj.* free from error; correct or true. You're *right;* I was wrong.

> **accurate** without errors or mistakes; correct. The weather report was *accurate* about the start of the snowfall.
>
> **correct** free from error; agreeing with fact or truth. She was the only contestant with the *correct* answer.
>
> **exact** very accurate; precise; completely correct. The bus driver asked for *exact* change.
>
> **precise** strictly accurate; being exactly what is called for or needed. The directions to your house were *precise*.
>
> **other synonyms:** fitting, suitable, proper
>
> **antonyms:** wrong, mistaken

rude *adj.* not polite; ill-mannered. Grandma specializes in talking to *rude* children.

> **discourteous** without good manners; rude. It's quite *discourteous* to shout.
>
> **impolite** not having or showing good manners. Grace became *impolite* after they accused her of stealing.
>
> **antonyms:** polite, courteous

S

sad *adj.* feeling or showing unhappiness, sorrow, or gloom. Everyone became *sad* when summer camp ended.
> **depressed** low in spirits; sad. He has been *depressed* since you moved away.
> **downcast** low in spirits; sad. Must you be so *downcast* at your son's wedding?
> **wretched** very unhappy; deeply distressed. He felt *wretched* about the news.
> **antonyms:** *See* happy.

same *adj.* being exactly like something else. We were born on the *same* day.
> **equal** the same in size, amount, quality, value, or rank. One hundred cents is *equal* to one dollar.
> **equivalent** equal in value, effect, force, or meaning. A quarter is *equivalent* to five nickels.
> **identical** one and the same; the very same. Their cars are *identical*.
> **antonym:** different

say *v.* to make known or express in words; state. What did Marva *say* about my new dress?
> **declare** to make known publicly or formally; announce. Ronnie has *declared* his intention to win.

state to express or explain fully in words. I will *state* my opinion in a letter to the newspaper editor on Tuesday.
> **other synonyms:** proclaim, exclaim, talk, speak; *see also* tell.

scared *adj.* afraid; alarmed. Are you *scared* of the dark?
> **afraid** feeling fear; frightened. They're *afraid* to fly.
> **fearful** filled with fear; afraid. He is *fearful* of crossing the street by himself.
> **frightened** suddenly alarmed or scared. Were you *frightened* by the noise?
> **terrified** filled with terror; very scared. Albert and Raymond were *terrified* after watching the horror movie.
> **other synonyms:** petrified, aghast

see *v.* to become aware of or notice with the eyes. Did you *see* them copying your answers?
> **observe** to see or notice. He said he *observed* two students painting the principal's office when he passed by.
> **perceive** to become aware of through sight or other senses. I *perceive* you won't be here for long.
> **view** to look at or see. We *viewed* the entire air show.
> **other synonyms:** *See* look.

shy *adj.* uncomfortable in the presence of others; bashful. Why do you act *shy* whenever you're around Doug?
> **bashful** uncomfortable in the presence of strangers; very shy. Children sometimes act *bashful* around me.
> **demure** quiet and modest, often in an artificial way. Ann acts *demure* whenever boys are around.
> **timid** showing a lack of courage, boldness, or self-confidence. They were *timid* in front of the principal.
> **antonym:** bold

smart *adj.* bright; intelligent; having learned a lot. That boy is very *smart* for his age.
> **clever** mentally sharp and alert; having a keen mind; quick-witted. Is she as *clever* as she says she is?
> **intelligent** able to learn, understand, and reason. An *intelligent* student can sometimes get by with little study.
> **shrewd** clever or sharp in practical matters. Denise was *shrewd* in getting Dianne to give up her overstuffed sandwich.
> **sly** clever about tricky or secret matters. The *sly* child hid the puppy from his parents.
> **antonym:** stupid

smile *v.* to make a facial expression that shows happiness, amusement, friendliness, or sympathy. She *smiled*, and everyone laughed.
> **beam** to smile in a joyful way. The boys *beamed* when they saw the girls.
> **grin** to smile broadly. We *grinned* when we were told the test had been canceled.
> **simper** to smile in a silly, artificial way. The salesclerk *simpered* at all the customers.
> **antonyms:** frown, scowl

strange *adj.* differing from the usual or the ordinary; odd. The car made a *strange,* loud sound.
> **bizarre** strikingly out of the ordinary; startlingly odd. The costumes were quite *bizarre.*
> **odd** not ordinary. That's an *odd* outfit!
> **peculiar** strange or odd, but in an interesting or curious way. I like your *peculiar* ability to write backward.
> **other synonyms:** weird; *see also* unusual.

strong *adj.* having great strength or physical power. She has *strong* arms.
> **brawny** strong and muscular. Two years of exercise made her *brawny.*
> **muscular** having well-developed muscles; strong. He is *muscular* but thin.
> **powerful** having great strength, influence, or authority. The *pow-*

erful athlete won eight gold and two silver medals.
antonym: weak

surprised *adj.* feeling sudden wonder or astonishment. They were *surprised* by his comment.

    amazed overwhelmed with wonder or surprise. He was *amazed* at the size of the cruise ship.

    astonished shocked; greatly surprised. Everyone was *astonished* when he quit the team.

    astounded greatly surprised; stunned. He was *astounded* by the amount of money he had spent in one day.

swear *v.* to make a solemn promise. He *swore* he would return before midnight.

    pledge to promise solemnly or formally. They *pledged* to stand by us to the end.

    vow to promise or pledge solemnly. They *vowed* to love each other forever.

T

take *v.* to get hold of in one's hands; grasp. The sign read, "Please *take* a number."

    grab to take roughly or rudely. She warned him never to *grab* her hand again.

    seize to take suddenly and by force. He *seized* my pencil as soon as I turned my back.

    snatch to take suddenly and quickly. I *snatched* it back from him immediately.

    antonyms: *See* give.

talk *See* say.

tell *v.* to give a detailed account of. Did she *tell* anyone about her trip?

    narrate to tell or relate. My friend *narrated* an interesting story about growing up in Sri Lanka.

    recount to tell in detail; narrate. The lawyer will ask the witness to *recount* what he saw when he testifies.

    relate to tell or report events or details. They *related* the incident to the police.

    other synonyms: *See* say.

think *v.* to use the mind to form opinions or judgments. I *think* I should leave this minute.

    contemplate to give long and close attention to. As he *contemplated* the painting, it began to make sense to him.

    muse to think in an idle, unconcerned manner. Eva *mused* about what Sam had said.

    ponder to consider or think over carefully. The scientist *pondered* the problem for several hours.

U

unusual *adj.* not usual, common, or ordinary. She gave me an *unusual* look when I asked her to dance.

> **exceptional** much above average in quality or ability. Jesse is an *exceptional* student.
> **extraordinary** beyond the ordinary; very unusual. The circus was *extraordinary*.
> **unique** having no equal or match; one of a kind. Many of the museum's collections are *unique*.
> **other synonyms:** uncommon, rare, abnormal, queer; *see also* strange.
> **antonyms:** usual, common; *see also* plain.

upset *adj.* anxious or uneasy; distressed. Bert was *upset* by the rules and regulations.

> **anxious** uneasy or fearful of what may happen. Exams sometimes make me *anxious*.
> **concerned** troubled or worried. We are deeply *concerned* about your attitude of late.
> **disturbed** in an unsettled state of mind. Maria was *disturbed* by the news about her aunt.
> **nervous** emotionally tense or restless; apprehensive or fearful. Carl was *nervous* today.
> **other synonyms:** agitated, distraught, worried
> **antonym:** calm

V

very *adv.* to a great extent. Today is *very* hot.

> **considerably** to a large or important degree. She said she was *considerably* more intelligent than her sister.
> **extremely** greatly or intensely. I am *extremely* delighted to have been invited.
> **somewhat** to some extent. She was *somewhat* convinced by the news report.

W

walk *v.* to move or travel on foot. Can we *walk* home together?

> **amble** to walk at a relaxed, leisurely pace. Jerry *ambled* across the lawn.
> **stride** to walk with long steps. He can *stride* faster than I can.
> **stroll** to walk in a relaxed or leisurely manner. They *stroll* to the park every Sunday.
> **strut** to walk in a vain or very proud way. We knew Stan had won by the way he *strutted* into the room.
> **other synonyms:** ramble, saunter, hike, parade, tread, step, pace, march

want *v.* to have a desire or wish for. She *wants* a better job.

> **crave** to want badly. They *crave*

seafood.

desire to have a strong wish for. He *desires* a convertible.

wish to have a longing or strong need or desire for something. They *wished* they were back on vacation.

wet *adj.* covered or soaked with water or other liquid. I don't want you running in the house in your *wet* clothes!

> **damp** slightly wet. The leak in the roof made the bed *damp*.
> **moist** damp; slightly wet. Leave the oven on, the cake is still *moist*.
> **sopping** dripping; extremely wet. His hair was *sopping* when

he came to dinner.

other synonyms: drenched, soggy, dank

antonym: dry

yell *v.* to call or cry out loudly. Gail *yelled* to us from the window.

> **bellow** to cry out in a loud, deep voice. The boy *bellowed* as if he were in pain.
> **scream** to cry out in a loud, shrill, piercing way. Nicole *screamed* when Dan frightened her.
> **shout** to cry out loudly. You needn't *shout*—I'm right here.

> *A **glossary** is a small, special dictionary that is sometimes found at the back of certain kinds of books—like this one. The glossary explains words and phrases used in the book that the authors consider especially important. To save you the trouble of looking through the book for the places where each word is used or of going to your dictionary to find it, the authors provide a list of these important words and their definitions so that you can look them all up in one handy place.*

Writing Terms

audience the reader or readers for whom something is written

brainstorming a way to focus a writing topic by writing or listing any thoughts that come to mind about the topic

charting a way to organize and classify ideas and information by gathering them under different headings—especially useful in comparing and contrasting

checklist a list of items, such as tasks or topic details, that can be used as an organizer and as a reference source. *See also* listing.

chronological order the arrangement of events in the order in which they occur in time. *See also* time order.

clarity the exactness with which the ideas and purpose of a piece of writing are expressed

clustering a way to explore ideas by gathering details related to the specific writing topic

coherence the orderly arrangement of ideas in a piece of writing

compare to explain how two or more things are alike

conference a meeting between the writer and a partner or a teacher, or in a group, to ask and answer questions about the writing in progress, with the purpose of improving it

contrast to explain how two or more things are different

description a piece of writing that creates a clear and vivid picture of a person, a place, or a thing

detail sentences sentences that tell more about the main idea of a paragraph

diagram a visual or graphic presentation of information; often used to organize information during prewriting. A Venn diagram is particularly useful for comparing and contrasting.

drafting the act of capturing ideas on paper; a stage in the recursive process of writing during which the writer gets his or her basic ideas down on paper

elaboration a writing strategy in which details and images are added to a piece of writing in order to give the topic fuller treatment

entertaining writing a piece of writing, often humorous or suspenseful, that amuses, intrigues, diverts, or engages the reader for the particular purpose of entertainment

explanation a piece of writing that presents the facts about a subject in a clear and logical way and explains to the reader how and why something occurs

freewriting a way to generate ideas by simply writing continuously for a specified time, without stopping to elaborate or to correct errors

informative writing a piece of writing that presents information to a reader that is organized in a clear, accurate, complete, and coherent way

instructions an explanation or a set of directions for how to do something. The steps in a set of instructions are arranged in a logical way so that other people can repeat the activity.

letter a way to communicate informally or formally with someone in writing. A friendly letter has five parts, each of which gives the person who receives the letter important information, and is personal in nature. A business letter has six parts and is written to an audience often unknown to the writer.

listing a way to organize your thoughts by writing them down and putting them in order—possibly by numbering them

logical order an arrangement of ideas in an order that makes sense and is easy for the reader to follow

outline a way to organize topic-related ideas in the order in which they will be discussed—especially useful in organizing a research report

overall impression the general idea or feeling expressed in a description

paragraph a group of sentences that develops one main idea

personal narrative a piece of writing in which the writer tells about something that has happened in his or her life

persuasive writing writing that encourages an audience to share the writer's beliefs, opinions, or point of view

prewriting the stage in the writing process in which the writer chooses a topic, explores ideas, gathers information, and organizes material before drafting

prewriting strategies particular ways of gathering, exploring, planning, and organizing ideas before writing a first draft. *See entries for individual prewriting strategies:* brainstorming, charting, clustering, freewriting, listing, outline, story chart, *and* time line.

proofreading to review writing in order to correct errors in punctuation, capitalization, spelling, and grammar

publishing to share written work with an audience—for example, by reading it aloud, contributing it to a school paper, or posting it on a bulletin board

purpose the writer's reason for writing—for example, to explain, to entertain, or to persuade

reflective writing a piece of writing in which the writer's personal thoughts, ideas, or feelings become an important part of the form. That form can be a poem, a story, or an essay, for example.

report a piece of writing that provides information about a specific subject. A **book review** is a report that gives information about a book the writer has read, as well as the writer's opinions about it. A **research report** summarizes information about a subject from many sources.

revising to improve a draft by adding or deleting information, combining and reordering sentences, or changing word choice to suit purpose and audience

sensory details in a description, the details that appeal to the reader's five senses—sight, hearing, touch, taste, and smell

story chart a way to gather ideas and details under headings important for the writing of a story—setting, characters, plot, problem/solution, and conclusion, for example

style a writer's use of language and sentence structure to create a particular tone

summary an account that tells the most important ideas in what has been read or observed by the writer. A summary can include information from one source or from multiple sources.

supporting details facts, examples, or sensory details that give more information about the main idea of a paragraph

time line a way to organize the events of a narrative in chronological order

time order the arrangement of events in a composition according to when they occur in time—also called **chronological order.** Some time-order words are *first, next, then,* and *last.*

tone the feeling or attitude a writer expresses toward the subject of a composition through his or her particular style of writing. For example, a writer's tone may be formal, informal, humorous, or critical.

topic sentence the sentence that states the main idea of an informative, explanatory, or persuasive paragraph

transition words words or phrases that may help writers to compare and contrast, such as *on the one hand* and *on the other hand;* also, words that link sentences in a narrative, such as *finally* and *in the meantime*

voice the quality of a piece of writing that makes it distinctively the writer's own

writing process the recursive stages involved in writing, which usually include prewriting, writing a draft, revising, proofreading, and publishing

Language Terms

abstract noun a common noun that names ideas or feelings that cannot be seen or touched

    Joan's *honor* was at stake.

action verb a word that expresses action

    He *walked* down the boulevard.

adjective a word that modifies, or describes, a noun or a pronoun

    The *small* dog played with me.

adjective phrase a prepositional phrase that modifies a noun or a pronoun

    The house *with the green shutters* is for sale.

adverb a word that modifies a verb, an adjective, or another adverb

    The actor performed *adequately.*

adverb phrase a prepositional phrase that modifies, or describes, a verb, an adjective, or an adverb

    The firefighter ran *into the blazing building.*

antecedent a word or group of words to which a pronoun refers

    Jane is good at tennis, and *she* swims well, too.

appositive a word or group of words that follows and identifies a noun

    John Jamison, *the class president,* is my friend.

article a special adjective—*a, an,* or *the*

    The dog growled at *a* man in *an* automobile.

common noun a noun that names any person, place, or thing

    When will the *coach* arrive?

complete predicate words that tell what the subject of a sentence does or is

    Stan *broke the record for the high jump.*

complete subject all the words that tell whom or what the sentence is about

    Chess and checkers are my favorite games.

compound sentence a sentence that contains two sentences joined by a semicolon or by a comma and the word *and, or,* or *but*

    Simone went to the mall, and she bought a dress.

concrete noun a noun that names things you can see or touch

    Ryan motioned to the *chairperson.*

conjunction a word that joins other words or groups of words in a sentence
Jan *and* Mark worked together.

demonstrative adjective an adjective that points out something or describes a noun by answering the question *which one?* or *which ones?*
That book is the one I want to borrow.

direct object a noun or a pronoun that receives the action of the verb
Ed gave a *speech* to the class.

essential clause an adjective clause needed to clarify sentence meaning
The marathon is the only race *that I ran this year.*

gerund a verb form that ends in *ing* and is used as a noun
Swimming is my favorite activity.

helping verb a verb that helps the main verb to express action
Lee *has* searched for the missing puzzle piece.

indefinite pronoun a pronoun that does not refer to a particular person, place, or thing
Does *anyone* have a book I can borrow?

independent clause a group of words that contains one complete subject and one complete predicate and can stand alone as a sentence
I will wait for you at the corner.

indirect object a noun or pronoun that answers the question *to whom? for whom? to what?* or *for what?* after an action verb
Linda gave *her* a lovely book.

infinitive the base form of a verb preceded by the word *to*, often used as a noun
To begin is often the hardest part.

interjection a word or a group of words that expresses strong feeling
Oops! Be careful of the slippery pavement.

interrogative pronoun a pronoun that introduces an interrogative sentence
Who is absent today?

linking verb a verb that connects the subject of a sentence to a noun or an adjective in the predicate
Joan *is* captain of the team.

nonessential clause an adjective clause not needed to clarify meaning
  The marathon, *which I ran this year,* was held in November.

noun a word that names a person, place, or thing
  The *child* saw a *clown* at the *circus.*

object of a preposition a noun or a pronoun that follows the preposition in a prepositional phrase
  I saw a man in the *window.*

object pronoun a pronoun that is used as the object of a preposition, a direct object, or an indirect object
  Please give the message to *me.*

participial phrase a group of words that includes a participle and other words that complete its meaning, all acting together as an adjective
  Feeling sad, I played some polka music.

participle a verb form used as an adjective
  She drank some *bottled* water.

possessive noun a noun that shows ownership
  The *dog's* collar was loose.

possessive pronoun a pronoun that shows who or what owns something
  His jacket is red.

predicate adjective an adjective that follows a linking verb and describes the subject
  The girl is *smart.*

predicate noun a noun that follows a linking verb and describes the subject
  Tamu is the *president.*

preposition a word that relates a noun or a pronoun to another word
  She gave me a box *of* stationery.

prepositional phrase a group of words that begins with a preposition and ends with a noun or a pronoun
  The book *on the shelf* is mine.

pronoun a word that takes the place of one or more nouns and the words that go with the nouns

She gave *me* a book.

proper adjective an adjective formed from a proper noun

She bought a *Mexican* basket.

proper noun a noun that names a particular person, place, or thing

The *Painted Desert* is magnificent.

run-on sentence two or more sentences that have been joined incorrectly

I bought a cake yesterday it was chocolate.

sentence a group of words that expresses a complete thought

Mother planted flowers in the garden.

sentence fragment a group of words that does not express a complete thought

Flowers in the garden.

subject pronoun a pronoun that is used as the subject of a sentence

She likes baseball very much.

subordinate clause a group of words that has a subject and a predicate but cannot stand alone as a complete sentence

Because we were late, we waited for the intermission.

Literary Terms

alliteration the repetition of the same first letter or initial consonant sound in a series of words

He clasps the crag with crooked hands.

autobiography the story of a person's life, written by that person

biography the story of a real person's life, written by someone else

character sketch a long description of a character that tries to present a very thorough and vivid portrait

characters the people (or animals) who participate in the action of a story or a play

concrete poem a poem whose shape suggests the subject of the poem

dialog the conversations the characters have in a story or a play

fiction written work that tells about imaginary characters and events. Works of fiction can include novels, plays, poems, short stories, science fiction, folktales, fairy tales, myths, and fables.

figurative language words used in unusual rather than in exact or expected ways, frequently in poetry. **Simile** and **metaphor** are two common forms of figurative language.

free verse a poem that sounds like ordinary speech and has no regular rhythm or rhyme

haiku a poem of 3 lines and usually 17 syllables, in which the poet often reflects on life or nature

hyperbole the use of extreme exaggeration in speaking or writing, usually not meant to be taken seriously

idiom an expression with a special meaning different from the literal meanings of the individual words that make up the expression
    Time flies.

imagery the use of word pictures—images—in writing, to make a description more vivid through especially precise or colorful language

limerick an English verse form consisting of five lines that rhyme *aabba*. The third and fourth lines have two stresses, and the other lines have three stresses.

lyrics the words of a song

lyric poem a fairly short poem expressing the personal mood, feeling, or reflections of a single speaker

metaphor a figure of speech in which a comparison is made without using the word *like* or *as*
    The field was a green blanket.

meter the regular pattern of beats in a poem

nonfiction written work that deals with real situations, people, or events. Nonfiction works include biographies, autobiographies, articles, editorials, and news stories.

onomatopoeia the formation of words and images in imitation of actual sounds the *whizz* of the skates

personification a description in which human qualities are given to something that is not human

    The leaves chased each other across the playground.

plot the action or sequence of events in a story, a novel, a play, or a narrative poem

proverb a short, familiar saying that expresses a common truth or a wise observation

repetition the use of the same word, phrase, or sound more than once, for emphasis or effect, in a piece of writing

rhyme the repetition of syllables that sound alike, especially at the ends of lines of poetry

    The wrinkled sea beneath him crawls;
    He watches from his mountain walls.

rhythm a pattern of stressed and unstressed syllables, like a regular musical beat, especially in a poem or a song

    And hand in hand, on the edge of the sand,
    They danced by the light of the moon.

setting the time and place in which the events of a story occur

simile a figure of speech in which a comparison is made using the word *like* or *as*
    The kite soared *like* a bird.

stanza a group of lines in a poem that forms a complete unit, like a paragraph in a piece of prose writing

story a piece of writing that has a sequence of events, or **plot**. The **characters** are the people in the story. The **setting** is where and when the story takes place.

tall tale a story in which the characters are larger than life and able to perform extraordinary feats. Exaggeration is used in a tall tale.

tanka a poem of 5 lines and usually 31 syllables (5, 7, 5, 7, 7) that frequently expresses the poet's reflections on a subject from life or nature

theme the main idea or meaning of a complete piece of writing

tone the total effect of the language, word choices, and sentence structure used by a writer to express a certain feeling or attitude toward the subject

> *Every writer needs resources. The books listed in this bibliography are books about writing or books that writers would find very useful. You might want to see if they are in your library.*

How I Came to Be a Writer

by Phyllis Reynolds, published by Macmillan Publishing Company, New York, 1987.

This book details the career of one writer from stories written in grade school through her first published pieces to novels written to date.

How to Write a Great School Report

by Elizabeth James and Carol Barkin, published by Lothrop, Lee and Shepard Books, New York, 1983.

This streamlined volume tells you everything you need to know about how to research and organize your reports. It also gives tips about making your reports interesting.

How to Write Your Best Book Report

by Carol Barkin and Elizabeth James, published by Lothrop, Lee and Shepard, New York, 1986.

This neat book gives ideas for making reports better, from choosing a good book to read to letting you know where to get help.

How Writers Write

by Pamela Lloyd, published by Heinemann Educational Books, Inc., Portsmouth, New Hampshire, 1987.

This book includes conversations with many writers such as Beverly Cleary, Stephen Kellogg, Seymour Simon, and Jane Yolen. The writers talk about how they get ideas for their writing and why they write.

Student Thesaurus

by Elizabeth A. Ryan, published by Troll Associates, Mahwah, New Jersey, 1990.
This is a treasure-trove of words that will make your writing sparkle! There are over 2,000 entries in this thesaurus—more than enough to help you say exactly what you want to say.

Where Do You Get Your Ideas? Helping Young Writers Begin

by Sandy Asher, published by Walker and Company, New York, 1987.
This book offers helpful information about keeping a journal as well as other interesting ideas for journalists-to-be.

Wild Words and How to Tame Them

by Sandy Asher, published by Walker and Company, New York, 1989.
This is a useful tool for all writers. Taming wild words may even become a favorite thing to do!

Word Works

by Catherine Berger Kay, published by Little, Brown and Company, Boston, 1989.
Loaded with illustrations and engaging writing, this book is filled to the brim with information about words—why we have them, why we need them, and how we use them.

Write Your Own Story

by Vivian Dubrovin, published by Franklin Watts, New York, 1984.
This little volume offers many practical tips about fiction writing.

Writing American English

by Bernard Seward, published by Alemany Press, Hayward, California, 1982.
This is an indispensable volume with loads of information for all writers, from those just beginning to those with loads of experience.

Writing for Kids

by Carol L. Benjamin, published by Harper and Row Junior Books, New York, 1985.
This is a handy book for all young writers, loaded with important hints and information.

Writing Your Own Plays

by Carol Korty, published by Charles Scribner's Sons, New York, 1986.
Carol Korty's practical handbook for the young playwright includes choosing a story, preparing a first draft, developing ideas, and outlining.

You Can Be an Author

by Philly Murtha, published by Creative Education, Inc., Mankato, Minnesota, 1985.
Yes, you can! Helpful tips and information to start you on your way to authorship can be found in this volume.

The Young Writer's Handbook

by Susan and Stephen Tchudi, published by Aladdin Books, New York, 1984.
This handy reference is a practical guide for the beginner who is serious about writing. The book even includes addresses of places that publish students' writing!

Acknowledgments The publisher has made every effort to trace the ownership of all copyrighted selections found in this book and to make full acknowledgment of their use. The publisher gratefully acknowledges permission to reprint the following copyrighted material:

From SEVEN BLACK AMERICAN SCIENTISTS by Robert C. Hayden. Text copyright © 1970, by Robert C. Hayden. Reprinted with permission of Addison-Wesley Publishing Company, Inc.

"Your Heart and How It Works" by American Heart Association. Copyright © 1979 American Heart Association. Reproduced with permission of American Heart Association.

"Space" by Evangelina Vigil-Piñón first published in THE COMPUTER IS DOWN. Copyright © 1987 by Arte Publico Press of the University of Houston. Reprinted by permission of the publisher.

From "Remember the Dream" a song by S. Tyrell, J. Sample, and S. Tyrell. Published by Sunstruck Music (BMI) and Tyrell Music Group, Inc. (BMI). Used by permission. All rights reserved.

"The Last Wolf" by Mary TallMountain from THERE IS NO WORD FOR GOODBYE. Published by *The Blue Cloud Quarterly*. Reprinted by permission of the publisher.

"Energy of the Future" letter by Jean Cannon from COBBLESTONE Magazine, October 1990. Published by Cobblestone Publishing, Inc. Reprinted by permission of Jean Cannon.

"The City is So Big" by Richard García. Copyright © 1973 by Richard García. Reprinted by permission of the author.

"Living in a Solar House" by Cynthia Boston from COBBLESTONE Magazine, October 1990, *Energy Powering Our Nation* © 1990, Cobblestone Publishing, Inc., Peterborough, NH 03458. Reprinted by permission of the publisher.

From "The Love Letter" by Jack Finney originally published in THE SATURDAY EVENING POST, 1959. Copyright © 1959, renewed 1987 by Jack Finney. Reprinted by permission of Don Congdon Associates, Inc.

"Put a Little Love in Your Heart" by Jimmy Holiday, Randy Myers & Jackie De Shannon. Copyright © 1969 UNART MUSIC CORPORATION. All Rights Assigned to EMI CATALOGUE PARTNERSHIP. All Rights Controlled and administered by EMI UNART CATALOG INC. International Copyright Secured. Made in USA. All Rights Reserved. Reprinted by permission of CPP/BELWIN, INC., 15800 NW 48th Avenue, PO Box 4340, Miami, FL 33014.

"Cricket League Contest Rules" from CRICKET Magazine, April 1990 issue, vol. 17, no. 8. Copyright © 1990 by Carus Corporation. Reprinted by permission of CRICKET Magazine.

From BLACK WOMEN WRITERS AT WORK by Claudia Tate. Copyright © 1983 by permission of the Continuum Publishing Company.

"Serenity/Suavidades" by Gabriela Mistral from SELECTED POEMS OF GABRIELA MISTRAL translated by Doris Dana. Copyright © 1961, 64, 70, 71 by Doris Dana. Reprinted by permission of Joan Daves Agency.

From MAHINHIN, A TALE OF THE PHILIPPINES, by Antonio E. Santa Elena. Copyright 1984 by Antonio E. Santa Elena, Reprinted by permission of Downey Place Publishing House, Inc.

From "A Letter to a Child Like Me" by José Torres from PARADE MAGAZINE, Feb. 24, 1991. Reprinted by permission of Agins, Dolgin, Siegel & Bernstein.

Recipe for "Curried Red Snapper with Vegetables" by Donald Cambell from ESSENCE Magazine, Oct. 1991 issue. Published by Essence Communications, Inc. Reprinted by permission of the publisher.

"If There Be Sorrow" by Mari Evans from I AM A BLACK WOMAN. Copyright © 1970 by Mari Evans. Published by William Morrow & Company. Reprinted by permission of Mari Evans.

"Letter to the U.S. Government" by Chief Seattle from THE FABER BOOK OF LETTERS, edited by Felix Pryor.

From CONTEMPORARY AUTHORS, Volume 13–16, edited by Clara D. Kinsman. Copyright © 1965, 1966, 1975 by Gale Research Inc. Reprinted by permission of the publisher.

From SOMETHING ABOUT THE AUTHORS, Volume 32, 48 and 56, edited by Ann Commire. Copyright © 1983, 1987, 1989 by Gale Research Inc. Reprinted by permission of the publisher.

From ANIMAL COMMUNICATION, OPPOSING VIEWPOINTS by Jacci Cole. Copyright © 1989 by Greenhaven Press, Inc. Reprinted by permission of the publisher.

From "The Marble Champ" from BASEBALL IN APRIL AND OTHER STORIES by Gary Soto. Copyright © 1990 by Gary Soto. Published by Harcourt Brace Jovanovich, Publishers. Reprinted by permission of the publisher.

A letter to the editor from Amanda Jayne Harkrader as it appeared in SPORTS ILLUSTRATED FOR KIDS, September 1991. Reprinted by permission of Amanda Jayne Harkrader.

Text excerpt p. 19 from SWEETWATER by Laurence Yep. Text copyright © 1973 by Laurence Yep. Reprinted by permission of HarperCollins Publishers, Inc.

Text excerpt "I had Never Been . . . and Wondered If I Should Go Back" from THE INK-KEEPER'S APPRENTICE by Allen Say. Copyright © 1979 by Allen Say. Reprinted by permission of HarperCollins Publishers, Inc.

Excerpt from HIGHER THAN HOPE by Fatima Meer. Copyright © 1990 by Fatima Meer. Reprinted by permission of HarperCollins Publishers, Inc.

Excerpt from GIFTS OF PASSAGE by Santha Rama Rau. Copyright © 1951, 1952, 1954, 1955, 1957, 1958, 1960, 1961 by Vasanthi Rama Rau Bowers. Reprinted by permission of HarperCollins Publishers, Inc.

From LETTERS OF E.B. WHITE by E.B. White. Copyright © 1976 by E.B. White. Reprinted by permission of HarperCollins, Inc.

Untitled poem from THE COMPLETE POEMS OF EMILY DICKINSON edited by Thomas H. Johnson, Cambridge, Mass.: The Belknap Press of Harvard University, Copyright © 1951, 1955, 1979, 1983 by the President and Fellows of Harvard College. Reprinted by permission of the publishers and the Trustee of Amherst College.

From "The Circuit" by Francisco Jiménez from THE ARIZONA QUARTERLY, Autumn 1973. Reprinted by permission of the author.

From BLUE HIGHWAYS: A JOURNEY INTO AMERICA by William Least Heat-Moon. Copyright © 1982 by William Least Heat-Moon. Reprinted by permission of Little, Brown and Company.

"Ballad of the Morning Streets" by Amiri Baraka from TALKING TO THE SUN. Copyright © 1969 by Amiri Baraka. Reprinted by permission of Sterling Lord Literistic, Inc.

Story summary of ANPAO: AN AMERICAN INDIAN ODYSSEY by Jamake Highwater from THROUGH THE EYES OF A CHILD by Donna E. Norton. Copyright © 1991 by Macmillan Publishing Company. Reprinted by permission of Macmillan Publishing Company, a division of Macmillan, Inc.

From SALLY RIDE p. 45 by Carolyn Blacknall. Copyright © 1984 by Dillon Press. Reprinted by permission of Dillon Press, an Imprint of Macmillan Publishing Company.

Diagram of a cell nucleus from MERRILL LIFE SCIENCE. Copyright 1993 by the Glencoe Division of Macmillan/McGraw-Hill Publishing Company. Reprinted by permission of the publisher.

"Kidnap Poem" from THE WOMEN AND THE MEN by Nikki Giovanni. Text copyright © 1970, 1974, 1975 by Nikki Giovanni. Reprinted by permission of William Morrow & Company, Inc.

From "Sacrifices of the High Andes" by Juan Schobinger from NATURAL HISTORY Magazine, April 1991. Copyright the American Museum of Natural History, 1991. Reprinted by permission from NATURAL HISTORY.

From "After 17 Years, Cicadas Prepare for their Roaring Return" by Jane E. Brody from THE NEW YORK TIMES, May 12, 1987. Copyright © 1987 by The New York Times Company. Reprinted by permission.

"Golden Monkeys" by Diane Ackerman from THE NEW YORKER Magazine, June 24, 1991. Reprinted by permission of the publisher; © 1991 by Diane Ackerman.

From SOUND-SHADOWS OF THE NEW WORLD by Ved Mehta. Copyright © 1985 by Ved Mehta. Reprinted by permission of W. W. Norton & Company, Inc.

Odate, "The Soul of the Tool" ASIAN ART Magazine, Summer, 1991, pg. 2. Copyright 1991, ASIAN ART, Oxford University Press. Used by permission.

From EDITH JACKSON by Rosa Guy. Copyright © Rosa Guy, 1978. Published by Viking Press. Reprinted by permission of Ellen Levine Agency.

From THE WRITER IN ALL OF US by June Gould. Copyright © 1989 by June Gould. Published by E.P. Dutton, a division of Penguin USA. Reprinted by permission of the publisher.

From ANNO'S SUNDIAL by Mitsumasa Anno. Copyright © 1985 by Mitsumasa anno. Reprinted by permission of Philomel Books.

Excerpt from THE JESSE OWENS STORY by Jesse Owens with Paul G. Neimark. Copyright © 1970 by Jesse Owens and Paul G. Neimark. Reprinted by permission of The Putnam Publishing Group.

From ALWAYS TO REMEMBER by Brent Ashabranner. Copyright © 1988 by Brent Ashabranner. Reprinted by permission of G.P. Putnam's Sons.

From THE BLACK STALLION by Walter Farley. Copyright © 1941 by Walter Farley. Copyright renewed 1969 by Walter Farley. Reprinted by permission of Random House, Inc.

From WOLF ROLAND by Julia Cunningham. Copyright © 1983 by Julia Cunningham. Reprinted by permission of Pantheon Books, a division of Random House, Inc.

Recipe "Purée of Parsnips" from JULIA CHILD AND COMPANY by Julia Child. Copyright © 1978 by Julia Child. Reprinted by Permission of Alfred A. Knopf, Inc.

From "A Worn Path" by Eudora Welty from A CURTAIN OF GREEN AND OTHER STORIES. Copyright © 1941 by Eudora Welty, renewed in 1969 by Eudora Welty. Reprinted by permission of Russell & Volkening Inc. as agents for the author.

"Lost" by Bruce Ignacio from SOUTH DAKOTA REVIEW, Summer 1969. Reprinted by permission of the editor.

From "The Firefly" by Li Po. Reprinted from A GARDEN OF PEONIES translated by Henry H. Hart. Copyright 1938 by the Board of Trustees of the Leland Stanford Junior University. Copyright renewed 1966 by Henry S. Hart. Reprinted by permission of the publisher, Stanford University Press.

From "More About Colors and Light" from LOOKING AT SENSES by David Suzuki with Barbara Hehner. Copyright © 1986 by David Suzuki and Barbara Hehner. Published by Stoddart Publishing Co. Limited. Reprinted by permission of the publisher.

For cartoon from THE AUTHORITATIVE CALVIN AND HOBBES by Bill Watterson. CALVIN AND HOBBES copyright 1988 UNIVERSAL PRESS SYNDICATE. Reprinted with permission. All rights reserved.

From book jacket blurb from SUSHI AND SOURDOUGH by Tooru J. Kanazawa. Copyright © 1989 by Tooru Kanazawa. Published by University of Washington Press. Reprinted by permission of the publisher.

WHICH WAY FREEDOM? by Joyce Hansen, book jacket blurb. Copyright © 1986 by Joyce Hansen Nelson. Published by Walker Publishing Company, Inc. Reprinted by permission of the publisher.

From "From Country Smiles to City Stares" by Ellen Goodman from THE BOSTON GLOBE, September 9, 1982. Copyright © 1982, The Boston Globe Newspaper Co./Washington Post Writers Group. Reprinted by permission.

"Making Eyes" from THE SCIENCE BOOK by Sara Stein. Copyright © 1979 by Sara Stein. Published by Workman Publishing Company, Inc., 708 Broadway, New York NY 10003. Reprinted by permission of the publisher.

"Dolphin Facts" from THE KIDS' WORLD ALMANAC OF ANIMALS AND PETS by Deborah G. Felder. Copyright © 1989 by Deborah G. Felder. Reprinted with permission of Pharos Books, New York, NY.

"Adopt an Acre. It's Habitat Forming" from ZOO LIFE, Summer 1991. Published by San Francisco Zoo. Reprinted by permission of Eco System Survival Plan.

Quote from "Allan Houser" by Sally Eauclaire. Published in SOUTHWEST ART, August 1991. Reprinted by permission of the publisher.

From GARFIELD FOOD FOR THOUGHT by Jim

Davis. GARFIELD reprinted by permission of UFS, Inc.

Cartoon from YOU'RE YOU, CHARLIE BROWN by Charles Shulz. PEANUTS reprinted by permission of UFS, Inc.

Book review of RYAN WHITE: MY OWN STORY from PUBLISHERS WEEKLY of 04/19/91. Copyright © Reed Publishing USA. Reprinted by permission from PUBLISHER'S WEEKLY.

Cover illustration from THE PEOPLE COULD FLY: AMERICAN BLACK FOLKTALES, told by Virginia Hamilton and illustrated by Leo and Diane Dillon. Cover illustration copyright © 1985 by Leo and Diane Dillon. Reprinted by permission of Alfred A. Knopf, Inc.

From "45 Years in Culture and Creative Writing" by Gwendolyn Brooks from EBONY Magazine, November 1990 issue. Reprinted by permission of the author.

"Mother to Son" from SELECTED POEMS OF LANGSTON HUGHES by Langston Hughes. Copyright © 1926 by Alfred A. Knopf, Inc. and renewed in 1954 by Langston Hughes. Reprinted by permission of the publisher.

From "Three Days to See" by Helen Keller. Material has been reprinted with permission from the American Foundation for the Blind, 15 West 16th Street, New York, NY 10011.

Cover of ALL JAHDU STORYBOOK by Virginia Hamilton, illustrated by Barry Moser. Illustration copyright © 1991 by Pennyroyal Press, Inc. Reprinted by permission of Harcourt Brace Jovanovich, Inc.

Excerpt from ALL JAHDU STORYBOOK BY Virginia Hamilton. Text copyright © 1991 by Virginia Hamilton. Reprinted by permission of Harcourt Brace Jovanich, Inc.

From "The Three Mosquiteers" from STORIES FROM EL BARRIO by Piri Thomas. Copyright © 1978 by Piri Thomas. Reprinted by permission of Alfred A. Knopf, Inc.

Review from MUSIC AND YOU. Copyright © 1991 Macmillan/McGraw-Hill School Publishing Company, a division of Macmillan, Inc. Reprinted by permission of the publisher.

"The Serenity of Stones" by N. Scott Momaday from CARRIERS OF THE DREAM WHEEL compiled by Duane Niatum. Reprinted by permission of N. Scott Momaday.

From "The Slim Butte Ghost" by Virginia Driving Hawk Sneve. Copyright © by Virginia Driving Hawk Sneve. Reprinted by permission of the author.

Quote by Gary Soto from CONTEMPORARY AUTHORS, Volume 125, Hal May and Susan M. Trosky, editors. Copyright © 1989 by Gale Research, Inc. Reprinted by permission of the publisher.

Story summary of SONG OF TREES by Mildred Taylor from EXCITING, FUNNY, SCARY, SHORT, DIFFERENT, AND SAD BOOKS KIDS LIKE ABOUT ANIMALS, SCIENCE, SPORTS, FAMILIES, SONGS AND OTHER THINGS edited by Frances Laverne Carroll and Mary Meacham. Copyright © 1984 by the American Library Association.

From SIGNS OF SPRING by Laurel Lee. Copyright © 1980 by Laurel Lee.

"Tosa Diary" excerpt from ANTHOLOGY OF JAPANESE LITERATURE FROM THE EARLIEST ERA TO THE MID-NINETEENTH CENTURY edited by Donald Keene. Copyright © 1955 by Grove Press, Inc.

From BRING ME A UNICORN, DIARIES AND LETTERS OF ANNE MORROW LINDBERGH. Copyright © 1971, 1972 by Anne Morrow Lindbergh.

From NILDA by Nicholasa Mohr. Copyright © 1973 by Nicholasa Mohr.

From SHANE by Jack Schaefer. Copyright 1949 by Jack Schaefer.

From WON'T KNOW TILL I GET THERE by Walter Dean Myers. Copyright © Walter Dean Myers, 1982.

From MY DIARY—MY WORLD by Elizabeth Yates. Copyright © 1981 by Elizabeth Yates.

ILLUSTRATION Carlos Aguirre, xi b.r., 37-43, 45-50; Rick Allen, 239, 247, 254, 258, 264, 268, 275, 281; Andrea Baruffi, xiv t.l., 113-119, 121-128; Daniel Baxter, 303-304, 314, 322-323, 332, 349-350; Federico Botana, xx b.l., 294, 308-309, 317, 327, 339; Doug Bowles, 205; Isabella von Buol, 82, 174; Abby Carter, 336; Raul Colon, xii t.l., 51-53, 57, 61-62, 64-66; Alicia Czechowski, xv t.l., 143-149, 151, 153-158; Jeffrey Fisher, x l., 3, 5, 7-11; Allen Garns, 211-212, 222, 233-234; Susan Greenstein, 242, 249, 257, 263, 267, 272; Moira Hahn, xiii t.l., 83-98; Celeste Henriquez, xvi t.l., 175-181, 183-184, 186, 188-190; Sophia Latto, 368; Kristen Miller, 191; Yan Nascimbene, 301, 311, 320-321, 336, 344; Gregory Nemec, 195 l.; Massato Nishimura, x r., 13-19; Michael O'Shaughnessy, xiii b.r., 99-105, 107-112; Lisa Palombo, 209-210, 217, 225, 235-236; Rodica Prato, xxi r., 378; Art Ruiz, xi t.l., 21-25, 27, 31, 34-36; Paul Schulenburg, xviii l., xxi b.l., 213-214, 227, 229-230, 353, 364-365, 370-371, 382, 398, 408, 410; Ken Spengler, xiv b.r., 129-135, 140-142; Heidi Stevens, xx t., 306-307, 315, 318-319, 334-335, 341, 343; Lynn Tanaka, 241, 250, 261, 274, 276; Dan Wiemer, xviii b.r., xix, 243, 245, 253, 255, 270, 279; Dean Williams, 207-208, 219-221, 237-238; Jean Wisenbaugh, 380; Mary Worcester, xxii, 372.

PHOTOGRAPHY All photographs are by Macmillan/McGraw-Hill School Division (MMSD) except as noted below.

Author's Pages: i: Monica Stevenson for MMSD; t. inset. Carlo Ontal. ii-ix: Monica Stevenson for MMSD. Table of Contents: xii: Lizzie Himmel for MMSD. xv: Heungman for MMSD. xvi: Russ Kinne/Comstock. Unit 2: 23, 24: Andy Sacks for MMSD. Unit 3: 39, 40: School District Office, Salt Lake City, UT. Unit 4: 53, 54: Scott Harvey for MMSD. Unit 5: 67–81: Lizzie Himmel for MMSD. 69: t.r. and 70: b. Lee Balgemann for MMSD. Unit 6: 85, 86: Doug Crouch for MMSD. Unit 7: 101, 102: Michael Fritz for MMSD. Unit 9: 131, 132: Andy Sacks for MMSD. Unit 10: 145, 146: Kelly James for MMSD. Unit 11: 159–173: Heungman for MMSD. 161: t.r. and 162: t.l. Walter P. Calahan for MMSD. Unit 12: 177, 178: Lee Balgemann. Writers' Gallery: 193: Vincent Van Gogh Collection, The Museum of Modern Art, "The Starry Night" 1889, Acquired through the Lillie P. Bliss Bequest. 195: b. John Nieto, Courtesy J. Cacciola Galleries, NY. 196: t.r. Beryl Bidwell/Tony Stone Worldwide. 198: t. Robert Delaunay Collection, The Museum of Modern Art, NY/"Simultaneous Contracts: Sun and Moon" 1913. Mrs. Simon Guggenheim Fund. 200: Russ Kinne/Comstock. 201: Diego Rivera, Los Angeles County Museum of Art, Los Angeles, County Fund. 202: J.H. Robinson/Photo Researchers.

PROGRAM DESIGN Carbone Smolan Associates

COVER ILLUSTRATION Gary Kelley